The Book of

COMMON PRAYER

of the

CHURCH

Proposed for Use in

THE ANTIOCHIAN
WESTERN RITE VICARIATE

Together with the Psalter

or

Psalms of David

APOLOGIA ANGLICANA
BOSTON, MASSACHUSETTS
A. D. MMXXV

Table of Contents

Copyright

ISBN: 978-1-969461-00-2 (Paperback)
ISBN: 978-1-969461-01-9 (eBook)

Library of Congress Control Number: 2025918491

Edited by J. P. 'Augustine' Watson (Augustine@ApologiaAnglicana.org). Front cover designed by Matthew Taylor (@semperadiuvans).

PLEASE NOTE THAT THIS IS NOT CURRENTLY AN OFFICIAL TEXT OF THE ANTIOCHIAN WESTERN RITE VICARIATE.

We are thankful to have such great giants upon whose shoulders we stand. These works are used in this Book according to fair use, where their content is not already in the public domain. What was used from the book, or in what way it was consulted, is described under each citation.

Davis, C. Lance, ed. *The Anglican Office Book*. 2nd edition. Chester: Whithorn Press, 2023. *Lessons and Psalms in the Daily Office Lectionary, which are not provided in the 1928 Book of Common Prayer. The Invitatory antiphon for Septuagesimatide. Some of the text and Rubrics for the Minor Hours. Other Daily Office propers.*

The American Missal: Revised & Expanded. Glendale: Lancelot Andrewes Press, 2010. *The Collect for Our Lady of Walsingham.*

The Armed Forces Division of the Protestant Episcopal Church. *The Armed Forces Prayer Book*. New York: The Church Pension Fund, 1951.

The Prayer for the Armed Forces.

The English Missal for the Laity. London: W. Knott & Sons Limited, 1933. *The Thanksgiving for Holy Communion. Collects not used from the Prayer Book Tradition nor the Sarum Missal.*

The General Synod of the Anglican Church of Canada. *The Book of Common Prayer*. Toronto: Anglican Book Centre, 1962. *The Invitatory Antiphon for Lent.*

The Monastic Diurnal. Oxford University Press, 1932. *Office Rubrics. Ranking of Feast Days. Sacrament of Penance. Office of the Dead. Preparation for Holy Communion. Office of St. Mary on Saturday.*

Dedication

This *2025 Proposed BCP Office* is dedicated to Patriarch JOHN X, 171st Successor of St. Peter, Head of the Church, and Patriarch of Antioch.

And we are beyond thankful for our Christ-loving, God-fearing, and faithful-caring Chief Bishop and Metropolitan SABA. For his support of the Western Rite continues our endeavours, lightens our hearts, and shows his divine charity for his flock.

And for our faithful, compassionate, and righteous Bishop JOHN, we must send up everlasting praise and thanksgiving unto the Most Holy Trinity. For through him has the daily care, discipline, and concern for the Vicariate been carried. Through him have so many of us flocked for refuge under the See of St. Peter within the Holy Orthodox Catholic Church. And through him have we been intimately cared and nourished.

Finally, we must thank our Lord and God and Saviour Jesus Christ for our beloved Priests, Deacons, and all Clergy in the Vicariate for their tireless care, concern, and work for our salvation. Chiefly among them must surely be our pious and religious Abbot Theodore of Ladyminster, as well as our blessed archpriests, The Very Reverend Fathers Edward Hughes, John Fenton, Lester Bundy, Patrick Cardine, and Christopher Nerreau.

We also wish to express our deep love for our brethren in the British Isles, keeping the life of the Western Rite, Fathers Augustine and James.

Let us for ever bless the Father and the Son and the Holy Ghost, together with all the Saints, chiefly of blessed Mary ever-Virgin, blessed John Baptist, and the holy Apostles Peter and Paul, for our fathers in the faith. May God, through the merits and prayers of the Saints, bless and preserve us now and for ever. Amen.

AND I SAY ALSO UNTO THEE, THAT THOU ART PETER, AND UPON THIS ROCK I WILL BUILD MY CHURCH; AND THE GATES OF HELL SHALL NOT PREVAIL AGAINST IT. AND I WILL GIVE UNTO THEE THE KEYS OF THE KINGDOM OF HEAVEN: AND WHATSOEVER THOU SHALT BIND ON EARTH SHALL BE BOUND IN HEAVEN: AND WHATSOEVER THOU SHALT LOOSE ON EARTH SHALL BE LOOSED IN HEAVEN.

Foreword

THE publication of this edition of the Book of Common Prayer, carefully edited and directed toward those in the Antiochian Western Rite Vicariate, marks a contemplative moment of continued growth of the Orthodox Catholic faith in North America and in the territories of British Christendom. Much has already been written about the nearly universal acceptance of the Western Rite among our Holy Fathers in modern times, and so this foreword is not concerned with such a topic. The message I hope to leave with the faithful is the importance of beauty, and the importance of Orthodox Christianity being the Great Healer of nations.

The Orthodox Church has always emphasized the importance of beauty in the salvation of mankind, for as it says in the Epistle of James,

> Every good gift and every perfect gift is from above, and cometh down from the Father of lights, with whom is no variableness, neither shadow of turning. —James 1:17

In our homeland of North America, many of us have been led to Orthodoxy by the beauty of the English tradition of prayer which was given to our forefathers (according to the flesh) by way of our English and Scottish heritage. As the peoples of the British Isles arrived in the colonial New World, so too did their prayer tradition which was rooted in a deep connection to the blessed Dowry of Mary, that is, the Albion of Saint Alfred and the Three Holy Patrons: St. Edmund, St. Edward, and St. Gregory the Great. Even the Congregationalists, Puritans, and "Low Churchmen" could not avoid retaining an echo of the ancient Liturgy within their houses of prayer.

This deep connection to the England once known as Mary's Dowry is what allowed for beauty to thrive in a deeply desolate new world. Amidst the darkness of isolation and uncertainty, New Englanders and Southern Americans built lasting houses of prayer adorned with the beauty of Christ's Name and images of His saints. Within those halls, the men and women of an uncertain new world prayed the collects, hymns, and prayers of an ancient inheritance, albeit commingled with new and unfamiliar doctrines and liturgics that set a broad path against what was once dedicated to the very Narrow Way of Christ. In modern times, the Christians of the English tradition have found themselves near shipwreck and in danger of losing the beauty of their rich past. Though the valuable buildings, real-estate, and stained glass have passed on to "the Religion of the Future," as our holy father St. Seraphim of Platina called it, the prayers and liturgical life of English Christians can be still be made firm in the life giving Water of Christ. This life giving water runs out from the side of the Living Christ, from His Church, which boldly proclaims the Catholic faith without shame.

The thirst for the living water of the ancient Orthodoxy of the Christian life was never fully stomped out by the errors of the dialectical tension of Roman Catholicism and Anglicanism. Much has been said before about the elegant writing of William Laud, Richard Hooker, Lancelot Andrewes, and George Herbert. And so I wish to offer a sometimes forgotten example from the Right Reverend William Seabury of Connecticut. Rt. Rev. Seabury was the first Anglican bishop consecrated in the United States and, writing in favor of aligning the American Anglican ethos with that of the Scottish prayerbook, he wrote:

> The grand fault in that [1662] office [of Holy Communion] is the deficiency of a more formal oblation of the elements, and of the invocation of the Holy Ghost to sanctify and bless them. The Consecration is made to consist merely in the Priest's laying his hands on the elements and pronouncing "This is my body," etc., which words are not consecration at all, nor were they addressed by Christ to the Father, but were declarative to the Apostles . . . The efficacy of Baptism, of Confirmation, of Orders, is ascribed to the Holy Ghost, and His energy is implored for that purpose; and why he should not be invoked in the consecration of the Eucharist, especially as all the old Liturgies are full to the point, I cannot conceive. —*The Life and Correspondence of Samuel Seabury*, p. 354

We see in this early American bishop a desire to return to the ancient liturgies, to live within the uncreated energies experienced and preached by St. Paul, and to find what had been lost after the Great Schism and the deeply regrettable brother wars of the Reformation which led to the destruction, desolation, and murder of European Christianity.

Herein we find the purpose of the 2025 Proposed Book of Common Prayer: to bring forth the Good, to let go of all that which is contrary to the Truth, and to heal what is infirm. Following carefully the recommendations of the fathers of the Antiochian and Russian Orthodox Churches, the 2025 Proposed Book of Common Prayer has only sought to remain loyal to what the Orthodox Church has already observed and ruled. Recalling the conclusion to the Russian Observations on the American Prayerbook, it is worth restating their findings:

Foreword

The committee, after reviewing these "Observations," allowed in general the possibility that if Orthodox parishes, composed of former Anglicans, were organized in America, they might be allowed, at their desire, to perform their worship according to the "Book of Common Prayer," but only on condition that the following corrections were made in the spirit of the Orthodox Church. —*Russian Observations upon the American Prayer Book* 2:VI

The 2025 Proposed Book of Common Prayer is not a restoration project, nor is it a historical recreation. Rather it is a spiritual surgery for those of the Anglican patrimony who seek communion with the One, Holy, Catholic, and Apostolic Church and to retain that which the ancient Church provided, influenced, and now attempts to sustain.

Continued prayers are also asked for all those of the Western Rite, so that a spirit of pretest, pride, or confusion may never yoke itself to the Latin and English presence within the Orthodox world. All things are submitted to the Holy Church so that Christ may judge, through His living Mystical Body.

The Blessings of Our Lord Jesus Christ,

The Reverend Father Justin Slaughter Doty
Priest, St. Euphemia Orthodox Christian Church
Overseeing St. Botolph Orthodox Chapel

Editor's Preface

Gregory, when he looked upon the youthful Angles, said: They have the countenance of Angels, and such as these should be of the fellowship of the Angels in heaven. —Mattins Antiphon for the Feast of Pope St. Gregory the Great

s Americans, we have inherited many fruits of the great work of Pope St. Gregory the Great in sending St. Augustine of Canterbury to reëvangelise Kent. In the following centuries, that blessed island realised great spiritual growth and maturity, even in the face of paganism and heresies. Unfortunately, along with the rest of the West, she was dragged into a great schism and only partially healed by internal reformation.

Because of this, we are greatly blessed to have received again that same great work in its ancient fulness. The Orthodox Church, in her great solicitude and care for the salvation of all men, has visited even America to bring the precious and inestimable gift of Our Lord's Good News, so that we may 'worship the Father in spirit and truth'.

It is towards this end that we are joyful to present this Book for the praying of the Daily Office. This is part of a larger project, the proposal of an official Book of Common Prayer for use in the Antiochian Western Rite Vicariate. It has been well-received by the clergy in the Vicariate, already being used in some of our churches, and we hope for a quick reception and official approbation.

With this Book, we wish to provide widely the opportunity to pray the Daily Office, according to the English Orthodox tradition, in an accessible manner. Those familiar with the Prayer Book Tradition will find it delightfully similar to the 1928 Book of Common Prayer's Daily Office. This Book, providing what is necessary for most people to pray the Office, contains: the Hours, the Psalter, the Collects for Sundays and Red Letter Days, and other rites and ceremonies which may prove beneficial in your prayer life.

We are sure that this Book will help you encounter Christ Himself, the Source and Goal of all prayer. Please pray for us as we pray for you.

On the Feast of Our Lady of Walsingham

Pax Christi,

Mr. Augustine Watson, MSt
Chief Editor, Apologia Anglicana

Rubrics

PREFACE

IN the Christian life, the Holy Sacrifice of the Mass and the Daily Office serve as the highest modes of prayer. Due to their solemnity, it is important to attend carefully to their proper celebration.

Through the Mass, the highest sacrifice is offered unto the Most Holy Trinity, and Christ is made substantially present upon the Altar. In the Office, the Christian obediently, faithfully, and joyfully observes the Sacred Scriptures' exhortation to offer the morning and evening sacrifice.

The Christian who prays this Book, both layman and cleric, must keep the rubrics and their purpose within these prayers in mind. At the same time, however, the rubrics are to help the Christian offer his Sacrifice with loving care and faithfulness, not to bog him down with obligations. The Rites and Rubrics in this Book are laid out in a manner that should be accessible, especially after a few uses, lest 'there be more business to find out what should be read, than to read it when it be found out.'

GENERAL RUBRICS

Amen When the word *Amen* is in italics, it should be said by the Congregation in response to the Minister's prayer.

Antecommunion It may occur that a community lacks a Priest on Sunday or another day where the Service of Holy Communion is desired. In such a case, Mattins and the Great Litany should first be said, followed by the Rite of Antecommunion.

NOTE, Mattins, the Great Litany, and Antecommunion should all be led by the Minister in the same place as the Office, not at the Altar.

Collects When several proper Collects are said, only the first and the last receive the full ending.

Commemorations When multiple Feast Days overlap on the same day, the Office will be of the Feast Day of highest rank. The other Feast Day(s) will then be commemorated (or, in some cases, suppressed or transferred). Commemoration consists of praying the highest-ranking Feast Day's collect first followed by the lower ranking Feast Day(s)' collect.

Conclusion of Collects When the Collect is addressed to God the Father, the ending is 'Through Jesus Christ thy Son our Lord, who liveth and reigneth with thee, in the unity of the Holy Ghost, God, throughout all ages, world without end. Amen.'

Rubrics

If in the beginning of the Collect the Son be mentioned: 'Through the same Jesus Christ thy Son our Lord; who liveth and reigneth with thee in the unity of the Holy Ghost, God, throughout all ages, world without end. Amen.'

If at the end of the Collect the Son be mentioned: 'Who liveth and reigneth with thee in the unity of the Holy Ghost, God, throughout all ages, world without end. Amen.'

If the Collect be addressed to the Son: 'Who livest and reignest with the Father, in the unity of the Holy Ghost, God, throughout all ages, world without end. Amen.'

If the Collect be addressed to the Holy Spirit: 'Who livest and reignest with the Father and the Son, God, throughout all ages, world without end. Amen.'

When the Holy Spirit is mentioned in the Collect: 'In the unity of the same Holy Ghost, etc.'

Dominus Vobiscum The Minister may only proclaim the *Dominus vobiscum* (The Lord be with you) if he be in Major Orders. Otherwise, he must instead lead with the *Domine, exaudi orationem nostram* (O Lord, hear our prayer) wherever the *Dominus vobiscum* appears, or omit it entirely if it would be said twice consecutively.

Ferial Commemorations In Advent & Lent, the propers for the First Sunday of Advent and Ash Wednesday may be said when commemoration of their season's respective Feria is indicated.

Gloria Patri During Passiontide, the *Gloria Patri* is omitted in the Invitatory of Mattins, Responsory of the Minor Hours, and Introit. During the Sacred Triduum, the *Gloria Patri* is wholly omitted.

Latin In much of this Book, Latin is provided alongside the English. The Latin may always be used instead of the English, unless otherwise determined by the Ordinary. When Latin is not provided, but great devotion exists for the Latin language, the Latin which serves as the base text (such as the Liber Precum Publicarum, Breviarium Monasticum, Missale, & Rituale) may be used, with great concern for the catechesis and participation of the People.

Liturgical Seasons For the purpose of the rubrics, these festive seasons are referenced:

Rubrics

- Christmastide: From I Evensong of Christmas Day until I Evensong of Epiphany Day, exclusive.
- Epiphanytide: From I Evensong of Epiphany Day until I Evensong of Septuagesima Sunday, exclusive.
- Septuagesimatide (Pre-Lent): From I Evensong of Septuagesima Sunday until Mattins of Ash Wednesday, exclusive.
- Lent: From Mattins of Ash Wednesday until I Evensong of Passion Sunday, exclusive.
- Passiontide: From I Evensong of Passion Sunday until Mattins of Maundy Thursday, exclusive.
- Sacred Triduum: From Mattins of Maundy Thursday until I Evensong of Easter Sunday, exclusive.
- Eastertide (Paschaltide): From I Evensong of Easter Sunday until I Evensong of Trinity Sunday, exclusive.
- Trinitytide: From I Evensong of Trinity Sunday until I Evensong of the First Sunday of Advent, exclusive.

Minor Feast Days Since only I and II Doubles are provided here in this Book (with some exceptions), the rubrics will be geared towards those. When the Office or Mass is celebrated with the rest of the Feast Days, the rubrics of the *Prayer Book Hymnal* should be consulted.

Mode of Recitation Wherever it is indicated something be read, it may also be chanted, except for the Fore-Office and the Prayers after the Third Collect.

Office Rubrics

Collects The Collect to be said during the Office is provided in the relevant Proper.

Ferial Days The Ferial Office, that is, the Simple Office of the occurrent Season, is always said on weekdays in Lent, on Ember Days, and on Rogation Monday, unless a I or II Double occur, in which case the Office is of the Feast with Commemoration of the Feria.

On weekdays in Advent and between Septuagesima and Ash Wednesday, and on Common Vigils, the Ferial Office is always said unless a Double Feast or Octave occur, and then Commemoration is made of such Ferias.

Rubrics

If a Simple Octave Day occur on one of these Ferias, it is only commemorated.

In like manner throughout the year the Office is of the Feria on those weekdays on which there does not occur a Double Feast, an Octave, or the Office of St. Mary on Saturday.

Gloria Patri After every Psalm and the indicated Canticles, except in the Office of the Dead or where otherwise indicated, the *Gloria Patri* should be said.

It is customary to reverence the Trinity by bowing one's head during the *Gloria Patri*, instead of crossing oneself.

Lectionary The Lessons and Psalms for the days of the Church Year are provided in the lectionary, according to the Rankings of Feast Days (p. xii).

NOTE, The proper psalms for Second Class and lower Sundays are optional.

Octaves The Office of an Octave is said (or Commemoration thereof made, when it is hindered by a Feast or a Sunday) through eight continuous days in Octaves of Feasts of the I Class. Octaves of Feasts of the II Class, which are Simple Octaves, are kept only on the Octave Day itself, with the rite of a Simple, unless hindered by a more worthy Office; but no notice is taken of the days within the Octave. If any Octave is not ended before Ash Wednesday, the Vigil of Pentecost, or 17 December, no notice is taken of it thenceforth.

A Simple Octave Day occurring within an Octave is only commemorated.

Octave Days On the Octave Day, except for the proper Psalms and Lessons, the Office is said as on the day of the Feast, unless otherwise noted. On a Simple Octave Day the Office is Simple.

On Sundays within Privileged Octaves, the Office is said as directed in the Proper of Season. On Sundays within Common Octaves, the Office is of the Sunday with Commemoration of the Octave.

Office of the Dead The Office of the Dead may be prayed in addition to the Daily Office. It may also be prayed instead of the Daily Office on an ordinary Feria, a Memorial, or a Feast of Simple rank.

The Office of the Dead may also replace the Daily Office of rank Double or lower on the day of death and the day of burial.

Rubrics

Office of the Dead Antiphons The Antiphons are not doubled except on 2 November; on the day of a burial; on the day after receiving tidings of a death; on the third, seventh, and thirtieth days; on the anniversary (even when transferred); and whenever the Office is celebrated solemnly.

Office of the Dead Lessons The lessons are always read without introduction or conclusion.

Office of Our Lady on Saturday On all Saturdays—except in Advent, Septuagesimatide, Lent, and on Ember Days—unless the Office be of a Double Feast (even transferred), or of an occurrent Octave or Vigil, or of a Sunday anticipated according to the rubrics, the Office is of St. Mary.

Scripture Verse Numbers When a lesson or psalm is listed with only one verse (such as John 1:45 or Psalm 102:15), the Minister reads the that verse and the verses following for the rest of the chapter.

Suffrages The Suffrages in the Minor Hours are not said on Feast Days Double or higher.

Sunday Collects If the Office be of a Feria without a proper Collect, then the Collect of the preceding Sunday is read.

Third Lesson In accordance with pious custom, after the Second Canticle in the Major Hours, but before the Creed, it is fitting for a patristic lesson to be read from the Feast Day's Second or Third Nocturn in Monastic or Sarum Matins.

Vigils The Office of a Vigil is only said at Mattins.

If a Vigil fall on a Sunday (except for the Vigils of Nativity & Epiphany), it is said or commemorated on the preceding Saturday.

Ranking of Days

EAST Days are ranked in order of priority. This is important, since it determines both what is prayed in the changeable parts of the Office (the Propers) and how to determine which Feast outranks the other(s) when Feast Days overlap on the same day.

The rankings for all of the Feast Days throughout the year are provided in the Kalendar (p. xvi). However, there are some rankings which are not provided there or may need to be explained. For most people, it is expedient to order a yearly Ordo from the Antiochian Western Rite Vicariate which lays out the correct ordering for each day. However, to determine it without an Ordo, important rankings are described here.

- Feast Days

    First Class Double (I Double)

    Second Class Double (II Double)

    Greater Double

    Double Feasts of Double and higher have I and II Evensong, beginning with I Evensong and ending with Compline of the following day.

    Semidouble Sundays and days within Common Octaves are Semidouble. The Semidouble Office begins with I Evensong and ends with Compline of the following day.

    Memorial No Office is to be said for a Memorial, but on the day on which they are noted in the Kalendar, Commemoration only is made of them at I Evensong and Mattins; except on II Doubles, on which Commemoration of the Memorial is omitted at Evensong; and on I Doubles, on which no Commemoration is made of Memorials.

    Simple The Office is Simple on weekdays when the Office is of the Feria, and on the Octave Day of a Simple Octave.

    The Simple Office begins with I Evensong, and ends with None of the following day.

- Ferial Days

    First Class Feria No Feast Day may be celebrated. Begins at Mattins.

    – Ash Wednesday
    – Holy Monday
    – Holy Tuesday

Ranking of Days

- Holy Wednesday

Second Class Feria Only I and II Doubles may be celebrated, lesser Feast Days being commemorated. Begins at Mattins.

- Ember Days
- Rogation Monday
- Weekdays in Lent & Passion Week

Greater Feria Begins at Mattins.

- Weekdays in Advent

Feria Begins when the Office of the preceding day ceases. The Ferial Office ends at None if a Double or Simple follow.

- Octaves

  - Privileged Octaves

  First Order Privileged Octaves The Feast Day, and second & third days of the Octave, are I Double. The rest of the Octave until the Octave Day is Semidouble. The Octave Day is I Double. Feast Days cannot outrank the Days within the Octave, nor the Octave Day.
  A I or II Double is transferred to the first unhindered day after the Octave; other Feasts are commemorated, except on the Feast Day and the two following days.

  - Easter Octave

  - Whitsun Octave

  Second Order Privileged Octaves The Feast Day is I Double. The Days within the Octave are Semidouble, being only out-ranked by I Double, with the Octave commemorated. The Octave Day is Greater Double, and gives place only to a I Double of universal observance.

  - Epiphany Octave

  - Corpus Christi Octave

  Third Order Privileged Octaves Days within the Octave are trumped by any feast over Simple. Any Double Feast within this Octave has its Office with Commemoration of the Octave, but on the Octave Day of the Ascension only a I or II Double is kept, with Commemoration of the Octave.

  - Christmas Octave

Ranking of Days

* Ascension Octave
- Common Octaves
  The Days within the Octave are Semidouble. A Double Feast occurring within a Common Octave has its Office with Commemoration of the Octave, unless otherwise noted.
  NOTE, Common Octaves are not commemorated during Lent.
  * Conception of the BVM Octave
  * Assumption Octave
  * Nativity of St. John Baptist Octave
  * Solemnity of St. Joseph Octave
  * Sts. Peter & Paul Octave
  * All Hallows Octave
  * The Octave of the principal patron saint of a church, cathedral, order, town, diocese, province, or nation.
- Simple Octaves
  The Feast Day is II Double. The Octave Day is Simple. The Days within the Octave are not commemorated.
  * St. Stephen Octave
  * St. John the Evangelist Octave
  * Holy Innocents Octave
  * St. Lawrence Octave
  * Nativity of the B.V.M. Octave
  * Divine Compassion Octave
  * An Octave of Secondary Patrons

• Sundays

First Class Sundays of the First Class give place to no Feast. A I or II Double Feast Day falling on a Sunday of the First Class is transferred to the first unhindered day.

NOTE, When I or II Double Feast Day falls on (or is transferred to) Monday, I Evensong is of the Feast Day with a commemoration of the Sunday. Otherwise, it is of the Sunday with a commemoration of the Feast Day.

- First Sunday of Advent
- Sundays in Lent & Passiontide

Ranking of Days

- Easter Sunday
- Low Sunday
- Whitsunday

Second Class Sundays of the Second Class give place only to I Doubles, and the Sunday is commemorated.

- Second Sunday of Advent
- Third Sunday of Advent
- Fourth Sunday of Advent
- Septuagesima Sunday
- Sexagesima Sunday
- Quinquagesima Sunday

All Other Sundays On lesser Sundays, the Office is of the Sunday unless a Double I or II Class occur thereon, when the Office is of the Feast with Commemoration of the Sunday.

- Privileged Vigils

First Class Vigils of the First Class are preferred over any other Feast Day.

- Vigil of the Nativity of Our Lord
- Vigil of Whitsunday

Second Class Vigils of the Second Class are preferred over any Feast Day, except I & II Doubles and Feasts of Our Lord.

- Vigil of Epiphany

- Common Vigils

Non-privileged Vigils are preferred over any Feast Day, except Doubles & above or an Octave.

Kalendar of the Church Year

Kalendar of the Church Year

26 | St. Polycarp of Smyrna, Bishop & Martyr, *Memorial*
27 | St. John Chrysostom, Bishop, Confessor, & Doctor, *Double*
28 | St. Cyril of Alexandria, Bishop, Confessor, & Doctor, *Double*
     | The Second Feast of St. Agnes, Virgin Martyress, *Memorial*
29 |
30 | St. Martina, Virgin Martyress, *Memorial*
31 | (Earliest Date of Septuagesima)

FEBRUARY

1 | St. Ignatius of Antioch, Bishop & Martyr, *Double*
   | St. Bridget of Ireland, Virgin, *Memorial*
2 | Purification of the Blessed Virgin Mary, *2ⁿᵈ Double*
3 | St. Blaise, Bishop & Martyr, *Memorial*
4 | The New Martyrs of Russia, *Memorial*
   | St. Joseph of Aleppo, Martyr, *Memorial*
5 | St. Agatha, Virgin Martyress, *Greater Double*
6 | St. Dorothea, Virgin Martyress, *Memorial*
   | St. Photius, Bishop & Confessor, *Memorial*
7 | St. Romuald, Abbot, *Double*
8 |
9 | St. Apollonia of Alexandria, Virgin Martyress, *Memorial*
10 | St. Scholastica, Virgin, *2ⁿᵈ Double*
11 | Pope St. Gregory II, Bishop & Confessor, *Memorial*
12 |
13 |
14 | St. Valentine, Priest & Martyr, *Memorial*
15 | Sts. Faustinus & Jovita, Martyrs, *Memorial*
16 |
17 | (Earliest Date of Lent)
18 | St. Simeon of Jerusalem, Bishop & Martyr, *Memorial*
19 |
20 |
21 |
22 | Chair of St. Peter at Antioch, *2ⁿᵈ Double*
   | Commemoration of St. Paul, *Commemoration*
23 | Vigil of St. Matthias, *Vigil*
24 | St. Matthias, Apostle, *2ⁿᵈ Double*
25 | St. Walburga of Heidenheim, Virgin, *Memorial*
26 | Pope St. Alexander of Alexandria, Bishop & Confessor, *Memorial*
27 | St. Raphael of Brooklyn, Bishop & Confessor, *Greater Double*

Kalendar of the Church Year

28 |

MARCH

1 | St. David of Wales, Bishop & Confessor, *Memorial*
2 | St. Chad, Bishop & Confessor, *Memorial*
3 |
4 | Pope St. Lucius I, Bishop & Martyr, *Memorial*
5 |
6 | St. Perpetua & Felicitas, Martyrs, *Double*
 | (Latest Date of Septuagesima)
7 |
8 |
9 | St. Gregory of Nyssa, Bishop, Confessor, & Doctor, *Memorial*
10 | The Forty Holy Martyrs, *Memorial*
11 |
12 | Pope St. Gregory, Bishop, Confessor, & Martyr, *2ⁿᵈ Double*
13 |
14 |
15 |
16 |
17 | St. Patrick, Bishop & Confessor, *Double*
 | St. Joseph of Arimathea, Confessor, *Memorial*
18 | St. Cyril of Jerusalem, Bishop, Confessor, & Doctor, *Double*
 | St. Edward, King & Martyr, *Memorial*
19 | St. Joseph, Spouse of the Blessed Virgin Mary, Confessor, *1ˢᵗ Double*
20 | St. Cuthbert, Bishop & Confessor, *Double*
21 | St. Benedict, Abbot, *2ⁿᵈ Double*
22 |
23 | (Latest Date of Lent)
24 | St. Gabriel the Archangel, *Greater Double*
25 | The Annunciation of the Blessed Virgin Mary, *1ˢᵗ Double*
26 |
27 | St. John Damascene, Confessor & Doctor, *Double*
28 |
29 |
30 | St. John Climacus, Abbot, *Memorial*
31 | St. Innocent of Alaska, Bishop & Confessor, *Memorial*

APRIL

1 |
2 |

Kalendar of the Church Year

3	
4	St. Isidore of Seville, Bishop, Confessor, & Doctor, *Double* (Earliest Date of Easter)
5	
6	
7	St. Tikhon of Moscow, Bishop & Confessor, *1ˢᵗ Double*, Common Octave
8	
9	
10	
11	Pope St. Leo the Great, Bishop, Confessor, & Doctor, *Double*
12	
13	St. Hermengild, Martyr, *Memorial*
14	St. Justin, Martyr, *Memorial*
	St. Tiburtius, Valerian, & Maximus, Martyrs, *Memorial*
15	
16	
17	Pope St. Anicetus, Bishop & Martyr, *Memorial*
18	
19	
20	
21	
22	Pope Sts. Soter & Caius, Bishops & Martyrs, *Memorial*
23	St. George, Martyr, *1ˢᵗ Double*, Common Octave
24	Day II within the Octave of St. George, *Semidouble*
25	St. Mark, Evangelist, *2ⁿᵈ Double*
	Day III within the Octave of St. George, *Semidouble*
26	Day IV within the Octave of St. George, *Semidouble*
	Sts. Cletus & Marcellinus, Martyrs, *Memorial*
27	Day V within the Octave of St. George, *Semidouble*
28	Day VI within the Octave of St. George, *Semidouble*
	St. Vitalis, Martyr, *Memorial*
29	Day VII within the Octave of St. George, *Semidouble*
30	Octave Day of St. George, *Greater Double*
May	
1	Sts. Philip & James, Apostles, *2ⁿᵈ Double*
2	St. Athanasius, Bishop, Confessor, & Doctor, *Double*
3	Invention of the Holy Cross, *2ⁿᵈ Double*
	Sts. Pope Alexander (Bishop), Eventius, Theodulus (Martyrs), & Juvenalis (Bishop & Confessor), *Memorial*

Kalendar of the Church Year

4	St. Monica, Widow, *Memorial*
5	
6	St. John before the Latin Gate, *Greater Double*
7	St. Alexis Toth, Priest & Confessor, *Memorial*
8	The Apparition of St. Michael the Archangel, *Greater Double*
	Pope St. Boniface IV, Bishop & Confessor, *Memorial*
	(Latest Date of Easter)
9	St. Gregory Nazianzen, Bishop, Confessor, & Doctor, *Double*
10	Sts. Gordian & Epimachus, Martyrs, *Memorial*
11	
12	Sts. Nereus, Achilles, Domitilla, & Pancras, Martyrs, *Memorial*
13	
14	St. Boniface of Tarsus, Martyr, *Memorial*
15	
16	
17	
18	St. Venantius, Martyr, *Double*
19	St. Pudentiana, Virgin, *Memorial*
20	
21	
22	St. Romanus, Abbot, *Memorial*
23	
24	St. Vincent of Lerins, Confessor, *Memorial*
25	Pope St. Urban, Bishop & Martyr, *Memorial*
26	St. Augustine of Canterbury, Bishop & Confessor, *Double*
	Pope St. Eleutherius, Bishop & Martyr, *Memorial*
27	St. Bede the Venerable, Confessor & Doctor, *Double*
	Pope St. John I, Bishop & Martyr, *Memorial*
28	
29	
30	Pope St. Felix I, Bishop & Martyr, *Memorial*
31	St. Petronilla, Virgin, *Memorial*
JUNE	
1	
2	St. Marcellinus, Peter, & Erasmus, Martyrs, *Memorial*
3	
4	
5	St. Boniface, Bishop & Martyr, *Double*
6	
7	

Kalendar of the Church Year

8	
9	St. Columba of Iona, Abbot, *Double*
	Sts. Primus & Felician, Martyrs, *Memorial*
10	St. Margaret of Scotland, Queen & Widow, *Memorial*
11	St. Barnabas, Apostle, *Greater Double*
12	Sts. Basilides, Cyrinus, Nabor, & Nazarius, Martyrs, *Memorial*
13	
14	St. Basil the Great, Bishop, Confessor, & Doctor, *Greater Double*
15	Sts. Vitus, Modestus, & Crescentia, Martyrs, *Memorial*
16	
17	
18	St. Ephrem the Syrian, Deacon, Confessor, & Doctor, *Double*
	Sts. Marcus & Marcellianus, Martyrs, *Memorial*
19	Sts. Gervase & Protase, Martyrs, *Memorial*
20	Pope St. Silverius, Bishop & Martyr, *Memorial*
21	
22	St. Alban, Protomartyr of England, *Double*
	St. Paulinus, Bishop & Confessor, *Memorial*
23	Vigil of St. John Baptist, *Vigil*
	St. Etheldreda, Queen & Virgin, *Memorial*
24	Nativity of St. John Baptist, *1st Double*, Common Octave
25	Day II within the Octave of St. John Baptist, *Semidouble*
26	Sts. John & Paul, Martyrs, *Double*
	Day III within the Octave of St. John Baptist, *Semidouble*
27	Day IV within the Octave of St. John Baptist, *Semidouble*
28	Day V within the Octave of St. John Baptist, *Semidouble*
	Vigil of Sts. Peter & Paul, *Vigil*
	Pope St. Leo II, Bishop & Confessor, *Memorial*
29	Sts. Peter & Paul, Apostles, *1st Double*, Common Octave
	Day VI within the Octave of St. John Baptist, *Semidouble*
30	Commemoration of St. Paul, Apostle, *Greater Double*
	Commemoration of St. Peter, Apostle, *Commemoration*
	Day VII within the Octave of St. John Baptist, *Semidouble*
JULY	
1	Most Precious Blood of Our Lord Jesus Christ, *2nd Double*
	Octave Day of St. John Baptist, *Greater Double*
	Day III within the Octave of Sts. Peter & Paul, *Semidouble*
2	Visitation of the Blessed Virgin Mary, *2nd Double*
	St. John of San Francisco, Bishop & Confessor, *Memorial*

Kalendar of the Church Year

	Sts. Processus & Martinian, Martyrs, *Memorial*
	Day IV within the Octave of Sts. Peter & Paul, *Semidouble*
3	St. Irenæus of Lyon, Bishop & Martyr, *Double*
	Day V within the Octave of Sts. Peter & Paul, *Semidouble*
4	Day VI within the Octave of Sts. Peter & Paul, *Semidouble*
5	Day VII within the Octave of Sts. Peter & Paul, *Semidouble*
6	The Octave Day of Sts. Peter & Paul, *Greater Double*
7	Sts. Cyril & Methodius, Bishops & Confessors, *Double*
8	
9	
10	Seven Holy Brothers, with Sts. Rufina & Secunda, Martyrs, *Memorial*
	Sts. Joseph of Damascus (Priest) & Companions, Martyrs, *Memorial*
11	Pope St. Pius I, Bishop & Martyr, *Memorial*
	[Solemnity of St. Benedict (Monastics & Oblates only)], *Greater Double*
12	Sts. Nabor & Felix, Martyrs, *Memorial*
13	Pope St. Anacletus, Bishop & Martyr, *Memorial*
14	
15	St. Vladimir of Kiev, King & Confessor, *Double*
16	Sts. Nicholas & Habib Khasha, Martyrs, *Memorial*
17	St. Alexius, Confessor, *Memorial*
18	Translation of St. Raphael of Brooklyn, *Double*
	St. Sergius of Radonezh, Abbot, *Memorial*
	Sts. Symphorosa & Her Seven Sons, Martyrs, *Memorial*
19	St. Seraphim of Sarov, Priest & Confessor, *Memorial*
20	St. Elias the Prophet, Confessor, *Double*
	St. Margaret of Antioch, Virgin Martyress, *Memorial*
21	St. Praxedes, Virgin, *Memorial*
22	St. Mary Magdalene, Penitent, *Greater Double*
23	St. John Cassian, Abbot, *Memorial*
	St. Apollinaris of Ravenna, Bishop & Martyr, *Memorial*
	St. Liborius, Bishop & Confessor, *Memorial*
24	Vigil of St. James, *Vigil*
	St. Christina, Virgin Martyress, *Memorial*
25	St. James, Apostle, *2nd Double*
	St. Christopher, Martyr, *Memorial*
26	St. Anne, Mother of the Blessed Virgin Mary, *2nd Double*
27	St. Pantaleon, Martyr, *Memorial*
28	Sts. Nazarius, Celsus, Martyrs; Pope St. Victor, Bishop & Martyr; & Pope St. Innocent, Bishop & Confessor, *Memorial*

Kalendar of the Church Year

29 | St. Martha of Bethany, Virgin, *Double*
Sts. Pope Felix II (Bishop), Simplicius, Faustinus, & Beatrice, Martyrs, *Memorial*
30 | Sts. Abdon & Sennen, Martyrs, *Memorial*
31 |

AUGUST

1 | Chains of St. Peter, Apostle, *Greater Double*
Commemoration of St. Paul, Apostle, *Commemoration*
Holy Maccabees, Martyrs, *Memorial*
2 | Pope St. Stephen, Bishop & Martyr, *Memorial*
3 | The Invention of St. Stephen, Protomartyr, *Double*
4 |
5 | Dedication of Our Lady of the Snows, *Greater Double*
St. Oswald, King & Martyr, *Memorial*
6 | Transfiguration of Our Lord Jesus Christ, *2ⁿᵈ Double*
Sts. Pope Sixtus II (Bishop & Martyr), Felicissimus, & Agapitus (Deacons), Martyrs, *Memorial*
7 | Most Holy Name of Jesus, *2ⁿᵈ Double*
St. Donatus, Bishop & Martyr, *Memorial*
8 | Sts. Cyriacus, Largus, & Smaragdus, Martyrs, *Memorial*
9 | Vigil of St. Lawrence, *Vigil*
St. Romanus, Martyr, *Memorial*
10 | St. Lawrence, Deacon & Martyr, *2ⁿᵈ Double*, Simple Octave
11 | Sts. Tiburtius & Susanna, Martyrs, *Memorial*
12 |
13 | St. Maximus of Constantinople, Confessor, *Double*
Sts. Hippolytus & Cassian, Martyrs, *Memorial*
14 | Vigil of the Assumption, *Vigil*
St. Eusebius, Priest & Confessor, *Memorial*
15 | Assumption of the Blessed Virgin Mary, *1ˢᵗ Double*, Common Octave
16 | St. Joachim, Father of the Blessed Virgin Mary, *2ⁿᵈ Double*
17 | Day III within the Octave of the Assumption, *Semidouble*
Octave Day of St. Lawrence, *Simple*
18 | Day IV within the Octave of the Assumption, *Semidouble*
St. Helen, Empress, *Memorial*
St. Agapitus, Martyr, *Memorial*
19 | Day V within the Octave of the Assumption, *Semidouble*
20 | Day VI within the Octave of the Assumption, *Semidouble*
21 | Day VII within the Octave of the Assumption, *Semidouble*

Kalendar of the Church Year

22	Octave Day of the Assumption, *Greater Double*
	St. Timothy (Bishop), Hippolytus, & Symphorian, Martyrs, *Memorial*
23	Vigil of St. Bartholomew, *Vigil*
24	St. Bartholomew, Apostle, *2nd Double*
25	
26	Pope St. Zephyrinus, Bishop & Martyr, *Memorial*
27	
28	St. Augustine of Hippo, Bishop, Confessor, & Doctor, *Greater Double*
	St. Hermes, Martyr, *Memorial*
29	Decollation of St. John Baptist, *Greater Double*
	St. Sabina, Martyr, *Memorial*
30	Sts. Felix & Adauctus, Martyrs, *Memorial*
31	St. Aidan of Lindisfarne, Bishop & Confessor, *Memorial*

SEPTEMBER

1	St. Giles, Abbot, *Memorial*
	Twelve Holy Brothers, Martyrs, *Memorial*
2	St. Stephen of Hungary, King & Confessor, *Memorial*
3	
4	St. Gorazde of Prague, Bishop & Martyr, *Double*
5	
6	
7	
8	Nativity of the Blessed Virgin Mary, *2nd Double*, Simple Octave
	St. Hadrian, Martyr, *Memorial*
9	St. Gorgonius, Martyr, *Memorial*
10	
11	Sts. Protus & Hyacinth, Martyrs, *Memorial*
12	Most Holy Name of Mary, *Greater Double*
13	
14	Exaltation of the Holy Cross, *Greater Double*
15	Seven Sorrows of the Blessed Virgin Mary, *2nd Double*
	St. Nicomedes, Martyr, *Memorial*
16	Sts. Pope Cornelius & Cyprian, Bishops and Martyrs, *Double*
	Sts. Euphemia, Lucy, & Geminian, Martyrs, *Memorial*
17	
18	
19	Sts. Januarius & Companions, Martyrs, *Double*
	St. Theodore of Canterbury, Bishop & Confessor, *Memorial*
20	Sts. Eustace & Companions, Martyrs, *Double*

Kalendar of the Church Year

	Vigil of St. Matthew, *Vigil*
21	St. Matthew, Apostle & Evangelist, *2nd Double*
22	Sts. Maurice & Companions, Martyrs, *Memorial*
23	Pope St. Linus, Bishop & Martyr, *Memorial*
	St. Thecla, Virgin Martyress, *Memorial*
24	
25	
26	Sts. Cyprian & Justina, Martyrs, *Memorial*
27	Sts. Cosmas & Damian, Martyrs, *Memorial*
28	St. Wenceslaus, Martyr, *Memorial*
29	Dedication of St. Michael the Archangel, *1st Double*
30	St. Jerome, Priest, Confessor, & Doctor, *Greater Double*
	St. Gregory of Armenia, Bishop & Confessor, *Memorial*

October

1	St. Remigius, Bishop & Confessor, *Memorial*
2	Holy Guardian Angels, *Greater Double*
3	
4	
5	Sts. Placidus & Companions, Martyrs, *Double*
6	
7	The Holy Rosary of the Blessed Virgin Mary, *Greater Double*
	Pope St. Mark of Rome, Bishop & Confessor, *Memorial*
	Sts. Sergius, Bacchus, Marcellus, & Apuleius, Martyrs, *Memorial*
8	
9	Sts. Denys, Rusticus, & Eleutherius, Martyrs, *Memorial*
10	
11	Motherhood of the Blessed Virgin Mary, *2nd Double*
12	St. Wilfrid, Bishop & Confessor, *Memorial*
13	St. Edward, King & Confessor, *Memorial*
14	Pope St. Callistus, Bishop & Martyr, *Double*
15	Our Lady of Walsingham, *Double*
16	
17	
18	St. Luke, Evangelist, *2nd Double*
19	St. Frideswide, Virgin, *Memorial*
20	
21	St. Hilarion, Abbot, *Memorial*
	Sts. Ursula & Companions, Martyrs, *Memorial*
22	

Kalendar of the Church Year

23	
24	St. Raphael the Archangel, *Greater Double*
25	Sts. Chrysanthus & Daria, Martyrs, *Memorial*
26	Pope St. Evaristus, Bishop & Martyr, *Memorial*
27	Vigil of Sts. Simon & Jude, *Vigil*
28	Sts. Simon & Jude, Apostles, *2ⁿᵈ Double*
29	
30	
31	Vigil of All Hallows, *Vigil*

NOVEMBER

1	All Hallows, *1ˢᵗ Double*, Common Octave
2	All Souls, *Double*
	Day II within the Octave of All Hallows, *Semidouble*
3	Day III within the Octave of All Hallows, *Semidouble*
	St. Winifred, Virgin Martyress, *Memorial*
4	Day IV within the Octave of All Hallows, *Semidouble*
	Sts. Vitalis & Agricola, Martyrs, *Memorial*
5	Day V within the Octave of All Hallows, *Semidouble*
	St. Elizabeth, Mother of St. John Baptist, *Memorial*
6	Day VI within the Octave of All Hallows, *Semidouble*
7	Day VII within the Octave of All Hallows, *Semidouble*
	St. Willibrord, Bishop & Confessor, *Memorial*
8	Octave Day of All Hallows, *Greater Double*
	Four Crowned Martyrs, *Memorial*
9	Dedication of the Basilica of St. Saviour, *Greater Double*
	St. Theodore Tyro, Martyr, *Memorial*
10	Sts. Tryphon, Respicius, & Nympha, Martyrs, *Memorial*
11	St. Martin of Tours, Bishop & Confessor, *Greater Double*
	St. Mennas, Martyr, *Memorial*
12	Pope St. Martin I, Bishop & Martyr, *Memorial*
13	St. Britius of Tours, Bishop & Confessor, *Memorial*
14	St. Gregory Palamas, Bishop & Confessor, *Memorial*
15	
16	
17	St. Gregory the Wonder-worker, Bishop & Confessor, *Memorial*
	St. Hilda of Whitby, Virgin, *Memorial*
18	Dedication of the Basilica of the Holy Apostles Peter & Paul, *Greater Double*
19	Pope St. Pontianus, Bishop & Martyr, *Memorial*

Kalendar of the Church Year

20 | St. Edmund, King & Martyr, *Double*
21 | Presentation of the Blessed Virgin Mary, *Greater Double*
    | St. Gelasius, Bishop & Confessor, *Memorial*
    | St. Columbanus, Abbot, *Memorial*
22 | St. Cecilia, Virgin Martyress, *Greater Double*
23 | Pope St. Clement, Bishop & Martyr, *Double*
    | St. Felicitas, Martyr, *Memorial*
24 | St. Chrysogonus, Martyr *Memorial*
25 | St. Catherine of Alexandria, Virgin Martyress, *Double*
26 | St. Peter of Alexandria, Bishop & Martyr, *Memorial*
27 |
28 |
29 | Vigil of St. Andrew, *Vigil*
    | St. Saturninus, Bishop & Martyr, *Memorial*
30 | St. Andrew, Apostle, *2ⁿᵈ Double*

DECEMBER

1 |
2 | St. Peter Chrysologus, Bishop, Confessor, & Doctor, *Double*
    | St. Bibiana, Virgin Martyress, *Memorial*
3 |
4 | St. Barbara, Virgin Martyress, *Memorial*
5 | St. Sabbas of Judæa, Abbot , *Memorial*
6 | St. Nicholas, Bishop & Confessor, *Double*
7 | St. Ambrose of Milan, Bishop, Confessor, & Doctor, *Greater Double*
8 | Conception of the Blessed Virgin Mary, *2ⁿᵈ Double*, Common Octave
9 | Day II within the Octave of the Conception, *Semidouble*
10 | Day III within the Octave of the Conception, *Semidouble*
    | Pope St. Melchiades, Bishop & Martyr, *Memorial*
11 | Day IV within the Octave of the Conception, *Semidouble*
    | Pope St. Damasus, Bishop & Confessor, *Memorial*
12 | Day V within the Octave of the Conception, *Semidouble*
13 | St. Lucy, Virgin Martyress, *Greater Double*
    | Day VI within the Octave of the Conception, *Semidouble*
    | St. Herman of Alaska, Priest & Confessor, *Memorial*
14 | Day VII within the Octave of the Conception, *Semidouble*
15 | Octave Day of the Conception of the Blessed Virgin Mary, *Greater Double*
16 | St. Eusebius of Vercelli, Bishop & Martyr, *Memorial*
17 |

Kalendar of the Church Year

18	Expectation of the Blessed Virgin Mary, *Double*
19	
20	Vigil of St. Thomas, *Vigil*
21	St. Thomas, Apostle, *2nd Double*
22	
23	
24	Vigil of the Nativity of Our Lord, *1st Vigil*
25	Nativity of Our Lord, *1st Double*, *3rd* Octave
	St. Anastasia, Virgin Martyress, *Commemoration*
26	St. Stephen, Protomartyr, *2nd Double*, Simple Octave
	Day II within the Nativity Octave, *Semidouble*
27	St. John, Apostle & Evangelist, *2nd Double*, Simple Octave
	Day III within the Nativity Octave, *Semidouble*
28	Holy Innocents, Martyrs, *2nd Double*, Simple Octave
	Day IV within the Nativity Octave, *Semidouble*
29	Day V within the Nativity Octave, *Semidouble*
30	Day VI within the Nativity Octave, *Semidouble*
31	St. Sylvester, Bishop & Confessor, *Double*
	Day VII within the Nativity Octave, *Semidouble*

DAILY OFFICE LECTIONARY

Lectionary

Proper of Season

Day	Psalms	Lesson 1	Lesson 2
ADVENT I			
Mattins	8,50	Is 55	Lk 1:57
Evensong	96,97	Is 60:1-11,18-end	Jn 1:15-28
Monday			
Mattins	-	Gn 1:1-2:3	Mk 1:1-20
Evensong	-	1 Kgs 11:1-25	Rev 4
Tuesday			
Mattins	-	Gn 2:4-14	Mk 1:21
Evensong	-	1 Kgs 11:26	Rev 5
Wednesday			
Mattins	-	Gn 2:15	Mk 2
Evensong	-	1 Kgs 12	Rev 6
Thursday			
Mattins	-	Gn 3	Mk 3
Evensong	-	1 Kgs 13	Rev 7
Friday			
Mattins	-	Gn 4:1-15	Mk 4:1-34
Evensong	-	1 Kgs 14:1-20	Rev 8
Saturday			
Mattins	-	Gn 4:16	Mk 4:35-5:20
ADVENT II			
Evensong	36,57	1 Kgs 15:25-16:7	Rev 9
Mattins	80,82	Is 35	Lk 4:14-32
Evensong	25,26	Jdgs 16:21	Lk 6:27-42
Monday			
Mattins	-	Gn 6	Mk 5:21
Evensong	-	1 Kgs 16:8	Rev 10
Tuesday			
Mattins	-	Gn 7:1-12	Mk 6:1-29
Evensong	-	1 Kgs 17	Rev 11:1-18
Wednesday			
Mattins	-	Gn 7:13	Mk 6:30
Evensong	-	1 Kgs 18	Rev 11:19-12:end
Thursday			
Mattins	-	Gn 8:1-19	Mk 7

Lectionary
Proper of Season

Day	Psalms	Lesson 1	Lesson 2
Evensong	-	1 Kgs 19	Rev 13
Friday			
Mattins	-	Gn 8:20-9:19	Mk
Evensong	-	1 Kgs 20:1-25	Rev 14
Saturday			
Mattins	-	Gn 9:20 & 11:1-9	Mk 8:1-21
ADVENT III			
Evensong	96,97,98	1 Kgs 20:26	Rev 15-16
Mattins	52,53	Is 40:1-11	Lk 3:1-18
Evensong	93,94	Is 61	Mt 9:35-10:7
Monday			
Mattins	-	2 Esd 6:38-55	Mk 8:22-9:1
Evensong	-	1 Kgs 21	Rev 17
Tuesday			
Mattins	-	Ecclus 42:15-43:10	Mk 9:2-37
Evensong	-	1 Kgs 22:1-28	Rev 18
Ember Wednesday			
Mattins	15,24,26	Mal 1:6-2:7	Jn 1:29
Evensong	84,132,134	Dt 18:13	2 Tim 1:1-2:7
Thursday			
Mattins	-	Ecclus 16:24-17:15	Mk 9:38-10:16
Evensong	-	1 Kgs 22:29	Rev 19
Ember Friday			
Mattins	15,24,26	Mal 3:1-12	Mt 9:1-17
Evensong	84,132,134	1 Sam 3	2 Tim 2:8
Ember Saturday			
Mattins	15,24,26	Mal 3:13-4:end	Lk 6:12-23
Evensong	84,132,134	Jer 1	2 Tim 3:14-4:8
ADVENT IV			
Mattins	98,99	Is 52:1-10	Mt 25:1-13
Evensong	101,103	1 Kgs 17:1-16	Mt 3:1-12
Monday			
Mattins	-	Is 1:1-20	Mk 10:17
Evensong	-	Dt 18:9	Rev 20-21:8
Tuesday			
Mattins	-	Is 2:1-21	Mk 11:
Evensong	-	Mic 3:5-4:7	Rev 21:9-22:end
Wednesday			
Mattins	-	Is 2:22-3:15	Mk 12:1-27

Lectionary

Day	Psalms	Lesson 1	Lesson 2
Evensong	-	Joel 3:9	Lk 1:1-25
Thursday			
Mattins	-	Is 5:1-17	Mk 12:28
Evensong	-	Ezek 12:21	Lk 1:26-38
Friday			
Mattins	-	Is 5:18	Mk 13
Evensong	-	Zech 2:10	Lk 1:39-56
Saturday			
Mattins	-	Is 9:8-10:4	Mt 1:18
CHRISTMAS			
Evensong	2,8,144	Mic 5:2-7	Lk 1:57
Mattins	19,45,85	Is 9:2-7	Lk 2:1-20
Evensong	89:1-30,110,132	Is 7:10-16	Titus 2:11-3:7
ST. STEPHEN			
Mattins	118	2 Chron 24:15-25	Acts 6
Evensong	30,31:1-6	Wis 4:7-15	Acts 7:59-8:8
ST. JOHN EVANGELIST			
Mattins	23,24	Ex 33:7	Jn 13:20-35
Evensong	97	Is 6:1-8	Rev 4
HOLY INNOCENTS			
Mattins	8,26	Jer 31:1-17	Mt 18:1-14
Evensong	19,126	2 Chron 22:8	Mk 10:13-27
CHRISTMAS I			
Mattins	2,8	1 Sam 1:20	Lk 2:22-40
Evensong	89:1-30	Is 9:2-7	Lk 2:1-19
29 December			
Mattins	-	Is 10:33-11:9	1 Jn 1:1-2:6
Evensong	-	Ezek 34:1-16	Lk 2:21-40
30 December			
Mattins	-	Is 11:10-12:end	1 Jn 2:7-17
Evensong	-	Ezek 34:17	Mt 2:1-12
31 December			
Mattins	-	Is 25:1-9	1 Jn 2:18
CIRCUMCISION			
Evensong	105	Dt 10:12-11:1	Mt 2:13
Mattins	40:1-16,90	Ex 6:2-8	Mt 1:18
Evensong	65,103	Gn 32:22-30	Rev 19:11-16
CHRISTMAS II			
Mattins	85,87	Ex 2:1-10	Mt 2:13

Day	Psalms	Lesson 1	Lesson 2
Evensong	90,91	Prv 31:10-29	Lk 2:15-32
MOST HOLY NAME OF JESUS			
Evensong	146,147	Is 7:10-14	Phil 2:5-11
Mattins	9,19,24	Is 28:9-22	1 Jn 3
Evensong	110,111,112	Jer 23:1-6	Lk 2:41
3 January			
Mattins	-	Is 29:9-19	1 Jn 3:18-4:6
Evensong	-	Jer 30:1-11	Jn 1:1-28
4 January			
Mattins	-	Is 32:1-8,16-18	1 Jn 4:7
Evensong	-	Jer 30:15-22	Jn 1:29
5 January			
Mattins	-	Is 35	1 Jn 5
EPIPHANY			
Evensong	19,67	Num 24:15-24	Mt 28:16
Mattins	46,47,48	Is 60	Mt 3:13
Evensong	72,117,135	Is 49:1-13	Jn 2:1-11
Monday			
Mattins	-	Is 42:5-12	Gal 1
Evensong	-	Jer 31:1-9	Jn 2:12
Tuesday			
Mattins	-	Is 45:11-23	Gal 2
Evensong	-	Jer 31:27-37	Jn 3:1-21
Wednesday			
Mattins	-	Is 55	Gal 3
Evensong	-	Jer 33:14	Jn 3:22
Thursday			
Mattins	-	Is 56:1-8	Gal 4:1-5:1
Evensong	-	Ezek 36:1-15	Jn 4:1-26
Friday			
Mattins	-	Is 61	Gal 5:2
Evensong	-	Zeph 3:7	Jn 4:27
Saturday			
Mattins	-	Is 66:1-2,10-14,18-23	Gal 6
Evensong	-	Zech 14:1-9	Jn 5:1-24
EPIPHANY I			
Mattins	47,48	Gn 28:10	Mt 2:1-11
Evensong	66,67	1 Sam 2:1-11,26	Mt 18:1-5,10-14

Lectionary

Day	Psalms	Lesson 1	Lesson 2
Monday			
Mattins	-	Gn 11:27-12:9	Rom 1:1-15
Evensong	-	2 Kgs 1	Jn 5:25
Tuesday			
Mattins	-	Gn 12:10	Rom 1:16
Evensong	-	2 Kgs 2	Jn 6:1-21
Wednesday			
Mattins	-	Gn 13	Rom 2:1-16
Evensong	-	2 Kgs 3	Jn 6:22-40
Thursday			
Mattins	-	Gn 14	Rom 2:17
Evensong	-	2 Kgs 4:1-25a	Jn 6:41
Friday			
Mattins	-	Gn 15	Rom 3:1-18
Evensong	-	2 Kgs 4:25b	Jn 7:1-30
Saturday			
Mattins	-	Gn 16	Rom 3:19
Evensong	-	2 Kgs 5	Jn 7:31
EPIPHANY II			
Mattins	96,97	Ex 3:1-15	Mk 9:2-13
Evensong	45,46	Neh 2:1-11	Acts 5:17-32
Monday			
Mattins	-	Gn 17	Rom 4:1-13
Evensong	-	2 Kgs 6	Jn 8:1-30
Tuesday			
Mattins	-	Gn 18	Rom 4:14
Evensong	-	2 Kgs 7	Jn 8:31
Wednesday			
Mattins	-	Gn 19:1-29	Rom 5:1-11
Evensong	-	2 Kgs 8	Jn 9:1-23
Thursday			
Mattins	-	Gn 19:30-20:end	Rom 5:12
Evensong	-	2 Kgs 9	Jn 9:24
Friday			
Mattins	-	Gn 21:1-21	Rom 6:1-14
Evensong	-	2 Kgs 10	Jn 10:1-21
Saturday			
Mattins	-	Gn 21:22	Rom 6:15
Evensong	-	2 Kgs 11	Jn 10:22

Lectionary

Proper of Season

Day	Psalms	Lesson 1	Lesson 2
EPIPHANY III			
Mattins	20,21	1 Sam 3:1-18	Mk 10:13-16,35-45
Evensong	27,29	Jonah 3-4	Acts 10:1-35,44-end
Monday			
Mattins	-	Gn 22	Rom 7:1-12
Evensong	-	2 Kgs 12	Jn 11:1-27
Tuesday			
Mattins	-	Gn 23	Rom 7:13
Evensong	-	Jonah 1-2	Jn 11:28-44
Wednesday			
Mattins	-	Gn 24:1-28	Rom 8:1-11
Evensong	-	Jonah 3-4	Jn 11:45
Thursday			
Mattins	-	Gn 24:29-52	Rom 8:11-25
Evensong	-	2 Kgs 13	Jn 12:1-19
Friday			
Mattins	-	Gn 24:53	Rom 8:26
Evensong	-	Amos 1:1-2:3	Jn 12:20-36
Saturday			
Mattins	-	Gn 25:7-11,19-end	Rom 9:1-18
Evensong	-	Amos 2:4	Jn 12:37
EPIPHANY IV			
Mattins	75,76	1 Kgs 18:1,17-39	Mk 1:32
Evensong	107	Num 22:1-35	Matt 23:16-26
Monday			
Mattins	-	Gn 26	Rom 9:19
Evensong	-	Amos 3-4	Jn 13:1-19
Tuesday			
Mattins	-	Gn 27:1-25	Rom 10:1-10
Evensong	-	Amos 5	Jn 13:20
Wednesday			
Mattins	-	Gn 27:26	Rom 10:11
Evensong	-	Amos 6	Jn 14
Thursday			
Mattins	-	Gn 28	Rom 11:1-11
Evensong	-	Amos 7	Jn 15
Friday			
Mattins	-	Gn 29:1-20	Rom 11:12-24
Evensong	-	Amos 8	Jn 16

Lectionary

Day	Psalms	Lesson 1	Lesson 2
Saturday			
Mattins	-	Gn 29:21	Rom 11:25
Evensong	-	Amos 9	Jn 17
EPIPHANY V			
Mattins	63,65	1 Kgs 18:41-19:end	Mk 8:22-9:1
Evensong	78	Num 23:1-26	Acts 5:1-11
Monday			
Mattins	-	Gn 30:1-24	Rom 12
Evensong	-	Hos 4	Jn 18:1-27
Tuesday			
Mattins	-	Gn 30:25-31:3	Rom 13
Evensong	-	Hos 5-6	Jn 18:28-19:16
Wednesday			
Mattins	-	Gn 31:4-24	Rom 14:1-18
Evensong	-	Hos 10	Jn 19:17
Thursday			
Mattins	-	Gn 31:25	Rom 14:19-15:12
Evensong	-	Hos 11	Jn 20:1-18
Friday			
Mattins	-	Gn 32	Rom 15:13
Evensong	-	Hos 13-14	Jn 20:19
Saturday			
Mattins	-	Gn 33	Rom 16
Evensong	-	2 Kgs 14	Jn 21
EPIPHANY VI			
Mattins	146,147	Dan 3:8	Mk 10:46
Evensong	148,149,150	Num 24:2	Lk 10:1-16
Monday			
Mattins	-	Wis 1:1-14,2:23-end	2 Pet 1
Evensong	-	2 Kgs 15	Heb 1
Tuesday			
Mattins	-	Wis 4:7-15	2 Pet 2
Evensong	-	2 Kgs 17:1-23	Heb 2
Wednesday			
Mattins	-	Wis 6:1-21	2 Pet 3
Evensong	-	2 Kgs 17:24	Heb 3
Thursday			
Mattins	-	Wis 6:22-7:14	Jude
Evensong	-	Nah 1	Heb 3

Lectionary *Proper of Season*

Day	Psalms	Lesson 1	Lesson 2
Friday			
Mattins	-	Wis 8:1-18	2 Jn
Evensong	-	Nah 2	Heb 4
Saturday			
Mattins	-	Wis 9:1-16	3 Jn
Evensong	-	Nah 3	Heb 5
EPIPHANY VII			
Mattins	75,76	2 Esd 16:53-67	Jas 4
Evensong	107	Bar 3:1-14	Mt 21:33
Monday			
Mattins	-	Prv 22:17	Mk 9:2-29
Evensong	-	Ecclus 28	Heb 6
Tuesday			
Mattins	-	Prv 23:19	Mk 9:30
Evensong	-	Ecclus 29	Heb 7:1-17
Wednesday			
Mattins	-	Prv 24:1-22	Mk 10:1-31
Evensong	-	Ecclus 35	Heb 7:18
Thursday			
Mattins	-	Prv 24:23	Mk 10:32
Evensong	-	Eccles 1	Heb 8
Friday			
Mattins	-	Prv 25	Acts 8:14
Evensong	-	Eccles 2	Heb 9:1-10
Saturday			
Mattins	-	Prv 26	Acts 9:1-22
Evensong	-	Eccles 3	Heb 9:11
EPIPHANY VIII			
Mattins	63,65	Prayer of Manasses	Jas 5
Evensong	78	Bar 4:36-5:end	Mt 23:1-22
Monday			
Mattins	-	Prv 27	Acts 13:33
Evensong	-	Eccles 5	Heb 10:1-18
Tuesday			
Mattins	-	Prv 28	Acts 14
Evensong	-	Eccles 6:1-7:8	Heb 10:19
Wednesday			
Mattins	-	Prv 29	Rev 17
Evensong	-	Eccles 8:1-15	Heb 11:1-16

Lectionary

Day	Psalms	Lesson 1	Lesson 2
Thursday			
Mattins	-	Prv 30:1-16	Rev 18
Evensong	-	Eccles 8:16-9:end	Heb 11:17
Friday			
Mattins	-	Prv 30:17	Rev 19
Evensong	-	Eccles 10	Heb 12
Saturday			
Mattins	-	Prv 31	Rev 20
Evensong	-	Eccles 11-12	Heb 13
SEPTUAGESIMA			
Mattins	8,148	Josh 6:1-21	Lk 7:1-10
Evensong	104	Lam 1:1-12	Mt 23:29-24:2
Monday			
Mattins	-	Gn 34	Phil 1:1-11
Evensong	-	1 Kgs 14:21	Mt 5:1-20
Tuesday			
Mattins	-	Gn 35-36:8	Phil 1:12
Evensong	-	1 Kgs 15:1-24	Mt 5:21
Wednesday			
Mattins	-	Gn 37	Phil 2:1-13
Evensong	-	2 Chron 19:4-end,20:30-end	Mt 6:1-18
Thursday			
Mattins	-	Gn 38	Phil 2:14
Evensong	-	2 Chron 21	Mt 6:19
Friday			
Mattins	-	Gn 39	Phil 3
Evensong	-	2 Chron 22	Mt 7:1-27
Saturday			
Mattins	-	Gn 40	Phil 4
Evensong	-	2 Chron 23	Mt 13:24-52
SEXAGESIMA			
Mattins	33,93	1 Sam 17:17	Mt 10:32-39
Evensong	139	2 Sam 22:1-12,33-36	Acts 12:1-17
Monday			
Mattins	-	Gn 41:1-36	Jas 1:1-15
Evensong	-	2 Chron 24	Mt 15:1-20
Tuesday			
Mattins	-	Gn 41:37	Jas 1:16
Evensong	-	2 Chron 25	Mt 18:1-14

Day	Psalms	Lesson 1	Lesson 2
Wednesday			
Mattins	-	Gn 42:1-17	Jas 2:1-12
Evensong	-	2 Chron 26:1-5-27:end	Mt 18:15
Thursday			
Mattins	-	Gn 42:18	Jas 2:12
Evensong	-	2 Kgs 16	Mt 20:1-16
Friday			
Mattins	-	Gn 43:1-14	Jas 3:1-13
Evensong	-	2 Chron 30:1-15,25-end	Mt 22:1-14
Saturday			
Mattins	-	Gn 43:15	Jas 3:13-4:6
Evensong	-	2 Chron 32:1-23	Mt 25:1-13
QUINQUAGESIMA			
Mattins	15,16	Ruth 1:1-17	Jn 15:1-17
Evensong	111,112	Is 63:7-9,14-16	1 Jn 4
Monday			
Mattins	-	Gn 44	Jas 4:7
Evensong	-	2 Kgs 20	Mt 25:14-30
Tuesday			
Mattins	-	Gn 45:1-15	Jas 5
Evensong	-	Mic 6	Mt 25:31
ASH WEDNESDAY			
Mattins	6,32,38	Is 58	Lk 15
Evensong	102,130,143	Is 1:2-20	Lk 3:1-22
Thursday			
Mattins	-	Gn 45:16	1 Cor 1
Evensong	-	2 Chron 33	Lk 4:1-29
Friday			
Mattins	-	Gn 46:1-7,26-end	1 Cor 2-3
Evensong	-	2 Kgs 22:1-23:3	Lk 4:30-5:16
Saturday			
Mattins	-	Gn 47	1 Cor 4
Evensong	-	2 Kgs 23:21-35	Lk 5:17
LENT I			
Mattins	51,54	2 Sam 11:1-12:13	Lk 18:10-14
Evensong	119:1-32	1 Sam 26:5	Mk 1:9-28
Monday			
Mattins	-	Gn 48	1 Cor 5-6:11
Evensong	-	Hab 1:1-2:4	Lk 6:1-26

Lectionary

Day	Psalms	Lesson 1	Lesson 2
Tuesday			
Mattins	-	Gn 49	1 Cor 6:12-7:16
Evensong	-	Jer 13	Lk 6:27
Ember Wednesday			
Mattins	15,24,26	1 Sam 2:27-35	Lk 10:1-24
Evensong	84,132,134	Jer 26	2 Cor 3
Thursday			
Mattins	-	Gn 50	1 Cor 7:17
Evensong	-	Jer 36	Lk 7:1-23
Ember Friday			
Mattins	15,24,26	Ezek 33:1-20	Mt 10:1-23
Evensong	84,132,134	Amos 7:1-15	2 Cor 4:1-5:4
Ember Saturday			
Mattins	15,24,26	Ezek 44:4-16,23-24	Mt 10:24
Evensong	84,132,134	Neh 8:1-12	2 Cor 5:5-6:10
LENT II			
Mattins	6,38	1 Kgs 21:1-20	Mk 10:17-31
Evensong	119:33-72	1 Sam 19:1-18	Mt 21:33
Monday			
Mattins	-	Wis 9:17-10:14	1 Cor 8-9:23
Evensong	-	2 Kgs 23:36-24:17	Lk 7:24
Tuesday			
Mattins	-	Ex 1	1 Cor 9:24-10:22
Evensong	-	Jer 24	Lk 8:1-25
Wednesday			
Mattins	-	Ex 2	1 Cor 10:23-11:16
Evensong	-	Jer 29:1-14	Lk 8:26
Thursday			
Mattins	-	Ex 3	1 Cor 11:17
Evensong	-	Jer 21	Lk 9:1-17
Friday			
Mattins	-	Ex 4:1-26	1 Cor 12:1-26
Evensong	-	Jer 18	Lk 9:18-36
Saturday			
Mattins	-	Ex 4:27-5:21	1 Cor 12:27-13:end
Evensong	-	Jer 19:1-20:6	Lk 9:37
LENT III			
Mattins	56,86	Gn 50:7-21	Mt 18:21
Evensong	119:73-104	Gn 27:1-38	Mt 20:1-28

Lectionary *Proper of Season*

Day	Psalms	Lesson 1	Lesson 2
Monday			
Mattins	-	Ex 5:22-6:13	1 Cor 14:1-19
Evensong	-	Jer 27	Lk 10:1-24
Tuesday			
Mattins	-	Ex 6:28-7:25	1 Cor 14:20
Evensong	-	Jer 28	Lk 10:25
Wednesday			
Mattins	-	Ex 8:1-19	1 Cor 15:1-22
Evensong	-	Jer 34	Lk 11:1-28
Thursday			
Mattins	-	Ex 8:20	1 Cor 15:20-34
Evensong	-	Jer 35	Lk 11:29
Friday			
Mattins	-	Ex 9:1-12	1 Cor 15:35
Evensong	-	Jer 37	Lk 12:1-12
Saturday			
Mattins	-	Ex 9:13	1 Cor 16
Evensong	-	Jer 38	Lk 12:13-34
LENT IV			
Mattins	142,143	2 Sam 18:5	Lk 15:11
Evensong	119:105-144	Gn 13	Mt 7:13
Monday			
Mattins	-	Ex 10:1-20	2 Cor 1:1-22
Evensong	-	2 Kgs 24:18-25:11,20-22	Lk 12:35
Tuesday			
Mattins	-	Ex 10:21-11:10	2 Cor 1:23-2:end
Evensong	-	Jer 39:11-40:end	Lk 13:1-17
Wednesday			
Mattins	-	Ex 12:1-28	2 Cor 3:1-4:6
Evensong	-	Jer 41	Lk 13:18
Thursday			
Mattins	-	Ex 12:29	2 Cor 4:7-5:10
Evensong	-	Jer 42	Lk 14:1-24
Friday			
Mattins	-	Ex 13	2 Cor 5:11-6:10
Evensong	-	Jer 43	Lk 14:25
Saturday			
Mattins	-	Ex 14	2 Cor 6:11-7:end
Evensong	-	Jer 44	Lk 15

Lectionary

Day	Psalms	Lesson 1	Lesson 2
PASSION SUNDAY			
Mattins	42,43	Gn 22:1-13	Jn 10:1-16
Evensong	119:145-176	1 Kgs 8:22-53	Jn 17
Passion Monday			
Mattins	-	Wis 10:15-11:4	2 Cor 8:1-22
Evensong	-	Dan 1	Lk 16:1-18
Passion Tuesday			
Mattins	-	Ex 15:1-21	2 Cor 8:23-9:end
Evensong	-	Dan 3	Lk 16:19-17:10
Passion Wednesday			
Mattins	-	Ex 15:22-16:10	2 Cor 10
Evensong	-	Dan 4	Lk 17:11
Passion Thursday			
Mattins	-	Ex 16:11	2 Cor 11
Evensong	-	Dan 5	Lk 18:1-17
Passion Friday			
Mattins	-	Ex 17	2 Cor 12
Evensong	-	Dan 6	Lk 18:18
Passion Saturday			
Mattins	-	Ex 18	2 Cor 13
Evensong	-	Dan 9	Lk 19:1-28
PALM SUNDAY			
Mattins	97,110	Zech 9:9-16	Mk 11:1-11
Evensong	22,23	Is 52:13-53:end	Lk 19:28b-44
Holy Monday			
Mattins	6,32,38	Num 20:1-13	1 Cor 10:1-13
Evensong	42,43	Is 5:1-7	Lk 19:45-20:40
Holy Tuesday			
Mattins	51,55	Num 21:1-9	Jn 3:1-21
Evensong	102,130	Is 2:2-5	Lk 21
Holy Wednesday			
Mattins	138,139	Is 42:1-12	Jn 10:11-18
Evensong	140,141	Gn 37:3-28	Lk 22:1-6
Maundy Thursday			
Mattins	81,116	Jer 31:31-34	Jn 13:1-17,33-35
Evensong	142,143	Ex 16:4-15	Lk22:7-22,39-54
Good Friday			
Mattins	22:1-19,40:1-16,54	Gn 22:1-18	Jn 18

Day	Psalms	Lesson 1	Lesson 2
Evensong	64,69:1-22,88	Is 52:13-53:end	Lk 23:13-47
Easter Even			
Mattins	4,16,17	Job 14:1-15	Rom 6:3-11
EASTER DAY			
Evensong	27,30,31	Ex 12:1-14	Lk 23:50
Mattins	2,57,111	Is 51:9-16	Lk 24:1-12
Evensong	113,114,118	Ex 15:1-21	Mt 28:1-10,16-end
Easter Monday			
Mattins	-	Ex 19:1-15	Mk 16:1-8
Evensong	-	Is 40	Lk 24:13-35
Easter Tuesday			
Mattins	-	Ex 19:16-20:26	Jn 20:1-18
Evensong	-	Is 41	Lk 24:36-49
Easter Wednesday			
Mattins	-	Ex 21:1-32	Mk 8:27-9:1
Evensong	-	Is 42	Jn 20:19
Easter Thursday			
Mattins	-	Ex 21:33-22:31	Mk 9:2-13,30-32
Evensong	-	Is 43	Jn 21:1-14
Easter Friday			
Mattins	-	Ex 23	Mk 10:32-45
Evensong	-	Is 44	Jn 21:15
Easter Saturday			
Mattins	-	Ex 24	Mk 14:17,22-28
Evensong	-	Is 45	Mk 16:9
EASTER I			
Mattins	110,111	2 Kgs 4:18-37	Lk 24:13-35
Evensong	2,57	Job 19:1,13-27a	Jn 14:1-14
Monday			
Mattins	-	Ex 25:1-22	1 Pet 1:1-21
Evensong	-	Is 46	Mk 5:22
Tuesday			
Mattins	-	Ex 25:23	1 Pet 1:22-2:10
Evensong	-	Is 47	Lk 7:11-16
Wednesday			
Mattins	-	Ex 31	1 Pet 2:11
Evensong	-	Is 48	Jn 11:1-44

Lectionary

Day	Psalms	Lesson 1	Lesson 2
Thursday			
Mattins	-	Ex 32:1-24	1 Pet 3
Evensong	-	Is 49	Jn 5:19-30
Friday			
Mattins	-	Ex 32:25-33:23	1 Pet 4
Evensong	-	Is 50	Jn 6:25-58
Saturday			
Mattins	-	Ex 34:1-14,27-35	1 Pet 5
Evensong	-	Is 51	Mk 13:18-27
EASTER II			
Mattins	21,23	2 Sam 1:19	Jn 20:24
Evensong	116,117	Ezek 34:11-16,30-31	Jn 10:1-11
Monday			
Mattins	-	Ex 35:20-36:1	Col 1
Evensong	-	Is 52	Acts 3:12
Tuesday			
Mattins	-	Ex 40:17	Col 2
PATRONAGE OF ST. JOSEPH			
Evensong	110,117,146	Gn 39:1-5	Mt 1:18
Mattins	1,2,3	Gn 41:38-43	Mt 2:13
Evensong	112,116,126	Gn 49:22-26	Lk 2:41
Thursday			
Mattins	-	Num 9	Col 3
Evensong	-	Is 53	Acts 17:22-31
Friday			
Mattins	-	Num 10:1-13,29-end	Col 4
Evensong	-	Is 54	Acts 26:1-23
Saturday			
Mattins	-	Num 11:1-30	Philemon
Evensong	-	Is 55	Acts 9:32
EASTER III			
Mattins	120,121,122	2 Sam 12:15b-23	Jn 21:1-19
Evensong	123,124,125	Ex 14:5	Rom 6:1-18
Monday			
Mattins	-	Num 11:31-12:16	Eph 1:1-2:3
Evensong	-	Is 56	1 Cor 15:1-11
Tuesday			
Mattins	-	Num 13:1-3,17-25	Eph 2:4
Evensong	-	Is 57	1 Cor 15:12-22

Day	Psalms	Lesson 1	Lesson 2
Wednesday			
Mattins	-	Num 13:26-14:10	Eph 3
Evensong	-	Is 58	2 Cor 5:5
Thursday			
Mattins	-	Num 14:11-25	Eph 4:1-16
Evensong	-	Is 59	Rom 1:1-12
Friday			
Mattins	-	Num 14:26	Eph 4:17
Evensong	-	Is 60	Rom 6:1-13
Saturday			
Mattins	-	Num 16:1-40	Eph 5:1-21
Evensong	-	Is 61	Rom 14:1-9
EASTER IV			
Mattins	126,127,128	2 Esd 2:42-47	Jn 11:17-39a,41-44
Evensong	129,130,131	Gn 8:6-12,15-16,9:8-16	Mk 12:18-27a
Monday			
Mattins	-	Num 16:41-17:11	Eph 5:22-6:9
Evensong	-	Is 62	Phil 3:7
Tuesday			
Mattins	-	Num 17:12-18:24	Eph 6:10
Evensong	-	Is 63	2 Cor 1:1-10
Wednesday			
Mattins	-	Num 20:1-21	Heb 1:1-12
Evensong	-	Is 64	2 Cor 4:6-5:1
Thursday			
Mattins	-	Num 20:22-21:9	Heb 1:13-2:13
Evensong	-	Is 65:1-12	Rom 8:1-17
Friday			
Mattins	-	Num 21:10-35	Heb 2:14-3:end
Evensong	-	Is 65:13	1 Cor 15:35
Saturday			
Mattins	-	Num 22:1-14	Heb 4:1-13
Evensong	-	Is 66	Rev 21:1-7
EASTER V			
Mattins	146,147	Ezek 37:1-14	Lk 24:36-49
Evensong	132,133,134	Job 14:1-15	Mt 19:16-29
Rogation Monday			
Mattins	-	Dt 28:1-14	Mt 6:24
Evensong	-	Dt 8	Jas 1:1-17

Day	Psalms	Lesson 1	Lesson 2
Rogation Tuesday			
Mattins	-	Is 64	Lk 11:1-13
Evensong	-	1 Kgs 8:22-40	Jas 4
Vigil of the Ascension			
Mattins	-	Jer 14	Jn 6:27-63
ASCENSION THURSDAY			
Evensong	93,99	Gn 5:18-24	Eph 4:1-13
Mattins	8,15,21	2 Kgs 2:1-15	Heb 4:14-5:10
Evensong	24,47,108:1-6	Dan 7:9-14	Lk 24:44
Friday			
Mattins	-	Num 22:15-35	Heb 5:11-6:end
Evensong	-	Obadiah	1 Pet 3:8
Saturday			
Mattins	-	Num 22:36-23:26	Heb 7
Evensong	-	Hab 1	Phil 2:1-11
SUNDAY WITHIN ASCENSION OCTAVE			
Mattins	108,110	2 Kgs 2:1-22	Acts 1:1-14
Evensong	46,47	Dt 34	Jn 14:15-27
Monday			
Mattins	-	Num 23:27-24:25	Heb 8:1-9:12
Evensong	-	Hab 2	Jn 14:1-14
Tuesday			
Mattins	-	Num 25	Heb 9:11
Evensong	-	Hab 3	Jn 14:15
Wednesday			
Mattins	-	Num 26:1-4,52-56,63-end; 27:12	Heb 10:1-34
Evensong	-	Zeph 1	Jn 15:1-16
Thursday			
Mattins	-	Num 32:1-33	Heb 10:35-11:22
Evensong	-	Zeph 2	Jn 15:17-16:11
Friday			
Mattins	-	Dt 31:1-13,24-26	Heb 11:23-12:2
Evensong	-	Zeph 3	Jn 16:12
Saturday			
Mattins	-	Dt 32:48-end;34	Heb 12:1-13
WHITSUNDAY			
Evensong	46,133	2 Esd 13	Jn 17
Mattins	48,68	Joel 2:28	Jn 3:1-16
Evensong	104,145	Gn 2:7-10,15-24	Acts 2:14-24,36-39

Lectionary

Proper of Season

Day	Psalms	Lesson 1	Lesson 2
Whit-Monday			
Mattins	-	Gn 11:1-9	Heb 12:14
Evensong	-	Ezek 11:14	Acts 2:38
Whit-Tuesday			
Mattins	-	Is 10:33-11:10	Heb 13
Evensong	-	Ezek 47:1-12	Acts 3:1-4:4
EMBER WEDNESDAY			
Mattins	15,24,26	Ezek 2:1-3:14	Eph 4:1-16
Evensong	84,132,134	Is 52:1-10	Acts 4:5-31
Whit-Thursday			
Mattins	-	Ezek 3:15	Gal 5:16-6:8
Evensong	-	Jer 31:27-37	Acts 4:32-5:11
EMBER FRIDAY			
Mattins	15,24,26	Jer 33:14	Jn 20:19-29
Evensong	84,132,134	Jer 42:1-12	Acts 5:12
EMBER SATURDAY			
Mattins	15,24,26	Is 61	Mt 28:16
Evensong	84,132,134	Zech 7:1-10	Acts 6
TRINITY SUNDAY			
Mattins	29,33	Gn 1:1-2:3	Jn 1:1-18
Evensong	93,97,150	Job 38:1-7,42:1-5	Rev 19:5-16
Monday			
Mattins	-	Josh 1	Mt 3
Evensong	-	Ezra 1	Acts 7:1-53
Tuesday			
Mattins	-	Josh 2	Mt 4
Evensong	-	Ezra 3-4:6,24	Acts 7:54-8:13
Wednesday			
Mattins	-	Josh 3-4	Mt 5:1-16
CORPUS CHRISTI			
Evensong	113,117,146	Gn 14:18-20	Mk 14:22-25
Mattins	20,23,24	Prv 9:1-6	1 Cor 10:15-17
Evensong	147,148	Ex 16:14-18	Jn 6:47-58
Friday			
Mattins	-	Josh 5	Mt 5:17-32
Evensong	-	Haggai 1-2:9	Acts 8:14
Saturday			
Mattins	-	Josh 6	Mt 5:33
Evensong	-	Haggai 2:10	Acts 9

Lectionary

Day	Psalms	Lesson 1	Lesson 2
TRINITY I			
Mattins	1,5	Is 6:1-8	Acts 9:1-22
Evensong	2,3,4	Is 40:12	Acts 17:16
Monday			
Mattins	-	Josh 7	Mt 6:1-18
Evensong	-	Zech 1	Acts 10
Tuesday			
Mattins	-	Josh 8	Mt 6:19
Evensong	-	Zech 2-3	Acts 11
Wednesday			
Mattins	-	Josh 9	Mt 7:1-20
Evensong	-	Zech 4	Acts 12-13:3
Thursday			
Mattins	-	Josh 10:1-28	Mt 7:21-8:13

Day	Psalms	Lesson 1	Lesson 2
COMPASSION OF OUR LORD			
Evensong	22,28,30	Lam 3:22-33	Eph 1:3
Mattins	34,45,72	Is 12:1-6	Jn 15:9-16
Evensong	84,85,86	Is 63:7-9	Eph 3:14-19

or

Day	Psalms	Lesson 1	Lesson 2
Friday			
Evensong	-	Haggai	Lk 4:16
Mattins	-	Num 34	Mk 1:40-2:12
Evensong	-	Dan 3:16	2 Tim 3

Day	Psalms	Lesson 1	Lesson 2
Saturday			
Mattins	-	Josh 10:29	Mt 8:14-27
Evensong	-	Zech 5-6	Acts 13:4
TRINITY II			
Mattins	12,13	Gn 3	Rev 3:7
Evensong	10,11	Ex 20:1-17	Mk 12:28-34a
Monday			
Mattins	-	Josh 11	Mt 8:28-9:1
Evensong	-	Ezra 5	Acts 14
Tuesday			
Mattins	-	Josh 14	Mt 9:2-17
Evensong	-	Ezra 6:1-12	Acts 15

Lectionary Proper of Season

Day	Psalms	Lesson 1	Lesson 2
Wednesday			
Mattins	-	Josh 18:1-10,20:1-21:3	Mt 9:18-34
Evensong	-	Ezra 6:13	Acts 16
Thursday			
Mattins	-	Josh 21:43-22:20	Mt 9:35-10:15
Evensong	-	Zech 7	Acts 17
Friday			
Mattins	-	Josh 22:21-23:13	Mt 10:16-11:1
Evensong	-	Zech 8	Acts 18
Saturday			
Mattins	-	Josh 23:14-24:end	Mt 11:2-19
Evensong	-	Ezra 4:7-23	Acts 19
TRINITY III			
Mattins	16,17	Gn 4:2b-10	1 Cor 13
Evensong	18	Gn 18:1-10,16-19	Acts 26:1-2,8-19
Monday			
Mattins	-	Jdgs 1:1-28	Mt 11:20
Evensong	-	Neh 1	Acts 20
Tuesday			
Mattins	-	Jdgs 2	Mt 12:1-21
Evensong	-	Neh 2	Acts 21:1-16
Wednesday			
Mattins	-	Jdgs 3	Mt 12:22-37
Evensong	-	Neh 4:1-11	Acts 21:17-36
Thursday			
Mattins	-	Jdgs 4	Mt 12:38
Evensong	-	Neh 4:12	Acts 21:37-22:29
Friday			
Mattins	-	Jdgs 5	Mt 13:1-23
Evensong	-	Neh 5	Acts 22:30-23:end
Saturday			
Mattins	-	Jdgs 6:1-24	Mt 13:24-43
Evensong	-	Neh 6:1-16	Acts 24
TRINITY IV			
Mattins	19,20	Gn 37:2-35	Mt 5:1-16
Evensong	24,25	Dt 10:12-11:1	Jn 8:21-36
Monday			
Mattins	-	Jdgs 6:25	Mt 13:44
Evensong	-	Ezra 7:1,6-end	Acts 25

Lectionary

Day	Psalms	Lesson 1	Lesson 2
Tuesday			
Mattins	-	Jdgs 7	Mt 14:1-21
Evensong	-	Ezra 8:15,21-32,36	Acts 26
Wednesday			
Mattins	-	Jdgs 8	Mt 14:22
Evensong	-	Ezra 9	Acts 27:1-26
Thursday			
Mattins	-	Jdgs 9:1-21	Mt 15:1-20
Evensong	-	Ezra 10:1-17	Acts 27:27
Friday			
Mattins	-	Jdgs 9:22	Mt 15:21
Evensong	-	Neh 8:1-12	Acts 28:1-15
Saturday			
Mattins	-	Jdgs 10	Mt 16:1-12
Evensong	-	Neh 8:13	Acts 28:16
TRINITY V			
Mattins	21,23	Gn 41:1-49,54-end	Mt 25:14-30
Evensong	26,27	Ex 6:1-13	Mk 9:14-29
Monday			
Mattins	-	Jdgs 11:1-17	Mt 16:13
Evensong	-	Neh 9:1-21	1 Thess 1
Tuesday			
Mattins	-	Jdgs 11:18	Mt 17:1-13
Evensong	-	Neh 9:22	1 Thess 2
Wednesday			
Mattins	-	Jdgs 12	Mt 17:14
Evensong	-	Neh 10:28-11:2	1 Thess 3
Thursday			
Mattins	-	Jdgs 13	Mt 18:1-20
Evensong	-	Neh 12:27-31,37-40,43-end	1 Thess 4:1-12
Friday			
Mattins	-	Jdgs 14	Mt 18:21
Evensong	-	Neh 13:1-14	1 Thess 4:13-5:13
Saturday			
Mattins	-	Jdgs 15	Mt 19:1-15
Evensong	-	Neh 13:15-22	1 Thess 5:14
TRINITY VI			
Mattins	28,29	Gn 42	Mt 5:38-6:15
Evensong	30,31	Ecclus 2	Mt 14:22-33

1

Lectionary

Proper of Season

Day	Psalms	Lesson 1	Lesson 2
Monday			
Mattins	-	Jdgs 16	Mt 19:16
Evensong	-	Est 1	2 Thess 1
Tuesday			
Mattins	-	Jdgs 17-18:13	Mt 20:1-16
Evensong	-	Est 2	2 Thess 2
Wednesday			
Mattins	-	Jdgs 18:14	Mt 20:17
Evensong	-	Est 3	2 Thess 3
Thursday			
Mattins	-	Jdgs 19	Mt 21:1-17
Evensong	-	Est 4	Gal 1
Friday			
Mattins	-	Jdgs 20:1-36a	Mt 21:18-32
Evensong	-	Est 13:8	Gal 2
Saturday			
Mattins	-	Jdgs 20:36b-21:end	Mt 21:33
Evensong	-	Est 14	Gal 3:1-15
TRINITY VII			
Mattins	32,36	Gn 43	Mt 25:31
Evensong	33,34	Tob 4:5-11,16	Mt 6:1-4,19-21
Monday			
Mattins	-	Ruth 1	Mt 22:1-14
Evensong	-	Est 5	Gal 3:16
Tuesday			
Mattins	-	Ruth 2	Mt 22:15-33
Evensong	-	Est 6:1-12	Gal 4:1-18
Wednesday			
Mattins	-	Ruth 3	Mt 22:34
Evensong	-	Est 6:13-7:end	Gal 4:19-5:1
Thursday			
Mattins	-	Ruth 4:1-17	Mt 23:1-12
Evensong	-	Est 8	Gal 5:2-15
Friday			
Mattins	-	1 Sam 1:1-20	Mt 23:13-26
Evensong	-	Est 16	Gal 5:16
Saturday			
Mattins	-	1 Sam 1:21-2:21	Mt 23:27
Evensong	-	Est 9:20-10:end	Gal 6

Lectionary

Day	Psalms	Lesson 1	Lesson 2
TRINITY VIII			
Mattins	39,41	Gn 44:18-45:15	Mt 7:1-12
Evensong	37	Gn 18:20	Lk 11:5-13
Monday			
Mattins	-	1 Sam 2:21	Mt 24:1-28
Evensong	-	Zech 9:9-16	1 Cor 1
Tuesday			
Mattins	-	1 Sam 3	Mt 24:29
Evensong	-	Zech 10	1 Cor 2
Wednesday			
Mattins	-	1 Sam 4	Mt 25:1-30
Evensong	-	Zech 11 & 13:7-end	1 Cor 3
Thursday			
Mattins	-	1 Sam 5	Mt 25:31
Evensong	-	Zech 12:1-8	1 Cor 4
Friday			
Mattins	-	1 Sam 6:1-7:2	Mt 26:1-16
Evensong	-	Zech 12:9-13:6	1 Cor 5-6:end
Saturday			
Mattins	-	1 Sam 7:3	Mt 26:17-35
Evensong	-	Zech 14	1 Cor 7:1-24
TRINITY IX			
Mattins	46,47	Ex 32:1-24	Jn 4:1-30
Evensong	44,45	Jonah 1:1-2:1,10	Acts 27:14
Monday			
Mattins	-	1 Sam 8	Mt 26:36-56
Evensong	-	Mal 1	1 Cor 7:25
Tuesday			
Mattins	-	1 Sam 9:1-10:1	Mt 26:57
Evensong	-	Mal 2:1-9	1 Cor 8
Wednesday			
Mattins	-	1 Sam 10:17-11:13	Mt 27:1-26
Evensong	-	Mal 2:10-16	1 Cor 9
Thursday			
Mattins	-	1 Sam 11:14-12:end	Mt 27:27-56
Evensong	-	Mal 2:17-3:6	1 Cor 10
Friday			
Mattins	-	1 Sam 13	Mt 27:57
Evensong	-	Mal 3:7-12	1 Cor 11

Day	Psalms	Lesson 1	Lesson 2
Saturday			
Mattins	-	1 Sam 14:1-23	Mt 28
Evensong	-	Mal 3:13-4:end	1 Cor 12:1-26
TRINITY X			
Mattins	61,62	Jdgs 5	Rom 12:9
Evensong	48,49	Joshua 24:14-28	Lk 9:46
Monday			
Mattins	-	1 Sam 14:24	Lk 3:1-22
Evensong	-	Dan 2:1-24	1 Cor 12:27-13:end
Tuesday			
Mattins	-	1 Sam 15	Lk 3:23-4:13
Evensong	-	Dan 2:25	1 Cor 14:1-20
Wednesday			
Mattins	-	1 Sam 16	Lk 4:14-32
Evensong	-	Dan 7	1 Cor 14:20
Thursday			
Mattins	-	1 Sam 17:1-30	Lk 4:33
Evensong	-	Dan 8	1 Cor 15:1-34
Friday			
Mattins	-	1 Sam 17:31-53	Lk 5:1-16
Evensong	-	Dan 10	1 Cor 15:35
Saturday			
Mattins	-	1 Sam 17:54-18:9	Lk 5:17
Evensong	-	Dan 11:1-4,12:1-end	1 Cor 16
TRINITY XI			
Mattins	63,64	1 Sam 16	Mk 4:35-5:20
Evensong	54,55	Gn 24:1-38,50-54,61-end	Mt 19:1-9
Monday			
Mattins	-	1 Sam 18:10	Lk 6:1-19
Evensong	-	1 Macc 1:1-28	2 Cor 1:1-22
Tuesday			
Mattins	-	1 Sam 19	Lk 6:20
Evensong	-	1 Macc 1:29-58	2 Cor 1:23-2:end
Wednesday			
Mattins	-	1 Sam 20:1-23	Lk 7:1-16
Evensong	-	1 Macc 2:1-30	2 Cor 3:1-4:6
Thursday			
Mattins	-	1 Sam 20:24	Lk 7:16-35
Evensong	-	1 Macc 2:31-48	2 Cor 4:7-5:10

Lectionary

Day	Psalms	Lesson 1	Lesson 2
Friday			
Mattins	-	1 Sam 21:1-22:2	Lk 7:36
Evensong	-	1 Macc 2:49	2 Cor 5:11-6:10
Saturday			
Mattins	-	1 Sam 22:3	Lk 8:1-21
Evensong	-	1 Macc 3:1-26	2 Cor 6:11-7:end
Trinity XII			
Mattins	76,77	1 Sam 20:11	Lk 10:25-37
Evensong	71,72	1 Sam 8	Lk 14:7-24
Monday			
Mattins	-	1 Sam 23	Lk 8:22-39
Evensong	-	1 Macc 3:42	2 Cor 8:1-22
Tuesday			
Mattins	-	1 Sam 24	Lk 8:40
Evensong	-	1 Macc 4:1-25	2 Cor 8:23-9:end
Wednesday			
Mattins	-	1 Sam 25:1-22	Lk 9:1-17
Evensong	-	1 Macc 4:36	2 Cor 10
Thursday			
Mattins	-	1 Sam 25:23	Lk 9:18-36
Evensong	-	1 Macc 6:1-16	2 Cor 11
Friday			
Mattins	-	1 Sam 26	Lk 9:37-50
Evensong	-	1 Macc 8:1-29	2 Cor 12
Saturday			
Mattins	-	1 Sam 27:1-28:2	Lk 9:51
Evensong	-	1 Macc 14:4-19,38-47	2 Cor 13
Trinity XIII			
Mattins	81,82	1 Sam 24	Mt 5:17-26
Evensong	73	Ex 17:8-13	Acts 20:17
Monday			
Mattins	-	1 Sam 28:3	Lk 10:1-24
Evensong	-	Dt 4:1-24	Rom 1
Tuesday			
Mattins	-	1 Sam 29	Lk 10:25
Evensong	-	Dt 4:25-40	Rom 2
Wednesday			
Mattins	-	1 Sam 30	Lk 11:1-13
Evensong	-	Dt 5:1-22	Rom 3

Lectionary *Proper of Season*

Day	Psalms	Lesson 1	Lesson 2
Thursday			
Mattins	-	1 Sam 31	Lk 11:14-28
Evensong	-	Dt 5:23	Rom 4
Friday			
Mattins	-	2 Sam 1	Lk 11:29
Evensong	-	Dt 6	Rom 5
Saturday			
Mattins	-	2 Sam 2:1-11	Lk 12:1-12
Evensong	-	Dt 7:1-11	Rom 6
TRINITY XIV			
Mattins	84,85	2 Sam 23:8-17	Mt 26:1-13
Evensong	74	1 Kgs 22:10-18,29-37	Mt 11:2-19
Monday			
Mattins	-	2 Sam 2:12	Lk 12:13-34
Evensong	-	Dt 7:12	Rom 7
Tuesday			
Mattins	-	2 Sam 3:1,17-end	Lk 12:35-48
Evensong	-	Dt 8	Rom 8:1-17
Wednesday			
Mattins	-	2 Sam 4	Lk 12:49
Evensong	-	Dt 10:12-11:1	Rom 8:18
Thursday			
Mattins	-	2 Sam 5	Lk 13:1-17
Evensong	-	Dt 11:2-12	Rom 9:1-18
Friday			
Mattins	-	2 Sam 6	Lk 13:18
Evensong	-	Dt 11:13	Rom 9:19
Saturday			
Mattins	-	2 Sam 7	Lk 14:1-14
Evensong	-	Dt 12:1-14	Rom 10
TRINITY XV			
Mattins	96,97	1 Kgs 3:5	Mt 10:2-16
Evensong	79,80	1 Kgs 20:28	Mk 9:33
Monday			
Mattins	-	2 Sam 8	Lk 14:15-24
Evensong	-	Dt 12:17	Rom 11
Tuesday			
Mattins	-	2 Sam 9	Lk 14:25
Evensong	-	Dt 14:22	Rom 12

Lectionary

Day	Psalms	Lesson 1	Lesson 2
Wednesday			
Mattins	-	2 Sam 10	Lk 15:1-10
Evensong	-	Dt 15:1-15	Rom 13
Thursday			
Mattins	-	2 Sam 11	Lk 15:11
Evensong	-	Dt 16:1-12	Rom 14
Friday			
Mattins	-	2 Sam 12	Lk 16:1-18
Evensong	-	Dt 16:13-20	Rom 15
Saturday			
Mattins	-	2 Sam 13	Lk 16:19
Evensong	-	Dt 17:8	Rom 16
TRINITY XVI			
Mattins	98,99	Dan 5:1-9,13-30	Lk 12:13-21
Evensong	89	Gn 32:24-30	Eph 6:10-20
Monday			
Mattins	-	2 Sam 14:1-20	Lk 17:1-10
Evensong	-	Dt 18:9	Eph 1
Tuesday			
Mattins	-	2 Sam 14:21	Lk 17:11-19
Evensong	-	Dt 19:1-15	Eph 2
Wednesday			
Mattins	-	2 Sam 15:1-12	Lk 17:20
Evensong	-	Dt 24:14	Eph 3
Thursday			
Mattins	-	2 Sam 15:13-29	Lk 18:1-14
Evensong	-	Dt 26	Eph 4:1-24
Friday			
Mattins	-	2 Sam 15:30	Lk 18:15-30
Evensong	-	Dt 27:1-10	Eph 4:25-5:14
Saturday			
Mattins	-	2 Sam 16	Lk 18:31
Evensong	-	Dt 28:1-14	Eph 5:15-6:9
TRINITY XVII			
Mattins	91,92	Dan 6:1-23	Rom 8:14-18,31-end
Evensong	105	Ruth 2	Jn 8:1-11
Monday			
Mattins	-	2 Sam 17:1-14	Lk 19:1-10
Evensong	-	Dt 29	Eph 6:10

Lectionary

Day	Psalms	Lesson 1	Lesson 2
Tuesday			
Mattins	-	2 Sam 17:15	Lk 19:11-28
Evensong	-	Dt 30	Col 1
Wednesday			
Mattins	-	2 Sam 18:1-18	Lk 19:29
Evensong	-	Dt 31:30-32:43	Col 2
Thursday			
Mattins	-	2 Sam 18:19	Lk 20:1-19
Evensong	-	Dt 33	Col 3:1-4:1
Friday			
Mattins	-	2 Sam 19:1-15	Lk 20:20-38
Evensong	-	Lev 19:1-18,32-end	Col 4:2
Saturday			
Mattins	-	2 Sam 19:16-30	Lk 20:39-21:4
Evensong	-	Lev 26:1-12	Philemon
TRINITY XVIII			
Mattins	111,112	Eccles 12	Lk 2:41
Evensong	106	Ex 34:27	1 Jn 2:24-3:2
Monday			
Mattins	-	2 Sam 19:31-20:2	Lk 21:5-24
Evensong	-	Job 1	Phil 1:1-11
Tuesday			
Mattins	-	2 Sam 20:3	Lk 21:25
Evensong	-	Job 2	Phil 1:12
Wednesday			
Mattins	-	2 Sam 21	Lk 22:1-13
Evensong	-	Job 3	Phil 2:1-13
Thursday			
Mattins	-	2 Sam 23:1-23	Lk 22:14-38
Evensong	-	Job 4	Phil 2:14
Friday			
Mattins	-	2 Sam 24	Lk 22:39-53
Evensong	-	Job 5	Phil 3
Saturday			
Mattins	-	1 Chron 21:1-17	Lk 22:54
Evensong	-	Job 6	Phil 4
TRINITY XIX			
Mattins	114,115	2 Kgs 5	Jn 13:1-15
Evensong	107	Ecclus 38:1-15	Mt 8:1-13

Lectionary

Day	Psalms	Lesson 1	Lesson 2
Monday			
Mattins	-	1 Chron 21:18-22:4	Lk 23:1-26
Evensong	-	Job 8	1 Tim 1
Tuesday			
Mattins	-	1 Chron 22:5	Lk 23:27-46
Evensong	-	Job 9	1 Tim 2
Wednesday			
Mattins	-	1 Kgs 1:5-21	Lk 23:47
Evensong	-	Job 11	1 Tim 3
Thursday			
Mattins	-	1 Kgs 1:22-37	Lk 24:1-12
Evensong	-	Job 12:1-24	1 Tim 4
Friday			
Mattins	-	1 Kgs 1:38	Lk 24:13-35
Evensong	-	Job 15	1 Tim 5
Saturday			
Mattins	-	1 Chron 23:1-6,24-end	Lk 24:36
Evensong	-	Job 16	1 Tim 6
TRINITY XX			
Mattins	116,117	2 Kgs 6:8-17	Jn 9:1-38
Evensong	118	Mic 4:1-7	Jas 3
Monday			
Mattins	-	1 Chron 28	Jn 1:1-18
Evensong	-	Job 18	Titus 1:1-2:10
Tuesday			
Mattins	-	1 Chron 29:1-19	Jn 1:19-34
Evensong	-	Job 19:1-27a	Titus 2:11-3:end
Wednesday			
Mattins	-	1 Chron 29:20	Jn 1:35
Evensong	-	Job 20	2 Tim 1
Thursday			
Mattins	-	1 Kgs 2:1-27	Jn 2:1-11
Evensong	-	Job 21	2 Tim 2
Friday			
Mattins	-	1 Kgs 2:28-35	Jn 2:12
Evensong	-	Job 22	2 Tim 3
Saturday			
Mattins	-	1 Kgs 2:36	Jn 3:1-21
Evensong	-	Job 23:1-24:1	2 Tim 4

Lectionary

Day	Psalms	Lesson 1	Lesson 2
Trinity XXI			
Mattins	120,121,122	Wis 3:1-9	Rev 21:1-7,10-11a,22-end
Evensong	133,134,135	1 Kgs 19:1-18	Mt 11:16
Monday			
Mattins	-	1 Kgs 3:1-15	Jn 3:22
Evensong	-	Job 25-26	Jas 1:1-15
Tuesday			
Mattins	-	1 Kgs 3:16	Jn 4:1-26
Evensong	-	Job 28	Jas 1:16
Wednesday			
Mattins	-	1 Kgs 4:21	Jn 4:27
Evensong	-	Job 29:1-30:1	Jas 2
Thursday			
Mattins	-	1 Kgs 5:1-12	Jn 5:1-24
Evensong	-	Job 31	Jas 3
Friday			
Mattins	-	1 Kgs 5:13-6:1,11-14	Jn 5:25
Evensong	-	Job 32	Jas 4
Saturday			
Mattins	-	1 Kgs 6:37-7:14	Jn 6:1-21
Evensong	-	Job 33	Jas 5
Trinity XXII			
Mattins	123,124,125	Ecclus 44:1-14	Heb 11:1-3,17-12:2
Evensong	136,138	Is 1:10-20	Lk 5:36-6:10
Monday			
Mattins	-	1 Kgs 8:1-21	Jn 6:22-40
Evensong	-	Job 34	1 Pet 1:1-21
Tuesday			
Mattins	-	1 Kgs 8:22-53	Jn 6:41
Evensong	-	Job 36:5-25	1 Pet 1:22-2:10
Wednesday			
Mattins	-	1 Kgs 8:54	Jn 7:1-30
Evensong	-	Job 36:27-37:end	1 Pet 2:11-3:7
Thursday			
Mattins	-	1 Kgs 9:1-9	Jn 7:31
Evensong	-	Job 38:1-36	1 Pet 3:8
Friday			
Mattins	-	1 Kgs 9:10	Jn 8:1-30
Evensong	-	Job 40	1 Pet 4

Lectionary

Day	Psalms	Lesson 1	Lesson 2
Saturday			
Mattins	-	1 Kgs 10:1-15,21-24	Jn 8:31
Evensong	-	Job 42	1 Pet 5
TRINITY XXIII			
Mattins	126,127,128	Job 1:1-21	2 Cor 11:18-30
Evensong	140,141	Ex 33:7-19	Heb 1:1-12
Monday			
Mattins	-	Prv 1:1-19	Jn 9:1-23
Evensong	-	Ecclus 1:1-20	Heb 1:13-2:13
Tuesday			
Mattins	-	Prv 1:20	Jn 9:24
Evensong	-	Ecclus 1:21-2:end	Heb 2:14-3:11
Wednesday			
Mattins	-	Prv 2	Jn 10:1-21
Evensong	-	Ecclus 3:1-15	Heb 3:12-4:13
Thursday			
Mattins	-	Prv 3:1-18	Jn 10:22
Evensong	-	Ecclus 4:1-19	Heb 4:14-5:end
Friday			
Mattins	-	Prv 3:19	Jn 11:1-27
Evensong	-	Ecclus 6:4-17	Heb 6
Saturday			
Mattins	-	Prv 4:1-13	Jn 11:28-44
Evensong	-	Ecclus 6:18	Heb 7:1-17
TRINITY XXIV			
Mattins	129,130,131	Is 5:1-7	Lk 8:4-15
Evensong	144,145	1 Sam 28:7-20	Lk 16:19
Monday			
Mattins	-	Prv 4:14	Jn 11:45
Evensong	-	Ecclus 7:1-18	Heb 7:18
Tuesday			
Mattins	-	Prv 5	Jn 12:1-19
Evensong	-	Ecclus 9:15-10:8	Heb 8:1-12
Wednesday			
Mattins	-	Prv 6	Jn 12:20-36
Evensong	-	Ecclus 10:12-24	Heb 8:13-9:12
Thursday			
Mattins	-	Prv 7	Jn 12:37
Evensong	-	Ecclus 14:20-15:end	Heb 9:11

Lectionary *Proper of Season*

Day	Psalms	Lesson 1	Lesson 2
Friday			
Mattins	-	Prv 8	Jn 13:1-19
Evensong	-	Ecclus 24:1-22	Heb 10:1-18
Saturday			
Mattins	-	Prv 9	Jn 13:20
Evensong	-	Ecclus 26:1-6,13-21	Heb 10:19
SUNDAY NEXT BEFORE ADVENT			
Mattins	146,147	2 Kgs 19:14-36	Mt 6:19
Evensong	148,149,150	Mic 6:1-8	Jas 1:12
Monday			
Mattins	-	Ecclus 44:1-15	Rev 1:1-8
Evensong	-	2 Esd 3:4-27	2 Jn
Tuesday			
Mattins	-	Ecclus 44:16-45:5	Rev 1:9
Evensong	-	Ecclus 48:1-16	3 Jn
Wednesday			
Mattins	-	Ecclus 46	Rev 2:1-11
Evensong	-	Ecclus 48:17-49:end	Jude
Thursday			
Mattins	-	Ecclus 47:1-11	Rev 2:12
Evensong	-	2 Esd 2:33	2 Pet 1
Friday			
Mattins	-	Ecclus 47:12	Rev 3:1-13
Evensong	-	2 Esd 7:19-35	2 Pet 2
Saturday			
Mattins	-	2 Esd 16:54-67	Rev 3:14
Evensong	-	Tob 13	2 Pet 3

Lessons for the Autumnal Ember Days

Day	Psalms	Lesson 1	Lesson 2
Wednesday			
Mattins	15,24,26	Gn 14:13-20	Heb 4:14-5:10
Evensong	84,132,134	1 Kgs 19	1 Tim 3
Friday			
Mattins	15,24,26	Num 17:1-18:7	Lk 12:35-48
Evensong	84,132,134	2 Kgs 2:1-22	1 Tim 4
Saturday			
Mattins	15,24,26	Dt 14:22	1 Cor 9:7
Evensong	84,132,134	Ezek 34:1-16	Titus 1:1-2:8

Lectionary

Feasts of the Year

Feast	Proper Psalms	Lesson 1	Lesson 2
ST. ANDREW			
30 November			
I Evensong	102:15,117	Is 49:1-13	1 Cor 4:1-16
Mattins	34	Num 10:29	Jn 1:29-42
II Evensong	96,100	Is 55	Jn 12:20-36
CONCEPTION OF THE B.V.M.			
8 December			
I Evensong	113,122,127	Gen 3:1-15	Gal 4:1-7
Mattins	8,19,24	Mic 5:2-5	Mt 1:20-23
II Evensong	146,147	1 Sam 2:1-11	Heb 2:9
ST. THOMAS			
21 December			
I Evensong	23,121	2 Kgs 6:8-23	Jn 11:1-16
Mattins	27	2 Kgs 7	Jn 14:1-14
II Evensong	112,113	Heb 1:1-2:4	Mk 16
CONVERSION OF ST. PAUL			
25 January			
I Evensong	1,19	Wis 5:1-16	Gal 1
Mattins	66	Ecclus 39:1-10	2 Tim 3:10-4:8
II Evensong	67,138	Jer 1:1-10	Acts 26:1-23
PURIFICATION			
2 February			
I Evensong	48,138	Ex 13:11-16	Heb 10:1-10
Mattins	20,86,87	1 Sam 1:20	Gal 3:15-4:7
II Evensong	84,113,134	Lev 12	1 Jn 3:1-8
CHAIR OF ST. PETER AT ANTIOCH			
22 February			
I Evensong	146,147	Ezek 3:4-11	Acts 4:8-20
Mattins	47,61,74	Ezek 2:1-7	Acts 11:1-18
II Evensong	113,126,139	Ezek 34:11-16	Jn 21:15-22
ST. MATTHIAS			
24/25 February			
I Evensong	33	1 Kgs 2:26-31	Lk 10:1-20
Mattins	15,24	1 Sam 2:27	Lk 12:16-40
II Evensong	145	Is 22:15-24	1 Jn 2:15

Lectionary *Proper of Saints*

Feast	Proper Psalms	Lesson 1	Lesson 2
POPE ST. GREGORY THE GREAT			
12 March			
I Evensong	1,2,4	Ecclus 39:1-10	Jn 21:15-17
Mattins	15,21,24	Is 61	Mt 5:13-19
II Evensong	96,97,98	Is 52:1-10	Jn 20:19-23
ST. JOSEPH, SPOUSE OF THE B.V.M.			
19 March			
I Evensong	110,117,146	Gn 39:1-5	Mt 1:18
Mattins	1,2,3	Gn 41:38-43	Mt 2:13
II Evensong	112,116,126	Gn 49:22-26	Lk 2:41
ST. BENEDICT			
21 March			
I Evensong	1,2,4	Ecclus 44:1-15	Jn 21:15-17
Mattins	15,21,24	Is 61	Mt 19:27-29
II Evensong	96,97,98	Is 52:1-10	Jn 20:19-23
ANNUNCIATION OF THE B.V.M.			
25 March			
I Evensong	113	Gn 3:1-15	Rev 12
Mattins	89:1-30	Gn 18:1-14	Jn 1:1-18
II Evensong	131,132,138	1 Sam 1:21-2:10	Lk 1:39-56
ST. TIKHON			
7 April			
I Evensong	23,100	Ecclus 50:5,11-21	Jn 21:15-17
Mattins	132	Is 61	Mt 10:1-20
II Evensong	111,112	Is 52:1-10	Jn 20:19-23
ST. GEORGE			
23 April			
I Evensong	1,2,4	Wis 5:1-7,15-20	Lk 21:10-19
Mattins	15,21,24	Jer 17:7-8	Jn 15:1-7
II Evensong	64,65,92	Ecclus 31:8-11	Rev 7:9
ST. MARK			
25 April			
I Evensong	67,96	Ecclus 2	Acts 12:24-13:13
Mattins	102:15	Is 62	1 Pet 5
II Evensong	19,112	Ezek 1:2-14	2 Tim 4:1-18
STS. PHILIP & JAMES			
1 May			
I Evensong	119:33-48	Ecclus 14:20-15:10	Jn 6:1-14
Mattins	139	Is 43:1-12	Jn 1:45

Feast	Proper Psalms	Lesson 1	Lesson 2
II Evensong	27	Is 61	Acts 15:1-31
Invention of the Holy Cross			
3 May			
I Evensong	8,21,24	Is 42:1-9	Phil 2:5-11
Mattins	30,47,66	Is 53:4	Col 2:9-15
II Evensong	76,96,97	Dt 21:18-23	Gal 3:10-14
St. John before the Latin Gate			
6 May			
I Evensong	19,34,45	Ecclus 15:1-6	Rev 1:9
Mattins	47,61,64	Ex 33:9-19	Jn 13:21-35
II Evensong	75,97,99	Is 6:1-8	1 Jn 5:1-12
St. Barnabas			
11 June			
I Evensong	112,146	Ecclus 31:3-11	Acts 4:23
Mattins	1,15	2 Esd 2:33	Acts 9:23-31
II Evensong	97,100	Dt 33:8-11,26-end	Acts 14
St. John Baptist			
24 June			
I Evensong	103	Jdgs 13	Lk 1:5-25
Mattins	82,98	Mal 3:1-12	Mt 3
II Evensong	24,96	1 Kgs 21:17	Mk 6:14-29
Sts. Peter & Paul			
29 June			
I Evensong	118	Ezek 3:4-14	Mt 4:12
Mattins	22:23,67	Ezek 34:1-16	Jn 21:1-22
II Evensong	23,146	Zech 3	1 Pet 4:12-5:11
Commemoration of St. Paul			
30 June			
Mattins	47,61,64	Is 45:18	2 Cor 11:18-31
II Evensong	75,97,99	Is 49:1-13	Phil 1:12-30
Precious Blood			
1 July			
I Evensong	1,2,3,4	Ex 12:1-14	Heb 9:11
Mattins	16,64,94	Is 63:1-9	Mt 27:1-25
II Evensong	23,30,88	Lev 3	Mt 26:20-30
Visitation of the B.V.M.			
2 July			
I Evensong	113,122,127	Songs 2:1-6	Lk 1:5-25
Mattins	45,46,87	Is 7:10-14	Lk 1:26-38

Feast	Proper Psalms	Lesson 1	Lesson 2
II Evensong	146,147	Songs 2:7-14	Lk 1:39-45
St. Mary Magdalene			
22 July			
I Evensong	113,117,146	Is 52:7-10	Mk 15:40-16:10
Mattins	63,93,100	Song 3:1-4,8:1-17	Lk 8:1-3
II Evensong	110,116,126	Zeph 3:14	Jn 20:1-10
St. James			
25 July			
I Evensong	112,113	1 Sam 22:6-19	Mk 1:14-22
Mattins	34	Jer 26:1-11	Mt 10:16
II Evensong	33	2 Kgs 1:1-15	Lk 9:46
St. Anne			
26 July			
I Evensong	113,122,127	Prov 31:10	2 Tim 1:1-10
Mattins	45,46,87	1 Sam 1:1-20	Rom 12:1-17
II Evensong	96,97,98	1 Sam 1:21-2:11	2 Jn
St. Peter in Chains			
1 August			
I Evensong	113,117,146	Jer 1:11-19	Acts 12:5-11
Mattins	75,97,99	Dan 3:19-28	2 Cor 1:3-11
II Evensong	116,126,139	Gn 22:1-19	1 Pet 1:13-21
Transfiguration			
6 August			
I Evensong	29,97	Ex 24	Mk 9:2-13
Mattins	27,61,93	Mal 3:16-4:end	Rev 1
II Evensong	84,99,133	Ex 34:29	2 Cor 3
Most Holy Name of Jesus			
7 August			
Evensong	146,147	Is 7:10-14	Phil 2:5-11
Mattins	9,19,24	Mic 6:3-8	Col 3:12-7
Evensong	110,111,112	Ex 34:1-8	Acts 3:1-12
St. Lawrence			
10 August			
I Evensong	1,2,4	Ecclus 51:1-12	Lk 21:10-19
Mattins	15,17,21	Ecclus 14:20-15:6	Jn 12:24-26
II Evensong	24,64,92	Job 5:8-21	Rev 7:9
Assumption of the B.V.M.			
15 August			
I Evensong	146,147	Songs 2:10	Jn 19:25-27

Lectionary

Feast	Proper Psalms	Lesson 1	Lesson 2
Mattins	45,46,87	Songs 2:1-4	Rev 11:19-12:6
II Evensong	148,149,150	Ecclus 24:7-12	Rev 7:9-17
ST. JOACHIM			
16 August			
I Evensong	1,2,3	Ecclus 31:8-11	Lk 12:42-44
Mattins	4,5,8	Ecclus 32:14-16	Mt 25:31-36
II Evensong	15,21,24	Ecclus 34:13-17	Jn 13:12-17
ST. BARTHOLOMEW			
24 August			
I Evensong	1,15	Is 66:1-2,18-23	Lk 6:12-23
Mattins	91	Gn 28:10	Jn 1:43
II Evensong	46,102:15	Mic 4:1-7	1 Pet 1:22-2:10
DECOLLATION OF ST. JOHN BAPTIST			
29 August			
I Evensong	113,117,146	Is 1:4-9	Jn 3:22-30
Mattins	63,93,100	Ezek 3:4-11	Mt 11:2-19
II Evensong	110,116,126	Wis 5:15-20	Lk 12:1-12
THE NATIVITY OF THE B.V.M.			
8 September			
I Evensong	113,122,126	Songs 1:1-8	Lk 1:26-38
Mattins	45,46,87	Songs 1:9	Rom 1:1-4
II Evensong	146,147	Prv 9:1-6	Lk 11:27-28
EXALTATION OF THE HOLY CROSS			
14 September			
I Evensong	8,21,24	Num 21:4-9	Jn 3:1-17
Mattins	30,47,66	Is 26:12-15	Gal 6:12-17
II Evensong	76,96,97	Is 6:1-8	Phil 2:5-11
SEVEN SORROWS OF THE B.V.M.			
15 September			
I Evensong	3,11,31	Lam 1:2,20-21	Lk 2:33-35
Mattins	22,56,42	Lam 2:13-18	Lk 2:41-51
II Evensong	64,6,46	Judith 13:17	Rev 11:19-12:5
ST. MATTHEW			
21 September			
I Evensong	65,117	Wis 7:21-8:1	Lk 5:27-32
Mattins	119:1-16	1 Kgs 19	Mt 19:16
II Evensong	19,112	Is 52:1-10	Rom 10:1-15

Lectionary

Feast	Proper Psalms	Lesson 1	Lesson 2
ST. MICHAEL			
29 September			
I Evensong	8,150	Job 38	Heb 1:13-2:10
Mattins	91,103	Gn 32:24-30	Acts 12:1-17
II Evensong	34,148	Dan 12	Rev 14:1-13
GUARDIAN ANGELS			
2 October			
I Evensong	8,11,15	Gn 31:45-32:2	Rev 14:6-12
Mattins	19,24,34	Ex 23:20-23	Acts 27:13-25
II Evensong	96,97,103	Is 6:1-8	Mt 4:1-11
HOLY ROSARY OF THE B.V.M.			
7 October			
I Evensong	8,19,24	Ecclus 24:7-12	Mt 1:18-25
Mattins	45,46,87	Ecclus 24:13-17	Lk 2:25-35
II Evensong	96,97,98	Ecclus 24:18-24	Gal 4:4-7
MOTHERHOOD OF THE B.V.M.			
11 October			
I Evensong	48,138	Ex 13:11-16	Heb 10:1-10
Mattins	20,86,87	1 Sam 1:20	Gal 3:15-4:7
II Evensong	84,113,134	Lev 12	1 Jn 3:1-8
OUR LADY OF WALSINGHAM			
15 October			
I Evensong	84,87	Ex 40:17-35	Jn 2:1-22
Mattins	116,122	1 Kgs 8:1-21	Jn 19:23-27
II Evensong	132,138	Ezra 5:9-15	1 Cor 3:11-23
ST. LUKE			
18 October			
I Evensong	103	Ecclus 38:1-14	Acts 15:36-16:15
Mattins	67,96	Ezek 1:1-14	Lk 1:1-4
II Evensong	147	Ezek 47:1-12	Col 4:2
ST. RAPHAEL			
24 October			
I Evensong	9,11,15	Tob 4:19-5:8	Jn 5:1-4
Mattins	30,34,47	Tob 12:1-15	Rev 8:1-5
II Evensong	97,99,103	Ex 23:20-23	Rev 10:1-7
STS. SIMON & JUDE			
28 October			
I Evensong	66	Is 44:1-8,21-26	Mark 6:1-13
Mattins	118	Is 28:9-16	Eph 2

Lectionary

Feast	Proper Psalms	Lesson 1	Lesson 2
II Evensong	62,121	Jer 3:12-18	Jn 14:15
CHRIST THE KING			
Last Sunday in October			
I Evensong	146,147	Jer 23:5-8	Lk 1:26-33
Mattins	72,89:1-36	Jer 10:1-10	Rev 19:1-16
II Evensong	110,111,113	Dan 4:34-37	1 Tim 6:1-16
ALL HALLOWS			
1 November			
I Evensong	97,148	Ecclus 44:1-15	Heb 11:32-12:11
Mattins	1,15,146	Wis 3:1-9	Rev 19:1-16
II Evensong	112,121,149	Dt 33:1-5,26-end	Rev 21:1-22:5

Common of Saints

❡ When, for some reason, a Feast Day (not mentioned in this lectionary) is elevated to II Double or higher, these Commons are used.

Feast	Proper Psalms	Lesson 1	Lesson 2
Bishop			
I Evensong	23,100	Ecclus 50:5,11-21	Jn 21:15-17
Mattins	132	Is 61	Mt 10:1-20
II Evensong	111,112	Is 52:1-10	Jn 20:19-23
Confessor			
I Evensong	121,124	Ecclus 2:1-11	Lk 12:1-12
Mattins	3,8	Jer 15:15	Eph 4:1-13
II Evensong	118	Is 49:1-12	Acts 4:5-13
Martyr			
I Evensong	138,146	Ecclus 51:7-12	Lk 21:10-19
Mattins	30	Job 19:23-27	Lk 6:20-36
II Evensong	116	Job 5:8-21	Rev 7:9
Virgin			
I Evensong	45	Jer 31:1-14	Mt 25:1-13
Mattins	96,97	Is 54:1-5,11-14	Lk 10:38
II Evensong	113,122	Joel 2:28	Mt 13:44-52
Matron			
I Evensong	148	Esth 4:1,5-17	Lk 23:50-24:10
Mattins	85	Prov 31:10	Rom 12
II Evensong	34	Is 49:14-21	2 Jn
Dedication of a Church			
I Evensong	84	Hg 2:1-9	1 Cor 3:9-17
Mattins	132	1 Kgs 8:22-30	Jn 10:22-30
II Evensong	48,122	Gn 28:10-12,16-17	Heb 10:19-25

❡ Note, For the Blessed Virgin Mary, the proper psalms and lessons from her Nativity are used.

Daily Office

Alternative Psalter Arrangement

¶ For those who also pray the Minor Hours, it may be desired to have a more robust cursus of the Psalms during Mattins and Evensong, which do not overlap with the Psalms of the Minor Hours. The following arrangement is provided for such a situation.

¶ Note, The proper Psalms for Feast Days and obligatory Sundays take priority.

¶ Note, The First Sunday of Advent & Palm Sunday always begin 'Week 1'.

WEEK I	WEEK II
Sunday	Sunday
Mattins. Psalms 63, 66, 67, 93, 96, 97. *Evensong.* Psalms 84, 85, 104.	*Mattins.* Psalms 98, 99, 100, 148, 149, 150.
Monday	*Evensong.* Psalms 110, 111, 112, 113, 114, 115.
Mattins. Psalms 1, 2, 3, 5, 6, 7, 8. *Evensong.* Psalms 69, 70, 71, 72.	Monday
Tuesday	*Mattins.* Psalms 35, 36, 37, 38. *Evensong.* Psalms 106, 107, 108, 109.
Mattins. Psalms 9, 10, 11, 12, 13, 14. *Evensong.* Psalms 73, 74, 75, 76, 77.	Tuesday
Wednesday	*Mattins.* Psalms 39, 40, 41, 42, 43. *Evensong.* Psalms 116, 117, 118, 120, 121, 122, 123, 124.
Mattins. Psalms 15, 16, 17, 18. *Evensong.* Psalms 78, 79, 80, 81.	Wednesday
Thursday	*Mattins.* Psalms 44, 45, 46, 47, 48, 49. *Evensong.* Psalms 125, 126, 127, 128, 129, 130, 131.
Mattins. Psalms 19, 20, 21, 22, 23. *Evensong.* Psalms 82, 83, 86, 87, 88.	Thursday
Friday	*Mattins.* Psalms 50, 51, 52, 53, 55. *Evensong.* Psalms 132, 133, 135, 136, 137, 138.
Mattins. Psalms 24, 25, 26, 27, 28, 29. *Evensong.* Psalms 89, 90, 92, 94.	Friday
Saturday	*Mattins.* Psalms 56, 57, 58, 59, 60, 61. *Evensong.* Psalms 139, 140, 141, 142, 143.
Mattins. Psalms 30, 31, 32, 33, 34. *Evensong.* Psalms 101, 102, 103, 105.	Saturday
	Mattins. Psalms 62, 64, 65, 68. *Evensong.* Psalms 144, 145, 146, 147.

DAILY OFFICE

Daily Office

Fore-Office

¶ The Minister shall begin Morning and Evening Prayer by reading one or more of the following Sentences of Scripture.

¶ On any day, save a Day of Fasting or Abstinence, or on any day when the Litany or Holy Communion is immediately to follow, the Minister may, at his discretion, pass at once from the Sentences to the Lord's Prayer and Angelic Salutation, which may never be omitted.

General

When the wicked man turneth away from his wickedness that he hath committed, and doeth that which is lawful and right, he shall save his soul alive.

I acknowledge my transgressions, and my sin is ever before me.

Hide thy face from my sins, and blot out all mine iniquities.

The sacrifices of God are a broken spirit: a broken and a contrite heart, O God, thou wilt not despise.

Rend your heart, and not your garments, and turn unto the Lord your God: for he is gracious and merciful, slow to anger, and of great kindness, and repenteth him of the evil.

To the Lord our God belong mercies and forgivenesses, though we have rebelled against him; neither have we obeyed the voice of the Lord our God, to walk in his laws which he set before us.

O Lord, correct me, but with judgment; not in thine anger, lest thou bring me to nothing.

Repent ye; for the Kingdom of Heaven is at hand.

I will arise and go to my father, and will say unto him, Father, I have sinned against heaven, and before thee, and am no more worthy to be called thy son.

Enter not into judgment with thy servant, O Lord; for in thy sight shall no man living be justified.

If we say that we have no sin, we deceive ourselves, and the truth is not in us; but if we confess our sins, God is faithful and just to forgive us our sins, and to cleanse us from all unrighteousness.

Morning

The LORD is in his holy temple: let all the earth keep silence before him.

I was glad when they said unto me, We will go into the house of the LORD.

Let the words of my mouth, and the meditation of my heart, be alway acceptable in thy sight, O LORD, my strength and my redeemer.

O send out thy light and thy truth, that they may lead me, and bring me unto thy holy hill, and to thy dwelling.

Thus saith the high and lofty One that inhabiteth eternity, whose name is Holy; I dwell in the high and holy place, with him also that is of a contrite and humble spirit, to revive the spirit of the humble, and to revive the heart of the contrite ones.

The hour cometh, and now is, when the true worshippers shall worship the Father in spirit and in truth: for the Father seeketh such to worship him.

Grace be unto you, and peace, from God our Father, and from the Lord Jesus Christ.

Evening

The LORD is in his holy temple: let all the earth keep silence before him.

LORD, I have loved the habitation of thy house, and the place where thine honour dwelleth.

Let my prayer be set forth in thy sight as the incense; and let the lifting up of my hands be an evening sacrifice.

O worship the LORD in the beauty of holiness; let the whole earth stand in awe of him.

Let the words of my mouth, and the meditation of my heart, be alway acceptable in thy sight, O LORD, my strength and my redeemer.

Seek ye the Lord while he may be found, call ye upon him while he is near: let the wicked forsake his way and the unrighteous man his thoughts: and let him return unto the Lord, and he will have mercy upon him: and to our God, for he will abundantly pardon.

Advent

Repent ye, for the Kingdom of heaven is at hand.

Watch ye, for ye know not when the master of the house cometh, at even, or at midnight, or at the cock-crowing, or in the morning: lest coming suddenly he find you sleeping.

Prepare ye the way of the LORD, make straight in the desert a highway for our God.

Christmastide

Behold, I bring you good tidings of great joy, which shall be to all people. For unto you is born this day in the city of David a Saviour, which is Christ the Lord.

Behold, the tabernacle of God is with men, and he will dwell with them, and they shall be his people, and God himself shall be with them, and be their God.

Herein was the love of God manifested in us, that God hath sent his only begotten Son into the world, that we might live through him.

Epiphanytide

From the rising of the sun even unto the going down of the same my Name shall be great among the Gentiles; and in every place incense shall be offered unto my Name, and a pure offering: for my Name shall be great among the heathen, saith the LORD of hosts.

And the Gentiles shall come to thy light, and kings to the brightness of thy rising.

The earth shall be filled with the knowledge of the glory of the LORD, as the waters cover the sea.

Septuagesimatide

The Lord is high above all heathen : and his glory above the heavens.

Daily Office

Lent

He shall deliver thee from the snare of the hunter. And from the noisome pestilence.

Passiontide

God commendeth his love toward us, in that, while we were yet sinners, Christ died for us.

Is it nothing to you, all ye that pass by? behold, and see if there be any sorrow like unto my sorrow which is done unto me, wherewith the LORD hath afflicted me.

Draw nigh unto my soul and save it. O deliver me because of mine enemies.

Eastertide

He is risen. The Lord is risen indeed.

Thanks be to God, which giveth us the victory through our Lord Jesus Christ.

If ye then be risen with Christ, seek those things which are above, where Christ sitteth on the right hand of God.

Ascensiontide

Seeing that we have a great High Priest, that is passed into the heavens, Jesus the Son of God, let us come boldly unto the throne of grace, that we may obtain mercy, and find grace to help in time of need.

Christ is not entered into the holy places made with hands, which are the figures of the true; but into heaven itself, now to appear in the presence of God for us.

I ascend to my Father, and your Father. And to my God, and your God. Alleluia.

Whitsuntide

Ye shall receive power, after that the Holy Ghost is come upon you: and ye shall be witnesses unto me both in Jerusalem, and in all Judæa, and in Samaria, and unto the uttermost part of the earth.

There is a river, the streams whereof shall make glad the city of God, the holy place of the tabernacles of the Most High.

The love of God hath been shed abroad in our hearts through the Holy Spirit which was given unto us.

Trinity Sunday

Holy, holy, holy, Lord God Almighty, which was, and is, and is to come.

Holy, holy, holy, is the LORD of hosts: the whole earth is full of his glory.

God is love; and he that abideth in love abideth in God and God in him.

Apostle

Thou hast given an heritage unto those that fear thy Name, O Lord.

Martyr

Thou hast crowned him, O Lord, with glory and worship.

Bishop, Confessor, or Doctor

The righteous shall flourish like a palm-tree: and shall spread abroad like a cedar in Libanus.

Abbot or Monk

O ye holy and humble men of heart, bless ye the Lord: praise and exalt him above all for ever.

Virgin

In thy grace and in thy beauty, go forth, ride prosperously and reign.

Matron

God is in the midst of her, therefore shall she not be removed : God shall help her, and that right early.

Blessed Virgin Mary

Thou art the holy Mother of God, O Mary, ever Virgin.

Blessed Sacrament

I have eaten my honeycomb with my honey. I have drunk my wine with my milk. (Alleluia.)

Dedication of a Church

My house shall be called the house of prayer.

EXHORTATION TO PENITENCE

EARLY beloved brethren, the Scripture moveth us, in sundry places, to acknowledge and confess our manifold sins and wickedness; and that we should not dissemble nor cloak them before the face of Almighty God our heavenly Father; but confess them with an humble, lowly, penitent, and obedient heart; to the end that we may obtain forgiveness of the same, by his infinite goodness and mercy. And although we ought, at all times, humbly to acknowledge our sins before God; yet ought we chiefly so to do, when we assemble and meet together to render thanks for the great benefits that we have received at his hands, to set forth his most worthy praise, to hear his most holy Word, and to ask those things which are requisite and necessary, as well for the body as the soul. Wherefore I pray and beseech you, as many as are here present, to accompany me with a pure heart, and humble voice, unto the throne of the heavenly grace, saying—

or,

BELOVED, we are come together in the presence of Almighty God and of the whole company of heaven to offer unto him through our Lord Jesus Christ our worship and praise and thanksgiving; to make confession of our sins; to pray, as well for others as for ourselves, that we may know more truly the greatness of God's love and shew forth in our lives the fruits of his grace; and to ask on behalf of all men such things as their well-being doth require. Wherefore let us kneel in silence, and remember God's presence with us now.

¶ If the exhortation be omitted, to be said in its place: Let us humbly confess our sins unto Almighty God.

Daily Office

GENERAL CONFESSION

⁋ To be said by the whole Congregation, after the Minister, all kneeling.

LMIGHTY and most merciful Father; We have erred, and strayed from thy ways like lost sheep. We have followed too much the devices and desires of our own hearts. We have offended against thy holy laws. We have left undone those things which we ought to have done; And we have done those things which we ought not to have done; And there is no health in us. But thou, O Lord, have mercy upon us, miserable offenders. Spare thou those, O God, who confess their faults. Restore thou those who are penitent; According to thy promises declared unto mankind in Christ Jesus our Lord. And grant, O most merciful Father, for his sake; That we may hereafter live a godly, righteous, and sober life, To the glory of thy holy Name. Amen.

DECLARATION OF ABSOLUTION

⁋ To be made by the Priest alone, standing; the People still kneeling.

⁋ But NOTE, That the Priest, at his discretion, may use, instead of what follows, the Absolution from the Order for the Holy Communion.

LMIGHTY God, the Father of our Lord Jesus Christ, who desireth not the death of a sinner, but rather that he may turn from his wickedness and live, hath given power, and commandment, to his Ministers, to declare and pronounce to his people, being penitent, the Absolution and Remission of their sins. He pardoneth and ✠ absolveth all those who truly repent, and unfeignedly believe his holy Gospel.

Wherefore let us beseech him to grant us true repentance, and his Holy Spirit, that those things may please him which we do at this present; and that the rest of our life hereafter may be pure and holy; so that at the last we may come to his eternal joy; through Jesus Christ our Lord. *Amen.*

or,

HE Almighty and merciful Lord grant you Absolution ✠ and Remission of all your sins, true repentance, amendment of life, and the grace and consolation of the Holy Spirit. Amen.

¶ If no Priest be present, the Minister saying the Service shall read the following, that Minister and the People still kneeling.

RANT, we beseech thee, merciful Lord, to thy faithful people pardon and peace, that they may be cleansed from all their sins, and serve thee with a quiet mind. Through Jesus Christ thy Son our Lord, who liveth and reigneth with thee, in the unity of the Holy Ghost, God, throughout all ages, world without end. *Amen.*

LORD'S PRAYER & ANGELIC SALUTATION

¶ Then the Minister shall kneel, and say the Lord's Prayer & Angelic Salutation; the People still kneeling, and repeating them with him, both here, and wheresoever else they are used in Divine Service.

UR Father, who art in heaven, Hallowed be thy Name. Thy kingdom come. Thy will be done on earth, As it is in heaven. Give us this day our daily bread. And forgive us our trespasses, As we forgive those who trespass against us. And lead us not into temptation; But deliver us from evil: For thine is the kingdom, and the power, and the glory, for ever and ever. Amen.

AIL Mary, full of grace; The Lord is with thee; Blessed art thou amongst women, And blessed is the fruit of thy womb, Jesus. Holy Mary, Mother of God, Pray for us sinners, now and at the hour of our death. Amen.

Daily Office

The Order for Daily Morning Prayer

℣. O Lord, † open thou our lips.

℟. And our mouth shall show forth thy praise.

℣. O God, ✠ make speed to save us.

℟. O Lord, make haste to help us.

℣. Dómine, † lábia nostra apéries.

℟. Et os nostrum annuntiábit laudem tuam.

℣. Deus, ✠ in adjutórium nostrum inténde.

℟. Dómine, ad adjuvándum nos festína.

¶ Here, all standing up, the Minister shall say,

℣. Glory be to the Father, and to the Son, and to the Holy Ghost.

℟. As it was in the beginning, is now, and ever shall be, world without end. Amen.

℣. Praise ye the Lord.

℟. The Lord's Name be praised.

℣. Glória Patri, et Fílio, * et Spirítui Sancto:

℟. Sicut erat in princípio, et nunc, et semper, * et in sǽcula sæculórum. Amen.

℣. Laudáte Dominum.

℟. Sit Nomen Dómini Benedíctum.

¶ Then shall be said or sung the following Psalm; except on those days for which an Anthem is appointed; and except also, when Psalm 95 may occur in the course of the Psalms.

¶ But NOTE, That on Ash Wednesday and Good Friday the Venite may be omitted.

¶ On the days hereafter named, immediately before and after the Venite may be sung or said,

Advent. Our King and Saviour draweth nigh; * O come, let us adore him.

Christmastide. Alleluia. Unto us a child is born; * O come, let us adore him. Alleluia.

Epiphanytide & Transfiguration. The Lord hath manifested forth his glory; * O come, let us adore him.

Septuagesimatide. Let us come before the presence of the Lord with thanksgiving; * O come, let us adore him.

Lent. The goodness of God leadeth to repentance; * O come, let us adore him.

Passiontide. Christ our Lord became obedient unto death; * O come, let us adore him.

Eastertide. Alleluia. The Lord is risen indeed; * O come let us adore him. Alleluia.

Ascensiontide. Alleluia. Christ the Lord ascended into heaven; * O come, let us adore him. Alleluia.

Whitsuntide. Alleluia. The Spirit of the Lord filleth the world; * O come, let us adore him. Alleluia.

Father, Son, and Holy Ghost, One God; * O come, let us adore him.
Feasts of Our Lord & Our Lady. The Word was made flesh; * O come, let us adore him.
Other Feast Days of Semidouble or higher. The Lord is glorious in his saints; * O come, let us adore him.

Venite, exultemus Domino.

O come, let us sing unto the Lord : let us heartily rejoice in the strength of our salvation.

2 Let us come before his presence with thanksgiving : and shew ourselves glad in him with psalms.

3 For the Lord is a great God : and a great King above all gods.

4 In his hand are all the corners of the earth : and the strength of the hills is his also.

5 The sea is his, and he made it : and his hands prepared the dry land.

6 O come, let us worship and fall down : and kneel before the Lord our Maker.

7 For he is the Lord our God : and we are the people of his pasture, and the sheep of his hand.

8 To-day if ye will hear his voice, harden not your hearts : as in the provocation, and as in the day of temptation in the wilderness.

9 When your fathers tempted me : proved me, and saw my works.

10 Forty years long was I grieved with this generation, and said : It is a people that do err in their hearts, for they have not known my ways;

11 Unto whom I sware in my wrath : that they should not enter into my rest.

ENÍTE, exsultémus Dómino, jubilémus Deo, salutári nostro:

Præoccupémus fáciem ejus in confessióne, et in psalmis jubilémus ei.

Quóniam Deus magnus Dóminus, et Rex magnus super omnes deos, quóniam non repéllet Dóminus plebem suam:

Quia in manu ejus sunt omnes fines terræ, et altitúdines móntium ipse cónspicit.

Quóniam ipsíus est mare, et ipse fecit illud, et áridam fundavérunt manus ejus

Veníte, adorémus, et procidámus ante Deum: plorémus coram Dómino, qui fecit nos,

Quia ipse est Dóminus, Deus noster; nos autem pópulus ejus, et oves páscuæ ejus.

Hódie, si vocem ejus audiéritis, nolíte obduráre corda vestra, sicut in exacerbatióne secúndum diem tentatiónis in desérto: ubi tentavérunt me patres vestri, probavérunt et vidérunt ópera mea.

Quadragínta annis próximus fui generatióni huic, et dixi; Semper hi errant corde, ipsi vero non cognovérunt vias meas: quibus jurávi in ira mea; Si introíbunt in réquiem meam.

❡ Then shall follow a Portion of the Psalms, according to the Use of this Church. And at the end of every Psalm, and likewise at the end of the Venite, daily Old Testament Canticle, Athanasian Creed, and Benedictus, shall be sung or said the Gloria Patri.

℣. Glory be to the Father, and to the Son, * and to the Holy Ghost.

℟. As it was in the beginning, is now, and ever shall be, * world without end. Amen.

℣. Glória Patri, et Fílio, * et Spirítui Sancto:

℟. Sicut erat in princípio, et nunc, et semper, * et in sǽcula sæculórum. Amen.

❡ Verses 8-11 of the Venite may be replaced with the following.

O worship the Lord in the beauty of holiness : let the whole earth stand in awe of him.

For he cometh, for he cometh to judge the earth : and with righteousness to judge the world, and the people with his truth.

Tóllite hóstias, et introíte in átria ejus: * adoráte Dóminum in átrio sancto ejus.

Judicábit orbem terræ in æquitáte, * et pópulos in veritáte sua.

❡ After the Venite, a Hymn may be sung.

❡ Then shall be read the First Lesson, according to the Table or Calendar. And NOTE, That before every Lesson, the Minister shall say, Here beginneth *such a Chapter* (or *Verse of such a Chapter*) of *such a Book*; and after every Lesson, Here endeth the First (or Second) Lesson.

Te Deum laudamus

❡ The Te Deum is prayed on all Sundays (outside Advent & Lent) and Feast Days (Semidouble or higher).

NOTE, The Old Testament Canticle (p. 21) may be said instead of the Te Deum.

E praise thee, O God; we acknowledge thee to be the Lord.

All the earth doth worship thee, the Father everlasting.

To thee all Angels cry aloud; the Heavens, and all the Powers therein;

To thee Cherubim and Seraphim continually do cry,

Holy, Holy, Holy, Lord God of

E Deum laudámus: * te Dóminum confitémur.

Te ætérnum Patrem * omnis terra venerátur.

Tibi omnes Ángeli, * tibi Cæli, et univérsæ Potestátes

Tibi Chérubim et Séraphim * incessábili voce proclámant:

Sanctus, Sanctus, Sanctus * Dóminus Deus Sábaoth.

Sabaoth;

Heaven and earth are full of the Majesty of thy glory.

The glorious company of the Apostles praise thee.

The goodly fellowship of the Prophets praise thee.

The noble army of Martyrs praise thee.

The holy Church throughout all the world doth acknowledge thee;

The Father of an infinite Majesty;

Thine honourable, true and only Son;

Also the Holy Ghost the Comforter.

THOU art the King of Glory, O Christ.

Thou art the everlasting Son of the Father.

When thou tookest upon thee to deliver man, thou didst not abhor the Virgin's womb.

When thou hadst overcome the sharpness of death, thou didst open the Kingdom of Heaven to all believers.

Thou sittest at the right hand of God, in the glory of the Father.

We believe that thou shalt come to be our Judge.

We therefore pray thee, help thy servants, whom thou hast redeemed with thy precious blood.

Make them to be numbered with thy Saints, in glory everlasting.

LORD, save thy people, and bless thine heritage.

Govern them and lift them up for ever.

Pleni sunt cæli et terra * majestátis glóriæ tuæ.

Te gloriósus * Apostolórum chorus,

Te Prophetárum * laudábilis númerus,

Te Mártyrum candidátus * laudat exércitus.

Te per orbem terrárum * sancta confitétur Ecclésia,

Patrem * imménsæ majestátis;

Venerándum tuum verum * et únicum Fílium;

Sanctum quoque * Paráclitum Spíritum.

U Rex glóriæ, * Christe.

Tu Patris * sempitérnus es Fílius.

Tu, ad liberándum susceptúrus hóminem: * non horruísti Vírginis úterum.

Tu, devícto mortis acúleo, * aperuísti credéntibus regna cælórum.

Tu ad déxteram Dei sedes, * in glória Patris.

Judex créderis * esse ventúrus.

Te ergo quǽsumus, tuis fámulis súbveni, * quos pretióso sánguine redemísti.

Ætérna fac cum Sanctis tuis * in glória numerári.

ALVUM fac pópulum tuum, Dómine, * et bénedic hereditáti tuæ.

Et rege eos, * et extólle illos usque in ætérnum.

Per síngulos dies * benedícimus te.

Et laudámus nomen tuum in sǽculum, * et in sǽculum sǽculi.

Dignáre, Dómine, die isto * sine peccáto nos custodíre.

Day by day we magnify thee;
And we worship thy Name ever,
world without end.

Vouchsafe, O Lord, to keep us this
day without sin.

O Lord, have mercy upon us, have
mercy upon us.

O Lord, let thy mercy lighten upon
us, as our trust is in thee.

O Lord, in thee have I trusted; let
me never be confounded.

Miserére nostri, Dómine, * miserére
nostri.

Fiat misericórdia tua, Dómine, super nos, * quemádmodum sperávimus
in te.

In te, Dómine, sperávi: * non con-
fúndar in ætérnum.

BENEDICITE, OMNIA OPERA DOMINI.

❡ The Benedicite is prayed on all Sundays in Advent & Lent, and on Days below Semidouble.

NOTE, The Old Testament Canticle (p. 21) may be said instead of the Benedicite.

 ALL ye Works of the Lord,
bless ye the Lord: * praise
him, and magnify him for
ever.

O ye Angels of the Lord, bless ye the
Lord: * praise him, and magnify him
for ever.

 YE Heavens, bless ye the Lord: *
praise him, and magnify him
for ever.

O ye Waters that be above the firmament, bless ye the Lord: * praise him,
and magnify him for ever.

O all ye Powers of the Lord, bless
ye the Lord: * praise him, and magnify
him for ever.

O ye Sun and Moon, bless ye the
Lord: * praise him, and magnify him
for ever.

O ye Stars of heaven, bless ye the
Lord: * praise him, and magnify him
for ever.

O ye Showers and Dew, bless ye the

 ENEDÍCITE, ómnia ópera Dómini, Dómino: * laudáte et
superexaltáte eum in sæcula.

Benedícite, Ángeli Dómini, Dómino: * laudáte et superexaltáte eum in
sæcula.

 ENEDÍCITE, cæli, Dómino: *
laudáte et superexaltáte eum
in sæcula.

Benedícite, aquæ omnes, quæ super
cælos sunt, Dómino: * laudáte et superexaltáte eum in sæcula.

Benedícite, omnes virtútes Dómini, Dómino: * laudáte et superexaltáte
eum in sæcula.

Benedícite, sol et luna, Dómino: *
laudáte et superexaltáte eum in sæcula.

Benedícite, stellæ cæli, Dómino: *
laudáte et superexaltáte eum in sæcula.

Benedícite, omnis imber et ros, Dómino: * laudáte et superexaltáte eum
in sæcula.

Benedícite, omnes spíritus Dei, Dó-

Lord: * praise him, and magnify him for ever.

O ye winds of God, bless ye the Lord: * praise him, and magnify him for ever.

O ye Fire and Heat, bless ye the Lord * praise him, and magnify him for ever.

O ye Winter and Summer, bless ye the Lord: * praise him, and magnify him for ever.

O ye Dews and Frosts, bless ye the Lord: * praise him, and magnify him for ever.

O ye Frost and Cold, bless ye the Lord: * praise him, and magnify him for ever.

O ye Ice and Snow, bless ye the Lord * praise him, and magnify him for ever.

O ye Nights and Days, bless ye the Lord: * praise him, and magnify him for ever.

O ye Light and Darkness, bless ye the Lord: * praise him, and magnify him for ever.

O ye Lightnings and Clouds, bless ye the Lord * praise him, and magnify him for ever.

LET the Earth bless the Lord: * yea, let it praise him, and magnify him for ever.

O ye Mountains and Hills, bless ye the Lord: * praise him, and magnify him for ever.

O all ye Green Things upon the earth, bless ye the Lord: * praise him, and magnify him for ever.

O ye Wells, bless ye the Lord: * praise him, and magnify him for ever.

mino: * laudáte et superexaltáte eum in sǽcula.

Benedícite, ignis et æstus, Dómino: * laudáte et superexaltáte eum in sǽcula.

Benedícite, frigus et æstus, Dómino: * laudáte et superexaltáte eum in sǽcula.

Benedícite, rores et pruína, Dómino: * laudáte et superexaltáte eum in sǽcula.

Benedícite, gelu et frigus, Dómino: * laudáte et superexaltáte eum in sǽcula.

Benedícite, glácies et nives, Dómino: * laudáte et superexaltáte eum in sǽcula.

Benedícite, noctes et dies, Dómino: * laudáte et superexaltáte eum in sǽcula.

Benedícite, lux et ténebræ, Dómino: * laudáte et superexaltáte eum in sǽcula.

Benedícite, fúlgura et nubes, Dómino: * laudáte et superexaltáte eum in sǽcula.

ENEDÍCAT terra Dóminum: * laudet et superexáltet eum in sǽcula.

Benedícite, montes et colles, Dómino: * laudáte et superexaltáte eum in sǽcula.

Benedícite, univérsa germinántia in terra, Dómino: * laudáte et superexaltáte eum in sǽcula.

Benedícite, fontes, Dómino: * laudáte et superexaltáte eum in sǽcula.

Benedícite, mária et flúmina, Dómino: * laudáte et superexaltáte eum in sǽcula.

O ye Seas and Floods, bless ye the Lord: * praise him, and magnify him for ever.

O ye Whales, and all that move in the waters, bless ye the Lord: * praise him, and magnify him for ever.

O all ye Fowls of the air, bless ye the Lord: * praise him, and magnify him for ever.

O all ye Beasts and Cattle, bless ye the Lord: * praise him, and magnify him for ever.

O ye Children of Men, bless ye the Lord: * praise him, and magnify him for ever.

LET Israel bless the Lord: * praise him, and magnify him for ever.

O ye Priests of the Lord, bless ye the Lord: * praise him, and magnify him for ever.

O ye Servants of the Lord, bless ye the Lord: * praise him, and magnify him for ever.

O ye Spirits and Souls of the Righteous, bless ye the Lord: * praise him, and magnify him for ever.

O ye holy and humble Men of heart, bless ye the Lord: * praise him, and magnify him for ever.

ET us bless the Father, and the Son, and the Holy Ghost: * praise him, and magnify him for ever.

Benedícite, cete, et ómnia, quæ movéntur in aquis, Dómino: * laudáte et superexaltáte eum in sǽcula.

Benedícite, omnes vólucres cæli, Dómino: * laudáte et superexaltáte eum in sǽcula.

Benedícite, omnes béstiæ et pécora, Dómino: * laudáte et superexaltáte eum in sǽcula.

Benedícite, fílii hóminum, Dómino: * laudáte et superexaltáte eum in sǽcula.

ENEDÍCAT Israël Dóminum: * laudet et superexáltet eum in sǽcula.

Benedícite, sacerdótes Dómini, Dómino: * laudáte et superexaltáte eum in sǽcula.

Benedícite, servi Dómini, Dómino: * laudáte et superexaltáte eum in sǽcula.

Benedícite, spíritus, et ánimæ justórum, Dómino: * laudáte et superexaltáte eum in sǽcula.

Benedícite, sancti, et húmiles corde, Dómino: * laudáte et superexaltáte eum in sǽcula.

ENEDICÁMUS Patrem et Fílium cum Sancto Spíritu: * laudémus et superexaltémus eum in sǽcula.

¶ Then shall be read, in like manner, the Second Lesson, taken out of the New Testament, according to the Table or Calendar.

¶ After which may be sung or said a Hymn.

BENEDICTUS

¶ Then shall be sung or said the Hymn following.

LESSED ✠ be the Lord God of Israel; * for he hath visited and redeemed his people;

And hath raised up a mighty salvation for us, * in the house of his servant David;

As he spake by the mouth of his holy Prophets, * which have been since the world began;

That we should be saved from our enemies, * and from the hand of all that hate us.

To perform the mercy promised to our forefathers, * and to remember his holy covenant;

To perform the oath which he sware to our forefather Abraham, * that he would give us;

That we being delivered out of the hand of our enemies * might serve him without fear;

In holiness and righteousness before him, * all the days of our life.

And thou, child, shalt be called the prophet of the Highest: * for thou shalt go before the face of the Lord to prepare his ways;

To give knowledge of salvation unto his people * for the remission of their sins,

Through the tender mercy of our God; * whereby the day-spring from on high hath visited us;

To give light to them that sit in darkness, and in the shadow of death, * and to guide our feet into the way of peace.

ENEDÍCTUS ✠ Dóminus, Deus Israël: * quia visitávit, et fecit redemptiónem plebi suæ:

Et eréxit cornu salútis nobis: * in domo David, púeri sui.

Sicut locútus est per os sanctórum, * qui a sǽculo sunt, prophetárum ejus:

Salútem ex inimícis nostris, * et de manu ómnium, qui odérunt nos.

Ad faciéndam misericórdiam cum pátribus nostris: * et memorári testaménti sui sancti.

Jusjurándum, quod jurávit ad Ábraham patrem nostrum, * datúrum se nobis:

Ut sine timóre, de manu inimicórum nostrórum liberáti, * serviámus illi.

In sanctitáte, et justítia coram ipso, * ómnibus diébus nostris.

Et tu, puer, Prophéta Altíssimi vocáberis: * præíbis enim ante fáciem Dómini, paráre vias ejus:

Ad dandam sciéntiam salútis plebi ejus: * in remissiónem peccatórum eórum:

Per víscera misericórdiæ Dei nostri: * in quibus visitávit nos, óriens ex alto:

Illumináre his, qui in ténebris, et in umbra mortis sedent: * ad dirigéndos pedes nostros in viam pacis.

Daily Office

APOSTLES' CREED

❡ Then shall be said the Apostles' Creed, by the Minister and the People, standing. NOTE, the Nicene Creed may be said instead of the Apostles' (p. 145).

❡ Upon these Feasts; Christmas Day, the Epiphany, Saint Matthias, Easter Day, Ascension Day, Whitsunday, Saint John Baptist, Saint James, Saint Bartholomew, Saint Matthew, Saint Simon and Saint Jude, Saint Andrew, and upon Trinity Sunday, shall be sung or said, instead of the Apostle's Creed, the Athanasian Creed (p. 37).

I BELIEVE in God the Father Almighty, Maker of heaven and earth: And in Jesus Christ his only Son our Lord: Who was conceived by the Holy Ghost, Born of the Virgin Mary: Suffered under Pontius Pilate, Was crucified, dead, and buried: He descended into hell; The third day he rose again from the dead: He ascended into heaven, And sitteth on the right hand of God the Father Almighty: From thence he shall come to judge the quick and the dead.

I believe in the Holy Ghost: The holy Catholic Church; The Communion of Saints: The Forgiveness of sins: The Resurrection of the body: ✠ And the Life everlasting. Amen.

CREDO in Deum, Patrem omnipoténtem, Creatórem cǽli et terræ. Et in Jesum Christum, Fílium ejus únicum, Dóminum nostrum: qui concéptus est de Spíritu Sancto, natus ex María Vírgine, passus sub Póntio Piláto, crucifíxus, mórtuus, et sepúltus: descéndit ad ínferos; tértia die resurréxit a mórtuis; ascéndit ad cælos; sedet ad déxteram Dei Patris omnipoténtis: inde ventúrus est judicáre vivos et mórtuos.

Credo in Spíritum Sanctum, sanctam Ecclésiam cathólicam, Sanctórum communiónem, remissiónem peccatórum, carnis ✠ resurrectiónem, vitam ætérnam. Amen.

❡ And after that, these Prayers following, the People devoutly kneeling; the Minister first pronouncing,

℣. The Lord be with you.
or, O Lord, hear our prayer.

℟. And with thy spirit.
or, And let our cry come unto thee.
℣. Let us pray.
℣. Lord, have mercy upon us.
℟. Christ, have mercy upon us.
℣. Lord, have mercy upon us.

℣. Dóminus vobíscum.
vel, Dómine, exáudi oratiónem nostram.

℟. Et cum spíritu tuo.
vel, Et clamor noster ad te véniat.
℣. Orémus.
℣. Kýrie, eléison.
℟. Christe, eléison.
℣. Kýrie, eléison.

LORD'S PRAYER

UR Father, who art in heaven, Hallowed be thy Name. Thy kingdom come. Thy will be done on earth, As it is in heaven. Give us this day our daily bread. And forgive us our trespasses, As we forgive those who trespass against us. And lead us not into temptation; But deliver us from evil. Amen.

ATER noster, qui es in cælis, sanctificétur nomen tuum: advéniat regnum tuum: fiat volúntas tua, sicut in cælo et in terra. Panem nostrum quotidiánum da nobis hódie: et dimítte nobis débita nostra, sicut et nos dimíttimus debitóribus nostris: et ne nos indúcas in tentatiónem: sed líbera nos a malo. Amen.

PRECES

℣. O Lord, show thy mercy upon us.

℟. And grant us thy salvation.

℣. O Lord, save the *State*.

℟. And mercifully hear us when we call upon thee.

℣. Endue thy Ministers with righteousness.

℟. And make thy chosen people joyful.

℣. O Lord, save thy people.

℟. And bless thine inheritance.

℣. Give peace in our time, O Lord.

℟. For it is thou, Lord, only, that makest us dwell in safety.

℣. O God, make clean our hearts within us.

℟. And take not thy Holy Spirit from us.

℣. Osténde nobis, Dómine, misericórdiam tuam.

℟. Et salutáre tuum da nobis.

℣. Dómine salvam fac *Civitatem*.

℟. Et exáudi nos cum invocámus te.

℣. Sacerdótes tui induántur Justítia.

℟. Et sancti tui exúltent.

℣. Salvum fac Pópulum tuum, Dómine.

℟. Et bénedic Hæreditáti tuæ.

℣. Da pacem Dómine in diébus nostris.

℟. Quóniam tu, Dómine, singuláriter in spe constituísti me.

℣. Cor mundum crea in nobis, O Deus.

℟. Et Spíritum Sanctum tuum ne áuferas a nobis.

¶ Then shall follow the Collect(s) for the Day, except when the Communion Service is read; and then the Collect(s) for the Day shall be omitted here.

A Collect for Peace

GOD, who art the author of peace and lover of concord, in knowledge of whom standeth our eternal life, whose service is perfect freedom; Defend us thy humble servants in all assaults of our enemies; that we, surely trusting in thy defence, may not fear the power of any adversaries, through the might of Jesus Christ our Lord. *Amen.*

A Collect for Grace

LORD, our heavenly Father, Almighty and everlasting God, who hast safely brought us to the beginning of this day; Defend us in the same with thy mighty power; and grant that this day we fall into no sin, neither run into any kind of danger; but that all our doings, being ordered by thy governance, may be righteous in thy sight; through Jesus Christ our Lord. *Amen.*

Conclusion

℣. The Lord be with you.
or, O Lord, hear our prayer.

℣. Dóminus vobíscum.
vel, Dómine, exáudi oratiónem nostram.

℟. And with thy spirit.
or, And let our cry come unto thee.

℟. Et cum spíritu tuo.
vel, Et clamor noster ad te véniat.

℣. Let us bless the Lord (alleluia, alleluia.)

℣. Benedicámus Dómino (allelúja, allelúja.)

℟. Thanks be to God (alleluia, alleluia.)

℟. Deo grátias (allelúja, allelúja.)

℣. May the souls ✠ of the faithful departed, through the mercy of God, rest in peace.

℣. Fidélium ánimæ ✠ per misericórdiam Dei requiéscant in pace.

℟. Amen.

℟. Amen.

¶ The following Prayers shall be omitted here when the Great Litany is said, and may be omitted when the Holy Communion is to follow.

¶ And NOTE, That the Minister may here end the Morning Prayer with such intercessions taken out of this Book, as he shall think fit, or with the Grace.

AFTER THE THIRD COLLECT

❡ The Prayer for the Head of State (p. 70) is here said.

A Prayer for the Clergy and People

LMIGHTY and everlasting God, from whom cometh every good and perfect gift; Send down upon our Bishops, and other Clergy, and upon the Congregations committed to their charge, the healthful Spirit of thy grace; and, that they may truly please thee, pour upon them the continual dew of thy blessing. Grant this, O Lord, for the honour of our Advocate and Mediator, Jesus Christ. *Amen.*

❡ Additional Prayers (p. 70) may here be said.

A Prayer for all Sorts & Conditions of Men

GOD, the Creator and Preserver of all mankind, we humbly beseech thee for all sorts and conditions of men; that thou wouldest be pleased to make thy ways known unto them, thy saving health unto all nations. More especially we pray for thy holy Church universal; that it may be so guided and governed by thy good Spirit, that all who profess and call themselves Christians may be led into the way of truth, and hold the faith in unity of spirit, in the bond of peace, and in righteousness of life. Finally, we commend to thy fatherly goodness all those who are any ways afflicted, or distressed, in mind, body, or estate; (*especially those for whom our prayers are desired;) that it may *This may be said when any desire the prayers of the Congregation.* please thee to comfort and relieve them, according to their several necessities; giving them patience under their sufferings, and a happy issue out of all their afflictions. And this we beg for Jesus Christ's sake. *Amen.*

A General Thanksgiving

❡ The General Thanksgiving may be said by the Congregation with the Minister.

LMIGHTY God, Father of all mercies, we, thine unworthy servants, do give thee most humble and hearty thanks for all thy goodness and loving-kindness to us and to all men; (*to those who desire now to *This may be said when any desire to return thanks for mercies vouchsafed to them.* offer up their praises and thanksgivings for thy late mercies vouchsafed unto them.) We bless thee for our creation, preservation, and all the blessings of this life; but above all, for thine inestimable love in the redemption of the world by our Lord Jesus Christ; for the means of grace, and for the hope of glory. And, we beseech thee, give us that due sense of all thy mercies, that our hearts may be unfeignedly thankful; and that we show forth thy praise, not only with our lips, but in our lives, by giving up our selves to thy service, and by walking before thee in holiness and righteousness all our days; through Jesus Christ our Lord, to whom, with thee and the Holy Ghost, be all honour and glory, world without end. *Amen.*

¶ The Thanksgivings (p. 82) may here be offered.

A Prayer of St. Chrysostom

LMIGHTY God, who hast given us grace at this time with one accord to make our common supplications unto thee; and dost promise that when two or three are gathered together in thy Name thou wilt grant their requests; Fulfil now, O Lord, the desires and petitions of thy servants, as may be most expedient for them; granting us in this world knowledge of thy truth, and in the world to come life everlasting. *Amen.*

The Grace

HE grace of our Lord Jesus Christ, ✠ and the love of God, and the fellowship of the Holy Ghost, be with us all evermore. *Amen.*

HERE ENDETH THE ORDER OF MORNING PRAYER.

Old Testament Canticles

❡ The Festal Canticle is prayed on Feast Days Semidouble & higher and the Saturday Office of St. Mary.

MONDAY FERIAL CANTICLE

Confitebor tibi

LORD, I will praise thee, though thou wast angry with me; * thine anger is turned away, and thou comfortedst me.

Behold, God is my salvation; * I will trust, and not be afraid:

For the Lord Jehovah is my strength and my song; * he also is become my salvation.

Therefore with joy shall ye draw water out of the wells of salvation: * and in that day shall ye say, Praise the Lord, call upon his Name,

Declare his doings among the people, * make mention that his Name is exalted.

Sing unto the Lord; for he hath done excellent things: * this is known in all the earth.

Cry out and shout, thou inhabitant of Sion: * for great is the Holy One of Israel in the midst of thee.

MONDAY FESTAL CANTICLE

Benedictus es, Domine

LESSED be thou, Lord God of Israel * our father, for ever and ever.

Thine, O Lord is the greatness, and the power, and the glory, † and the vic-tory, and the majesty: * for all that is in the heaven and in the earth is thine;

Thine is the kingdom, O Lord, * and thou art exalted as head above all.

Both riches and honour come of thee, * and thou reignest over all;

And in thine hand is power and might; * and in thine hand it is to make great, and to give strength unto all.

Now therefore, our God, we thank thee, and praise thy glorious name.

TUESDAY FERIAL CANTICLE

Ego dixi

SAID in the cutting off of my days, † I shall go to the gates of the grave: * I am deprived of the residue of my years.

I said, I shall not see the Lord, † even the Lord, in the land of the living: * I shall behold man no more with the inhabitants of the world.

Mine age is departed, * and is removed from me as a shepherd's tent;

I have cut off like a weaver my life: † he will cut me off with pining sickness: * from day even to night wilt thou make an end of me.

I reckoned till morning, † that, as a lion, so will he break all my bones: * from day even to night wilt thou make an end of me.

Like a crane or a swallow, so did I chatter: * I did mourn as a dove.

Mine eyes fail with looking upward: * O Lord, I am oppressed; undertake for me.

What shall I say? † he hath both spoken unto me, and himself hath done it: * I shall go softly all my years in the bitterness of my soul.

O Lord, by these things men live, † and in all these things is the life of my spirit: * so wilt thou recover me, and make me to live.

Behold, for peace I had great bitterness: † but thou hast in love to my soul delivered it from the pit of corruption: * for thou hast cast all my sins behind thy back.

For the grave cannot praise thee, † death can not celebrate thee: * they that go down into the pit cannot hope for thy truth.

The living, the living, he shall praise thee, as I do this day: * the father to the children shall make known thy truth.

The Lord was ready to save me: * therefore we will sing my songs to the stringed instruments all the days of our life in the house of the Lord.

scattered us among them.

There declare his greatness, and extol him before all the living: * for he is our Lord, and he is the God our Father for ever.

And he will scourge us for our iniquities, * and will have mercy again, and will gather us out of all nations, among whom he hath scattered us.

If ye turn to him with your whole heart, and with your whole mind, † and deal uprightly before him, * then will he turn unto you, and will not hide his face from you.

Therefore see what he will do with you, and confess him with your whole mouth, and praise the Lord of might, * and extol the everlasting King.

In the land of my captivity do I praise him, * and declare his might and majesty to a sinful nation.

O ye sinners, turn and do justice before him: * who can tell if he will accept you, and have mercy on you?

I will extol my God, * and my soul shall praise the King of heaven, and shall rejoice in his greatness.

TUESDAY FESTAL CANTICLE

Magnus es, Domine

LESSED be God that liveth for ever, * and blessed be his kingdom.

For he doth scourge, and hath mercy: † he leadeth down to hell, and bringeth up again: * neither is there any that can avoid his hand.

Confess him before the Gentiles, ye children of Israel: * for he hath

WEDNESDAY FERIAL CANTICLE

Exsultavit cor meum

Y heart rejoiceth in the Lord,* mine horn is exalted in the Lord:

My mouth is enlarged over mine enemies; * because I rejoice in thy salvation.

There is none holy as the Lord: † for there is none beside thee: * neither is there any rock like our God.

Talk no more so exceeding proudly; * let not arrogancy come out of your mouth:

For the Lord is a God of knowledge, * and by him actions are weighed.

The bows of the mighty men are broken, * and they that stumbled are girded with strength.

They that were full have hired out themselves for bread; * and they that were hungry ceased:

So that the barren hath born seven; * and she that hath many children is waxed feeble.

The Lord killeth, and maketh alive: * he bringeth down to the grave, and bringeth up.

The Lord maketh poor, and maketh rich: * he bringeth low, and lifteth up.

He raiseth up the poor out of the dust, * and lifteth up the beggar from the dunghill,

To set them among princes, * and to make them inherit the throne of glory:

For the pillars of the earth are the Lord's, * and he hath set the world upon them.

He will keep the feet of his saints, † and the wicked shall be silent in darkness; * for by strength shall no man prevail.

The adversaries of the Lord shall be broken to pieces; * out of heaven shall he thunder upon them:

The Lord shall judge the ends of the earth; † and he shall give strength unto his King, * and exalt the horn of his Anointed.

WEDNESDAY FESTAL CANTICLE

Hymnum cantemus

WILL sing unto the Lord a new song: * O Lord, thou art great and glorious, wonderful in strength, and invincible.

Let all creatures serve thee: * for thou spakest, and they were made,

Thou didst send forth thy spirit, and it created them, * and there is none that can resist thy voice.

For the mountains shall be moved from their foundations with the waters, † the rocks shall melt as wax at thy presence: * yet thou art merciful to them that fear thee.

For all sacrifice is too little for a sweet savour unto thee: * but he that feareth the Lord is great at all times.

Woe to the nations that rise up against my kindred! * the Lord Almighty will take vengeance of them in the day of judgment.

THURSDAY FERIAL CANTICLE

Cantemus Domino

WILL sing unto the Lord, for he hath triumphed gloriously: * the horse and his rider hath he thrown into the sea.

The Lord is my strength and song, * and he is become my salvation:

He is my God, and I will prepare him an habitation; * my father's God, and I will exalt him.

The Lord is a man of war: * the Lord is his Name.

Pharaoh's chariots and his host hath he cast into the sea: * his chosen captains also are drowned in the Red Sea.

The depths have covered them: * they sank into the bottom as a stone.

Thy right hand, O Lord, is become glorious in power: * thy right hand, O Lord, hath dashed in pieces the enemy.

And in the greatness of thine excellency † thou hast overthrown them that rose up against thee: * thou sentest forth thy wrath, which consumed them as stubble.

And with the blast of thy nostrils the waters were gathered together, * the floods stood upright as an heap, and the depths were congealed in the heart of the sea.

The enemy said, † I will pursue, I will overtake, I will divide the spoil; * my lust shall be satisfied upon them;

I will draw my sword, * my hand shall destroy them.

Thou didst blow with thy wind, the sea covered them: * they sank as lead in the mighty waters.

Who is like unto thee, O Lord, among the gods? * who is like thee, glorious in holiness, fearful in praises, doing wonders?

Thou stretchedst out thy right hand, * the earth swallowed them.

Thou in thy mercy hast led forth the people which thou hast redeemed: * thou hast guided them in thy strength unto thy holy habitation.

The people shall hear, and be afraid: * sorrow shall take hold on the inhabitants of Palestina.

Then the dukes of Edom shall be amazed; * the mighty men of Moab, trembling shall take hold upon them; all the inhabitants of Canaan shall melt away.

Fear and dread shall fall upon them; † by the greatness of thine arm they shall be as still as a stone; * till thy people pass over, O Lord, till the people pass over, which thou hast purchased.

Thou shalt bring them in, and plant them in the mountain of thine inheritance, * in the place, O Lord, which thou hast made for thee to dwell in, in the Sanctuary, O Lord, which thy hands have established.

The Lord shall reign * for ever and ever.

For the horse of Pharaoh went in with his chariots and with his horsemen into the sea, * and the Lord brought again the waters of the sea upon them.

But the children of Israel went on dry land * in the midst of the sea.

THURSDAY FESTAL CANTICLE

Audite verbum

EAR the word of the Lord, O ye nations, * and declare it in the isles afar off,

And say, He that scattered Israel will gather him, * and keep him, as a shepherd doth his flock.

For the Lord hath redeemed Jacob, * and ransomed him from the hand of him that was stronger than he.

Therefore they shall come and sing in the height of Sion, * and shall flow together to the goodness of the Lord,

For wheat, and for wine, and for oil, * and for the young of the flock and of the herd:

And their soul shall be as a watered garden; * and they shall not sorrow any more at all.

Then shall the virgin rejoice in the dance, * both young men and old together:

For I will turn their mourning into joy, * and will comfort them, and make them rejoice from their sorrow.

And I will satiate the soul of the priests with fatness, * and my people shall be satisfied with my goodness, saith the Lord.

FRIDAY FERIAL CANTICLE

Domine audivi

LORD, I have heard thy speech, * and was afraid: O Lord, revive thy work in the midst of the years, † in the midst of the years make known; * in wrath remember mercy.

God came from Teman, * and the Holy One from mount Paran.

His glory covered the heavens, * and the earth was full of his praise.

And his brightness was as the light; † he had horns coming out of his hand: * and there was the hiding of his power.

Before him went the pestilence, * and burning coals went forth at his feet.

He stood, and measured the earth: * he beheld, and drove asunder the nations;

And the everlasting mountains were scattered, † the perpetual hills did bow: * his ways are everlasting.

I saw the tents of Cushan in affliction: * and the curtains of the land of Midian did tremble.

Was the Lord displeased against the rivers? * was thine anger against the rivers?

Was thy wrath against the sea, * that thou didst ride upon thine horses and thy chariots of salvation?

Thy bow was made quite naked, * according to the oaths of the tribes, even thy word.

Thou didst cleave the earth with rivers: * the mountains saw thee, and they trembled:

The overflowing of the water passed by: * the deep uttered his voice, and lifted up his hands on high.

The sun and moon stood still in their habitation: * at the light of thine arrows they went, and at the shining of thy glittering spear.

Thou didst march through the land in indignation, * thou didst thresh the heathen in anger.

Thou wentest forth for the salvation of thy people, * even for salvation with thine Anointed;

Thou woundedst the head out of the house of the wicked, * by discovering the foundation unto the neck.

Thou didst strike through with his staves the head of his villages: * they came out as a whirlwind to scatter me:

their rejoicing was as to devour the poor secretly.

Thou didst walk through the sea with thine horses, * through the heap of great waters.

When I heard, my belly trembled; * my lips quivered at the voice:

Rottenness entered into my bones, * and I trembled in myself, that I might rest in the day of trouble:

When he cometh up unto the people, * he will invade them with his troops.

Although the fig tree shall not blossom, * neither shall fruit be in the vines;

The labour of the olive shall fail, * and the fields shall yield no meat;

The flock shall be cut off from the fold, * and there shall be no herd in the stalls:

Yet I will rejoice in the Lord, * I will joy in the God of my salvation.

The Lord God is my strength, and he will make my feet like hinds' feet, * and he will make me to walk upon mine high places.

FRIDAY FESTAL CANTICLE

Vere tu es Deus absconditus

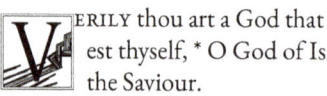ERILY thou art a God that hidest thyself, * O God of Israel, the Saviour.

They shall be ashamed, and also confounded, all of them: * they shall go to confusion together that are makers of idols.

But Israel shall be saved in the Lord with an everlasting salvation: * ye shall not be ashamed nor confounded world without end.

For thus saith the Lord that created the heavens; * God himself that formed the earth and made it;

He hath established it, he created it not in vain, * he formed it to be inhabited:

I am the Lord; * and there is none else.

I have not spoken in secret, * in a dark place of the earth:

I said not unto the seed of Jacob, Seek ye me in vain: * I the Lord speak righteousness, I declare things that are right.

Assemble yourselves and come; * draw near together, ye that are escaped of the nations:

They have no knowledge that set up the wood of their graven image, * and pray unto a god that cannot save.

Tell ye, and bring them near; † yea, let them take counsel together: * who hath declared this from ancient time? who hath told it from that time?

Have not I the Lord? and there is no God else beside me; * a just God and a Saviour; there is none beside me.

Look unto me, and be ye saved, all the ends of the earth: * for I am God, and there is none else.

I have sworn by myself, * the word is gone out of my mouth in righteousness, and shall not return,

That unto me every knee shall bow, * every tongue shall swear.

Surely, shall one say, in the Lord have I righteousness and strength: * even to him shall men come; and all that are incensed against him shall be ashamed.

In the Lord shall all the seed of Israel be justified, * and shall glory.

SATURDAY FERIAL CANTICLE

Audite cæli

IVE ear, O ye heavens, and I will speak; * and hear, O earth, the words of my mouth.

My doctrine shall drop as the rain, † my speech shall distil as the dew, * as the small rain upon the tender herb, and as the showers upon the grass:

Because I will publish the Name of the Lord: * ascribe ye greatness unto our God.

He is the Rock, his work is perfect: * for all his ways are judgment:

A God of truth and without iniquity, * just and right is he.

They have corrupted themselves, † their spot is not the spot of his children: * they are a perverse and crooked generation.

Do ye thus requite the Lord, O foolish people and unwise? * is not he thy father that hath bought thee? hath he not made thee, and established thee?

Remember the days of old, * consider the years of many generations:

Ask thy father, and he will shew thee; * thy elders, and they will tell thee.

When the Most High divided to the nations their inheritance, * when he separated the sons of Adam,

He set the bounds of the people * according to the number of the children of Israel.

For the Lord's portion is his people; * Jacob is the lot of his inheritance.

He found him in a desert land, * and in the waste howling wilderness;

He led him about, he instructed him, * he kept him as the apple of his eye.

As an eagle stirreth up her nest, fluttereth over her young, * spreadeth abroad her wings, taketh them, beareth them on her wings:

So the Lord alone did lead him, * and there was no strange god with him.

He made him ride on the high places of the earth, * that he might eat the increase of the fields;

And he made him to suck honey out of the rock, * and oil out of the flinty rock;

Butter of kine, and milk of sheep, * with fat of lambs, and rams of the breed of Bashan,

And goats, with the fat of kidneys of wheat; * and thou didst drink the pure blood of the grape.

But Jeshurun waxed fat, and kicked: * thou art waxen fat, thou art grown thick, thou art covered with fatness;

Then he forsook God which made him, * and lightly esteemed the Rock of his salvation.

They provoked him to jealousy with strange gods, * with abominations provoked they him to anger.

They sacrificed unto devils, not to God; * to gods whom they knew not, to new gods that came newly up, whom your fathers feared not.

Of the Rock that begat thee thou art unmindful, * and hast forgotten God that formed thee.

And when the Lord saw it, he abhorred them, * because of the provoking of his sons, and of his daughters.

And he said, I will hide my face from them, † I will see what their end shall be: * for they are a very froward generation, children in whom is no faith.

They have moved me to jealousy with that which is not God; * they have provoked me to anger with their vanities:

And I will move them to jealousy with those which are not a people; * I will provoke them to anger with a foolish nation.

Ignis succensus est

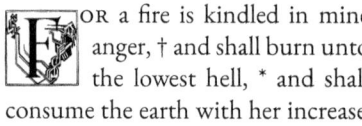OR a fire is kindled in mine anger, † and shall burn unto the lowest hell, * and shall consume the earth with her increase, and set on fire the foundations of the mountains.

I will heap mischiefs upon them; * I will spend mine arrows upon them.

They shall be burnt with hunger, * and devoured with burning heat, and with bitter destruction:

I will also send the teeth of beasts upon them, * with the poison of serpents of the dust.

The sword without, and terror within, † shall destroy both the young man and the virgin, * the suckling also with the man of gray hairs.

I said, I would scatter them into corners, * I would make the remembrance of them to cease from among men:

Were it not that I feared the wrath of the enemy, * lest their adversaries should behave themselves strangely,

And lest they should say, Our hand is high, * and the Lord hath not done all this.

For they are a nation void of counsel, * neither is there any understanding in them.

O that they were wise, that they understood this, * that they would consider their latter end!

How should one chase a thousand, † and two put ten thousand to flight, * except their Rock had sold them, and the Lord had shut them up?

For their rock is not as our Rock, * even our enemies themselves being judges.

For their vine is of the vine of Sodom, * and of the fields of Gomorrah:

Their grapes are grapes of gall, * their clusters are bitter:

Their wine is the poison of dragons, * and the cruel venom of asps.

Is not this laid up in store with me, † and sealed up among my treasures? * to me belongeth vengeance, and recompence;

Their foot shall slide in due time: * for the day of their calamity is at hand, and the things that shall come upon them make haste.

For the Lord shall judge his people, * and repent himself for his servants,

When he seeth that their power is gone, * and there is none shut up, or left.

And he shall say, Where are their

gods, * their rock in whom they trusted,

Which did eat the fat of their sacrifices, * and drank the wine of their drink offerings?

Let them rise up and help you, *and be your protection.

See now that I, even I, am he, * and there is no god with me:

I kill, and I make alive; † I wound, and I heal: * neither is there any that can deliver out of my hand.

For I lift up my hand to heaven, and say, * I live for ever.

If I whet my glittering sword, and mine hand take hold on judgment; * I will render vengeance to mine enemies, and will reward them that hate me.

I will make mine arrows drunk with blood, † and my sword shall devour flesh; * and that with the blood of the slain and of the captives, from the beginning of revenges upon the enemy.

Rejoice, O ye nations, with his people: * for he will avenge the blood of his servants,

And will render vengeance to his adversaries, * and will be merciful unto his land, and to his people.

SATURDAY FESTAL CANTICLE

Miserere nostri, Deus

❡ This Canticle is also used when Sunday Mattins is anticipated on Saturday evening.

AVE mercy upon us, O Lord God of all, and behold us: * and send thy fear upon all the nations that seek not after thee.

Lift up thy hand against the strange nations, * and let them see thy power.

As thou wast sanctified in us before them: * so be thou magnified among them before us.

And let them know thee, as we have known thee, * that there is no God but only thou, O God.

Shew new signs, and repeat thy wonders: * glorify thy hand and thy right arm, that they may set forth thy wondrous works.

Raise up indignation, and pour out wrath: * take away the adversary, and destroy the enemy.

Make the time short, remember the covenant, * and let them declare thy wonderful works.

Let him that escapeth be consumed by the rage of the fire; * and let them perish that oppress the people.

Smite in sunder the heads of the rulers of the heathen, * that say, There is none other but we.

Gather all the tribes of Jacob together, * and inherit thou them, as from the beginning.

Daily Office

Hour of Prime

❡ This service may be said at any convenient time before or after the saying of Morning Prayer, but not in substitution therefor.

℣. O God, ✠ make speed to save us.
℟. O Lord, make haste to help us.
℣. Glory be to the Father, and to the Son, and to the Holy Ghost.
℟. As it was in the beginning, is now, and ever shall be, world without end. Amen.
℣. Praise ye the Lord.
℟. The Lord's Name be praised.

Jam Lucis Ordo Sidere

ow that the daylight fills the sky,
We lift our hearts to God on high,
That he, in all we do or say,
Would keep us free from harm to-day:

Would guard our hearts and tongues from strife;
From anger's din would hide our life;
From all ill sights would turn our eyes,
Would close our ears from vanities:

Would keep our inmost conscience pure;
Our souls from folly would secure;
Would bid us check the pride of sense
With due and holy abstinence.

So we, when this new day is gone,
And night in turn is drawing on,
With conscience by the world un-stained

Shall praise his name for victory gained.

All laud to God the Father be;
All praise, eternal Son, to thee;
All glory, as is ever meet,
To God the holy Paraclete. Amen.

Psalm 54. *Deus, in nomine*

ave me, O God, for thy Name's sake : and avenge me in thy strength.

2 Hear my prayer, O God : and hearken unto the words of my mouth.

3 For strangers are risen up against me : and tyrants, which have not God before their eyes, seek after my soul.

4 Behold, God is my helper : the Lord is with them that uphold my soul.

5 He shall reward evil unto mine enemies : destroy thou them in thy truth.

6 An offering of a free heart will I give thee, and praise thy Name, O Lord : because it is so comfortable.

7 For he hath delivered me out of all my trouble : and mine eye hath seen his desire upon mine enemies.

℣. Glory be to the Father, and to the Son, and to the Holy Ghost.
℟. As it was in the beginning, is now, and ever shall be, world without end. Amen.

PSALM 119. *BEATI IMMACULATI*

LESSED are those that are un-defiled in the way : and walk in the law of the Lord.

2 Blessed are they that keep his testimonies : and seek him with their whole heart.

3 For they who do no wickedness : walk in his ways.

4 Thou hast charged : that we shall diligently keep thy commandments.

5 O that my ways were made so direct : that I might keep thy statutes!

6 So shall I not be confounded : while I have respect unto all thy commandments.

7 I will thank thee with an unfeigned heart : when I shall have learned the judgements of thy righteousness.

8 I will keep thy ceremonies : O forsake me not utterly.

℣. Glory be to the Father, and to the Son, and to the Holy Ghost.

℞. As it was in the beginning, is now, and ever shall be, world without end. Amen.

IN QUO CORRIGET?

HEREWITHAL shall a young man cleanse his way : even by ruling himself after thy word.

10 With my whole heart have I sought thee : O let me not go wrong out of thy commandments.

11 Thy words have I hid within my heart : that I should not sin against thee.

12 Blessed art thou, O Lord : O teach me thy statutes.

13 With my lips have I been telling : of all the judgements of thy mouth.

14 I have had as great delight in the way of thy testimonies : as in all manner of riches.

15 I will talk of thy commandments : and have respect unto thy ways.

16 My delight shall be in thy statutes : and I will not forget thy word.

℣. Glory be to the Father, and to the Son, and to the Holy Ghost.

℞. As it was in the beginning, is now, and ever shall be, world without end. Amen.

RETRIBUE SERVO TUO

DO well unto thy servant : that I may live, and keep thy word.

18 Open thou mine eyes : that I may see the wondrous things of thy law.

19 I am a stranger upon earth : O hide not thy commandments from me.

20 My soul breaketh out for the very fervent desire : that it hath alway unto thy judgements.

21 Thou hast rebuked the proud : and cursed are they that do err from thy commandments.

22 O turn from me shame and rebuke : for I have kept thy testimonies.

23 Princes also did sit and speak against me : but thy servant is occupied in thy statutes.

24 For thy testimonies are my delight : and my counsellors.

℣. Glory be to the Father, and to the Son, and to the Holy Ghost.

℞. As it was in the beginning, is now, and ever shall be, world without end. Amen.

Adhaesit pavimento

Y soul cleaveth to the dust : O quicken thou me, according to thy word.

26 I have acknowledged my ways, and thou heardest me : O teach me thy statutes.

27 Make me to understand the way of thy commandments : and so shall I talk of thy wondrous works.

28 My soul melteth away for very heaviness : comfort thou me according unto thy word.

29 Take from me the way of lying : and cause thou me to make much of thy law.

30 I have chosen the way of truth : and thy judgements have I laid before me.

31 I have stuck unto thy testimonies : O Lord, confound me not.

32 I will run the way of thy commandments : when thou hast set my heart at liberty.

℣. Glory be to the Father, and to the Son, and to the Holy Ghost.

℞. As it was in the beginning, is now, and ever shall be, world without end. Amen.

⁋ As in the ancient use of Prime, the Athanasian Creed (p. 37) may here be said, concluding with the Gloria Patri.

Chapter

Ferias Throughout the Year

Love the truth and peace, saith the Lord of hosts.

Sundays & Feast Days

Now unto the King eternal, immortal, invisible, the only wise God, be honour and glory for ever and ever.

Eastertide

O Lord, be gracious unto us; we have waited for thee: be thou our arm every morning, our salvation also in the time of trouble.

⁋ After the Chapter is said,

℞. Thanks be to God.

Short Respond

℣. Jesu Christ, Son of the living God, have mercy upon us;

℞. Jesu Christ, Son of the living God, have mercy upon us.

℣. Thou that sittest at the right hand of the Father;

℞. Have mercy upon us.

℣. Glory be to the Father, and to the Son, and to the Holy Ghost.

℞. Jesu Christ, Son of the living God, have mercy upon us.

℣. O Lord, arise, help us;

℞. And deliver us for thy name's sake.

SUFFRAGES

¶ The Suffrages are said, kneeling, on all Ferias outside of Eastertide.

℣. Lord, have mercy upon us.
℟. Christ, have mercy upon us.
℣. Lord, have mercy upon us.

Lord's Prayer

UR Father, who art in heaven, Hallowed be thy Name. Thy kingdom come. Thy will be done on earth, As it is in heaven. Give us this day our daily bread. And forgive us our trespasses, As we forgive those who trespass against us. And lead us not into temptation; But deliver us from evil. Amen.

¶ Then shall follow these Versicles and Responses.

℣. O let my mouth be filled with thy praise;
℟. That I may sing of thy glory and honour all the day long.
℣. Turn thy face from my sins, O Lord;
℟. And put out all my misdeeds.
℣. Make me a clean heart, O God;
℟. And renew a right spirit within me.
℣. Cast me not away from thy presence;
℟. And take not thy Holy Spirit from me.
℣. O give me the comfort of thy help again;
℟. And stablish me with thy free spirit.

Confession

¶ Then shall the Minister and People say together the Confession following,

CONFESS to God, to blessed Mary, to all the saints, and to you: that I have sinned exceedingly in thought, word, and deed, by my own fault. I beg holy Mary, all the Saints of God, and you, to pray for me.

¶ The Minister then stands and says,

LMIGHTY God, have mercy upon us, forgive us all our sins and deliver us from all evil, confirm and strengthen us in all goodness, and bring us to life everlasting. *Amen.*

¶ If a Priest be present, he shall stand and pronounce the following Absolution,

AY the Almighty and Merciful Lord grant unto you pardon ✠ and remission of all your sins, time for amendment of life, and the grace and comfort of the Holy Spirit. *Amen.*

℣. Wilt thou not turn again and quicken us, O God?
℟. That thy people may rejoice in thee.
℣. O Lord, show thy mercy upon us.
℟. And grant us thy salvation.
℣. Vouchsafe, O Lord, to keep us this day without sin;
℟. O Lord, have mercy upon us, have mercy upon us.

COLLECT

℣. O Lord, hear our prayer.

℟. And let our cry come unto thee.

Let us pray.

N this hour of this day, fill us, O Lord, with thy mercy; that going forth in thy strength, we may make our boast of thee all the day long. Through.

℣. The Lord be with you.

or, O Lord, hear our prayer.

℟. And with thy spirit.

or, And let our cry come unto thee.

℣. Let us bless the Lord.

℟. Thanks be to God.

HE Lord bless us, and preserve us from all evil, and bring us to everlasting life; and may the souls ✠ of the faithful departed, through the mercy of God, rest in peace. *Amen.*

❡ The Office of Prime may end here, or the following devotions may be added.

Pretiosa

❡ The Pretiosa is a laudable custom and may be added to Prime. The Martyrology reading for the Day may here be read. The following is then said.

℣. Right dear in the sight of the Lord.

℟. Is the death of his Saints.

AY holy Mary and all the Saints intercede for us to the Lord: that we may be worthy to obtain from him help and salvation, who liveth and reigneth for ever and ever. *Amen.*

℣. O God, ✠ make speed to save me.
℟. O Lord, make haste to help me.
℣. O God, ✠ make speed to save me.
℟. O Lord, make haste to help me.
℣. O God, ✠ make speed to save me.
℟. O Lord, make haste to help me.

℣. Glory be to the Father, and to the Son, and to the Holy Ghost.
℟. As it was in the beginning, is now, and ever shall be, world without end. Amen.
℣. Lord, have mercy upon us.
℟. Christ, have mercy upon us.
℣. Lord, have mercy upon us.

UR Father, who art in heaven, Hallowed be thy Name. Thy kingdom come. Thy will be done on earth, As it is in heaven. Give us this day our daily bread. And for-give us our trespasses, As we forgive those who trespass against us. And lead us not into temptation; But deliver us from evil. Amen.

℣. Let thy loving mercy come also unto us, O Lord.
℟. Even thy salvation, according unto thy word.
℣. And show thy servants thy work.
℟. And their children thy glory.
℣. And the glorious Majesty of the Lord our God be upon us.
℟. And prosper thou the work of our hands upon us: O prosper thou our handy-work.

Let us pray.

ALMIGHTY Lord and Everlasting God, vouchsafe, we beseech thee, to direct, sanctify, and govern, both our hearts and bodies in the ways of thy laws and in the works of thy commandments: that through thy most mighty protection, both here and ever, we may be preserved in body and soul; through our Lord and Saviour Jesus Christ. *Amen.*

℣. May the Divine Assistance remain always with us.
℟. Amen.

Daily Office

Commemoration of the Faithful Departed

❡ This Commemoration is a laudable custom, which may be said after any Hour.

℣. Let us commemorate our departed kinsfolk, neighbours, friends, and benefactors.

℟. May they rest in peace.

PSALM 130. *DE PROFUNDIS*

UT of the deep have I called unto thee, O Lord : Lord, hear my voice.

2 O let thine ears consider well : the voice of my complaint.

3 If thou, Lord, wilt be extreme to mark what is done amiss : O Lord, who may abide it?

4 For there is mercy with thee : therefore shalt thou be feared.

5 I look for the Lord; my soul doth wait for him : in his word is my trust.

6 My soul fleeth unto the Lord : before the morning watch, I say, before the morning watch.

7 O Israel, trust in the Lord, for with the Lord there is mercy : and with him is plenteous redemption.

8 And he shall redeem Israel : from all his sins.

℣. Rest eternal * grant unto them, O Lord.

℟. And let light perpetual * shine upon them.

℣. From the gate of hell.

℟. Deliver their souls, O Lord.

℣. May they rest in peace.

℟. Amen.

℣. O Lord hear my prayer.

℟. And let my cry come unto thee.

℣. The Lord be with you.

℟. And with thy spirit.

Let us pray.

GOD, the Giver of pardon and the Author of man's salvation: we humbly beseech thy mercy to grant that our kinsfolk, neighbours, friends, and benefactors who have departed out of this world, blessed Mary ever Virgin and all thy Saints praying for them, may attain to the fellowship of everlasting blessedness. Through.

℣. Rest eternal grant unto them, O Lord.

℟. And let light perpetual shine upon them.

℣. May they rest in peace.

℟. Amen.

Athanasian Creed

HOSOEVER would be saved : needeth before all things to hold fast the Catholick Faith.

2 Which Faith except a man keep whole and undefiled : without doubt he will perish eternally.

3 Now the Catholick Faith is this : that we worship one God in Trinity, and the Trinity in Unity;

4 Neither confusing the Persons : nor dividing the substance.

5 For there is one Person of the Father, another of the Son : another of the Holy Ghost;

6 But the Godhead of the Father, and of the Son, and of the Holy Ghost is all one : the glory equal, the majesty co-eternal.

7 Such as the Father is, such is the Son : and such is the Holy Ghost.

8 The Father uncreated, the Son uncreated : the Holy Ghost uncreated;

9 The Father infinite, the Son infinite : the Holy Ghost infinite;

10 The Father eternal, the Son eternal : the Holy Ghost eternal.

11 And yet there are not three eternals : but one eternal

12 As also there are not three uncreated, nor three infinites : but one infinite, and one uncreated.

13 So likewise the Father is almighty, the Son almighty : the Holy Ghost almighty;

14 And yet there are not three almighties : but one almighty.

15 So the Father is God, the Son God

UICÚMQUE vult salvus esse, * ante ómnia opus est, ut téneat cathólicam fidem:

Quam nisi quisque íntegram inviolatámque serváverit, * absque dúbio in ætérnum períbit.

Fides autem cathólica hæc est: * ut unum Deum in Trinitáte, et Trinitátem in unitáte venerémur.

Neque confundéntes persónas, * neque substántiam separántes.

Alia est enim persóna Patris, ália Fílii, * ália Spíritus Sancti:

Sed Patris, et Fílii, et Spíritus Sancti una est divínitas, * æquális glória, coætérna majéstas.

Qualis Pater, talis Fílius, * talis Spíritus Sanctus.

Increátus Pater, increátus Fílius, * increátus Spíritus Sanctus.

Imménsus Pater, imménsus Fílius, * imménsus Spíritus Sanctus.

Ætérnus Pater, ætérnus Fílius, * ætérnus Spíritus Sanctus.

Et tamen non tres ætérni, * sed unus ætérnus.

Sicut non tres increáti, nec tres imménsi, * sed unus increátus, et unus imménsus.

Simíliter omnípotens Pater, omnípotens Fílius, * omnípotens Spíritus Sanctus.

Et tamen non tres omnipoténtes, * sed unus omnípotens.

Ita Deus Pater, Deus Fílius, * Deus Spíritus Sanctus.

Ut tamen non tres Dii, * sed unus

: the Holy Ghost God;

16 And yet there are not three Gods : but one God.

17 So the Father is Lord, the Son Lord : the Holy Ghost Lord;

18 And yet there are not three Lords : but one Lord.

19 For like as we are compelled by the Christian verity : to confess each Person by himself to be both God and Lord;

20 So are we forbidden by the Catholick religion : to speak of three Gods or three Lords.

21 The Father is made of none : nor created, nor begotten.

22 The Son is of the Father : not made, nor created, but begotten.

23 The Holy Ghost is of the Father : not made, nor created, nor begotten, but proceeding.

24 There is therefore one Father, not three Fathers; one Son, not three Sons : one Holy Ghost, not three Holy Ghosts.

25 And in this Trinity there is no before or after : no greater or less;

26 But all three Persons are co-eternal together : and co-equal.

27 So that in all ways, as is aforesaid : both the Trinity is to be worshipped in Unity, and the Unity in Trinity.

28 He therefore that would be saved : let him thus think of the Trinity.

URTHERMORE it is necessary to eternal salvation : that he also believe faithfully the Incarnation of our Lord Jesus Christ.

30 Now the right faith is that we believe and confess : that our Lord Jesus

est Deus.

Ita Dóminus Pater, Dóminus Fílius, * Dóminus Spíritus Sanctus.

Et tamen non tres Dómini, * sed unus est Dóminus.

Quia, sicut singillátim unamquámque persónam Deum ac Dóminum confitéri christiána veritáte compélli-mur: * ita tres Deos aut Dóminos dícere cathólica religióne prohibémur.

Pater a nullo est factus: * nec creátus, nec génitus.

Fílius a Patre est: * non factus, nec creátus, sed génitus.

Spíritus Sanctus a Patre: * non factus, nec creátus, nec génitus, sed procédens.

Unus ergo Pater, non tres Patres: unus Fílius, non tres Fílii: * unus Spíritus Sanctus, non tres Spíritus Sancti.

Et in hac Trinitáte nihil prius aut postérius, nihil majus aut minus: * sed totæ tres persónæ coætérnæ sibi sunt et coæquáles.

Ita ut per ómnia, sicut jam supra dictum est, * et únitas in Trinitáte, et Trínitas in unitáte veneránda sit.

Qui vult ergo salvus esse, * ita de Trinitáte séntiat.

ED necessárium est ad ætérnam salútem, * ut Incarnatiónem quoque Dómini nostri Jesu Christi fidéliter credat.

Est ergo fides recta ut credámus et confiteámur, * quia Dóminus noster Jesus Christus, Dei Fílius, Deus et homo est.

Deus est ex substántia Patris ante sǽcula génitus: * et homo est ex substántia matris in sǽculo natus.

Christ, the Son of God, is both God and man.

31 He is God, of the substance of the Father, begotten before the worlds : and he is man, of the substance of his Mother, born in the world;

32 Perfect God : perfect man, of reasoning soul and human flesh subsisting;

33 Equal to the Father as touching his Godhead : less than the Father as touching his manhood.

34 Who although he be God and man : yet he is not two, but is one Christ ;

35 One however, not by conversion of Godhead into flesh : but by taking manhood into God;

36 One altogether : not by confusion of substance, but by unity of person.

37 For as reasoning soul and flesh is one man : so God and man is one Christ;

38 Who suffered for our salvation : descended into hell, rose again from the dead;

39 Ascended into heaven, sat down at the right hand of the Father : from whence he shall come to judge the quick and the dead.

40 At whose coming all men must rise again with their bodies : and shall give account for their own deeds.

41 And they that have done good will go into life eternal : they that have done evil into eternal fire.

THIS is the Catholick Faith : which except a man do faithfully and steadfastly believe, he cannot be saved.

Perféctus Deus, perféctus homo: * ex ánima rationáli et humána carne subsístens.

Æquális Patri secúndum divinitátem: * minor Patre secúndum humanitátem.

Qui licet Deus sit et homo, * non duo tamen, sed unus est Christus.

Unus autem non conversióne divinitátis in carnem, * sed assumptióne humanitátis in Deum.

Unus omníno, non confusióne substántiæ, * sed unitáte persónæ.

Nam sicut ánima rationális et caro unus est homo: * ita Deus et homo unus est Christus.

Qui passus est pro salúte nostra: descéndit ad ínferos: * tértia die resurréxit a mórtuis.

Ascéndit ad cælos, sedet ad déxteram Dei Patris omnipoténtis: * inde ventúrus est judicáre vivos et mórtuos.

Ad cujus advéntum omnes hómines resúrgere habent cum corpóribus suis; * et redditúri sunt de factis própriis ratiónem.

Et qui bona egérunt, ibunt in vitam ætérnam: * qui vero mala, in ignem ætérnum.

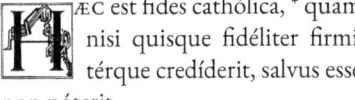ÆC est fides cathólica, * quam nisi quisque fidéliter firmitérque credíderit, salvus esse non póterit.

Daily Office

Hour of Terce

℣. O God, ✠ make speed to save us.

℟. O Lord, make haste to help us.

℣. Glory be to the Father, and to the Son, and to the Holy Ghost.

℟. As it was in the beginning, is now, and ever shall be, world without end. Amen.

℣. Praise ye the Lord.

℟. The Lord's Name be praised.

Nunc Sancte

OME Holy Ghost, with God the Son,
And God the Father, ever one:
Shed forth thy grace within our breast,
And dwell with us, a ready Guest.

By every power, by heart and tongue,
By act and deed, thy praise be sung;
Inflame with perfect love each sense,
That others' souls may kindle thence.

O Father, that we ask be done,
Through Jesus Christ, thine only Son;
Who, with the Holy Ghost and thee,
Shall live and reign eternally. Amen.

Legem pone

EACH me, O Lord, the way of thy statutes : and I shall keep it unto the end.

34 Give me understanding, and I shall keep thy law : yea, I shall keep it with my whole heart.

35 Make me to go in the path of thy commandments : for therein is my desire.

36 Incline my heart unto thy testimonies : and not to covetousness.

37 O turn away mine eyes, lest they behold vanity : and quicken thou me in thy way.

38 O stablish thy word in thy servant : that I may fear thee.

39 Take away the rebuke that I am afraid of : for thy judgements are good.

40 Behold, my delight is in thy commandments : O quicken me in thy righteousness.

℣. Glory be to the Father, and to the Son, and to the Holy Ghost.

℟. As it was in the beginning, is now, and ever shall be, world without end. Amen.

Et veniat super me

ET thy loving mercy come also unto me, O Lord : even thy salvation, according unto thy word.

42 So shall I make answer unto my blasphemers : for my trust is in thy word.

43 O take not the word of thy truth utterly out of my mouth : for my hope is in thy judgements.

44 So shall I alway keep thy law : yea, for ever and ever.

45 And I will walk at liberty : for I seek thy commandments.

46 I will speak of thy testimonies also, even before kings : and will not be ashamed.

47 And my delight shall be in thy commandments : which I have loved.

48 My hands also will I lift up unto thy commandments, which I have loved : and my study shall be in thy statutes.

℣. Glory be to the Father, and to the Son, and to the Holy Ghost.

℟. As it was in the beginning, is now, and ever shall be, world without end. Amen.

Memor esto servi tui

THINK upon thy servant, as concerning thy word : wherein thou hast caused me to put my trust.

50 The same is my comfort in my trouble : for thy word hath quickened me.

51 The proud have had me exceedingly in derision : yet have I not shrinked from thy law.

52 For I remembered thine everlasting judgements, O Lord : and received comfort.

53 I am horribly afraid : for the ungodly that forsake thy law.

54 Thy statutes have been my songs : in the house of my pilgrimage.

55 I have thought upon thy Name, O Lord, in the night-season : and have kept thy law.

56 This I had : because I kept thy commandments.

℣. Glory be to the Father, and to the Son, and to the Holy Ghost.

℟. As it was in the beginning, is now, and ever shall be, world without end. Amen.

Portio mea, Domine

HOU art my portion, O Lord : I have promised to keep thy law.

58 I made my humble petition in thy presence with my whole heart : O be merciful unto me, according to thy word.

59 I called mine own ways to remembrance : and turned my feet unto thy testimonies.

60 I made haste, and prolonged not the time : to keep thy commandments.

61 The congregations of the ungodly have robbed me : but I have not forgotten thy law.

62 At midnight I will rise to give thanks unto thee : because of thy righteous judgements.

63 I am a companion of all them that fear thee : and keep thy commandments.

64 The earth, O Lord, is full of thy mercy : O teach me thy statutes.

℣. Glory be to the Father, and to the Son, and to the Holy Ghost.

℟. As it was in the beginning, is now, and ever shall be, world without end. Amen.

Bonitatem fecisti

LORD, thou hast dealt graciously with thy servant : according unto thy word.

66 O learn me true understanding and knowledge : for I have believed thy commandments.

67 Before I was troubled, I went wrong : but now have I kept thy word.

68 Thou art good and gracious : O teach me thy statutes.

69 The proud have imagined a lie against me : but I will keep thy commandments with my whole heart.

70 Their heart is as fat as brawn : but my delight hath been in thy law.

71 It is good for me that I have been in trouble : that I may learn thy statutes.

72 The law of thy mouth is dearer unto me : than thousands of gold and silver.

℣. Glory be to the Father, and to the Son, and to the Holy Ghost.

℟. As it was in the beginning, is now, and ever shall be, world without end. Amen.

Manus tuae fecerunt me

HY hands have made me and fashioned me : O give me understanding, that I may learn thy commandments.

74 They that fear thee will be glad when they see me : because I have put my trust in thy word.

75 I know, O Lord, that thy judgements are right : and that thou of very faithfulness hast caused me to be troubled.

76 O let thy merciful kindness be my comfort : according to thy word unto thy servant.

77 O let thy loving mercies come unto me, that I may live : for thy law is my delight.

78 Let the proud be confounded, for they go wickedly about to destroy me :

but I will be occupied in thy commandments.

79 Let such as fear thee, and have known thy testimonies : be turned unto me.

80 O let my heart be sound in thy statutes : that I be not ashamed.

℣. Glory be to the Father, and to the Son, and to the Holy Ghost.

℟. As it was in the beginning, is now, and ever shall be, world without end. Amen.

Chapter

Feria Days Throughout the Year

Heal me, O Lord, and I shall be healed; save me, and I shall be saved: for thou art my praise.

Sundays & Feast Days

O the depth of the riches both of the wisdom and knowledge of God! How unsearchable are his judgements, and his ways past finding out!

Eastertide

For whatsoever is born of God overcometh the world: and this is the victory that overcometh the world, even our faith.

℟. Thanks be to God.

Short Respond

Ferias Throughout the Year

℣. Heal my soul, for I have sinned against thee.

℟. Heal my soul, for I have sinned against thee.

℣. I said, Lord, be merciful unto me.

℟. For I have sinned against thee.

℣. Glory be to the Father, and to the Son, and to the Holy Ghost.

℟. Heal my soul, for I have sinned against thee.

℣. Thou hast been my succour.

℟. Leave me not, neither forsake me, O God of my salvation.

Sundays, Feasts, & in Eastertide

℣. Incline my heart, O God, unto thy testimonies (alleluia, alleluia).

℟. Incline my heart, O God, unto thy testimonies (alleluia, alleluia).

℣. Turn away mine eyes, lest they behold vanity.

℟. Unto thy testimonies (alleluia, alleluia).

℣. Glory be to the Father, and to the Son, and to the Holy Ghost.

℟. Incline my heart, O God, unto thy testimonies (alleluia, alleluia).

℣. I said, Lord, be merciful unto me (alleluia).

℟. For I have sinned against thee (alleluia).

Suffrages

❡ The Suffrages are said, kneeling, on all Ferias outside of Eastertide.

℣. Lord, have mercy upon us.

℟. Christ, have mercy upon us.

℣. Lord, have mercy upon us.

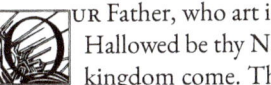UR Father, who art in heaven, Hallowed be thy Name. Thy kingdom come. Thy will be done on earth, As it is in heaven. Give us this day our daily bread. And forgive us our trespasses, As we forgive those who trespass against us. And lead us not into temptation; But deliver us from evil. Amen.

℣. Send out thy light and thy truth, that they may lead me.

℟. And bring me unto thy holy hill, and to thy dwelling.

℣. O let us live.

℟. And we shall call upon thy Name.

℣. Turn us again, O Lord God of hosts.

℟. Show the light of thy countenance, and we shall be whole.

Collects

℣. The Lord be with you.

or, O Lord, hear our prayer.

℟. And with thy spirit.

or, And let our cry come unto thee.

℣. Let us pray.

❡ The Collect(s) of the Day is here said, followed by this memorial Collect.

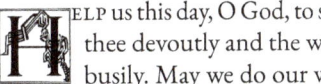ELP us this day, O God, to serve thee devoutly and the world busily. May we do our work wisely, give succour secretly, go to our meat appetitely, sit thereat discreetly, arise temperately, please our friends duly, go to our bed merrily, and sleep surely; for the joy of our Lord Jesus Christ. *Amen.*

℣. The Lord be with you.

or, O Lord, hear our prayer.

℟. And with thy spirit.

or, And let our cry come unto thee.

℣. Let us bless the Lord.

℟. Thanks be to God.

℣. May the souls ✠ of the faithful departed, through the mercy of God, rest in peace.

UNTO him that loved us, and washed us from our sins in his own blood, and hath made us kings and priests unto God and his Father, to him be glory and dominion for ever and ever. *Amen.*

Hour of Sext

℣. O God, ✠ make speed to save us.
℟. O Lord, make haste to help us.
℣. Glory be to the Father, and to the Son, and to the Holy Ghost.
℟. As it was in the beginning, is now, and ever shall be, world without end. Amen.
℣. Praise ye the Lord.
℟. The Lord's Name be praised.

RECTOR POTENS

GOD of truth, O Lord of might,
Who ord'rest time and change aright,
And send'st the early morning ray,
And light'st the glow of perfect day.

Extinguish thou each sinful fire,
And banish every ill desire:
And while thou keep'st the body whole,
Shed forth thy peace upon the soul.

O Father, that we ask be done,
Through Jesus Christ, thine only Son;
Who, with the Holy Ghost and thee,
Doth live and reign eternally. Amen.

DEFECIT ANIMA MEA

Y soul hath longed for thy salvation : and I have a good hope because of thy word.

82 Mine eyes long sore for thy word : saying, O when wilt thou comfort me?

83 For I am become like a bottle in the smoke : yet do I not forget thy statutes.

84 How many are the days of thy servant : when wilt thou be avenged of them that persecute me?

85 The proud have digged pits for me : which are not after thy law.

86 All thy commandments are true : they persecute me falsely; O be thou my help.

87 They had almost made an end of me upon earth : but I forsook not thy commandments.

88 O quicken me after thy lovingkindness : and so shall I keep the testimonies of thy mouth.

℣. Glory be to the Father, and to the Son, and to the Holy Ghost.
℟. As it was in the beginning, is now, and ever shall be, world without end. Amen.

IN AETERNUM. DOMINE

LORD, thy word : endureth for ever in heaven.

90 Thy truth also remaineth from one generation to another : thou hast laid the foundation of the earth, and it abideth.

91 They continue this day according to thine ordinance : for all things serve thee.

92 If my delight had not been in thy law : I should have perished in my trouble.

93 I will never forget thy commandments : for with them thou hast quickened me.

94 I am thine, O save me : for I have sought thy commandments.

95 The ungodly laid wait for me to destroy me : but I will consider thy testimonies.

96 I see that all things come to an end : but thy commandment is exceeding broad.

℣. Glory be to the Father, and to the Son, and to the Holy Ghost.

℟. As it was in the beginning, is now, and ever shall be, world without end. Amen.

Quomodo dilexi!

ORD, what love have I unto thy law : all the day long is my study in it.

98 Thou through thy commandments hast made me wiser than mine enemies : for they are ever with me.

99 I have more understanding than my teachers : for thy testimonies are my study.

100 I am wiser than the aged : because I keep thy commandments.

101 I have refrained my feet from every evil way : that I may keep thy word.

102 I have not shrunk from thy judgements : for thou teachest me.

103 O how sweet are thy words unto my throat : yea, sweeter than honey unto my mouth.

104 Through thy commandments I get understanding : therefore I hate all evil ways.

℣. Glory be to the Father, and to the Son, and to the Holy Ghost.

℟. As it was in the beginning, is now, and ever shall be, world without end. Amen.

Lucerna pedibus meis

HY word is a lantern unto my feet : and a light unto my paths.

106 I have sworn, and am stedfastly purposed : to keep thy righteous judgements.

107 I am troubled above measure : quicken me, O Lord, according to thy word.

108 Let the free-will offerings of my mouth please thee, O Lord : and teach me thy judgements.

109 My soul is alway in my hand : yet do I not forget thy law.

110 The ungodly have laid a snare for me : but yet I swerved not from thy commandments.

111 Thy testimonies have I claimed as mine heritage for ever : and why? they are the very joy of my heart.

112 I have applied my heart to fulfil thy statutes alway : even unto the end.

℣. Glory be to the Father, and to the Son, and to the Holy Ghost.

℟. As it was in the beginning, is now, and ever shall be, world without end. Amen.

Iniquos odio habui

HATE them that imagine evil things : but thy law do I love.

114 Thou art my defence and shield : and my trust is in thy word.

115 Away from me, ye wicked : I will keep the commandments of my God.

116 O stablish me according to thy word, that I may live : and let me not be disappointed of my hope.

117 Hold thou me up, and I shall be safe : yea, my delight shall be ever in thy statutes.

118 Thou hast trodden down all them that depart from thy statutes : for they imagine but deceit.

119 Thou puttest away all the ungodly of the earth like dross : therefore I love thy testimonies.

120 My flesh trembleth for fear of thee : and I am afraid of thy judgements.

℣. Glory be to the Father, and to the Son, and to the Holy Ghost.

℟. As it was in the beginning, is now, and ever shall be, world without end. Amen.

FECI JUDICIUM

DEAL with the thing that is lawful and right : O give me not over unto mine oppressors.

122 Make thou thy servant to delight in that which is good : that the proud do me no wrong.

123 Mine eyes are wasted away with looking for thy health : and for the word of thy righteousness.

124 O deal with thy servant according unto thy loving mercy : and teach me thy statutes.

125 I am thy servant, O grant me understanding : that I may know thy testimonies.

126 It is time for thee, Lord, to lay to thine hand : for they have destroyed thy law.

127 For I love thy commandments : above gold and precious stone.

128 Therefore hold I straight all thy commandments : and all false ways I utterly abhor.

℣. Glory be to the Father, and to the Son, and to the Holy Ghost.

℟. As it was in the beginning, is now, and ever shall be, world without end. Amen.

CHAPTER

Ferias Throughout the Year

Prove all things, hold fast to that which is good: abstain from all appearance of evil.

Sundays & Feast Days

There are three that bear record in heaven: The Father, the Word, and the Holy Ghost: and these three are one.

Eastertide

Who is he that overcometh the world, but he that believeth that Jesus is the Son of God? This is he that came by water and blood, even Jesus Christ.

℟. Thanks be to God.

SHORT RESPOND

Ferias Throughout the Year

℣. I will bless the Lord at all times.

℟. I will bless the Lord at all times.

℣. His praise shall ever be in my mouth.

℟. At all times.

℣. Glory be to the Father, and to the Son, and to the Holy Ghost.

℟. I will bless the Lord at all times.

℣. Behold, God is my helper.

℟. The Lord is with them that uphold my soul.

℣. O Lord, thy Word endureth for ever in heaven (alleluia, alleluia).

℞. O Lord, thy Word endureth for ever in heaven (alleluia, alleluia).

℣. Thy truth also remaineth from one generation to another.

℞. For ever in heaven (alleluia, alleluia).

℣. Glory be to the Father, and to the Son, and to the Holy Ghost.

℞. O Lord, thy Word endureth for ever in heaven (alleluia, alleluia).

℣. The Lord is my shepherd, therefore can I lack nothing (alleluia).

℞. He shall feed me in a green pasture (alleluia).

SUFFRAGES

❡ The Suffrages are said, kneeling, on all Ferias outside of Eastertide.

℣. Lord, have mercy upon us.

℞. Christ, have mercy upon us.

℣. Lord, have mercy upon us.

UR Father, who art in heaven, Hallowed be thy Name. Thy kingdom come. Thy will be done on earth, As it is in heaven. Give us this day our daily bread. And forgive us our trespasses, As we forgive those who trespass against us. And lead us not into temptation; But deliver us from evil. Amen.

℣. Hide not thy face from thy servant, for I am in trouble.

℞. O haste thee and hear me.

℣. Draw nigh unto my soul and save it.

℞. O deliver me, because of mine enemies.

℣. Arise, O Christ, and help us.

℞. And deliver us for thy Name's sake.

COLLECTS

℣. The Lord be with you.

or, O Lord, hear our prayer.

℞. And with thy spirit.

or, And let our cry come unto thee.

℣. Let us pray.

❡ The Collect(s) of the Day is here said, followed by this memorial Collect.

ORD Jesus, who didst stretch out thine arms of love on the hard wood of the Cross, that all men might come within the reach of thy saving embrace; clothe us in thy Spirit, that we, stretching forth our hands in loving labour for others, may bring those who know thee not to the knowledge and love of thee, who with the Father and the Holy Ghost livest and reignest ever one God, world without end. *Amen.*

℣. The Lord be with you.

or, O Lord, hear our prayer.

℞. And with thy spirit.

or, And let our cry come unto thee.

℣. Let us bless the Lord.

℞. Thanks be to God.

℣. May the souls ✠ of the faithful departed, through the mercy of God, rest in peace.

OW unto the King eternal, immortal, invisible, the only wise God, be honour and glory, for ever and ever. *Amen.*

Daily Office

Hour of None

℣. O God, ✠ make speed to save us.
℟. O Lord, make haste to help us.
℣. Glory be to the Father, and to the Son, and to the Holy Ghost.
℟. As it was in the beginning, is now, and ever shall be, world without end. Amen.
℣. Praise ye the Lord.
℟. The Lord's Name be praised.

RERUM DEUS

GOD, creation's secret force, Thyself unmoved, all motion's source, Who from the morn till evening ray, Through all its changes guid'st the day:

Grant us, when this short life is past, The glorious evening that shall last; That, by a holy death attained, Eternal glory may be gained.

O Father, that we ask be done, Through Jesus Christ, thine only Son; Who, with the Holy Ghost and thee, Doth live and reign eternally. Amen.

MIRABILIA

HY testimonies are wonderful : therefore doth my soul keep them.

130 When thy word goeth forth : it giveth light and understanding unto the simple.

131 I opened my mouth, and drew in my breath : for my delight was in thy commandments.

132 O look thou upon me, and be merciful unto me : as thou usest to do unto those that love thy Name.

133 Order my steps in thy word : and so shall no wickedness have dominion over me.

134 O deliver me from the wrongful dealings of men : and so shall I keep thy commandments.

135 Shew the light of thy countenance upon thy servant : and teach me thy statutes.

136 Mine eyes gush out with water : because men keep not thy law.

℣. Glory be to the Father, and to the Son, and to the Holy Ghost.
℟. As it was in the beginning, is now, and ever shall be, world without end. Amen.

JUSTUS ES, DOMINE

IGHTEOUS art thou, O Lord : and true is thy judgement.

138 The testimonies that thou hast commanded : are exceeding righteous and true.

139 My zeal hath even consumed me : because mine enemies have forgotten thy words.

140 Thy word is tried to the uttermost : and thy servant loveth it.

141 I am small, and of no reputation : yet do I not forget thy commandments.

142 Thy righteousness is an everlasting righteousness : and thy law is the truth.

143 Trouble and heaviness have taken hold upon me : yet is my delight in thy commandments.

144 The righteousness of thy testimonies is everlasting : O grant me understanding, and I shall live.

℣. Glory be to the Father, and to the Son, and to the Holy Ghost.

℟. As it was in the beginning, is now, and ever shall be, world without end. Amen.

Clamavi in toto corde meo

CALL with my whole heart : hear me, O Lord, I will keep thy statutes.

146 Yea, even unto thee do I call : help me, and I shall keep thy testimonies.

147 Early in the morning do I cry unto thee : for in thy word is my trust.

148 Mine eyes prevent the nightwatches : that I might be occupied in thy words.

149 Hear my voice, O Lord, according unto thy loving-kindness : quicken me, according as thou art wont.

150 They draw nigh that of malice persecute me : and are far from thy law.

151 Be thou nigh at hand, O Lord : for all thy commandments are true.

152 As concerning thy testimonies, I have known long since : that thou hast grounded them for ever.

℣. Glory be to the Father, and to the Son, and to the Holy Ghost.

℟. As it was in the beginning, is now, and ever shall be, world without end. Amen.

Vide humilitatem

CONSIDER mine adversity, and deliver me : for I do not forget thy law.

154 Avenge thou my cause, and deliver me : quicken me, according to thy word.

155 Health is far from the ungodly : for they regard not thy statutes.

156 Great is thy mercy, O Lord : quicken me, as thou art wont.

157 Many there are that trouble me, and persecute me : yet do I not swerve from thy testimonies.

158 It grieveth me when I see the transgressors : because they keep not thy law.

159 Consider, O Lord, how I love thy commandments : O quicken me, according to thy loving-kindness.

160 Thy word is true from everlasting : all the judgements of thy righteousness endure for evermore.

℣. Glory be to the Father, and to the Son, and to the Holy Ghost.

℟. As it was in the beginning, is now, and ever shall be, world without end. Amen.

Principes persecuti sunt

RINCES have persecuted me without a cause : but my heart standeth in awe of thy word.

162 I am as glad of thy word : as one that findeth great spoils.

163 As for lies, I hate and abhor them : but thy law do I love.

164 Seven times a day do I praise thee : because of thy righteous judgements.

165 Great is the peace that they have who love thy law : and they are not offended at it.

166 Lord, I have looked for thy saving health : and done after thy commandments.

167 My soul hath kept thy testimonies : and loved them exceedingly.

168 I have kept thy commandments and testimonies : for all my ways are before thee.

℣. Glory be to the Father, and to the Son, and to the Holy Ghost.

℞. As it was in the beginning, is now, and ever shall be, world without end. Amen.

Appropinquet deprecatio

ET my complaint come before thee, O Lord : give me understanding, according to thy word.

170 Let my supplication come before thee : deliver me, according to thy word.

171 My lips shall speak of thy praise : when thou hast taught me thy statutes.

172 Yea, my tongue shall sing of thy word : for all thy commandments are righteous.

173 Let thine hand help me : for I have chosen thy commandments.

174 I have longed for thy saving health, O Lord : and in thy law is my delight.

175 O let my soul live, and it shall praise thee : and thy judgements shall help me.

176 I have gone astray like a sheep that is lost : O seek thy servant, for I do not forget thy commandments.

℣. Glory be to the Father, and to the Son, and to the Holy Ghost.

℞. As it was in the beginning, is now, and ever shall be, world without end. Amen.

Chapter

Ferias Throughout the Year

Bear ye one another's burdens, and so fulfil the law of Christ.

Sundays & Feast Days

One Lord, one Faith, one Baptism, one God and Father of all, who is above all, and through all, and in you all.

Eastertide

There are three that bear witness in earth: the Spirit, and the Water, and the Blood: and these three agree in one.

℞. Thanks be to God.

Short Respond

Ferias Throughout the Year

℣. Deliver me, O Lord, and be merciful unto me.

℞. Deliver me, O Lord, and be merciful unto me.

℣. My foot standeth right; I will praise the Lord in the congregations.

℞. And be merciful unto me.

℣. Glory be to the Father, and to the Son, and to the Holy Ghost.

℞. Deliver me, O Lord, and be merciful unto me.

℣. I will praise thy Name, O Lord.

℞. For thou hast delivered me out of all my trouble.

Sundays, Feasts, & in Eastertide

℣. I call with my whole heart; hear me, O Lord (alleluia, alleluia).

℟. I call with my whole heart; hear me, O Lord (alleluia, alleluia).

℣. I will keep thy statutes.

℟. Hear me, O Lord (alleluia, alleluia).

℣. Glory be to the Father, and to the Son, and to the Holy Ghost.

℟. I will call with my whole heart; hear me, O Lord (alleluia, alleluia).

℣. Cleanse me, O Lord, from my secret faults (alleluia).

℟. Keep thy servant also from presumptuous sins (alleluia).

SUFFRAGES

❡ The Suffrages are said, kneeling, on all Ferias outside of Eastertide.

℣. Lord, have mercy upon us.

℟. Christ, have mercy upon us.

℣. Lord, have mercy upon us.

UR Father, who art in heaven, Hallowed be thy Name. Thy kingdom come. Thy will be done on earth, As it is in heaven. Give us this day our daily bread. And forgive us our trespasses, As we forgive those who trespass against us. And lead us not into temptation; But deliver us from evil. Amen.

℣. Cast me not away in the time of age.

℟. Forsake me not when my strength faileth me.

℣. Hide not thy face from me.

℟. Lest I be like unto them that go down into the pit.

℣. Quicken me, O Lord, for thy Name's sake.

℟. And for thy righteousness' sake bring my soul out of trouble.

COLLECTS

℣. The Lord be with you.

or, O Lord, hear our prayer.

℟. And with thy spirit.

or, And let our cry come unto thee.

℣. Let us pray.

❡ The Collect(s) of the Day is here said, followed by this memorial Collect.

ORD Jesus Christ, who for our sakes didst tread the paths of death; make known to us the way of life; that as thou wast reckoned with the transgressors in thy death, and with the rich in thy burial, so we, who are dead in trespasses and sins, may be raised up by thee to the land of true riches. Who livest and reignest with the Father and the Holy Ghost, ever one God, world without end. *Amen.*

℣. The Lord be with you.

or, O Lord, hear our prayer.

℟. And with thy spirit.

or, And let our cry come unto thee.

℣. Let us bless the Lord.

℟. Thanks be to God.

℣. May the souls ✠ of the faithful departed, through the mercy of God, rest in peace.

ow unto him that is able to keep us from falling and to present us faultless before the presence of his glory with exceeding joy; to the only wise God our Saviour be glory and majesty, dominion, and power, both now and ever. *Amen.*

The Order for Daily Evening Prayer

℣. O Lord, ✝ open thou our lips.

℟. And our mouth shall show forth thy praise.

℣. O God, ✠ make speed to save us.

℟. O Lord, make haste to help us.

℣. Dómine, ✝ lábia nostra apéries.

℟. Et os nostrum annuntiábit laudem tuam.

℣. Deus, ✠ in adjutórium nostrum inténde.

℟. Dómine, ad adjuvándum nos festína.

❡ Here, all standing up, the Minister shall say,

℣. Glory be to the Father, and to the Son, and to the Holy Ghost.

℟. As it was in the beginning, is now, and ever shall be, world without end. Amen.

℣. Praise ye the Lord.

℟. The Lord's Name be praised.

℣. Glória Patri, et Fílio, * et Spirítui Sancto:

℟. Sicut erat in princípio, et nunc, et semper, * et in sǽcula sæculórum. Amen.

℣. Laudáte Dominum.

℟. Sit Nomen Dómini Benedíctum.

❡ Then shall follow a Portion of the Psalms, according to the Use of this Church. And at the end of every Psalm, and likewise at the end of the Magnificat, Nunc dimittis, shall be sung or said the Gloria Patri, or else the Gloria in excelsis, as followeth, except during Advent, Septuagesimatide, & Lent.

GLORIA IN EXCELSIS

 LORY be to God on high, and on earth peace, good will towards men. We praise thee, we bless thee, we worship thee, we glorify thee, we give thanks to thee for thy great glory, O Lord God, heavenly King, God the Father Almighty.

O Lord, the only-begotten Son, Jesus Christ; O Lord God, Lamb of God, Son of the Father, that takest away the sins of the world, have mercy upon us. Thou that takest away the sins of the world, receive our prayer. Thou that sittest at the right hand of God the Father, have mercy upon us. For thou

 LÓRIA in excélsis Deo. Et in terra pax homínibus bonæ voluntátis. Laudámus te. Benedícimus te. Adorámus te. Glorificámus te. Grátias ágimus tibi propter magnam glóriam tuam. Dómine Deus, Rex cæléstis, Deus Pater omnípotens.

Dómine Fili unigénite, Jesu Christe. Dómine Deus, Agnus Dei, Fílius Patris. Qui tollis peccáta mundi, miserére nobis. Qui tollis peccáta mundi, súscipe deprecatiónem nostram. Qui sedes ad déxteram Patris, miserére nobis. Quóniam tu solus Sanctus. Tu solus Dóminus. Tu solus Altíssimus, Je-

only art holy; thou only art the Lord; thou only, O Christ, with the Holy Ghost, art ✠ most high in the glory of God the Father. Amen.

¶ Then shall be read the First Lesson, according to the Table or Calendar.

¶ After which may be sung or said a Hymn.

MAGNIFICAT

¶ Then shall be sung or said the Hymn following.

Y soul ✠ doth magnify the Lord, * and my spirit hath rejoiced in God my Saviour.

For he hath regarded * the lowliness of his handmaiden.

For behold, from henceforth * all generations shall call me blessed.

For he that is mighty hath magnified me; * and holy is his Name.

And his mercy is on them that fear him * throughout all generations.

He hath showed strength with his arm; * he hath scattered the proud in the imagination of their hearts.

He hath put down the mighty from their seat, * and hath exalted the humble and meek.

He hath filled the hungry with good things; * and the rich he hath sent empty away.

He remembering his mercy hath holpen his servant Israel; * as he promised to our forefathers, Abraham and his seed, for ever.

su Christe. Cum Sancto Spíritu ✠ in glória Dei Patris. Amen.

AGNÍFICAT ✠ ánima mea Dóminum.

Et exsultávit spíritus meus: * in Deo, salutári meo.

Quia respéxit humilitátem ancíllæ suæ: * ecce enim ex hoc beátam me dicent omnes generatiónes.

Quia fecit mihi magna qui potens est: * et sanctum nomen ejus.

Et misericórdia ejus, a progénie in progénies: * timéntibus eum.

Fecit poténtiam in brácchio suo: * dispérsit supérbos mente cordis sui.

Depósuit poténtes de sede: * et exaltávit húmiles.

Esuriéntes implévit bonis: * et dívites dimísit inánes.

Suscépit Israël púerum suum: * recordátus misericórdiæ suæ.

Sicut locútus est ad patres nostros: * Ábraham, et sémini ejus in sæcula.

¶ Then a Lesson of the New Testament, as it is appointed.

Daily Office

Nunc dimittis

¶ And after that shall be sung or said the Hymn called Nunc dimittis, as followeth.

ORD, ✠ now lettest thou thy servant depart in peace, * according to thy word.

For mine eyes have seen * thy salvation,

Which thou hast prepared * before the face of all people;

To be a light to lighten the Gentiles, * and to be the glory of thy people Israel.

UNC dimíttis ✠ servum tuum, Dómine, * secúndum verbum tuum in pace:

Quia vidérunt óculi mei * salutáre tuum,

Quod parásti * ante fáciem ómnium populórum,

Lumen ad revelatiónem géntium, * et glóriam plebis tuæ Israël.

Apostles' Creed

¶ Then shall be said the Apostles' Creed, by the Minister and the People, standing. NOTE, the Nicene Creed may be said instead of the Apostles' (p. 145).

BELIEVE in God the Father Almighty, Maker of heaven and earth: And in Jesus Christ his only Son our Lord: Who was conceived by the Holy Ghost, Born of the Virgin Mary: Suffered under Pontius Pilate, Was crucified, dead, and buried: He descended into hell; The third day he rose again from the dead: He ascended into heaven, And sitteth on the right hand of God the Father Almighty: From thence he shall come to judge the quick and the dead.

I believe in the Holy Ghost: The holy Catholic Church; The Communion of Saints: The Forgiveness of sins: The Resurrection of the body: ✠ And the Life everlasting. Amen.

REDO in Deum, Patrem omnipoténtem, Creatórem cæli et terræ. Et in Jesum Christum, Fílium ejus únicum, Dóminum nostrum: qui concéptus est de Spíritu Sancto, natus ex María Vírgine, passus sub Póntio Piláto, crucifíxus, mórtuus, et sepúltus: descéndit ad ínferos; tértia die resurréxit a mórtuis; ascéndit ad cælos; sedet ad déxteram Dei Patris omnipoténtis: inde ventúrus est judicáre vivos et mórtuos.

Credo in Spíritum Sanctum, sanctam Ecclésiam cathólicam, Sanctórum communiónem, remissiónem peccatórum, carnis ✠ resurrectiónem, vitam ætérnam. Amen.

Daily Office

¶ And after that, these Prayers following, the People devoutly kneeling; the Minister first pronouncing,

℣. The Lord be with you.

or, O Lord, hear our prayer.

℟. And with thy spirit.

or, And let our cry come unto thee.

℣. Let us pray.

℣. Lord, have mercy upon us.

℟. Christ, have mercy upon us.

℣. Lord, have mercy upon us.

℣. Dóminus vobíscum.

vel, Dómine, exáudi oratiónem nostram.

℟. Et cum spíritu tuo.

vel, Et clamor noster ad te véniat.

℣. Orémus.

℣. Kýrie, eléison.

℟. Christe, eléison.

℣. Kýrie, eléison.

LORD'S PRAYER

¶ Then the Minister, Clerks, and People—all kneeling—shall say the Lord's Prayer with a loud voice.

UR Father, who art in heaven, Hallowed be thy Name. Thy kingdom come. Thy will be done on earth, As it is in heaven. Give us this day our daily bread. And forgive us our trespasses, As we forgive those who trespass against us. And lead us not into temptation; But deliver us from evil. Amen.

ATER noster, qui es in cælis, sanctificétur nomen tuum: advéniat regnum tuum: fiat volúntas tua, sicut in cælo et in terra. Panem nostrum quotidiánum da nobis hódie: et dimítte nobis débita nostra, sicut et nos dimíttimus debitóribus nostris: et ne nos indúcas in tentatiónem: sed líbera nos a malo. Amen.

PRECES

¶ Then the Minister standing up shall say

℣. O Lord, show thy mercy upon us.

℟. And grant us thy salvation.

℣. O Lord, save the *State.*

℟. And mercifully hear us when we call upon thee.

℣. Endue thy Ministers with righteousness.

℟. And make thy chosen people joyful.

℣. Osténde nobis, Dómine, misericórdiam tuam.

℟. Et salutáre tuum da nobis.

℣. Dómine salvam fac *Civitatem.*

℟. Et exáudi nos cum invocámus te.

℣. Sacerdótes tui induántur Justítia.

℟. Et sancti tui exúltent.

℣. Salvum fac Pópulum tuum, Dómine.

℟. Et bénedic Hæreditáti tuæ.

℣. O Lord, save thy people.
℞. And bless thine inheritance.
℣. Give peace in our time, O Lord.
℞. For it is thou, Lord, only, that makest us dwell in safety.
℣. O God, make clean our hearts within us.
℞. And take not thy Holy Spirit from us.

℣. Da pacem Dómine in diébus nostris.
℞. Quóniam tu, Dómine, singuláriter in spe constituísti me.
℣. Cor mundum crea in nobis, O Deus.
℞. Et Spíritum Sanctum tuum ne áuferas a nobis.

¶ Then shall be said the Collect(s) of the Day, and after that the Collects and Prayers following.

A Collect for Peace

GOD, from whom all holy desires, all good counsels, and all just works do proceed; Give unto thy servants that peace which the world cannot give; that our hearts may be set to obey thy commandments, and also that by thee, we, being defended from the fear of our enemies, may pass our time in rest and quietness; through the merits of Jesus Christ our Saviour. *Amen.*

A Collect for Aid against Perils

IGHTEN our darkness, we beseech thee, O Lord; and by thy great mercy defend us from all perils and dangers of this night; for the love of thy only Son, our Saviour, Jesus Christ. *Amen.*

Conclusion

℣. The Lord be with you.
or, O Lord, hear our prayer.
℞. And with thy spirit.
or, And let our cry come unto thee.
℣. Let us bless the Lord (alleluia, alleluia.)
℞. Thanks be to God (alleluia, alleluia.)
℣. May the souls ✠ of the faithful departed, through the mercy of God, rest in peace.
℞. Amen.

℣. Dóminus vobíscum.
vel, Dómine, exáudi oratiónem nostram.
℞. Et cum spíritu tuo.
vel, Et clamor noster ad te véniat.
℣. Benedicámus Dómino (allelúja, allelúja.)
℞. Deo grátias (allelúja, allelúja.)
℣. Fidélium ánimæ ✠ per misericórdiam Dei requiéscant in pace.
℞. Amen.

¶ In places where it may be convenient, here followeth the Marian Anthem (p. 65).

¶ The Minister may here end the Evening Prayer with such Prayer, or Prayers, taken out of this Book, as he shall think fit.

AFTER THE THIRD COLLECT

¶ The Prayer for the Head of State (p. 70) is here said.

A Prayer for the Clergy and People

ALMIGHTY and everlasting God, from whom cometh every good and perfect gift; Send down upon our Bishops, and other Clergy, and upon the Congregations committed to their charge, the healthful Spirit of thy grace; and, that they may truly please thee, pour upon them the continual dew of thy blessing. Grant this, O Lord, for the honour of our Advocate and Mediator, Jesus Christ. *Amen.*

¶ Additional Prayers (p. 70) may here be said.

A Prayer for all Sorts & Conditions of Men

O GOD, the Creator and Preserver of all mankind, we humbly beseech thee for all sorts and conditions of men; that thou wouldest be pleased to make thy ways known unto them, thy saving health unto all nations. More especially we pray for thy holy Church universal; that it may be so guided and governed by thy good Spirit, that all who profess and call themselves Christians may be led into the way of truth, and hold the faith in unity of spirit, in the bond of peace, and in righteousness of life. Finally, we commend to thy fatherly goodness all those who are any ways afflicted, or distressed, in mind, *This may* body, or estate; (*especially those for whom our prayers are desired;) that it may *be said when* *any desire the* please thee to comfort and relieve them, according to their several necessities; *prayers of the* giving them patience under their sufferings, and a happy issue out of all their *Congregation.* afflictions. And this we beg for Jesus Christ's sake. *Amen.*

A General Thanksgiving

¶ The General Thanksgiving may be said by the Congregation with the Minister.

ALMIGHTY God, Father of all mercies, we, thine unworthy servants, do give thee most humble and hearty thanks for all thy goodness and *This may be* loving-kindness to us and to all men; (*to those who desire now to *said when any* offer up their praises and thanksgivings for thy late mercies vouchsafed unto *desire to return* *thanks for* *mercies vouch-* *safed to them.*

58

them.) We bless thee for our creation, preservation, and all the blessings of this life; but above all, for thine inestimable love in the redemption of the world by our Lord Jesus Christ; for the means of grace, and for the hope of glory. And, we beseech thee, give us that due sense of all thy mercies, that our hearts may be unfeignedly thankful; and that we show forth thy praise, not only with our lips, but in our lives, by giving up our selves to thy service, and by walking before thee in holiness and righteousness all our days; through Jesus Christ our Lord, to whom, with thee and the Holy Ghost, be all honour and glory, world without end. *Amen.*

¶ The Thanksgivings (p. 82) may here be offered.

A Prayer of St. Chrysostom

LMIGHTY God, who hast given us grace at this time with one accord to make our common supplications unto thee; and dost promise that when two or three are gathered together in thy Name thou wilt grant their requests; Fulfil now, O Lord, the desires and petitions of thy servants, as may be most expedient for them; granting us in this world knowledge of thy truth, and in the world to come life everlasting. *Amen.*

The Grace

HE grace of our Lord Jesus Christ, ✠ and the love of God, and the fellowship of the Holy Ghost, be with us all evermore. *Amen.*

HERE ENDETH THE ORDER OF EVENING PRAYER.

Daily Office

Hour of Compline

THE Lord Almighty grant us a quiet night and a perfect end.

℟. Amen.

RETHREN, be sober, be vigilant; because your adversary the devil, as a roaring lion, walketh about, seeking whom he may devour : Whom resist, steadfast in the faith. (1 Peter 5:8-9.)

℣. But thou, O Lord, have mercy upon us;

℟. Thanks be to God.

INTRODUCTION

℣. O God, ✠ make speed to save us.

℟. O Lord, make haste to help us.

℣. Glory be to the Father, and to the Son, and to the Holy Ghost.

℟. As it was in the beginning, is now, and ever shall be, world without end. Amen.

℣. Praise ye the Lord.

℟. The Lord's Name be praised.

PSALM 4. *CUM INVOCAREM*

EAR me when I call, O God of my righteousness : thou hast set me at liberty when I was in trouble; have mercy upon me, and hearken unto my prayer.

2 O ye sons of men, how long will ye blaspheme mine honour : and have such pleasure in vanity, and seek after leasing?

3 Know this also, that the Lord hath chosen to himself the man that is godly : when I call upon the Lord, he will hear me.

4 Stand in awe, and sin not : commune with your own heart, and in your chamber, and be still.

5 Offer the sacrifice of righteousness : and put your trust in the Lord.

6 There be many that say : Who will shew us any good?

7 Lord, lift thou up : the light of thy countenance upon us.

8 Thou hast put gladness in my heart : since the time that their corn and wine and oil increased.

9 I will lay me down in peace, and take my rest : for it is thou, Lord, only, that makest me dwell in safety.

℣. Glory be to the Father, and to the Son, and to the Holy Ghost.

℟. As it was in the beginning, is now, and ever shall be, world without end. Amen.

PSALM 31. *IN TE, DOMINE, SPERAVI*

N thee, O Lord, have I put my trust : let me never be put to confusion, deliver me in thy righteousness.

2 Bow down thine ear to me : make haste to deliver me.

3 And be thou my strong rock, and house of defence : that thou mayest save me.

4 For thou art my strong rock, and my castle : be thou also my guide, and lead me for thy Name's sake.

5 Draw me out of the net that they have laid privily for me : for thou art my strength.

6 Into thy hands I commend my spirit : for thou hast redeemed me, O Lord, thou God of truth.

℣. Glory be to the Father, and to the Son, and to the Holy Ghost.

℟. As it was in the beginning, is now, and ever shall be, world without end. Amen.

PSALM 91. *QUI HABITAT*

HOSO dwelleth under the defence of the most High : shall abide under the shadow of the Almighty.

2 I will say unto the Lord, Thou art my hope, and my strong hold : my God, in him will I trust.

3 For he shall deliver thee from the snare of the hunter : and from the noisome pestilence.

4 He shall defend thee under his wings, and thou shalt be safe under his feathers : his faithfulness and truth shall be thy shield and buckler.

5 Thou shalt not be afraid for any terror by night : nor for the arrow that flieth by day;

6 For the pestilence that walketh in darkness : nor for the sickness that destroyeth in the noon-day.

7 A thousand shall fall beside thee, and ten thousand at thy right hand : but it shall not come nigh thee.

8 Yea, with thine eyes shalt thou behold : and see the reward of the ungodly.

9 For thou, Lord, art my hope : thou hast set thine house of defence very high.

10 There shall no evil happen unto thee : neither shall any plague come nigh thy dwelling.

11 For he shall give his angels charge over thee : to keep thee in all thy ways.

12 They shall bear thee in their hands : that thou hurt not thy foot against a stone.

13 Thou shalt go upon the lion and adder : the young lion and the dragon shalt thou tread under thy feet.

14 Because he hath set his love upon me, therefore will I deliver him : I will set him up, because he hath known my Name.

15 He shall call upon me, and I will hear him : yea, I am with him in trouble; I will deliver him, and bring him to honour.

16 With long life will I satisfy him : and shew him my salvation.

℣. Glory be to the Father, and to the Son, and to the Holy Ghost.

℟. As it was in the beginning, is now, and ever shall be, world without end. Amen.

PSALM 134. *ECCE NUNC*

EHOLD now, praise the Lord : all ye servants of the Lord;

2 Ye that by night stand in the house of the Lord : even in the courts of the house of our God.

3 Lift up your hands in the sanctuary : and praise the Lord.

4 The Lord that made heaven and earth : give thee blessing out of Sion.

℣. Glory be to the Father, and to the Son, and to the Holy Ghost.

℟. As it was in the beginning, is now, and ever shall be, world without end. Amen.

CHAPTER

HOU, O Lord, art in the midst of us, and we are called by thy name. Leave us not, O Lord our God. ℟. Thanks be to God.

SHORT RESPOND

℣. Into thy hands, O Lord, I commend my spirit;

℟. Into thy hands, O Lord, I commend my spirit;

℣. For thou hast redeemed me, O Lord, thou God of truth.

℟. I commend my spirit.

℣. Glory be to the Father, and to the Son, and to the Holy Ghost;

℟. Into thy hands, O Lord, I commend my spirit.

TE LUCIS ANTE TERMINUM.

EFORE the ending of the day, Creator of the world we pray, That with thy wonted favour thou Wouldst be our guard and keeper now.

From all ill dreams defend our eyes, From nightly fears and fantasies Tread under foot our ghostly foe, That no pollution we may know.

O Father, that we ask be done, Through Jesus Christ, thine only Son; Who, with the Holy Ghost and thee, Doth live and reign eternally. Amen.

℣. Keep me as the apple of an eye;

℟. Hide me under the shadow of thy wings.

NUNC DIMITTIS

Ant. Preserve us, O Lord, waking, and guard us sleeping, that we may watch with Christ, and rest in peace.

ORD, ✠ now lettest thou thy servant depart in peace, * according to thy word.

For mine eyes have seen * thy salvation,

Which thou hast prepared * before the face of all people;

To be a light to lighten the Gentiles, * and to be the glory of thy people Israel.

℣. Glory be to the Father, and to the Son, and to the Holy Ghost.

℟. As it was in the beginning, is now, and ever shall be, world without end. Amen.

Ant. Preserve us, O Lord, waking, and guard us sleeping, that we may watch with Christ, and rest in peace.

SUFFRAGES

¶ The Suffrages are said, kneeling, on all Ferias outside of Eastertide.

℣. Lord, have mercy upon us.
℟. Christ, have mercy upon us.
℣. Lord, have mercy upon us.

Lord's Prayer

UR Father, who art in heaven, Hallowed be thy Name. Thy kingdom come. Thy will be done on earth, As it is in heaven. Give us this day our daily bread. And forgive us our trespasses, As we forgive those who trespass against us. And lead us not into temptation; But deliver us from evil. Amen.

Apostles' Creed

BELIEVE in God the Father Almighty, Maker of heaven and earth: And in Jesus Christ his only Son our Lord: Who was conceived by the Holy Ghost, Born of the Virgin Mary: Suffered under Pontius Pilate, Was crucified, dead, and buried: He descended into hell; The third day he rose again from the dead: He ascended into heaven, And sitteth on the right hand of God the Father Almighty: From thence he shall come to judge the quick and the dead.

I believe in the Holy Ghost: The holy Catholic Church; The Communion of Saints: The Forgiveness of sins: The Resurrection of the body: ✠ And the Life everlasting. Amen.

¶ Then shall follow these Versicles and Responses.

℣. Blessed art thou, Lord God of our fathers;
℟. To be praised and glorified above all for ever.
℣. Let us bless the Father, the Son, and the Holy Ghost;
℟. Let us praise him and magnify him for ever.
℣. Blessed art thou, O Lord, in the firmament of heaven;
℟. To be praised and glorified above all for ever.
℣. The Almighty and most merciful Lord guard us and give us his blessing.
℟. Amen.

Confession

¶ Then shall the Minister and People say together the Confession following,

CONFESS to God, to blessed Mary, to all the saints, and to you: that I have sinned exceedingly in thought, word, and deed, by my own fault. I beg holy Mary, all the Saints of God, and you, to pray for me.

¶ The Minister then stands and says,

LMIGHTY God, have mercy upon us, forgive us all our sins and deliver us from all evil, confirm and strengthen us in all goodness, and bring us to life everlasting. *Amen.*

¶ If a Priest be present, he shall stand and pronounce the following Absolution,

AY the almighty and merciful Lord grant unto you pardon ✠ and remission of all your sins, time for amendment of life, and the grace and comfort of the Holy Spirit. *Amen.*

℣. Wilt thou not turn again and quicken us, O God?

℟. That thy people may rejoice in thee.

℣. O Lord, show thy mercy upon us.

℟. And grant us thy salvation.

℣. Vouchsafe, O Lord, to keep us this day without sin;

℟. O Lord, have mercy upon us, have mercy upon us.

COLLECT

℣. O Lord, hear our prayer.

℟. And let our cry come unto thee.

Let us pray.

ISIT, we beseech thee, O Lord, this place, and drive from it all the snares of the enemy; let thy holy angels dwell herein to preserve us in peace; and may thy blessing be upon us evermore; through Jesus Christ our Lord. *Amen.*

or,

ORD Jesus Christ, Son of the living God, who at this evening hour didst rest in the sepulchre, and didst thereby sanctify the grave to be a bed of hope to thy people; Make us so to abound in sorrow for our sins, which were the cause of thy passion, that when our bodies lie in the dust, our souls may live with thee; who livest and reignest with the Father and the Holy Ghost, one God world without end. Amen.

CONCLUSION

℣. We will lay us down in peace and take our rest.

℟. For it is thou, Lord, only that makest us dwell in safety.

℣. The Lord be with you.

or, O Lord, hear our prayer.

℟. And with thy spirit.

or, And let our cry come unto thee.

℣. Let us bless the Lord.

℟. Thanks be to God.

HE Almighty and merciful Lord, the Father, ✠ the Son, and the Holy Ghost; bless and preserve us. *Amen.*

¶ The appropriate Marian Anthem (p. 65) shall be said or sung here.

Marian Anthems

ALMA REDEMPTORIS MATER

From I Evensong of Advent I until II Evensong of the Purification, inclusive.

RACIOUS Mother of our Redeemer, for ever abiding Heaven's gateway, and star of ocean,
O succour the people, who, though falling, strive to rise again.
Thou Maiden who barest thy holy Creator, to the wonder of all nature;
Ever Virgin, after, as before thou receivedst that Ave
From the mouth of Gabriel; have compassion on us sinners.

In Advent

℣. The Angel of the Lord announced unto Mary.

℟. And she conceived by the Holy Ghost.

Let us pray.

E beseech thee, O Lord, pour thy grace into our hearts: that, as we have known the incarnation of thy Son Jesus Christ by the message of an angel, so by his Cross and Passion we may be brought unto the glory of his Resurrection. Through the same Christ our Lord. *Amen.*

In Christmastide

℣. After Childbearing, O Virgin, thou didst remain inviolate.

℟. Intercede for us, O Mother of God.

LMA Redemptóris Mater, quæ pérvia cæli porta manes,
Et stella maris, succúrre cadénti,
Súrgere qui curat, pópulo: tu quæ genuísti,
Natúra miránte, tuum sanctum Genitórem,
Virgo prius ac postérius, Gabriélis ab ore
Sumens illud Ave, peccatórum miserére.

In Adventu

℣. Ángelus Dómini nuntiávit Maríæ.

℟. Et concépit de Spíritu Sancto.

Orémus.

RÁTIAM tuam, quǽsumus, Dómine, méntibus nostris infúnde: ut, qui, Ángelo nuntiánte, Christi Fílii tui incarnatiónem cognóvimus; per passiónem ejus et crucem, ad resurrectiónis glóriam perducámur. Per eúmdem Christum Dóminum nóstrum. *Amen.*

De Nativitate

℣. Post partum, Virgo, invioláta permansísti.

℟. Dei Génitrix, intercéde pro nobis.

Let us pray.

GOD, who by the fruitful virginity of Blessed Mary hast bestowed upon mankind the reward of eternal salvation: Grant, we beseech thee, that we may know the help of her intercession through whom we have been accounted worthy to receive the Author of our life, Jesus Christ thy Son our Lord. *Amen.*

Orémus.

EUS, qui salútis ætérnæ, beátæ Maríæ virginitáte fecúnda, humáno géneri prǽmia præstitísti: tríbue, quǽsumus; ut ipsam pro nobis intercédere sentiámus, per quam merúimus auctórem vitæ suscípere, Dóminum nóstrum Jesum Christum Fílium tuum. *Amen.*

AVE, REGINA CÆLORUM

From Compline of the Purification until Compline of Holy Wednesday, inclusive.

UEEN of the heavens, we hail thee,
Hail thee, Lady of all the Angels;
Thou the dawn, the door of morning
Whence the world's true light is risen:

Joy to thee, O Virgin glorious,
Beautiful beyond all other;
Hail and farewell, O most gracious,
Intercede for us alway to Jesus.

℣. Vouchsafe that I may praise thee, O holy Virgin.

℞. Give me strength against thine enemies.

Let us pray.

RANT us, O merciful God, protection in our weakness: that we who celebrate the memory of the holy Mother of God may, through the aid of her intercession, rise again from our sins. Through the same Christ our Lord. *Amen.*

VE, Regína cælórum,
Ave, Dómina Angelórum:
Salve radix, salve porta,
Ex qua mundo lux est orta:

Gaude, Virgo gloriósa,
Super omnes speciósa,
Vale, o valde decóra,
Et pro nobis Christum exóra.

℣. Dignáre me laudáre te, Virgo sacráta.

℞. Da mihi virtútem contra hostes tuos.

Orémus.

ONCÉDE, miséricors Deus, fragilitáti nostræ præsídium; ut, qui sanctæ Dei Genetrícis memóriam ágimus; intercessiónis ejus auxílio, a nostris iniquitátibus resurgámus. Per eúmdem Christum Dóminum nóstrum. *Amen.*

REGINA CÆLI

From Compline of Holy Saturday until I Evensong of Trinity Sunday, exclusive.

QUEEN of heaven, be joyful, alleluia; Because he whom so meetly thou barest, alleluia, Hath arisen, as he promised, alleluia: Pray for us to the Father, alleluia.

℣. Rejoice and be glad, O Virgin Mary, alleluia.

℟. For the Lord is risen indeed, alleluia.

Let us pray.

GOD, who, by the resurrection of thy Son Jesus Christ didst vouchsafe to give gladness unto the world: Grant, we beseech thee, that we, being holpen by the Virgin Mary, his Mother, may attain unto the joys of everlasting life. Through the same Christ our Lord. *Amen.*

EGÍNA cæli, lætáre, allelúja; Quia quem meruísti portáre, allelúja, Resurréxit, sicut dixit, allelúja: Ora pro nobis Deum, allelúja.

℣. Gaude et lætáre, Virgo María, allelúja.

℟. Quia surréxit Dóminus vere, allelúja.

Orémus.

EUS, qui per resurrectiónem Fílii tui, Dómini nostri Jesu Christi, mundum lætificáre dignátus es: præsta, quǽsumus; ut, per eíus Genetrícem Vírginem Maríam, perpétuæ capiámus gáudia vitæ. Per eúmdem Christum Dóminum nóstrum. *Amen.*

Salve Regina

From I Evensong of Trinity Sunday until I Evensong of Advent I, exclusive.

ARY, we hail thee, Mother and Queen compassionate; Mary, our comfort, life and hope, we hail thee.
To thee we exiles, children of Eve, lift our crying.
To thee we are sighing, as mournful and weeping,
We pass through this vale of sorrow.

Turn thou therefore, O our intercessor,
Those thine eyes of pity and lovingkindness upon us sinners.
Hereafter, when our earthly exile shall be ended,
Show us Jesus, the blessed fruit of thy womb.
O gentle, O tender, O gracious Virgin Mary.

℣. Pray for us, O holy Mother of God.
℟. That we may be made worthy of the promises of Christ.

Let us pray.

LMIGHTY and everlasting God, who by the cooperation of the Holy Ghost, didst prepare the body and soul of the glorious Virgin Mother Mary to become a habitation meet for thy Son: Grant that as we rejoice in her commemoration, we may be delivered by her loving intercession from our present evils and from eternal death. Through the same Christ our Lord. *Amen.*

ALVE, Regína, mater misericórdiæ;
Vita, dulcédo et spes nóstra, salve.
Ad te clamámus éxsules fílii Hevæ.
Ad te suspirámus geméntes et flentes
In hac lacrimárum valle.

Eja ergo, advocáta nostra,
Illos tuos misericórdes óculos ad nos convérte.
Et Jesum, benedíctum fructum ventris tui,
Nobis post hoc exsílium osténde.
O clemens, o pia, o dulcis Virgo María.

℣. Ora pro nobis, sancta Dei Génitrix.
℟. Ut digni efficiámur promissiónibus Christi.

Orémus.

MNÍPOTENS sempitérne Deus, qui gloriósæ Vírginis Matris Maríæ corpus et ánimam, ut dignum Fílii tui habitáculum éffici mererétur, Spíritu Sancto cooperánte, præparásti: da, ut, cujus commemoratióne lætámur, ejus pia intercessióne, ab instántibus malis et a morte perpétua liberémur. Per eúmdem Christum Dóminum nóstrum. *Amen.*

29

Prayers & Thanksgivings

Prayers

PRAYERS FOR THE UNITED STATES OF AMERICA

For the President of the United States, and all in Civil Authority

LORD, our heavenly Father, the high and mighty Ruler of the universe, who dost from thy throne behold all the dwellers upon earth; Most heartily we beseech thee, with thy favour to behold and bless thy servant THE PRESIDENT OF THE UNITED STATES, and all others in authority; and so replenish them with the grace of thy Holy Spirit, that they may always incline to thy will, and walk in thy way. Endue them plenteously with heavenly gifts; grant them in health and prosperity long to live; and finally, after this life, to attain everlasting joy and felicity; through Jesus Christ our Lord. *Amen.*

For Congress

¶ To be used during their Session.

OST gracious God, we humbly beseech thee, as for the people of these United States in general, so especially for their Senate and Represent-atives in Congress assembled; that thou wouldest be pleased to direct and prosper all their consultations, to the advancement of thy glory, the good of thy Church, the safety, honour, and welfare of thy people; that all things may be so ordered and settled by their endeavours, upon the best and surest foundations, that peace and happiness, truth and justice, religion and piety, may be established among us for all generations. These and all other necessaries, for them, for us, and thy whole Church, we humbly beg in the Name and mediation of Jesus Christ, our most blessed Lord and Saviour. *Amen.*

For a State Legislature

GOD, the fountain of wisdom, whose statutes are good and gracious and whose law is truth; We beseech thee so to guide and bless the Legislature of this *State,* that it may ordain for our governance only such things as please thee, to the glory of thy Name and the welfare of the people; through Jesus Christ, thy Son, our Lord. *Amen.*

For Courts of Justice

LMIGHTY God, who sittest in the throne judging right; We humbly beseech thee to bless the courts of justice and the magistrates in all this land; and give unto them the spirit of wisdom and understanding, that they may discern the truth and impartially administer the law in the fear of thee alone; through him who shall come to be our judge, thy Son, our Saviour, Jesus Christ. *Amen.*

Prayers

For the Military

LORD God of Hosts, stretch forth, we pray thee, thine almighty arm to strengthen and protect the Soldiers, Sailors, Marines, Airmen, Coast Guardsmen, and Guardians of our country; Support them in the day of battle, and in the time of peace keep them safe from all evil; endue them with courage and loyalty; and grant that in all things they may serve without reproach; through Jesus Christ our Lord. *Amen.*

¶ *or this.*

HEAVENLY Father, we commend to thy gracious care and keeping all the men and women in our Armed Forces at home and abroad. Defend them day by day with thy heavenly grace; strengthen them in their trials and temptations; give them courage to face the perils that beset them; and help them to know that none can pluck out of thy hand those who put their trust in thee; through Jesus Christ our Lord. *Amen.*

PRAYERS FOR CANADA & COMMONWEALTH

For the King's Majesty

LORD, our heavenly Father, high and mighty, King of kings, Lord of lords, the only Ruler of princes, who dost from thy throne behold all the dwellers upon earth: Most heartily we beseech thee with thy favour to behold our most gracious Sovereign Lord, King *CHARLES*; and so replenish him with the grace of thy Holy Spirit, that he may alway incline to thy will, and walk in thy way. Endue him plenteously with heavenly gifts; grant him in health and wealth long to live; strengthen him that he may vanquish and overcome all his enemies; and finally after this life he may attain everlasting joy and felicity; through Jesus Christ our Lord. *Amen.*

For the Royal Family

ALMIGHTY God, the fountain of all goodness, we humbly beseech thee to bless Queen *Camilla*, *William* Prince of Wales, the Princess of Wales, and all the Royal Family: Endue them with thy Holy Spirit; enrich them with thy heavenly grace; prosper them with all happiness; and bring them to thine everlasting kingdom; through Jesus Christ our Lord. *Amen.*

Prayers

For Parliament

MOST gracious God, we humbly beseech thee, as for this Commonwealth in general, so especially for the High Court of Parliament, *the Parliament of this Dominion, and the Legislature of this Province,* under our most religious and gracious King at this time assembled: That thou wouldest be pleased to direct and prosper all their consultations to the advancement of thy glory, the good of thy Church, the safety, honour, and welfare of our Sovereign and his Dominions; that all things may be so ordered and settled by their endeavours, upon the best and surest foundations, that peace and happiness, truth and justice, religion and piety, may be established among us for all generations. These and all other necessaries, for them, for us, and thy whole Church, we humbly beg in the Name and Mediation of Jesus Christ our most blessed Lord and Saviour. *Amen.*

For the Forces of the King

O LORD of Hosts, stretch forth, we pray thee, thine Almighty arm to strengthen and protect the forces of our King in every peril of sea, and land, and air; shelter them in the day of battle, and in time of peace keep them safe from all evil; endue them ever with loyalty and courage; and grant that in all things they may serve as seeing thee who art invisible; through Jesus Christ our Lord. *Amen.*

For the Commonwealth

ALMIGHTY God, who rulest in the kingdom of men, and hast given to our Sovereign Lord, King CHARLES, a great dominion in all parts of the earth: Draw together, we pray thee, in true fellowship the men of divers races, languages, and customs, who dwell therein, that, bearing one another's burdens, and working together in brotherly concord, they may fulfil the purpose of thy providence, and set forward thy everlasting kingdom. Pardon, we beseech thee our sins and shortcomings: keep far from us all selfishness and pride: and give us grace to employ thy good gifts of order and freedom to thy glory and the welfare of mankind; through Jesus Christ thy Son our Lord, to whom with thee and the Holy Ghost be all glory and dominion, world without end. *Amen.*

Prayers

For the Unity of God's People

GOD, the Father of our Lord Jesus Christ, our only Saviour, the Prince of Peace; Give us grace seriously to lay to heart the great dangers we are in by our unhappy divisions. Take away all hatred and prejudice, and whatsoever else may hinder us from godly union and concord: that as there is but one Body and one Spirit, and one hope of our calling, one Lord, one Faith, one Baptism, one God and Father of us all, so we may be all of one heart and of one soul, united in one holy bond of truth and peace, of faith and charity, and may with one mind and one mouth glorify thee; through Jesus Christ our Lord. *Amen.*

For those who are to be admitted into Holy Orders

¶ To be used in the Weeks preceding the stated Times of Ordination.

ALMIGHTY God, our heavenly Father, who hast purchased to thyself an universal Church by the precious blood of thy dear Son; Mercifully look upon the same, and at this time so guide and govern the minds of thy servants the Bishops and Pastors of thy flock, that they may lay hands suddenly on no man, but faithfully and wisely make choice of fit persons, to serve in the sacred Ministry of thy Church, And to those who shall be ordained to any holy function, give thy grace and heavenly benediction; that both by their life and doctrine they may show forth thy glory, and set forward the salvation of all men; through Jesus Christ our Lord. *Amen.*

For the Increase of the Ministry

ALMIGHTY God, look mercifully upon the world which thou hast redeemed by the blood of thy dear Son, and incline the hearts of many to dedicate themselves to the sacred ministry of thy Church; through the same thy Son Jesus Christ our Lord. *Amen.*

For Missions

GOD, who hast made of one blood all nations of men for to dwell on the face of the whole earth, and didst send thy blessed Son to preach peace to them that are far off and to them that are nigh; Grant that all men everywhere may seek after thee and find thee. Bring the nations into thy fold, and add the heathen to thine inheritance. And we pray thee shortly to accomplish the number of thine elect, and to hasten thy kingdom; through the same Jesus Christ our Lord. *Amen.*

Prayers

PRAYERS IN TIMES OF ILLNESS

In Time of Great Sickness and Mortality

ALMIGHTY God, the Lord of life and death, of sickness and health Regard our supplications, we humbly beseech thee; and, thou hast thought fit to visit us for our sins with great sickness and mortality, in the midst of thy judgment, O Lord, remember mercy. Have pity upon us miserable sinners, and withdraw from us the grievous sickness with which we are afflicted. May this thy fatherly correction have its due influence upon us, by leading us to consider how frail and uncertain our life is; that we may apply our hearts unto that heavenly wisdom which in the end will bring us to everlasting life; through Jesus Christ our Lord. *Amen.*

For a Sick Person

FATHER of mercies and God of all comfort, our only help in time of need; We humbly beseech thee to behold, visit, and relieve thy sick *servant N.* for whom our prayers are desired. Look upon *him* with the eyes of thy mercy; comfort *him* with a sense of thy goodness; preserve *him* from the temptations of the enemy; and give *him* patience under *his* affliction. In thy good time, restore *him* to health, and enable *him* to lead the residue of *his* life in thy fear, and to thy glory; and grant that finally *he* may dwell with thee in life everlasting; through Jesus Christ our Lord. *Amen.*

PRAYERS IN TIMES OF OTHER NECESSITIES

For Fruitful Seasons

¶ To be used on Rogation Sunday and the Rogation Days

ALMIGHTY God, who hast blessed the earth that it should be fruitful and bring forth whatsoever is needful for the life of man, and hast commanded us to work with quietness, and eat our own bread; Bless the labours of the husbandman, and grant such seasonable weather that we may gather in the fruits of the earth, and ever rejoice in thy goodness, to the praise of thy holy Name; through Jesus Christ our Lord. *Amen.*

For Rain

GOD, heavenly Father, who by thy Son Jesus Christ hast promised to all those who seek thy kingdom, and the righteousness thereof, all things necessary to their bodily sustenance; Send us, we beseech thee, in this our necessity, such moderate rain and showers, that we may receive the fruits of the earth to our comfort, and to thy honour; through Jesus Christ our Lord. *Amen.*

Prayers

For Fair Weather

LORD God, which for the sin of man didst once drown all the world, except eight persons, and afterward of thy great mercy, didst promise never to destroy it so again: We humbly beseech thee, that although we for our iniquities have worthily deserved this plague of rain and waters, yet, upon our true repentance, thou wilt send us such weather whereby we may receive the fruits of the earth in due season, and learn both by the punishment to amend our lives, and by the granting of our petition to give thee praise and glory: Through Jesu Christ our Lord. *Amen.*

For Every Man in his Work

LMIGHTY God, our heavenly Father, who declarest thy glory and showest forth thy handiwork in the heavens and in the earth; Deliver us, we beseech thee, in our several callings, from the service of mammon, that we may do the work which thou givest us to do, in truth, in beauty, and in righteousness, with singleness of heart as thy servants, and to the benefit of our fellow men; for the sake of him who came among us as one that serveth, thy Son, Jesus Christ our Lord. *Amen.*

For Christian Justice

LMIGHTY God, who hast created man in thine own image; Grant us grace fearlessly to contend against evil, and to make no peace with oppression; and, that we may reverently use our freedom, help us to employ it in the maintenance of justice among men and nations, to the glory of thy holy Name; through Jesus Christ our Lord. *Amen.*

In Time of Dearth and Famine

GOD, heavenly Father, whose gift it is that the rain doth fall, and the earth bring forth her increase; Behold, we beseech thee, the afflictions of thy people; increase the fruits of the earth by thy heavenly benediction; and grant that the scarcity and dearth, which we now most justly suffer for our sins, may, through thy goodness, be mercifully turned into plenty; for the love of Jesus Christ our Lord, to whom, with thee and the Holy Ghost, be all honour and glory, now and for ever. *Amen.*

Prayers

In Time of War and Tumults

ALMIGHTY God, King of all kings, and Governor of all things, whose power no creature is able to resist, to whom it belongeth justly to punish sinners, and to be merciful to those who truly repent; Save and deliver us, we humbly beseech thee, from the hands of our enemies; abate their pride, assuage their malice, and confound their devices; that we, being armed with thy defence, may be preserved evermore from all perils, to glorify thee, who art the only giver of all victory; through the merits of thy Son, Jesus Christ our Lord. *Amen.*

For a Person under Affliction

MERCIFUL God, and heavenly Father, who hast taught us in thy holy Word that thou dost not willingly afflict or grieve the children of men; Look with pity, we beseech thee, upon the sorrows of thy *servant* for whom our prayers are offered. Remember *him*, O Lord, in mercy; endue *his* soul with patience; comfort *him* with a sense of thy goodness; lift up thy countenance upon *him*, and give *him* peace; through Jesus Christ our Lord. *Amen.*

For a Person, or Persons, going to Sea

ETERNAL God, who alone spreadest out the heavens, and rulest the raging of the sea; We commend to thy almighty protection, thy *servant*, for whose preservation on the great deep our prayers are desired. Guard *him*, we beseech thee, from the dangers of the sea, from sickness, from the violence of enemies, and from every evil to which *he* may be exposed. Conduct *him* in safety to the haven where *he* would be, with a grateful sense of thy mercies; through Jesus Christ our Lord. *Amen.*

For Prisoners

GOD, who sparest when we deserve punishment, and in thy wrath rememberest mercy; We humbly beseech thee, of thy goodness, to comfort and succour all prisoners (especially those who are condemned to die). Give them a right understanding of themselves, and of thy promises; that, trusting wholly in thy mercy, they may not place their confidence anywhere but in thee. Relieve the distressed, protect the innocent, awaken the guilty; and forasmuch as thou alone bringest light out of darkness, and good out of evil, grant to these thy servants, that by the power of thy Holy Spirit they may be set free from the chains of sin, and may be brought to newness of life; through Jesus Christ our Lord. *Amen.*

Prayers

¶ or this.

MOST gracious and merciful God, we earnestly beseech thee to have pity and compassion upon these persons recommended to our prayers, who now lie under the sentence of the law and are appointed to die. Visit them, O Lord, with thy mercy and salvation convince them of the miserable condition they are in, by their sins and wickedness; and let thy powerful grace produce in them such a godly sorrow, and sincere repentance, as thou wilt be pleased to accept. Give them a strong and lively faith in thy Son, our blessed Saviour and make it effectual to the salvation of their souls. O Lord, in judgment remember mercy and whatever sufferings they are to endure in this world, yet deliver them, O God, from the bitter pains of eternal death. Pardon their sins, and save their souls, for the sake and merits of thy dear Son, our blessed Saviour and Redeemer. *Amen.*

PRAYERS FOR THE DEAD

For All the Faithful Departed

GOD, the Creator and Redeemer of all the faithful: grant unto the souls of thy servants and handmaids the remission of all their sins; that through devout supplications they may obtain the pardon they have always desired. Who with God the Father in the unity of the Holy Spirit livest and reignest God, world without end. *Amen.*

On the Day of Burial

BSOLVE, O Lord, we beseech thee, the soul of thy *servant N.*, that being dead to the world *he* may live unto thee: and whatsoever *he* hath done amiss in *his* earthly conversation through frailty of the flesh, do thou wipe away by the pardon of thy merciful goodness. Through.

For a Priest Departed

GOD, who hast made thy *servant N.* to flourish among the Ministers of Apostolic Succession in the honourable office of a Priest: grant, we beseech thee, that *he* may also be joined with them in a perpetual fellowship. Through.

Another Collect for a Priest Departed

RANT, we beseech thee, O Lord: that the soul of thy servant the Priest *N.*, whom while dwelling in this world thou didst adorn with holy gifts, may ever rejoice with glory in the heavenly mansions. Through.

Prayers

For a Father and Mother

GOD, who hast bidden us to honour our father and mother: of thy mercy have compassion on the *souls* of *my father and mother*; forgive *their* sins, and grant that *I* may behold *them* in the joy of eternal brightness. Through.

For Many Deceased

GOD, whose nature and property is ever to have mercy and to forgive: have compassion on the souls of thy servants and handmaids, and grant them the remission of all their sins; that being delivered from the bonds of mortality, they may be worthy to pass over into life. Through.

Another Collect for Many Deceased

RANT, we beseech thee, O Lord, to the souls of thy servants and hand-maids thy perpetual mercy: and let it profit them in eternity that they hoped and believed in thee. Through.

For a Man Departed

NCLINE thine ear, O Lord, unto our prayers, wherein we humbly entreat thy mercy: that thou wouldest appoint unto the soul of thy servant *N.*, which thou hast bidden to depart out of this world, a place in the land of life and peace; and wouldest make him a partaker with thy Saints. Through.

For a Woman Departed

E beseech thee, O Lord, of thy loving kindness have mercy upon the soul of thine handmaid *N.*: and now that she is released from the conta-gion of mortality, do thou restore her portion in everlasting salvation. Through.

Through the Year

GOD, who hast made thy servants to flourish among the Ministers of Apostolic Succession in the honourable offices of Bishopric and Priest-hood: grant, we beseech thee, that they may also be joined with them in a perpetual fellowship.

Prayers

❡ or this.

GOD, the Giver of pardon and the Author of man's salvation: we humbly beseech thy mercy to grant that the *brethren*, kinsfolk, and benefactors of our Congregation who have departed out of this world, blessed Mary ever Virgin and all thy Saints praying for them, may attain to the fellowship of everlasting blessedness.

❡ or this.

GOD, the Creator and Redeemer of all the faithful: grant unto the souls of thy servants and handmaids the remission of all their sins; that through devout supplications they may obtain the pardon they have always desired. Who with God the Father, in the unity of the Holy Spirit, livest and reignest God, world without end. *Amen.*

ADDITIONAL COLLECTS

❡ These Collects are said for the conclusion of Antecommunion. They may be said after the Collects of Morning and Evening Prayer, at the discretion of the Minister.

LORD Jesus Christ, who saidst unto thine Apostles, Peace I leave with you, my peace I give unto you; Regard not our sins, but the faith of thy Church; and grant to it that peace and unity which is according to thy will, who livest and reignest with the Father and the Holy Ghost, one God, world without end. *Amen.*

ASSIST us mercifully, O Lord, in these our supplications and prayers, and dispose the way of thy servants towards the attainment of everlasting salvation; that, among all the changes and chances of this mortal life, they may ever be defended by thy most gracious and ready help; through Jesus Christ our Lord. *Amen.*

GRANT, we beseech thee, Almighty God, that the words which we have heard this day with our outward ears, may, through thy grace, be so grafted inwardly in our hearts, that they may bring forth in us the fruit of good living, to the honour and praise of thy Name; through Jesus Christ our Lord. *Amen.*

DIRECT us, O Lord, in all our doings, with thy most gracious favour, and further us with thy continual help; that in all our works begun, continued, and ended in thee, we may glorify thy holy Name, and finally, by thy mercy, obtain everlasting life; through Jesus Christ our Lord. *Amen.*

Prayers

LMIGHTY God, the fountain of all wisdom, who knowest our necessities before we ask, and our ignorance in asking; We beseech thee to have compassion upon our infirmities; and those things which for our unworthiness we dare not, and for our blindness we cannot ask, vouchsafe to give us, for the worthiness of thy Son Jesus Christ our Lord. *Amen.*

LMIGHTY God, who hast promised to hear the petitions of those who ask in thy Son's Name; We beseech thee mercifully to incline thine ears to us who have now made our prayers and supplications unto thee; and grant that those things which we have faithfully asked according to thy will, may effectually be obtained, to the relief of our necessity, and to the setting forth of thy glory; through Jesus Christ our Lord. *Amen.*

A Bidding Prayer

To be used to preface Sermons, or on Special Occasions.

FTER a laudable custom of our Mother holy Church, ye shall kneel down, moving your hearts unto Almighty God, and making your special prayers for the three estates, concerning all Christian people, that is, for the Spirituality, the Temporality, and the souls departed.

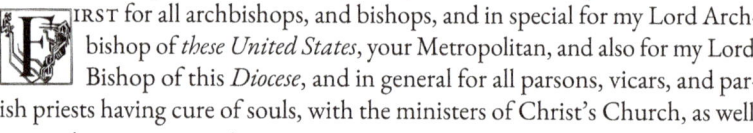IRST for all archbishops, and bishops, and in special for my Lord Archbishop of *these United States*, your Metropolitan, and also for my Lord Bishop of this *Diocese*, and in general for all parsons, vicars, and parish priests having cure of souls, with the ministers of Christ's Church, as well monastic as not monastic.

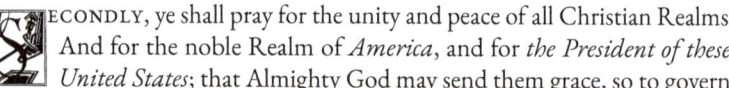ECONDLY, ye shall pray for the unity and peace of all Christian Realms. And for the noble Realm of *America*, and for *the President of these United States*; that Almighty God may send them grace, so to govern and rule the land, that it may be pleasing unto Almighty God, wealth and profit to the land, and salvation to their souls. Also ye shall pray for all those that have honoured the Church with light, lamp, vestment, or bell, or with any other ornaments, by which the service of Almighty God is the better maintained and kept. Furthermore ye shall pray for all true travellers and tillers of the earth, that truly and duly done their duty to God and holy Church, as they be bound to do.

Also ye shall pray for all manner of fruits that be done upon the ground, or shall be that Almighty God of his great pity and mercy may send such weather, that it may come to the sustenance of man. Ye shall pray also for all those that be in debt or deadly sin, that Almighty God may give them grace to come out thereof, and the sooner by our prayer. Also ye shall pray for all those that be sick or diseased, either in body or in soul, that the Almighty would send them

Prayers

the thing that is most profitable as well bodily as ghostly. Also ye shall pray for all pilgrims, and palmers, that have taken the way to Rome, to Saint James of Jerusalem, or to any other place: that Almighty God may give them grace to go safe, and to come safe, and give us grace to have part of their prayers, and they part of ours. Also ye shall pray for the holy Cross, that is in possession and hands of unrightful people; that God Almighty may send it into the hands of Christian people when it pleaseth him. Furthermore I commit unto your devout prayers, all women that be in our ladies' bonds: that Almighty God may send them grace, the child to receive the Sacrament of Baptism, and the mother purification. Also ye shall pray for the good man and woman, that this day giveth bread to make the holy loaf, and for all those that first began it, and them that longest continue. For these and for all true Christian people, every man and woman say the Lord's Prayer and the Angelic Salutation.

¶ The Priest and the People say,

UR Father, who art in heaven, Hallowed be thy Name. Thy kingdom come. Thy will be done on earth, As it is in heaven. Give us this day our daily bread. And forgive us our trespasses, As we forgive those who trespass against us. And lead us not into temptation; But deliver us from evil: For thine is the kingdom, and the power, and the glory, for ever and ever. Amen.

AIL Mary, full of grace; The Lord is with thee; Blessed art thou amongst women, And blessed is the fruit of thy womb, Jesus. Holy Mary, Mother of God, Pray for us sinners, now and at the hour of our death. Amen.

¶ The Priest then says,

E shall make a special prayer for your fathers' souls, for your mothers' souls, godfathers' souls and godmothers' souls, brothers' souls and sisters' souls, and for all your elders' souls, and for all the souls, that ye or I be bound to pray for, and specially for all the souls whose bones are buried in this Church or in this Churchyard, or in any other holy place, and especially for all the souls that bid the great mercy of Almighty God, that God for his great mercy release them of their pain, if it be his blessed will, and that our prayers may sum what stand them in stead; every man and woman of your charity help them with the Lord's Prayer and the Angelic Salutation.

¶ The Priest and the People then conclude the Bidding of the Bedes by saying the Lord's Prayer and Angelic Salutation once more.

Thanksgivings

A Thanksgiving to Almighty God for the Fruits of the Earth and all the other Blessings of his merciful Providence

MOST gracious God, by whose knowledge the depths are broken up, and the clouds drop down the dew; We yield thee unfeigned thanks and praise for the return of seed-time and harvest, for the increase of the ground and the gathering in of the fruits thereof, and for all the other blessings of thy merciful providence bestowed upon this nation and people. And, we beseech thee, give us a just sense of these great mercies; such as may appear in our lives by an humble, holy, and obedient walking before thee all our days; through Jesus Christ our Lord, to whom, with thee and the Holy Ghost, be all glory and honour, world without end. *Amen.*

The Thanksgiving of Women after Child-birth

¶ To be said when any Woman, being present in Church, shall have desired to return thanks to Almighty God for her safe deliverance.

ALMIGHTY God, we give thee humble thanks for that thou hast been graciously pleased to preserve, through the great pain and peril of childbirth, this woman, thy handmaid, who desireth now to offer her praises and thanksgivings unto thee. Grant, we beseech thee, most merciful Father, that she, through thy help, may both faithfully live and walk according to thy will in this life present, and also may be partaker of everlasting glory in the life to come; through Jesus Christ our Lord. *Amen.*

For Rain

GOD, our heavenly Father, by whose gracious providence the former and the latter rain descend upon the earth, that it may bring forth fruit for the use of man; We give thee humble thanks that it hath pleased thee to send us rain to our great comfort, and to the glory of thy holy Name; through Jesus Christ our Lord. *Amen.*

Thanksgivings

For Fair Weather

LORD God, who hast justly humbled us by thy late visitation of us with immoderate rain and waters, and in thy mercy hast relieved and comforted our souls by this seasonable and blessed change of weather; We praise and glorify thy holy Name for this thy mercy, and will always declare thy loving-kindness from generation to generation; through Jesus Christ our Lord. *Amen.*

For Peace, and Deliverance from our Enemies

ALMIGHTY God, who art a strong tower of defence unto thy servants against the face of their enemies; We yield thee praise and thanksgiving for our deliverance from those great and apparent dangers wherewith we were compassed. We acknowledge in thy goodness that we were not delivered over as a prey unto them; beseeching thee still to continue such thy mercies towards us, that all the world may know that thou art our Saviour and mighty Deliverer; through Jesus Christ our Lord. *Amen.*

For Restoring Public Peace at Home

ETERNAL God, our heavenly Father, who alone makest men to be of one mind in a house, and stillest the outrage of a violent and unruly people; We bless thy holy Name, that it hath pleased thee to appease the seditious tumults which have been lately raised up amongst us; most humbly beseeching thee to grant to all of us grace, that we may henceforth obediently walk in thy holy commandments; and, leading a quiet and peaceable life in all godliness and honesty, may continually offer unto thee our sacrifice of praise and thanksgiving for these thy mercies towards us; through Jesus Christ our Lord. *Amen.*

For Deliverance from great Sickness and Mortality

LORD God, who hast wounded us for our sins, and consumed us for our transgressions, by thy late heavy and dreadful visitation and now, in the midst of judgment remembering mercy, hast redeemed our souls from the jaws of death; We offer unto thy fatherly goodness ourselves, our souls and bodies which thou hast delivered, to be a living sacrifice unto thee, always praising and magnifying thy mercies in the midst of thy Church; through Jesus Christ our Lord. *Amen.*

Thanksgivings

For Recovery from Sickness

GOD, who art the giver of life, of health, and of safety; We bless thy Name, that thou hast been pleased to deliver from *his* bodily sickness this thy *servant*, who now desireth to return thanks unto thee, in the presence of all thy people. Gracious art thou, O Lord, and full of compassion to the children of men. May *his* heart be duly impressed with a sense of thy merciful goodness, and may *he* devote the residue of *his* days to an humble, holy, and obedient walking before thee; through Jesus Christ our Lord. *Amen.*

For a Child's Recovery from Sickness

LMIGHTY God and heavenly Father, we give thee humble thanks for that thou hast been graciously pleased to deliver from *his* bodily sickness the child in whose behalf we bless and praise thy Name, in the presence of all thy people. Grant, we beseech thee, O gracious Father, that *he*, through thy help, may both faithfully live in this world according to thy will, and also may be partaker of everlasting glory in the life to come; through Jesus Christ our Lord. *Amen.*

For a Safe Return from a Journey

OST gracious Lord, whose mercy is over all thy works; We praise thy holy Name that thou hast been pleased to conduct in safety, through the perils of the great deep, (*his* way,) this thy *servant*, who now desireth to return *his* thanks unto thee in thy holy Church. May *he* be duly sensible of thy merciful providence towards *him*, and ever express *his* thankfulness by a holy trust in thee, and obedience to thy laws; through Jesus Christ our Lord. *Amen.*

LITANIES & OFFICES OF THE CHURCH

Litanies & Offices

Great Litany

❡ To be used after the Third Collect at Morning or Evening Prayer; or before the Holy Communion; or separately.

GOD the Father, Creator of heaven and earth;

℟. Have mercy upon us.

O God the Son, Redeemer of the world;

℟. Have mercy upon us.

O God the Holy Ghost, Sanctifier of the faithful;

℟. Have mercy upon us.

O holy, blessed, and glorious Trinity, one God;

℟. Have mercy upon us.

HOLY Virgin Mary, Mother of God our Saviour Jesu Christ,

℟. Pray for us.

All holy Angels and Archangels, and all holy orders of blessed spirits.

℟. Pray for us.

All holy Patriarchs and Prophets, Apostles, Martyrs, Confessors and Virgins, and all the blessed company of heaven.

℟. Pray for us.

EMEMBER not, Lord, our offences, nor the offences of our forefathers; neither take thou vengeance of our sins: Spare us, good Lord, spare thy people, whom thou hast redeemed with thy most precious blood, and be not angry with us for ever.

℟. Spare us, good Lord.

From all evil and mischief; from sin; from the crafts and assaults of the devil; from thy wrath, and from everlasting damnation;

℟. Good Lord, deliver us.

From all blindness of heart; from pride, vainglory, and hypocrisy; from envy, hatred, and malice, and all uncharitableness.

℟. Good Lord, deliver us.

From all inordinate and sinful affections; and from all the deceits of the world, the flesh, and the devil,

℟. Good Lord, deliver us.

From lightning and tempest; from earthquake, fire, and flood; from plague, pestilence, and famine; from battle and murder, and from sudden death,

℟. Good Lord, deliver us.

From all sedition, privy conspiracy, and rebellion; from all false doctrine, heresy, and schism; from hardness of heart, and contempt of thy Word and Commandment,

℟. Good Lord, deliver us.

By the mystery of thy holy Incarnation; by thy holy Nativity and Circumcision; by thy Baptism, Fasting, and Temptation,

℟. Good Lord, deliver us.

By thine Agony and Bloody Sweat; by thy Cross and Passion; by thy precious Death and Burial; by thy glorious Resurrection and Ascension; and by the Coming of the Holy Ghost,

℟. Good Lord, deliver us.

In all time of our tribulation; in all time of our prosperity; in the hour of death, and in the day of judgment,

℟. Good Lord, deliver us.

E sinners do beseech thee to hear us, O Lord God; and that it may please thee to rule and govern thy holy Church universal in the right way;

℟. We beseech thee to hear us, good Lord.

❡ In the United States and its territories, the following is said,

That it may please thee so to rule the heart of thy servant, The President of the United States, that he may above all things seek thy honour and glory;

℟. We beseech thee to hear us, good Lord.

❡ In the British Commonwealth, the following is said,

That it may please thee to keep and strengthen in the true worshipping of thee, in righteousness and holiness of life, thy servant *CHARLES*, our most gracious King and Governor,

℟. We beseech thee to hear us, good Lord.

That it may please thee to rule his heart in thy faith, fear, and love, and that he may evermore have affiance in thee, and ever seek thy honour and glory,

℟. We beseech thee to hear us, good Lord.

That it may please thee to be his defender and keeper, giving him the victory over all his enemies,

℟. We beseech thee to hear us, good Lord.

That it may please thee to bless and preserve Queen *Camilla*, *William* Prince of Wales, the Princess of Wales, and all the Royal Family;

℟. We beseech thee to hear us, good Lord.

That it may please thee to bless and preserve all Christian Rulers and Magistrates; giving them grace to execute justice, and to maintain truth;

℟. We beseech thee to hear us, good Lord.

That it may please thee to bless and illuminate all Bishops, Priests, and Deacons, with true knowledge and understanding of thy Word; and that both by their preaching and living they may set it forth, and show it accordingly;

℞. We beseech thee to hear us, good Lord.

That it may please thee to send forth labourers into thy harvest;

℞. We beseech thee to hear us, good Lord.

That it may please thee to bless and keep all thy people;

℞. We beseech thee to hear us, good Lord.

That it may please thee to give to all nations unity, peace, and concord;

℞. We beseech thee to hear us, good Lord.

That it may please thee to give us an heart to love and fear thee, and diligently to live after thy commandments;

℞. We beseech thee to hear us, good Lord.

That it may please thee to give to all thy people increase of grace to hear meekly thy Word, and to receive it with pure affection, and to bring forth the fruits of the Spirit:

℞. We beseech thee to hear us, good Lord.

That it may please thee to bring into the way of truth all such as have erred, and are deceived;

℞. We beseech thee to hear us, good Lord.

That it may please thee to strengthen such as do stand; and to comfort and help the weak-hearted; and to raise up those who fall; and finally to beat down Satan under our feet;

℞. We beseech thee to hear us, good Lord.

That it may please thee to succour, help, and comfort, all who are in danger, necessity, and tribulation;

℞. We beseech thee to hear us, good Lord.

That it may please thee to preserve all who travel by land, by water, or by air, all women in child-birth, all sick persons, and young children; and to show thy pity upon all prisoners and captives;

℞. We beseech thee to hear us, good Lord.

That it may please thee to defend, and provide for, the fatherless children, and widows, and all who are desolate and oppressed;

℞. We beseech thee to hear us, good Lord.

That it may please thee to have mercy upon all men;

℞. We beseech thee to hear us, good Lord.

That it may please thee to forgive our enemies, persecutors, and slanderers, and to turn their hearts;

℞. We beseech thee to hear us, good Lord.

That it may please thee to give and preserve to our use the kindly fruits of the earth, so that in due time we may enjoy them;

℟. We beseech thee to hear us, good Lord.

That it may please thee to give us true repentance; to forgive us all our sins, negligences, and ignorances; and to endue us with the grace of thy Holy Spirit to amend our lives according to thy Holy Word;

℟. We beseech thee to hear us, good Lord.

Son of God, we beseech thee to hear us.

℟. Son of God, we beseech thee to hear us.

O Lamb of God, who takest away the sins of the world;

℟. Grant us thy peace.

O Lamb of God, who takest away the sins of the world;

℟. Have mercy upon us.

O Christ, hear us.

℟. O Christ, hear us.

Lord, have mercy upon us.

℟. Lord, have mercy upon us.

Christ, have mercy upon us.

℟. Christ, have mercy upon us.

Lord, have mercy upon us.

℟. Lord, have mercy upon us.

❡ Then shall the Minister, and the People with him, say the Lord's Prayer.

UR Father who art in heaven, Hallowed be thy Name. Thy kingdom come. Thy will be done on earth, As it is in heaven. Give us this day our daily bread. And forgive us our trespasses, As we forgive those who trespass against us. And lead us not into temptation; But deliver us from evil. Amen.

❡ The Minister may, at his discretion, omit all that followeth, to the Prayer, We humbly beseech thee, O Father, etc.

℣. O Lord, deal not with us according to our sins.

℟. Neither reward us according to our iniquities.

℣. Let us pray.

GOD, merciful Father, who despisest not the sighing of a contrite heart, nor the desire of such as are sorrowful; Mercifully assist our prayers which we make before thee in all our troubles and adversities, whensoever they oppress us; and graciously hear us, that those evils which the craft and subtilty of the devil or man worketh against us, may, by thy good providence, be brought to nought; that we thy servants, being hurt by no persecutions, may evermore give thanks unto thee in thy holy Church; through Jesus Christ our Lord.

℞. O Lord, arise, help us, and deliver us, for thy Name's sake.

GOD, we have heard with our ears, and our fathers have declared unto us, the noble works that thou didst in their days, and in the old time before them.

℞. O Lord, arise, help us, and deliver us, for thine honour.

℣. Glory be to the Father, and to the Son, and to the Holy Ghost;

℞. As it was in the beginning, is now, and ever shall be, world without end. Amen.

℣. From our enemies defend us, O Christ.

℞. Graciously look upon our afflictions.

℣. With pity behold the sorrows of our hearts.

℞. Mercifully forgive the sins of thy people.

℣. Favourably with mercy hear our prayers.

℞. O Son of David, have mercy upon us.

℣. Both now and ever vouchsafe to hear us, O Christ.

℞. Graciously hear us, O Christ; graciously hear us, O Lord Christ.

℣. O Lord, let thy mercy be showed upon us;

℞. As we do put our trust in thee.

℣. Let us pray.

E humbly beseech thee, O Father, mercifully to look upon our infirmities; and for the glory of thy Name, turn from us all those evils that we most justly have deserved; and grant, that in all our troubles we may put our whole trust and confidence in thy mercy, and evermore serve thee in holiness and pureness of living, to thy honour and glory; through our only Mediator and Advocate, Jesus Christ our Lord. *Amen.*

❡ The Minister may end the Litany here, or at his discretion add other Prayers from this Book.

A Penitential Office

❡ On the First Day of Lent, the Penitential Office is read immediately after the Great Litany during Morning Prayer. It may also be used during Evening Prayer or as a separate Office.

❡ The Penitential Office may be read at other times, at the discretion of the Minister.

❡ The Minister and the People kneeling, then shall be said by them this Psalm following.

PSALM 51. *MISERERE MEI, DEUS*

HAVE mercy upon me, O God, after thy great goodness : according to the multitude of thy mercies do away mine offences.

2 Wash me throughly from my wickedness : and cleanse me from my sin.

3 For I acknowledge my faults : and my sin is ever before me.

4 Against thee only have I sinned, and done this evil in thy sight : that thou mightest be justified in thy saying, and clear when thou art judged.

5 Behold, I was shapen in wickedness : and in sin hath my mother conceived me.

6 But lo, thou requirest truth in the inward parts : and shalt make me to understand wisdom secretly.

7 Thou shalt purge me with hyssop, and I shall be clean : thou shalt wash me, and I shall be whiter than snow.

8 Thou shalt make me hear of joy and gladness : that the bones which thou hast broken may rejoice.

9 Turn thy face from my sins : and put out all my misdeeds.

10 Make me a clean heart, O God : and renew a right spirit within me.

11 Cast me not away from thy presence : and take not thy holy Spirit from me.

12 O give me the comfort of thy help again : and stablish me with thy free Spirit.

13 Then shall I teach thy ways unto the wicked : and sinners shall be converted unto thee.

14 Deliver me from blood-guiltiness, O God, thou that art the God of my health : and my tongue shall sing of thy righteousness.

15 Thou shalt open my lips, O Lord : and my mouth shall shew thy praise.

16 For thou desirest no sacrifice, else would I give it thee : but thou delightest not in burnt-offerings.

17 The sacrifice of God is a troubled spirit : a broken and contrite heart, O God, shalt thou not despise.

18 O be favourable and gracious unto Sion : build thou the walls of Jerusalem.

19 Then shalt thou be pleased with the sacrifice of righteousness, with the burnt-offerings and oblations : then shall they offer young bullocks upon thine altar.

℣. Glory be to the Father, and to the Son, and to the Holy Ghost.

℞. As it was in the beginning, is now, and ever shall be, world without end. Amen.

❡ If the Litany hath been already said, the Minister may pass at once to O Lord, save thy servants; etc.

℣. Lord, have mercy upon us.

℞. Christ, have mercy upon us.

℣. Lord, have mercy upon us.

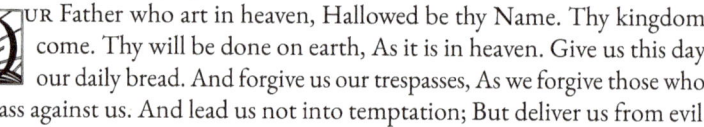UR Father who art in heaven, Hallowed be thy Name. Thy kingdom come. Thy will be done on earth, As it is in heaven. Give us this day our daily bread. And forgive us our trespasses, As we forgive those who trespass against us. And lead us not into temptation; But deliver us from evil. Amen.

℣. O Lord, save thy servants;

℞. That put their trust in thee.

℣. Send unto them help from above.

℞. And evermore mightily defend them.

℣. Help us, O God our Saviour.

℞. And for the glory of thy Name deliver us; be merciful to us sinners, for thy Name's sake.

℣. O Lord, hear our prayer.

℞. And let our cry come unto thee.

Let us pray.

LORD, we beseech thee, mercifully hear our prayers, and spare all those who confess their sins unto thee; that they, whose consciences by sin are accused, by thy merciful pardon may be absolved; through Christ our Lord. *Amen.*

MOST mighty God, and merciful Father, who hast compassion upon all men, and who wouldest not the death of a sinner, but rather that he should turn from his sin, and be saved; Mercifully forgive us our trespasses; receive and comfort us, who are grieved and wearied with the burden of our sins. Thy property is always to have mercy; to thee only it appertaineth to forgive sins. Spare us therefore, good Lord, spare thy people, whom thou hast redeemed; enter not into judgment with thy servants; but so turn thine anger from us, who meekly acknowledge our transgressions, and truly repent us of our faults, and so make haste to help us in this world, that we may ever live with thee in the world to come; through Jesus Christ our Lord. *Amen.*

❡ Then shall the People say this that followeth, with the Minister.

URN thou us, O good Lord, and so shall we be turned. Be favourable, O Lord, Be favourable to thy people, Who turn to thee in weeping, fasting, and praying. For thou art a merciful God, Full of compassion, Long-suffering, and of great pity. Thou sparest when we deserve punishment, And in thy wrath thinkest upon mercy. Spare thy people, good Lord, spare them, And let not thine heritage be brought to confusion. Hear us, O Lord, for thy mercy is great, And after the multitude of thy mercies look upon us; Through the merits and mediation of thy blessed Son, Jesus Christ our Lord. *Amen.*

❡ Then the Minister shall say,

GOD, whose nature and property is ever to have mercy and to forgive; Receive our humble petitions; and though we be tied and bound with the chain of our sins, yet let the pitifulness of thy great mercy loose us; for the honour of Jesus Christ, our Mediator and Advocate. *Amen.*

HE Lord bless us, and keep us. The Lord make his face to shine upon us, and be gracious unto us. The Lord lift up his countenance upon us, and give us peace, both now and evermore. *Amen.*

Litanies & Offices

Sacrament of Penance

¶ The Pentient begins with the following.

Bless me, Father, for I have sinned. ℣. The Lord be in thy heart and upon thy lips, that so thou mayest worthily confess all thy sins; In the Name of the Father, ✠ and of the Son, and of the Holy Ghost. Amen.

¶ The Penitent then confesses his sins using the following or similar formula:

I confess to God Almighty, to Blessed Mary Ever-Virgin, to blessed Michael the Archangel, to blessed John Baptist, to the holy Apostles Peter and Paul, to all the Saints, and to thee, Father, that I have sinned exceedingly in thought, word, and deed, by my fault, by my own fault, by my own most grievous fault,

Especially I accuse myself that since my last Confession, which was (Say how long) ago, I have committed the following sins. (Confess your sins and conclude with:)

For these and for all my other sins which I cannot now remember, I am heartily sorry, firmly purpose amendment, and humbly ask pardon of God; and of thee, my spiritual father, penance, counsel, and Absolution.

Wherefore I beg blessed Mary Ever-Virgin, blessed Michael the Archangel, blessed John Baptist, the holy Apostles Peter and Paul, all the Saints, and thee, father, to pray for me to the Lord our God.

¶ Here the Priest gives penance, counsel, and then absolution saying,

LMIGHTY God have mercy upon thee, forgive thee thy sins, and bring thee to everlasting life. *Amen.*

HE Almighty and merciful Lord grant thee pardon, ✠ absolution, and remission of thy sins. *Amen.*

UR Lord Jesus Christ, who hath left power to his Church to absolve all sinners who truly repent and believe in him, of his great mercy forgive thee thine offences: And by his authority committed to me, I absolve thee from all thy sins, In the Name of the Father, ✠ and of the Son, and of the Holy Ghost. *Amen.*

HE merits of the Passion of our Lord Jesus Christ, the prayers of his holy Mother the Blessed Virgin Mary, and of all the Saints, whatsoever good thou hast done, or evil thou hast endured, be unto thee for the remission of sins, the increase of grace, and the reward of eternal life: And the blessing of God Almighty, the Father, ✠ the Son, and the Holy Ghost, be upon thee and remain with thee for ever. *Amen.*

Go in peace, the Lord hath put away all thy sins. And pray for me, a sinner.

OFFICE OF THE DEAD

Office of the Dead

Vespers of the Dead

❡ Vespers begins with the Lord's Prayer and Angelic Salutation, unless it should follow the carrying of the body to the Church or Matins & Lauds of the occurrent Office, in which case the Office begins with the Antiphon.

PSALM 116. *DILEXI, QUONIAM*

Ant. I will walk † before the Lord in the land of the living.

AM well pleased : that the Lord hath heard the voice of my prayer;

2 That he hath inclined his ear unto me : therefore will I call upon him as long as I live.

3 The snares of death compassed me round about : and the pains of hell gat hold upon me.

4 I shall find trouble and heaviness, and I will call upon the Name of the Lord : O Lord, I beseech thee, deliver my soul.

5 Gracious is the Lord, and righteous : yea, our God is merciful.

6 The Lord preserveth the simple : I was in misery, and he helped me.

7 Turn again then unto thy rest, O my soul : for the Lord hath rewarded thee.

8 And why? thou hast delivered my soul from death : mine eyes from tears, and my feet from falling.

9 I will walk before the Lord : in the land of the living.

℣. Rest eternal * grant unto them, O Lord.

℟. And let light perpetual * shine upon them.

Ant. I will walk before the Lord in the land of the living.

PSALM 120. *AD DOMINUM*

Ant. Woe is me † that I am constrained to dwell with Mesech.

HEN I was in trouble I called upon the Lord : and he heard me.

2 Deliver my soul, O Lord, from lying lips : and from a deceitful tongue.

3 What reward shall be given or done unto thee, thou false tongue : even mighty and sharp arrows, with hot burning coals.

4 Woe is me, that I am constrained to dwell with Mesech : and to have my habitation among the tents of Kedar.

5 My soul hath long dwelt among them : that are enemies unto peace.

6 I labour for peace, but when I speak unto them thereof : they make them ready to battle.

℣. Rest eternal * grant unto them, O Lord.

℟. And let light perpetual * shine upon them.

Ant. Woe is me that I am constrained to dwell with Mesech.

PSALM 121. *LEVAVI OCULUS*

Ant. The Lord † shall preserve thee from all evil yea, it is even he that shall keep thy soul.

WILL lift up mine eyes unto the hills : from whence cometh my help.

2 My help cometh even from the Lord : who hath made heaven and earth.

3 He will not suffer thy foot to be moved : and he that keepeth thee will not sleep.

4 Behold, he that keepeth Israel : shall neither slumber nor sleep.

5 The Lord himself is thy keeper : the Lord is thy defence upon thy right hand;

6 So that the sun shall not burn thee by day : neither the moon by night.

7 The Lord shall preserve thee from all evil : yea, it is even he that shall keep thy soul.

8 The Lord shall preserve thy going out, and thy coming in : from this time forth for evermore.

℣. Rest eternal * grant unto them, O Lord.

℟. And let light perpetual * shine upon them.

Ant. The Lord shall preserve thee from all evil yea, it is even he that shall keep thy soul.

PSALM 130. *DE PROFUNDIS*

Ant. If thou, Lord, wilt be extreme † to mark what is done amiss, O Lord, who may abide it?

OUT of the deep have I called unto thee, O Lord : Lord, hear my voice.

2 O let thine ears consider well : the voice of my complaint.

3 If thou, Lord, wilt be extreme to mark what is done amiss : O Lord, who may abide it?

4 For there is mercy with thee : therefore shalt thou be feared.

5 I look for the Lord; my soul doth wait for him : in his word is my trust.

6 My soul fleeth unto the Lord : before the morning watch, I say, before the morning watch.

7 O Israel, trust in the Lord, for with the Lord there is mercy : and with him is plenteous redemption.

8 And he shall redeem Israel : from all his sins.

℣. Rest eternal * grant unto them, O Lord.

℟. And let light perpetual * shine upon them.

Ant. If thou, Lord, wilt be extreme to mark what is done amiss, O Lord, who may abide it?

Office of the Dead

PSALM 138. *CONFITEBOR TIBI*

Ant. Despise not then, † O Lord, the works of thine own hands.

WILL give thanks unto thee, O Lord, with my whole heart : even before the gods will I sing praise unto thee.

2 I will worship toward thy holy temple, and praise thy Name, because of thy loving-kindness and truth : for thou hast magnified thy Name and thy word above all things.

3 When I called upon thee, thou heardest me : and enduedst my soul with much strength.

4 All the kings of the earth shall praise thee, O Lord : for they have heard the words of thy mouth.

5 Yea, they shall sing in the ways of the Lord : that great is the glory of the Lord.

6 For though the Lord be high, yet hath he respect unto the lowly : as for the proud, he beholdeth them afar off.

7 Though I walk in the midst of trouble, yet shalt thou refresh me : thou shalt stretch forth thy hand upon the furiousness of mine enemies, and thy right hand shall save me.

8 The Lord shall make good his loving-kindness toward me : yea, thy mercy, O Lord, endureth for ever; despise not then the works of thine own hands.

℣. Rest eternal * grant unto them, O Lord.

℞. And let light perpetual * shine upon them.

Ant. Despise not then, O Lord, the works of thine own hands.

℣. I heard a voice from heaven, saying unto me.

℞. Blessed are the dead which die in the Lord.

MAGNIFICAT

Ant. All that the Father † giveth me shall come to me; and him that cometh to me, I will in no wise cast out.

Y soul ✠ doth magnify the Lord, * and my spirit hath rejoiced in God my Saviour.

For he hath regarded * the lowliness of his handmaiden.

For behold, from henceforth * all generations shall call me blessed.

For he that is mighty hath magnified me; * and holy is his Name.

And his mercy is on them that fear him * throughout all generations.

He hath showed strength with his arm; * he hath scattered the proud in the imagination of their hearts.

He hath put down the mighty from their seat, * and hath exalted the humble and meek.

He hath filled the hungry with good things; * and the rich he hath sent empty away.

He remembering his mercy hath holpen his servant Israel; * as he promised to our forefathers, Abraham and his seed, for ever.

℣. Rest eternal * grant unto them, O Lord.

℟. And let light perpetual * shine upon them.

Ant. All that the Father giveth me shall come to me; and him that cometh to me, I will in no wise cast out.

Lord's Prayer

❡ The Lord's Prayer is here said, in secret, kneeling, ending with,

℣. And lead us not into temptation.

℟. But deliver us from evil.

Psalm 146. *Lauda, anima mea*

❡ Psalm 146 is not said on All Souls Day, on the day of death or burial, nor at any time when the Office is recited with Double rite.

Raise the Lord, O my soul; while I live will I praise the Lord : yea, as long as I have any being, I will sing praises unto my God.

2 O put not your trust in princes, nor in any child of man : for there is no help in them.

3 For when the breath of man goeth forth he shall turn again to his earth : and then all his thoughts perish.

4 Blessed is he that hath the God of Jacob for his help : and whose hope is in the Lord his God;

5 Who made heaven and earth, the sea, and all that therein is : who keepeth his promise for ever;

6 Who helpeth them to right that suffer wrong : who feedeth the hungry.

7 The Lord looseth men out of prison : the Lord giveth sight to the blind.

8 The Lord helpeth them that are fallen : the Lord careth for the righteous.

9 The Lord careth for the strangers, he defendeth the fatherless and widow : as for the way of the ungodly, he turneth it upside down.

10 The Lord thy God, O Sion, shall be King for evermore : and throughout all generations.

℣. Rest eternal * grant unto them, O Lord.

℟. And let light perpetual * shine upon them.

Office of the Dead

RESPONSORY

℣. From the gate of hell.

℞. Deliver *his soul*, O Lord.

℣. May *he* rest in peace.

℞. Amen.

CONCLUSION

℣. O Lord, hear my prayer.

℞. And let my cry come unto thee.

℣. The Lord be with you.

℞. And with thy spirit.

℣. Let us pray.

❡ The appropriate collect is here said (p. 77).

℣. Rest eternal * grant unto them, O Lord.

℞. And let light perpetual * shine upon them.

℣. May they rest in peace.

℞. Amen.

HERE ENDETH THE ORDER OF VESPERS OF THE DEAD.

Office of the Dead

Matins of the Dead

❧ Matins begins with the Lord's Prayer, Angelic Salutation, and Apostles' Creed, unless it should follow the carrying of the body to the Church or Matins & Lauds of the occurrent Office, in which case the Office immediately begins with the Invitatory or the Antiphon of the Nocturn.

❧ The following Invitatory is only said when the Office of the Dead is recited with three Nocturns (even when the rite is Semidouble) or when one Nocturn only is said but with Double rite.

❧ The Nocturns placed below, or one Nocturn only, may be said as noted—except on the day of a burial (on which the first Nocturn is always to be said) and in the Commemoration of All the Faithful Departed.

VENITE, EXULTEMUS

Ant. The King unto whom all live, * O come, let us adore him.

Ant. The King unto whom all live, * O come, let us adore him.

COME, let us sing unto the Lord : let us heartily rejoice in the strength of our salvation.

2 Let us come before his presence with thanksgiving : and shew ourselves glad in him with psalms.

Ant. The King unto whom all live, * O come, let us adore him.

3 For the Lord is a great God : and a great King above all gods.

4 In his hand are all the corners of the earth : and the strength of the hills is his also.

Ant. O come, let us adore him.

5 The sea is his, and he made it : and his hands prepared the dry land.

6 O come, let us worship and fall down : and kneel before the Lord our Maker.

7 For he is the Lord our God : and we are the people of his pasture, and the sheep of his hand.

Ant. The King unto whom all live, * O come, let us adore him.

8 To-day if ye will hear his voice, harden not your hearts : as in the provocation, and as in the day of temptation in the wilderness.

9 When your fathers tempted me : proved me, and saw my works.

Ant. O come, let us adore him.

10 Forty years long was I grieved with this generation, and said : It is a people that do err in their hearts, for they have not known my ways;

11 Unto whom I sware in my wrath : that they should not enter into my rest.

Ant. The King unto whom all live, * O come, let us adore him.

℣. Rest eternal * grant unto them, O Lord.

℞. And let light perpetual * shine upon them.

Ant. O come, let us adore him.

Ant. The King unto whom all live, * O come, let us adore him.

NOCTURN I

¶ If only one Nocturn be said, Nocturn I is said on Sunday, Monday, & Thursday.

Psalm 5. Verba mea auribus.

Ant. Make thy way plain, † O Lord my God, before my face.

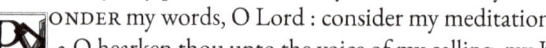

PONDER my words, O Lord : consider my meditation

2 O hearken thou unto the voice of my calling, my King, and my God : for unto thee will I make my prayer.

3 My voice shalt thou hear betimes, O Lord : early in the morning will I direct my prayer unto thee, and will look up.

4 For thou art the God that hast no pleasure in wickedness : neither shall any evil dwell with thee.

5 Such as be foolish shall not stand in thy sight : for thou hatest all them that work vanity.

6 Thou shalt destroy them that speak leasing : the Lord will abhor both the blood-thirsty and deceitful man.

7 But as for me, I will come into thine house, even upon the multitude of thy mercy : and in thy fear will I worship toward thy holy temple.

8 Lead me, O Lord, in thy righteousness, because of mine enemies : make thy way plain before my face.

9 For there is no faithfulness in his mouth : their inward parts are very wickedness.

10 Their throat is an open sepulchre : they flatter with their tongue.

11 Destroy thou them, O God; let them perish through their own imaginations : cast them out in the multitude of their ungodliness; for they have rebelled against thee.

12 And let all them that put their trust in thee rejoice : they shall ever be giving of thanks, because thou defendest them; they that love thy Name shall be joyful in thee;

13 For thou, Lord, wilt give thy blessing unto the righteous : and with thy favourable kindness wilt thou defend him as with a shield.

℣. Rest eternal * grant unto them, O Lord.

℞. And let light perpetual * shine upon them.

Ant. Make thy way plain, O Lord my God, before my face.

Psalm 6. Domine, ne in furore

Ant. Turn thee, † O Lord, and deliver my soul: for in death no man remembereth thee.

LORD, rebuke me not in thine indignation : neither chasten me in thy displeasure.

2 Have mercy upon me, O Lord, for I am weak : O Lord, heal me, for my bones are vexed.

3 My soul also is sore troubled : but, Lord, how long wilt thou punish me?

4 Turn thee, O Lord, and deliver my soul : O save me for thy mercy's sake.

5 For in death no man remembereth thee : and who will give thee thanks in the pit?

6 I am weary of my groaning; every night wash I my bed : and water my couch with my tears.

7 My beauty is gone for very trouble : and worn away because of all mine enemies.

8 Away from me, all ye that work vanity : for the Lord hath heard the voice of my weeping.

9 The Lord hath heard my petition : the Lord will receive my prayer.

10 All mine enemies shall be confounded, and sore vexed : they shall be turned back, and put to shame suddenly.

℣. Rest eternal * grant unto them, O Lord.

℟. And let light perpetual * shine upon them.

Ant. Turn thee, O Lord, and deliver my soul: for in death no man remembereth thee.

Psalm 7. Domine, Deus meus

Ant. Lest he devour † my soul like a lion, and tear it in pieces, while there is none to help.

LORD my God, in thee have I put my trust : save me from all them that persecute me, and deliver me;

2 Lest he devour my soul, like a lion, and tear it in pieces : while there is none to help.

3 O Lord my God, if I have done any such thing : or if there be any wickedness in my hands;

4 If I have rewarded evil unto him that dealt friendly with me : yea, I have delivered him that without any cause is mine enemy,

5 Then let mine enemy persecute my soul, and take me : yea, let him tread my life down upon the earth, and lay mine honour in the dust.

6 Stand up, O Lord, in thy wrath, and lift up thyself, because of the indignation of mine enemies : arise up for me in the judgement that thou hast commanded.

7 And so shall the congregation of the people come about thee : for their sakes therefore lift up thyself again.

8 The Lord shall judge the people; give sentence with me, O Lord : according to my righteousness, and according to the innocency that is in me.

9 O let the wickedness of the ungodly come to an end : but guide thou the just.

10 For the righteous God : trieth the very hearts and reins.

11 My help cometh of God : who preserveth them that are true of heart.

12 God is a righteous Judge, strong and patient : and God is provoked every day.

13 If a man will not turn, he will whet his sword : he hath bent his bow, and made it ready.

14 He hath prepared for him the instruments of death : he ordaineth his arrows against the persecutors.

15 Behold, he travaileth with mischief : he hath conceived sorrow, and brought forth ungodliness.

16 He hath graven and digged up a pit : and is fallen on himself into the destruction that he made for other.

17 For his travail shall come upon his own head : and his wickedness shall fall on his own pate.

18 I will give thanks unto the Lord, according to his righteousness : and I will praise the Name of the Lord most High.

℣. Rest eternal * grant unto them, O Lord.

℟. And let light perpetual * shine upon them.

Ant. Lest he devour my soul like a lion, and tear it in pieces, while there is none to help.

℣. From the gate of hell.

℟. Deliver their souls, O Lord.

¶ The Lord's Prayer is said secretly.

Lesson 1. Job 7:16

ET me alone; for my days are vanity. What is man, that thou shouldest magnify him? and that thou shouldest set thine heart upon him? And that thou shouldest visit him every morning, and try him every moment? How long wilt thou not depart from me, nor let me alone till I swallow down my spittle? I have sinned; what shall I do unto thee, O thou preserver of men? why hast thou set me as a mark against thee, so that I am a burden to myself? And why dost thou not pardon my transgression, and take away mine iniquity? for now shall I sleep in the dust; and thou shalt seek me in the morning, but I shall not be.

℟. I know † that my Redeemer liveth, and that he shall stand at the latter day upon the earth: * And in my flesh shall I see God my Saviour.

℣. Whom I shall see for myself, and mine eyes shall behold, and not another.

℟. And in my flesh shall I see God my Saviour.

Lesson 2. Job 10:1

MY soul is weary of my life; I will leave my complaint upon myself; I will speak in the bitterness of my soul. I will say unto God, Do not condemn me; shew me wherefore thou contendest with me. Is it good unto thee that thou shouldest oppress, that thou shouldest despise the work of thine hands, and shine upon the counsel of the wicked? Hast thou eyes of flesh? or seest thou as man seeth? Are thy days as the days of man? are thy years as man's days, That thou enquirest after mine iniquity, and searchest after my sin? Thou knowest that I am not wicked; and there is none that can deliver out of thine hand.

℟. Thou who didst raise Lazarus † already corrupting from the grave; * Grant them rest, O Lord, and a place of forgiveness.

℣. Thou who shalt come to judge the quick and the dead, and the world by fire.

℟. Grant them rest, O Lord, and a place of forgiveness.

Lesson 3. Job 10:8

THINE hands have made me and fashioned me together round about; yet thou dost destroy me. Remember, I beseech thee, that thou hast made me as the clay; and wilt thou bring me into dust again? Hast thou not poured me out as milk, and curdled me like cheese? Thou hast clothed me with skin and flesh, and hast fenced me with bones and sinews. Thou hast granted me life and favour, and thy visitation hath preserved my spirit.

℟. O Lord, † when thou comest to judge the earth, where shall I hide myself from the wrath of thy countenance? * For I have sinned grievously in my life.

℣. I am afraid of my transgressions, and I am ashamed before thee: when thou comest to judgment, O condemn me not.

℟. For I have sinned grievously in my life.

℣. Rest eternal grant unto them, O Lord: and let light perpetual shine upon them.

℟. For I have sinned grievously in my life.

❡ If only one Nocturn be said, Lauds begins immediately (p. 116).

NOCTURN II

Tuesday and Friday

Psalm 23. Dominus regit me.

Ant. He shall feed me † in a green pasture.

HE Lord is my shepherd : therefore can I lack nothing.

2 He shall feed me in a green pasture : and lead me forth beside the waters of comfort.

3 He shall convert my soul : and bring me forth in the paths of righteousness, for his Name's sake.

4 Yea, though I walk through the valley of the shadow of death, I will fear no evil : for thou art with me; thy rod and thy staff comfort me.

5 Thou shalt prepare a table before me against them that trouble me : thou hast anointed my head with oil, and my cup shall be full.

6 But thy loving-kindness and mercy shall follow me all the days of my life : and I will dwell in the house of the Lord for ever.

℣. Rest eternal * grant unto them, O Lord.

℟. And let light perpetual * shine upon them.

Ant. He shall feed me in a green pasture.

Psalm 25. Ad te, Domine, levavi

Ant. Remember not † the sins and offences of my youth, O Lord.

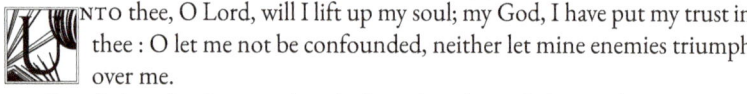NTO thee, O Lord, will I lift up my soul; my God, I have put my trust in thee : O let me not be confounded, neither let mine enemies triumph over me.

2 For all they that hope in thee shall not be ashamed : but such as transgress without a cause shall be put to confusion.

3 Shew me thy ways, O Lord : and teach me thy paths.

4 Lead me forth in thy truth, and learn me : for thou art the God of my salvation; in thee hath been my hope all the day long.

5 Call to remembrance, O Lord, thy tender mercies : and thy loving-kindnesses, which have been ever of old.

6 O remember not the sins and offences of my youth : but according to thy mercy think thou upon me, O Lord, for thy goodness.

7 Gracious and righteous is the Lord : therefore will he teach sinners in the way.

8 Them that are meek shall he guide in judgement : and such as are gentle, them shall he learn his way.

9 All the paths of the Lord are mercy and truth : unto such as keep his covenant and his testimonies.

10 For thy Name's sake, O Lord : be merciful unto my sin, for it is great.

11 What man is he that feareth the Lord : him shall he teach in the way that he shall choose.

12 His soul shall dwell at ease : and his seed shall inherit the land.

13 The secret of the Lord is among them that fear him : and he will shew them his covenant.

14 Mine eyes are ever looking unto the Lord : for he shall pluck my feet out of the net.

15 Turn thee unto me, and have mercy upon me : for I am desolate and in misery.

16 The sorrows of my heart are enlarged : O bring thou me out of my troubles.

17 Look upon my adversity and misery : and forgive me all my sin.

18 Consider mine enemies, how many they are : and they bear a tyrannous hate against me.

19 O keep my soul, and deliver me : let me not be confounded, for I have put my trust in thee.

20 Let perfectness and righteous dealing wait upon me : for my hope hath been in thee.

21 Deliver Israel, O God : out of all his troubles.

℣. Rest eternal * grant unto them, O Lord.

℟. And let light perpetual * shine upon them.

Ant. Remember not the sins and offences of my youth, O Lord.

Psalm 27. Dominus illuminatio

Ant. I believe † verily to see the goodness of the Lord in the land of the living.

THE Lord is my light and my salvation; whom then shall I fear : the Lord is the strength of my life; of whom then shall I be afraid?

2 When the wicked, even mine enemies and my foes, came upon me to eat up my flesh : they stumbled and fell.

3 Though an host of men were laid against me, yet shall not my heart be afraid : and though there rose up war against me, yet will I put my trust in him.

4 One thing have I desired of the Lord, which I will require : even that I may dwell in the house of the Lord all the days of my life, to behold the fair beauty of the Lord, and to visit his temple.

5 For in the time of trouble he shall hide me in his tabernacle : yea, in the secret place of his dwelling shall he hide me, and set me up upon a rock of stone.

6 And now shall he lift up mine head : above mine enemies round about me.

7 Therefore will I offer in his dwelling an oblation with great gladness : I will sing, and speak praises unto the Lord.

8 Hearken unto my voice, O Lord, when I cry unto thee : have mercy upon me, and hear me.

9 My heart hath talked of thee, Seek ye my face : Thy face, Lord, will I seek.

10 O hide not thou thy face from me : nor cast thy servant away in displeasure.

11 Thou hast been my succour : leave me not, neither forsake me, O God of my salvation.

12 When my father and my mother forsake me : the Lord taketh me up.

13 Teach me thy way, O Lord : and lead me in the right way, because of mine enemies.

14 Deliver me not over into the will of mine adversaries : for there are false witnesses risen up against me, and such as speak wrong.

15 I should utterly have fainted : but that I believe verily to see the goodness of the Lord in the land of the living.

16 O tarry thou the Lord's leisure : be strong, and he shall comfort thine heart; and put thou thy trust in the Lord.

℣. Rest eternal * grant unto them, O Lord.

℟. And let light perpetual * shine upon them.

Ant. I believe verily to see the goodness of the Lord in the land of the living.

℣. The Lord shall set them with the princes.

℟. Even with the princes of his people.

❡ The Lord's Prayer is said secretly.

Lesson 4. Job 13:22

HEN call thou, and I will answer: or let me speak, and answer thou me. How many are mine iniquities and sins? make me to know my transgression and my sin. Wherefore hidest thou thy face, and holdest me for thine enemy? Wilt thou break a leaf driven to and fro? and wilt thou pursue the dry stubble? For thou writest bitter things against me, and makest me to possess the iniquities of my youth. Thou puttest my feet also in the stocks, and lookest narrowly unto all my paths; thou settest a print upon the heels of my feet. And he, as a rotten thing, consumeth, as a garment that is moth eaten.

℟. Remember me, † O God, that my life is wind: * The eye of him that hath seen me shall see me no more.

℣. Out of the deep have I called unto thee, O Lord: Lord, hear my voice.

℟. The eye of him that hath seen me shall see me no more.

Lesson 5. Job 14:1

AN that is born of a woman is of few days, and full of trouble. He cometh forth like a flower, and is cut down: he fleeth also as a shadow, and continueth not. And dost thou open thine eyes upon such an one, and bringest me into judgment with thee? Who can bring a clean thing out of an unclean? not one. Seeing his days are determined, the number of his months are with thee, thou hast appointed his bounds that he cannot pass; Turn from him, that he may rest, till he shall accomplish, as an hireling, his day.

℟. Woe is me, † O Lord, for I have sinned grievously all the days of my life! O wretched man, what shall I do? Whither shall I flee, but unto thee, O my God? * Have mercy upon me, when thou comest at the day of judgment.

℣. My soul is sore troubled; but, Lord, be thou my helper.

℟. Have mercy upon me, when thou comest at the day of judgment.

Lesson 6. Job 14:13

THAT thou wouldest hide me in the grave, that thou wouldest keep me secret, until thy wrath be past, that thou wouldest appoint me a set time, and remember me! If a man die, shall he live again? all the days of my appointed time will I wait, till my change come. Thou shalt call, and I will answer thee: thou wilt have a desire to the work of thine hands. For now thou numberest my steps: dost thou not watch over my sin?

℟. Remember not † my trespasses, O Lord, * When thou shalt come to judge the world by fire.

℣. Make thy way plain before my face, O Lord my God.

℟. When thou shalt come to judge the world by fire.

℣. Rest eternal grant unto them, O Lord: and let light perpetual shine upon them.

℟. When thou shalt come to judge the world by fire.

❡ If only one Nocturn be said, Lauds begins immediately (p. 116).

NOCTURN III

Wednesday and Saturday

Psalm 40. Expectans expectavi

Ant. O Lord, † let it be thy pleasure to deliver me; make haste, O Lord, to help me.

WAITED patiently for the Lord : and he inclined unto me, and heard my calling.

2 He brought me also out of the horrible pit, out of the mire and clay : and set my feet upon the rock, and ordered my goings.

3 And he hath put a new song in my mouth : even a thanksgiving unto our God.

4 Many shall see it, and fear : and shall put their trust in the Lord.

5 Blessed is the man that hath set his hope in the Lord : and turned not unto the proud, and to such as go about with lies.

6 O Lord my God, great are the wondrous works which thou hast done, like as be also thy thoughts which are to us-ward : and yet there is no man that ordereth them unto thee:

7 If I should declare them, and speak of them : they should be more than I am able to express.

8 Sacrifice and meat-offering thou wouldest not : but mine ears hast thou opened.

9 Burnt-offerings, and sacrifice for sin, hast thou not required : then said I, Lo, I come,

10 In the volume of the book it is written of me, that I should fulfil thy will, O my God : I am content to do it; yea, thy law is within my heart.

11 I have declared thy righteousness in the great congregation : lo, I will not refrain my lips, O Lord, and that thou knowest.

12 I have not hid thy righteousness within my heart : my talk hath been of thy truth and of thy salvation.

13 I have not kept back thy loving mercy and truth : from the great congregation.

14 Withdraw not thou thy mercy from me, O Lord : let thy loving-kindness and thy truth alway preserve me.

15 For innumerable troubles are come about me; my sins have taken such hold upon me that I am not able to look up : yea, they are more in number than the hairs of my head, and my heart hath failed me.

16 O Lord, let it be thy pleasure to deliver me : make haste, O Lord, to help me.

17 Let them be ashamed and confounded together, that seek after my soul to destroy it : let them be driven backward and put to rebuke, that wish me evil.

18 Let them be desolate, and rewarded with shame : that say unto me, Fie upon thee, fie upon thee.

19 Let all those that seek thee be joyful and glad in thee : and let such as love thy salvation say alway, The Lord be praised.

20 As for me, I am poor and needy : but the Lord careth for me.

21 Thou art my helper and redeemer : make no long tarrying, O my God.

℣. Rest eternal * grant unto them, O Lord.

℟. And let light perpetual * shine upon them.

Ant. O Lord, let it be thy pleasure to deliver me; make haste, O Lord, to help me.

Psalm 41. Beatus qui intelligit

Ant. Heal my soul, † O Lord, for I have sinned against thee.

BLESSED is he that considereth the poor and needy : the Lord shall deliver him in the time of trouble.

2 The Lord preserve him, and keep him alive, that he may be blessed upon earth : and deliver not thou him into the will of his enemies.

3 The Lord comfort him, when he lieth sick upon his bed : make thou all his bed in his sickness.

4 I said, Lord, be merciful unto me : heal my soul, for I have sinned against thee.

5 Mine enemies speak evil of me : When shall he die, and his name perish?

6 And if he come to see me, he speaketh vanity : and his heart conceiveth falsehood within himself, and when he cometh forth he telleth it.

7 All mine enemies whisper together against me : even against me do they imagine this evil.

8 Let the sentence of guiltiness proceed against him : and now that he lieth, let him rise up no more.

9 Yea, even mine own familiar friend, whom I trusted : who did also eat of my bread, hath laid great wait for me.

10 But be thou merciful unto me, O Lord : raise thou me up again, and I shall reward them.

11 By this I know thou favourest me : that mine enemy doth not triumph against me.

12 And when I am in my health, thou upholdest me : and shalt set me before thy face for ever.

13 Blessed be the Lord God of Israel : world without end. Amen.

℣. Rest eternal * grant unto them, O Lord.

℟. And let light perpetual * shine upon them.

Ant. Heal my soul, O Lord, for I have sinned against thee.

Psalm 42. *Quemadmodum*

Ant. My soul is athirst for God, † yea, even for the living God: when shall I come to appear before the presence of the Lord.

IKE as the hart desireth the water-brooks : so longeth my soul after thee, O God.

2 My soul is athirst for God, yea, even for the living God : when shall I come to appear before the presence of God?

3 My tears have been my meat day and night : while they daily say unto me, Where is now thy God?

4 Now when I think thereupon, I pour out my heart by myself : for I went with the multitude, and brought them forth into the house of God;

5 In the voice of praise and thanksgiving : among such as keep holy-day.

6 Why art thou so full of heaviness, O my soul : and why art thou so disquieted within me?

7 Put thy trust in God : for I will yet give him thanks for the help of his countenance.

8 My God, my soul is vexed within me : therefore will I remember thee concerning the land of Jordan, and the little hill of Hermon.

9 One deep calleth another, because of the noise of the water-pipes : all thy waves and storms are gone over me.

10 The Lord hath granted his loving-kindness in the day-time : and in the night-season did I sing of him, and made my prayer unto the God of my life.

11 I will say unto the God of my strength, Why hast thou forgotten me : why go I thus heavily, while the enemy oppresseth me?

12 My bones are smitten asunder as with a sword : while mine enemies that trouble me cast me in the teeth;

13 Namely, while they say daily unto me : Where is now thy God?

14 Why art thou so vexed, O my soul : and why art thou so disquieted within me?

15 O put thy trust in God : for I will yet thank him, which is the help of my countenance, and my God.

℣. Rest eternal * grant unto them, O Lord.

℟. And let light perpetual * shine upon them.

Ant. My soul is athirst for God, yea, even for the living God: when shall I come to appear before the presence of the Lord.

℣. O deliver not the soul of thy turtle-dove unto the multitude of the enemies.

℟. Forget not the congregation of the poor for ever.

¶ The Lord's Prayer is said secretly.

Lesson 7. Job 17:1

MY breath is corrupt, my days are extinct, the graves are ready for me. Are there not mockers with me? and doth not mine eye continue in their provocation? Lay down now, put me in a surety with thee; who is he that will strike hands with me? My days are past, my purposes are broken off, even the thoughts of my heart. They change the night into day: the light is short because of darkness. If I wait, the grave is mine house: I have made my bed in the darkness. I have said to corruption, Thou art my father: to the worm, Thou art my mother, and my sister. And where is now my hope? as for my hope, who shall see it?

℟. The while I trespass daily † and have no repentance, the fear of death appalleth me: * Because in hell there is no redemption, have mercy upon me, O God, and save me.

℣. Save me, O God, for thy Name's sake, and deliver me in thy strength.

℟. Because in hell there is no redemption, have mercy upon me, O God, and save me.

Lesson 8. Job 19:20

MY bone cleaveth to my skin and to my flesh, and I am escaped with the skin of my teeth. Have pity upon me, have pity upon me, O ye my friends; for the hand of God hath touched me. Why do ye persecute me as God, and are not satisfied with my flesh? Oh that my words were now written! oh that they were printed in a book! That they were graven with an iron pen and lead in the rock for ever! For I know that my redeemer liveth, and that he shall stand at the latter day upon the earth: And though after my skin worms destroy this body, yet in my flesh shall I see God: Whom I shall see for myself, and mine eyes shall behold, and not another; though my reins be consumed within me.

℟. Judge me not, † O Lord, according to my deeds; for I have done nothing worthy in thy sight: wherefore I humbly beseech thy Majesty, * That thou, O God, mayest do away mine offences.

℣. Wash me throughly, O Lord, from mine unrighteousness, and cleanse me from my sin.

℞. That thou, O God, mayest do away mine offences.

Lesson 9. Job 10:18

WHEREFORE then hast thou brought me forth out of the womb? Oh that I had given up the ghost, and no eye had seen me! I should have been as though I had not been; I should have been carried from the womb to the grave. Are not my days few? cease then, and let me alone, that I may take comfort a little, Before I go whence I shall not return, even to the land of darkness and the shadow of death; A land of darkness, as darkness itself; and of the shadow of death, without any order, and where the light is as darkness.

RESPONSORY

¶ The following Responsory is said when only the Third Nocturn is said.

℞. Deliver me, O Lord, † from the paths of hell, thou that brakest in pieces the gates of brass; and visitedst hell, and gavest them light, that they might see thee, * Who dwelt in the pains of darkness.

℣. Crying out and saying, Thou art come, O our Redeemer.

℞. Who dwelt in the pains of darkness.

℣. Rest eternal grant unto them, O Lord: and let light perpetual shine upon them.

℞. Who dwelt in the pains of darkness.

¶ If only one Nocturn be said, Lauds begins immediately (p. 116).

¶ The following Responsory is said when three Nocturns are said.

℞. Deliver me, O Lord, † from death eternal in that day of trembling: * When heaven and earth shall be shaken: * When thou shalt come to judge the world by fire.

℣. Trembling taketh hold upon me, and fearfulness, as the sifting draweth on and the wrath to come.

℞. When heaven and earth shall be shaken.

℣. Ah, that day, that day of anger, of calamity and misery; Ah that great day, and exceeding bitter!

℞. When thou shalt come to judge the world by fire.

℣. Rest eternal grant unto them, O Lord: and let light perpetual shine upon them.

℟. Deliver me, O Lord, from death eternal in that day of trembling: When heaven and earth shall be shaken: When thou shalt come to judge the world by fire.

CONCLUSION

❧ The following Conclusion is said when Matins is separated from Lauds.

℣. The Lord be with you.

or, O Lord, hear our prayer.

℟. And with thy spirit.

or, And let our cry come unto thee.

❧ The appropriate collect is here said (p. 77).

℣. Rest eternal * grant unto them, O Lord.

℟. And let light perpetual * shine upon them.

℣. May they rest in peace.

℟. Amen.

HERE ENDETH THE ORDER OF MATINS OF THE DEAD.

Office of the Dead

Lauds of the Dead

❡ Before Lauds—if it be said separately from Matins—the Lord's Prayer and Angelic Salutation are said secretly. Otherwise, the Office begins at once with the Antiphon.

PSALM 51. *MISERERE MEI, DEUS*

Ant. The bones which thou hast broken † shall rejoice in the Lord.

HAVE mercy upon me, O God, after thy great goodness : according to the multitude of thy mercies do away mine offences.

2 Wash me throughly from my wickedness : and cleanse me from my sin.

3 For I acknowledge my faults : and my sin is ever before me.

4 Against thee only have I sinned, and done this evil in thy sight : that thou mightest be justified in thy saying, and clear when thou art judged.

5 Behold, I was shapen in wickedness : and in sin hath my mother conceived me.

6 But lo, thou requirest truth in the inward parts: and shalt make me to understand wisdom secretly.

7 Thou shalt purge me with hyssop, and I shall be clean : thou shalt wash me, and I shall be whiter than snow.

8 Thou shalt make me hear of joy and gladness : that the bones which thou hast broken may rejoice.

9 Turn thy face from my sins : and put out all my misdeeds.

10 Make me a clean heart, O God : and renew a right spirit within me.

11 Cast me not away from thy presence : and take not thy holy Spirit from me.

12 O give me the comfort of thy help again : and stablish me with thy free Spirit.

13 Then shall I teach thy ways unto the wicked : and sinners shall be converted unto thee.

14 Deliver me from blood-guiltiness, O God, thou that art the God of my health : and my tongue shall sing of thy righteousness.

15 Thou shalt open my lips, O Lord : and my mouth shall shew thy praise.

16 For thou desirest no sacrifice, else would I give it thee : but thou delightest not in burnt-offerings.

17 The sacrifice of God is a troubled spirit : a broken and contrite heart, O God, shalt thou not despise.

18 O be favourable and gracious unto Sion : build thou the walls of Jerusalem.

19 Then shalt thou be pleased with the sacrifice of righteousness, with the burnt-offerings and oblations : then shall they offer young bullocks upon thine altar.

℣. Rest eternal * grant unto them, O Lord.

℟. And let light perpetual * shine upon them.

Ant. The bones which thou hast broken shall rejoice in the Lord.

Psalm 65. *Te decet hymnus*

Ant. Thou, O Lord, † that hearest the prayer, unto thee shall all flesh come.

THOU, O God, art praised in Sion : and unto thee shall the vow be performed in Jerusalem.

2 Thou that hearest the prayer : unto thee shall all flesh come.

3 My misdeeds prevail against me : O be thou merciful unto our sins.

4 Blessed is the man whom thou choosest, and receivest unto thee : he shall dwell in thy court, and shall be satisfied with the pleasures of thy house, even of thy holy temple.

5 Thou shalt shew us wonderful things in thy righteousness, O God of our salvation : thou that art the hope of all the ends of the earth, and of them that remain in the broad sea.

6 Who in his strength setteth fast the mountains : and is girded about with power.

7 Who stilleth the raging of the sea : and the noise of his waves, and the madness of the people.

8 They also that dwell in the uttermost parts of the earth shall be afraid at thy tokens : thou that makest the outgoings of the morning and evening to praise thee.

9 Thou visitest the earth, and blessest it : thou makest it very plenteous.

10 The river of God is full of water : thou preparest their corn, for so thou providest for the earth.

11 Thou waterest her furrows, thou sendest rain into the little valleys thereof : thou makest it soft with the drops of rain, and blessest the increase of it.

12 Thou crownest the year with thy goodness : and thy clouds drop fatness.

13 They shall drop upon the dwellings of the wilderness : and the little hills shall rejoice on every side.

14 The folds shall be full of sheep : the valleys also shall stand so thick with corn, that they shall laugh and sing.

℣. Rest eternal * grant unto them, O Lord.

℟. And let light perpetual * shine upon them.

Ant. Thou, O Lord, that hearest the prayer, unto thee shall all flesh come.

Office of the Dead

PSALM 63. *DEUS, DEUS MEUS*

Ant. Thy right hand † hath upholden me, O Lord.

GOD, thou art my God : early will I seek thee.

2 My soul thirsteth for thee, my flesh also longeth after thee : in a barren and dry land where no water is.

3 Thus have I looked for thee in holiness : that I might behold thy power and glory.

4 For thy loving-kindness is better than the life itself : my lips shall praise thee.

5 As long as I live will I magnify thee on this manner : and lift up my hands in thy Name.

6 My soul shall be satisfied, even as it were with marrow and fatness : when my mouth praiseth thee with joyful lips.

7 Have I not remembered thee in my bed : and thought upon thee when I was waking?

8 Because thou hast been my helper : therefore under the shadow of thy wings will I rejoice.

9 My soul hangeth upon thee : thy right hand hath upholden me.

10 These also that seek the hurt of my soul : they shall go under the earth.

11 Let them fall upon the edge of the sword : that they may be a portion for foxes.

12 But the King shall rejoice in God; all they also that swear by him shall be commended : for the mouth of them that speak lies shall be stopped.

℣. Rest eternal * grant unto them, O Lord.

℟. And let light perpetual * shine upon them.

Ant. Thy right hand hath upholden me, O Lord.

EGO DIXI

Ant. From the gate of hell, † deliver my soul, O Lord.

SAID in the cutting off of my days, † I shall go to the gates of the grave: * I am deprived of the residue of my years.

I said, I shall not see the Lord, † even the Lord, in the land of the living: * I shall behold man no more with the inhabitants of the world.

Mine age is departed, * and is removed from me as a shepherd's tent;

I have cut off like a weaver my life: † he will cut me off with pining sickness: * from day even to night wilt thou make an end of me.

I reckoned till morning, † that, as a lion, so will he break all my bones: * from day even to night wilt thou make an end of me.

Like a crane or a swallow, so did I chatter: * I did mourn as a dove.

Mine eyes fail with looking upward: * O Lord, I am oppressed; undertake for me.

What shall I say? † he hath both spoken unto me, and himself hath done it: * I shall go softly all my years in the bitterness of my soul.

O Lord, by these things men live, † and in all these things is the life of my spirit: * so wilt thou recover me, and make me to live.

Behold, for peace I had great bitterness: † but thou hast in love to my soul delivered it from the pit of corruption: * for thou hast cast all my sins behind thy back.

For the grave cannot praise thee, † death can not celebrate thee: * they that go down into the pit cannot hope for thy truth.

The living, the living, he shall praise thee, as I do this day: * the father to the children shall make known thy truth.

The Lord was ready to save me: * therefore we will sing my songs to the stringed instruments all the days of our life in the house of the Lord.

℣. Rest eternal * grant unto them, O Lord.

℟. And let light perpetual * shine upon them.

Ant. From the gate of hell, deliver my soul, O Lord.

Psalm 150. *Laudate Dominum*

Ant. Let everything that hath breath † praise the Lord.

PRAISE God in his holiness : praise him in the firmament of his power. 2 Praise him in his noble acts : praise him according to his excellent greatness.

3 Praise him in the sound of the trumpet : praise him upon the lute and harp.

4 Praise him in the cymbals and dances : praise him upon the strings and pipe.

5 Praise him upon the well-tuned cymbals : praise him upon the loud cymbals.

6 Let every thing that hath breath : praise the Lord.

℣. Rest eternal * grant unto them, O Lord.

℟. And let light perpetual * shine upon them.

Ant. Let everything that hath breath praise the Lord.

℣. I heard a voice from heaven, saying unto me.

℟. Blessed are the dead which die in the Lord.

Office of the Dead

BENEDICTUS

Ant. I am the resurrection † and the life: he that believeth in me, though he were dead, yet shall he live: and whosoever liveth and believeth in me, shall never die.

BLESSED ✠ be the Lord God of Israel; * for he hath visited and redeemed his people;

And hath raised up a mighty salvation for us, * in the house of his servant David;

As he spake by the mouth of his holy Prophets, * which have been since the world began;

That we should be saved from our enemies, * and from the hand of all that hate us.

To perform the mercy promised to our forefathers, * and to remember his holy covenant;

To perform the oath which he sware to our forefather Abraham, * that he would give us;

That we being delivered out of the hand of our enemies * might serve him without fear;

In holiness and righteousness before him, * all the days of our life.

And thou, child, shalt be called the prophet of the Highest: * for thou shalt go before the face of the Lord to prepare his ways;

To give knowledge of salvation unto his people * for the remission of their sins,

Through the tender mercy of our God; * whereby the day-spring from on high hath visited us;

To give light to them that sit in darkness, and in the shadow of death, * and to guide our feet into the way of peace.

℣. Rest eternal * grant unto them, O Lord.

℟. And let light perpetual * shine upon them.

Ant. I am the resurrection and the life: he that believeth in me, though he were dead, yet shall he live; and whosoever liveth and believeth in me, shall never die.

LORD'S PRAYER

❡ The Lord's Prayer is said, in secret, kneeling, ending with,

℣. And lead us not into temptation.

℟. But deliver us from evil.

Psalm 130. *De profundis*

¶ Psalm 130 is not said on All Souls Day, on the day of death or burial, nor at any time when the Office is recited with Double rite.

UT of the deep have I called unto thee, O Lord : Lord, hear my voice.

2 O let thine ears consider well : the voice of my complaint.

3 If thou, Lord, wilt be extreme to mark what is done amiss : O Lord, who may abide it?

4 For there is mercy with thee : therefore shalt thou be feared.

5 I look for the Lord; my soul doth wait for him : in his word is my trust.

6 My soul fleeth unto the Lord : before the morning watch, I say, before the morning watch.

7 O Israel, trust in the Lord, for with the Lord there is mercy : and with him is plenteous redemption.

8 And he shall redeem Israel : from all his sins.

℣. Rest eternal * grant unto them, O Lord.

℟. And let light perpetual * shine upon them.

Responsory

℣. From the gate of hell.

℟. Deliver *his soul*, O Lord.

℣. May *he* rest in peace.

℟. Amen.

Conclusion

℣. O Lord, hear my prayer.

℟. And let my cry come unto thee.

℣. The Lord be with you.

℟. And with thy spirit.

¶ The appropriate collect is here said (p. 77).

℣. Rest eternal * grant unto them, O Lord.

℟. And let light perpetual * shine upon them.

℣. May they rest in peace.

℟. Amen.

Here endeth the Order of Lauds of the Dead.

EUCHARISTIC DEVOTIONS

Eucharistic Devotions

Benediction of the Blessed Sacrament

O Salutaris Hostia

❡ The Priest brings the Sacrament out of the Tabernacle with all kneeling, singing:

SAVING Victim op'ning wide * The Gate of heav'n to man below,
Our foes press on from ev'ry side, * Thine aid supply, thy strength bestow.
All praise and thanks to thee ascend * For evermore, blest One in Three;
O grant us life that shall not end, * In our true native land with thee. Amen.

SALUTÁRIS Hóstia, * Quæ cæli pandis óstium:
Bella premunt hostília, * Da robur, fer auxílium.
Uni trinóque Dómino * Sit sempitérna glória,
Qui vitam sine término * Nobis donet in pátria. Amen.

Tantum Ergo Sacramentum

❡ After a time for silence, the following Hymn is sung:

HEREFORE we, before him bending, * This great Sacrament revere;
Types and shadows have their ending, * For the newer rite is here;
Faith, our outward sense befriending, * Makes our inward vision clear.

Glory let us give and blessing * To the Father and the Son,
Honour, thanks, and praise addressing, * While eternal ages run;
Ever too his love confessing * Who from One with Both is One. Amen.

℣. Thou gavest them bread from heaven. (Alleluia)
℟. Containing in itself all sweetness. (Alleluia)

ÁNTUM ergo Sacraméntum * Venerémur cérnui,
Et antíquum documéntum, * Nóvo cédat rítui,
Præstet fídes suppleméntum * Sénsuum deféctui.

Genitóri, Genitóque, * Laus et jubilátio;
Sálus, hónor, vírtus quoque * Sit et benedíctio.
Procedénti ab unóque * Cómpar sit laudátio. Amen.

℣. Panem de cælis præstitísti eis. (Allelúja.)
℟. Omne delectaméntum in se habéntem. (Allelúja.)

Let us pray.

GOD, who in this wonderful Sacrament hast left us a perpetual Memorial of thy Passion: Grant us, we beseech thee, so to venerate the Sacred Mysteries of thy Body and Blood, that we may ever perceive within ourselves the fruit of thy redemption; who livest and reignest, world without end. *Amen.*

Orémus.

EUS, qui nobis sub sacraménto mirábili, passiónis tuæ memóriam reliquísti: tríbue, Quæsumus, ita nos córporis et sánguinis tui sacra mystéria venerári, ut redemptiónis tuæ fructum in nobis iúgiter sentiámus. Qui vivis et regnas in sæcula sæculorum. *Amen.*

DIVINE PRAISES

¶ All kneeling, the Priest blesses the People with the Blessed Sacrament. He then places it upon the Altar and says the Divine Praises, as followeth.

Blessed be God.

Blessed be his Holy Name.

Blessed be Jesus Christ, true God and true Man.

Blessed be the Name of Jesus.

Blessed be Jesus in the Most Holy Sacrament of the Altar.

Blessed be God the Holy Ghost, the Comforter.

Blessed be the Great Mother of God, Mary most Holy.

Blessed be the name of Mary, Virgin and Mother.

Blessed be Saint Joseph, her most chaste spouse.

Blessed be God in his Angels and in his Saints.

Benedíctus Deus.

Benedíctum Nomen Sanctum ejus.

Benedíctus Jesus Christus, verus Deus et verus homo.

Benedíctum Nomen Jesu.

Benedíctus Jesus in sanctíssimo altáris Sacraménto.

Benedíctus Sanctus Spíritus, Paraclítus.

Benedícta magna Mater Dei, María sanctíssima.

Benedíctum nomen Maríæ, Vírginis et Matris.

Benedíctus sanctus Joseph, ejus castíssimus Sponsus.

Benedíctus Deus in Angelis suis, et in Sanctis suis.

Eucharistic Devotions

PSALM 117. *LAUDATE DOMINUM*

¶ The Blessed Sacrament is replaced in the Tabernacle. All stand and pray the following,

Ant. Let us forever adore the Most Holy Sacrament. (Alleluia.)

PRAISE the LORD, all ye heathen : praise him, all ye nations.

For his merciful kindness is ever more and more toward us : and the truth of the LORD endureth for ever. Praise the LORD.

Glory be to the Father, and to the Son, * and to the Holy Ghost:

As it was in the beginning, is now, and ever shall be, * world without end. Amen.

Ant. Let us forever adore the Most Holy Sacrament. (Alleluia.)

Ant. Adorémus in ætérnum Sanctíssimum Sacramentum. (Allelúja.)

AUDÁTE Dóminum, omnes gentes: * laudáte eum, omnes pópuli:

Quóniam confirmáta est super nos misericórdia ejus: * et véritas Dómini manet in ætérnum.

Glória Patri, et Fílio, * et Spirítui Sancto.

Sicut erat in princípio, et nunc, et semper, * et in sǽcula sæculórum. Amen.

Ant. Adorémus in ætérnum Sanctíssimum Sacraméntum. (Allelúja.)

Preparation for Holy Communion

Psalms

EMEMBER not, † Lord, our offences, nor the offences of our forefathers; neither take thou vengeance of our sins. (Alleluia.)

E reminiscáris, † Dómine, delícta nostra, vel paréntum nostrórum, neque vindíctam sumas de peccátis nostris. (Allelúja.)

Psalm 84

HOW amiable are thy dwellings : thou Lord of hosts!

2 My soul hath a desire and longing to enter into the courts of the Lord : my heart and my flesh rejoice in the living God.

3 Yea, the sparrow hath found her an house, and the swallow a nest where she may lay her young : even thy altars, O Lord of hosts, my King and my God.

4 Blessed are they that dwell in thy house : they will be alway praising thee.

5 Blessed is the man whose strength is in thee : in whose heart are thy ways.

6 Who going through the vale of misery use it for a well : and the pools are filled with water.

7 They will go from strength to strength : and unto the God of gods appeareth every one of them in Sion.

8 O Lord God of hosts, hear my prayer : hearken, O God of Jacob.

9 Behold, O God our defender : and look upon the face of thine Anointed.

10 For one day in thy courts : is better than a thousand.

11 I had rather be a door-keeper in the house of my God : than to dwell in the tents of ungodliness.

UAM dilécta tabernácula tua, Dómine virtútum: * concupíscit, et déficit ánima mea in átria Dómini.

Cor meum, et caro mea * exsultavérunt in Deum vivum.

Étenim passer invénit sibi domum: * et turtur nidum sibi, ubi ponat pullos suos.

Altária tua, Dómine virtútum: * Rex meus, et Deus meus.

Beáti, qui hábitant in domo tua, Dómine: * in sǽcula sæculórum laudábunt te.

Beátus vir, cujus est auxílium abs te: * ascensiónes in corde suo dispósuit, in valle lacrimárum in loco, quem pósuit.

Étenim benedictiónem dabit legislátor, ibunt de virtúte in virtútem: * vidébitur Deus deórum in Sion.

Dómine, Deus virtútum, exáudi oratiónem meam: * áuribus pércipe, Deus Iacob.

Protéctor noster, áspice, Deus: * et réspice in fáciem Christi tui:

Quia mélior est dies una in átriis tuis, * super míllia.

Elégi abiéctus esse in domo Dei mei: * magis quam habitáre in tabernáculis

12 For the Lord God is a light and defence : the Lord will give grace and worship, and no good thing shall he withhold from them that live a godly life.

13 O Lord God of hosts : blessed is the man that putteth his trust in thee.

℣. Glory be to the Father, and to the Son, and to the Holy Ghost.

℞. As it was in the beginning, is now, and ever shall be, world without end. Amen.

peccatórum.

Quia misericórdiam, et veritátem díligit Deus: * grátiam et glóriam dabit Dóminus.

Non privábit bonis eos, qui ámbulant in innocéntia: * Dómine virtútum, beátus homo, qui sperat in te.

℣. Glória Patri, et Fílio, * et Spirítui Sancto:

℞. Sicut erat in princípio, et nunc, et semper, * et in sǽcula sæculórum. Amen.

Psalm 85

ORD, thou art become gracious unto thy land : thou hast turned away the captivity of Jacob.

2 Thou hast forgiven the offence of thy people : and covered all their sins.

3 Thou hast taken away all thy displeasure : and turned thyself from thy wrathful indignation.

4 Turn us then, O God our Saviour : and let thine anger cease from us.

5 Wilt thou be displeased at us for ever : and wilt thou stretch out thy wrath from one generation to another?

6 Wilt thou not turn again, and quicken us : that thy people may rejoice in thee?

7 Shew us thy mercy, O Lord : and grant us thy salvation.

8 I will hearken what the Lord God will say concerning me : for he shall speak peace unto his people, and to his saints, that they turn not again.

ENEDIXÍSTI, Dómine, terram tuam: * avertísti captivitátem Iacob.

Remisísti iniquitátem plebis tuæ: * operuísti ómnia peccáta eórum.

Mitigásti omnem iram tuam: * avertísti ab ira indignatiónis tuæ.

Convérte nos, Deus, salutáris noster: * et avérte iram tuam a nobis.

Numquid in ætérnum irascéris nobis? * aut exténdes iram tuam a generatióne in generatiónem?

Deus, tu convérsus vivificábis nos: * et plebs tua lætábitur in te.

Osténde nobis, Dómine, misericórdiam tuam: * et salutáre tuum da nobis.

Áudiam quid loquátur in me Dóminus Deus: * quóniam loquétur pacem in plebem suam.

Et super sanctos suos: * et in eos, qui convertúntur ad cor.

Verúmtamen prope timéntes eum salutáre ipsíus: * ut inhábitet glória in terra nostra.

9 For his salvation is nigh them that fear him : that glory may dwell in our land.

10 Mercy and truth are met together : righteousness and peace have kissed each other.

11 Truth shall flourish out of the earth : and righteousness hath looked down from heaven.

12 Yea, the Lord shall shew lovingkindness : and our land shall give her increase.

13 Righteousness shall go before him : and he shall direct his going in the way.

℣. Glory be to the Father, and to the Son, and to the Holy Ghost.

℞. As it was in the beginning, is now, and ever shall be, world without end. Amen.

Misericórdia, et véritas obviavérunt sibi: * justítia, et pax osculátæ sunt.

Véritas de terra orta est: * et justítia de cælo prospéxit.

Étenim Dóminus dabit benignitátem: * et terra nostra dabit fructum suum.

Justítia ante eum ambulábit: * et ponet in via gressus suos.

℣. Glória Patri, et Fílio, * et Spirítui Sancto:

℞. Sicut erat in princípio, et nunc, et semper, * et in sǽcula sæculórum. Amen.

Psalm 86

OW down thine ear, O Lord, and hear me : for I am poor, and in misery.

2 Preserve thou my soul, for I am holy : my God, save thy servant that putteth his trust in thee.

3 Be merciful unto me, O Lord : for I will call daily upon thee.

4 Comfort the soul of thy servant : for unto thee, O Lord, do I lift up my soul.

5 For thou, Lord, art good and gracious : and of great mercy unto all them that call upon thee.

6 Give ear, Lord, unto my prayer : and ponder the voice of my humble desires.

NCLÍNA, Dómine, aurem tuam, et exáudi me: * quóniam inops, et pauper sum ego.

Custódi ánimam meam, quóniam sanctus sum: * salvum fac servum tuum, Deus meus, sperántem in te.

Miserére mei, Dómine, quóniam ad te clamávi tota die: * lætífica ánimam servi tui, quóniam ad te, Dómine, ánimam meam levávi.

Quóniam tu, Dómine, suávis, et mitis: * et multæ misericórdiæ ómnibus invocántibus te.

Áuribus pércipe, Dómine, oratiónem meam: * et inténde voci deprecatiónis meæ.

7 In the time of my trouble I will call upon thee : for thou hearest me.

8 Among the gods there is none like unto thee, O Lord : there is not one that can do as thou doest.

9 All nations whom thou hadst made shall come and worship thee, O Lord : and shall glorify thy Name.

10 For thou art great, and doest wondrous things : thou art God alone.

11 Teach me thy way, O Lord, and I will walk in thy truth : O knit my heart unto thee, that I may fear thy Name.

12 I will thank thee, O Lord my God, with all my heart : and will praise thy Name for evermore.

13 For great is thy mercy toward me : and thou hast delivered my soul from the nethermost hell.

14 O God, the proud are risen against me : and the congregations of naughty men have sought after my soul, and have not set thee before their eyes.

15 But thou, O Lord God, art full of compassion and mercy : long-suffering, plenteous in goodness and truth.

16 O turn thee then unto me, and have mercy upon me : give thy strength unto thy servant, and help the son of thine handmaid.

17 Shew some token upon me for good, that they who hate me may see it and be ashamed : because thou, Lord, hast holpen me and comforted me.

℣. Glory be to the Father, and to the Son, and to the Holy Ghost.

℟. As it was in the beginning, is now, and ever shall be, world without end. Amen.

In die tribulatiónis meæ clamávi ad te: * quia exaudísti me.

Non est símilis tui in diis, Dómine: * et non est secúndum ópera tua.

Omnes gentes quascúmque fecísti, vénient, et adorábunt coram te, Dómine: * et glorificábunt nomen tuum.

Quóniam magnus es tu, et fáciens mirabília: * tu es Deus solus.

Deduc me, Dómine, in via tua, et ingrédiar in veritáte tua: * lætétur cor meum ut tímeat nomen tuum.

Confitébor tibi, Dómine, Deus meus, in toto corde meo, * et glorificábo nomen tuum in ætérnum:

Quia misericórdia tua magna est super me: * et eruísti ánimam meam ex inférno inferióri.

Deus, iníqui insurrexérunt super me, et synagóga poténtium quæsiérunt ánimam meam: * et non proposuérunt te in conspéctu suo.

Et tu, Dómine, Deus miserátor et miséricors, * pátiens, et multæ misericórdiæ, et verax,

Réspice in me, et miserére mei, * da impérium tuum púero tuo: et salvum fac fílium ancíllæ tuæ.

Fac mecum signum in bonum, ut vídeant qui odérunt me, et confundántur: * quóniam tu, Dómine, adjuvísti me, et consolátus es me.

℣. Glória Patri, et Fílio, * et Spirítui Sancto:

℟. Sicut erat in princípio, et nunc, et semper, * et in sǽcula sæculórum. Amen.

Psalm 116:10

BELIEVED, and therefore will I speak; but I was sore troubled : I said in my haste, All men are liars.

11 What reward shall I give unto the Lord : for all the benefits that he hath done unto me?

12 I will receive the cup of salvation : and call upon the Name of the Lord.

13 I will pay my vows now in the presence of all his people : right dear in the sight of the Lord is the death of his saints.

14 Behold, O Lord, how that I am thy servant : I am thy servant, and the son of thine handmaid; thou hast broken my bonds in sunder.

15 I will offer to thee the sacrifice of thanksgiving : and will call upon the Name of the Lord.

16 I will pay my vows unto the Lord, in the sight of all his people : in the courts of the Lord's house, even in the midst of thee, O Jerusalem. Praise the Lord.

℣. Glory be to the Father, and to the Son, and to the Holy Ghost.

℟. As it was in the beginning, is now, and ever shall be, world without end. Amen.

RÉDIDI, propter quod locútus sum: * ego autem humiliátus sum nimis.

Ego dixi in excéssu meo: * Omnis homo mendax.

Quid retríbuam Dómino, * pro ómnibus, quæ retríbuit mihi?

Cálicem salutáris accípiam: * et nomen Dómini invocábo.

Vota mea Dómino reddam coram omni pópulo ejus: * pretiósa in conspéctu Dómini mors sanctórum ejus:

O Dómine, quia ego servus tuus: * ego servus tuus, et fílius ancíllæ tuæ.

Dirupísti víncula mea: * tibi sacrificábo hóstiam laudis, et nomen Dómini invocábo.

Vota mea Dómino reddam in conspéctu omnis pópuli ejus: * in átriis domus Dómini, in médio tui, Jerúsalem.

℣. Glória Patri, et Fílio, * et Spirítui Sancto:

℟. Sicut erat in princípio, et nunc, et semper, * et in sǽcula sæculórum. Amen.

Psalm 130

UT of the deep have I called unto thee, O Lord : Lord, hear my voice.

2 O let thine ears consider well : the voice of my complaint.

E profúndis clamávi ad te, Dómine: * Dómine, exáudi vocem meam:

Fiant aures tuæ intendéntes, * in vocem deprecatiónis meæ.

3 If thou, Lord, wilt be extreme to mark what is done amiss : O Lord, who may abide it?

4 For there is mercy with thee : therefore shalt thou be feared.

5 I look for the Lord; my soul doth wait for him : in his word is my trust.

6 My soul fleeth unto the Lord : before the morning watch, I say, before the morning watch.

7 O Israel, trust in the Lord, for with the Lord there is mercy : and with him is plenteous redemption.

8 And he shall redeem Israel : from all his sins.

℣. Glory be to the Father, and to the Son, and to the Holy Ghost.

℞. As it was in the beginning, is now, and ever shall be, world without end. Amen.

EMEMBER not, Lord, our offences, nor the offences of our forefathers; neither take thou vengeance of our sins. (Alleluia.)

℣. Lord, have mercy upon us.

℞. Christ, have mercy upon us.

℣. Lord, have mercy upon us.

❡ The Lord's Prayer is said silently until,

℣. And lead us not into temptation.

℞. But deliver us from evil. Amen.

℣. I said, Lord, be merciful unto me.

℞. Heal my soul; for I have sinned against thee.

℣. Turn thee again, O Lord, at the last.

℞. And be gracious unto thy servants.

℣. O Lord, let thy mercy be shewed upon us.

Si iniquitátes observáveris, Dómine: * Dómine, quis sustinébit?

Quia apud te propitiátio est: * et propter legem tuam sustínui te, Dómine.

Sustínuit ánima mea in verbo ejus: * sperávit ánima mea in Dómino.

A custódia matutína usque ad noctem: * speret Israël in Dómino.

Quia apud Dóminum misericórdia: * et copiósa apud eum redémptio.

Et ipse rédimet Israël, * ex ómnibus iniquitátibus ejus.

℣. Glória Patri, et Fílio, * et Spirítui Sancto:

℞. Sicut erat in princípio, et nunc, et semper, * et in sǽcula sæculórum. Amen.

E reminiscáris, Dómine, delícta nostra, vel paréntum nostrórum, neque vindíctam sumas de peccátis nostris. (Allelúja.)

℣. Kýrie, eléison.

℞. Christe, eléison.

℣. Kýrie, eléison.

℣. Et ne nos indúcas in tentatiónem.

℞. Sed líbera nos a malo. Amen.

℣. Ego dixi: Dómine, miserére mei.

℞. Sana ánimam meam, quia peccávi tibi.

℣. Convértere, Dómine, aliquántulum.

℞. Et deprecáre super servos tuos.

℣. Fiat misericórdia tua, Dómine, super nos.

℟. As we do put our trust in thee.

℣. Let thy priests be clothed with righteousness.

℟. And let thy saints sing with joyfulness.

℣. Cleanse me, O Lord, from my secret faults.

℟. Keep thy servant also from presumptuous sins.

℣. O Lord, hear my prayer.

℟. And let my cry come unto thee.

℣. The Lord be with you.

℟. And with thy spirit.

Let us pray.

OST gracious God, incline thy merciful ears unto our prayers and by the grace of the Holy Spirit illumine our hearts, that we may worthily serve at thy holy Mysteries, and love thee with an everlasting love.

GOD, unto whom all hearts are open, all desires known, and from whom no secrets are hid: cleanse the thoughts of our hearts by the inspiration of thy Holy Spirit, that we may perfectly love thee and worthily magnify thy holy Name.

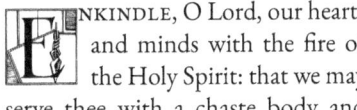NKINDLE, O Lord, our hearts and minds with the fire of the Holy Spirit: that we may serve thee with a chaste body and please thee with a clean heart.

E beseech thee, O Lord, that the Comforter, who proceedeth from thee, may enlighten our minds: and lead us into all truth, as thy Son hath promised.

℟. Quemádmodum sperávimus in te.

℣. Sacerdótes tui induántur justítiam.

℟. Et Sancti tui exsúltent.

℣. Ab occúltis meis munda me, Dómine.

℟. Et ab aliénis parce servo tuo.

℣. Dómine, exáudi oratiónem meam.

℟. Et clamor meus ad te véniat.

℣. Dóminus vobíscum.

℟. Et cum spíritu tuo.

Orémus.

URES tuæ pietátis, mitíssime Deus, inclína précibus nostris, et grátia Sancti Spíritus illúmina cor nostrum: ut tuis mystériis digne ministráre, teque ætérna caritáte dilígere mereámur.

EUS, cui omne cor patet et omnis volúntas lóquitur, et quem nullum latet secrétum: purífica per infusiónem Sancti Spíritus cogitatiónes cordis nostri: ut te perfécte dilígere, et digne laudáre mereámur.

RE igne Sancti Spíritus renes nostros et cor nostrum, Dómine: ut tibi casto córpore serviámus, et mundo corde placeámus.

ENTES nostras, quǽsumus, Dómine, Paráclitus, qui a te procédit, illúminet: et indúcat in omnem, sicut tuus promísit Fílius, veritátem.

DSIT nobis, quǽsumus, Dómine, virtus Spíritus Sancti: quæ et corda nostra cleménter expúrget et ab ómnibus tueátur advérsis.

Eucharistic Devotions

ET the power of the Holy Spirit come upon us, O Lord, we beseech thee: that he may both mercifully cleanse our hearts, and defend us from all adversities.

GOD, who didst teach the hearts of thy faithful people, by sending them the light of thy Holy Spirit: grant us by the same Spirit to have a right judgement in all things, and evermore to rejoice in his holy comfort.

URIFY our consciences, we beseech thee, O Lord, by thy visitation: that our Lord Jesus Christ thy Son, when he cometh, may find in us a mansion prepared for himself. Who with thee, in the unity of the Holy Spirit, liveth and reigneth God, world without end. Amen.

EUS, qui corda fidélium Sancti Spíritus illustratióne docuísti: da nobis in eódem Spíritu recta sápere; et de ejus semper consolatióne gaudére.

ONSCIÉNTIAS nostras, quǽsumus, Dómine, visitándo purífica: ut véniens Dóminus noster Jesus Christus, Fílius tuus, parátam sibi in nobis invéniat mansiónem: Qui tecum vivit et regnat.

PRAYER OF ST. AMBROSE

❡ In the following prayers, the sections in parentheses is said, unless he be a Priest preparing to celebrate Mass, in which case he should always say the text in the margin.

Sunday

[a] *teach me, thy unworthy servant, whom among thy other gifts, not for my own merit, but only our of the worthiness of thy mercy, thou hast deigned to call to the priestly office;*

[b] *handle*

SUPREME High Priest and true Chief Bishop, Jesus Christ, who didst offer thyself to God the Father a pure and spotless Victim upon the Altar of the Cross for us miserable sinners, and who didst give us thy Flesh to eat and thy Blood to drink, and didst ordain that Mystery in the power of the Holy Spirit, saying, This do, as often as ye shall do it, in remembrance of me; I pray thee, by that same Blood of thine, the great price of our salvation; I pray thee, by that wonderful and unspeakable love wherewith thou didst vouchsafe to love us, miserable and unworthy, as to wash us from our sins in thy Blood;[a] teach me, I pray thee, by thy Holy Spirit, to [approach][b] so great a Mystery with such reverence and honour, with such fear and devotion, as are due and fitting. Make me, through thy grace, always so to believe and understand, so to conceive and firmly hold, so to think and speak of this wondrous Mystery, as shall please thee and benefit my own soul. Let thy good Spirit enter into my heart, there silently to sound, and without clamour of words to speak all truth. For exceeding deep are thy Mysteries, and covered with a sacred veil. Of thy great mercy grant me to [assist at]^c the Solemnity of the Mass with a clean heart and *celebrate* a pure mind. Set free my heart from all unclean and unholy, all vain and hurtful thoughts. Defend me with the loving and faithful guard, the mighty protection of thy blessed Angels, that the enemies of all good may go away ashamed. By the virtue of this great Mystery and by the hand of thy holy Angel drive away from me and from all thy servants the hard spirit of pride and vain-glory, of impurity and uncleanness, of doubting and mistrust. Let them be confounded that persecute us: let them perish that make haste to destroy us.

Monday

KING of virgins and lover of chastity and innocence, extinguish in my body, by the dew of thy heavenly blessing, whatever may kindle the burning of wanton desire, that so one even purity of soul and body may abide in me. Mortify in my members the incitements of the flesh, and all lustful emotions, and give me true and persevering chastity with thine other gifts which please thee in truth, so that I may with chaste body and pure heart offer unto thee the sacrifice of praise. For with what contrition of heart and flowing of tears, with what reverence and awe, with what chastity of body and purity of soul, should that divine and heavenly Sacrifice be celebrated, wherein thy Flesh is eaten indeed, where thy Blood is drunk indeed, wherein things lowest and highest, earthly and divine, are united, where the holy Angels are present, where thou art in a marvellous and unspeakable manner both Priest and Sacrifice

Tuesday

HO can worthily [assist at]^d this Sacrifice unless thou, O God, makest him *celebrate* worthy? I know, O Lord, yea, truly do I know, and this do I confess to thy loving-kindness, that I am unworthy to approach so great a Mystery, by reason of my numberless sins and negligences; but I know and truly with my whole heart do I believe, and with my mouth confess, that thou canst make me worthy, who alone canst make clean one conceived of unclean seed, and canst make sinners to be righteous and holy. By this thine almighty power I beseech thee, O my God, to grant that I, a sinner, may [assist at]^e this Sacrifice *celebrate* with fear and trembling, with purity of heart and streams of tears, with spiritual gladness and heavenly joy; may my mind feel the sweetness of thy most blessed Presence, and the guardianship of thy holy Angels round about me.

Wednesday

OR now, O Lord, mindful of thy venerable Passion, I approach thine Altar, to offer thee that Sacrifice which thou hast instituted, and commanded us to offer in remembrance of thee for our salvation. Receive it, I beseech thee, O God Most High, for thy holy Church, and for the people whom thou hast purchased with thy Blood.^f If thou wilt graciously vouchsafe to behold^g the tribulations of the people, the perils of the nations, the groans of prisoners, the miseries of orphans, the necessities of strangers, the helplessness of the weak, the depression of the weary, the infirmities of the aged, the aspirations of the young, the vows of virgins, the lamentations of widows.

^f And since thou hast willed that I, a sinner, should be in the midst between thee and the same thy people, although thou perceivest in me the evidence of no good works, at least refuse not the service of the ministry which thou hast given me; let not the price of their salvation be wasted through my unworthiness, whose saving Victim and redemption thou didst deign to be.

^g Also I bring before thee, O Lord

Thursday

OR thou, O Lord, art merciful unto all and hatest nothing that thou hast made. Remember what is our nature, for thou art our Father, thou art our God. Be not angry with us for ever, nor withhold the multitude of thy mercies from us; for it is not in our righteousness that we humbly present our prayers before thy face, but because of thy great compassion. Take away from us our iniquities, and graciously kindle the fire of thy Holy Spirit within us. Take away our hearts of stone, and give us an heart of flesh, which may love thee, prefer thee, delight in thee, follow thee, and enjoy thee. We pray thee of thy mercy, O Lord, vouchsafe to shew the light of thy countenance unto thy family awaiting the service of thy holy Name; and that the good desires of none may be ineffectual, the petitions of none unfruitful, do thou put into our minds such prayers as thou mayest delight graciously to hear and answer.

Friday

E beseech thee also, O Lord, Holy Father, for the souls of the faithful departed; that this great Sacrament of thy love may be unto them health and salvation, joy and refreshment. Grant them this day, O Lord my God, a great and abundant feast of thee, the living Bread, which camest down from heaven, and givest life unto the world; even of thy holy and blessed Flesh, the Lamb without spot, that takest away the sins of the world; even of that Flesh, which was taken from the holy and glorious womb of the blessed Virgin Mary, and conceived of the Holy Ghost; and of that Fountain of mercy which by the soldier's spear flowed from thy most sacred Side; that after being fed and satisfied, refreshed and comforted, they may rejoice in thy praise and glory.

I pray thy mercy, O Lord, that on the bread to be offered unto thee may descend the fulness of thy blessing and the hallowing of thy Godhead. May there also descend the invisible and incomprehensible majesty of thy Holy Spirit, as it came down of old on the sacrifices of the fathers; which will both make our oblations thy Body and Blood, and teach us, [thy unworthy servants][h] to treat so great a Mystery with purity of heart and with tears of devotion, with reverence and trembling, so that thou mayest graciously and favourably receive this sacrifice[i] for the well-being of all, both living and departed.

[h] *me thy un-worthy priest,*

[i] *at my hands*

Saturday

NTREAT thee also, O Lord, by this most holy mystery of thy Body and Blood, wherewith we are daily fed and given to drink, washed and sanctified in thy Church, and are made partakers of the one supreme Divinity, grant unto me thy holy graces, that fulfilled therewith I may draw near to thine Altar with a good conscience; so that these heavenly Sacraments may be made unto me salvation and life; for thou hast said with thy holy and blessed mouth, 'The bread that I will give is my flesh, which I will give for the life of the world. I am the living bread which came down from heaven. If any man eat of this bread, he shall live for ever.'

O sweetest Bread, heal the palate of my heart, that I may taste the pleasant savour of thy love. Heal it of all infirmities, that I may find sweetness in nothing out of thee. O purest Bread, having all delight and all savour, which ever refreshest us, and never failest, let my heart feed on thee, and may my inmost soul be fulfilled with the sweetness of thy savour. The Angels feed upon thee fully: let the wayfaring man feed on thee according to his measure, that, refreshed with such a Viaticum, he fail not by the way. O holy Bread, O living Bread, O pure Bread, who camest down from heaven, and givest life unto the world, come into my heart, and cleanse me from all defilement of flesh and spirit. Enter into my soul; heal and cleanse me within and without; be the protection and continual health of my soul and body. Drive far from me all foes that lie in wait; Let them flee at the presence of thy power, so that being guarded without and within by thee, I may come to thy kingdom by a straight way: where, not as now in mysteries, but face to face, we shall behold thee: when thou shalt have delivered up the kingdom to God, even the Father, and shalt be God, all in all. Then shalt thou satisfy me with thyself in wondrous fulness, so that I shall never hunger nor thirst any more. Who with the same God the Father and the Holy Ghost livest and reignest, world without end. Amen.

ANOTHER PRAYER OF ST. AMBROSE

TO the Table of thy most sweet Feast, O loving Lord Jesus Christ, I, a sinner, presuming nothing on my own merits, but trusting in thy mercy and goodness, approach with fear and trembling. For my heart and my body are stained with many and grievous sins, my thoughts and my lips have not been carefully kept. Wherefore, O gracious God, O awful majesty, I, in my misery, being brought into a great strait, turn to thee, the Fountain of mercy, to thee I hasten to be healed, and flee under thy protection: and thee, before whom I cannot stand as my Judge, I long to have as my Saviour. To thee, O Lord, I show my wounds, to thee I discover my shame. I know my sins, many and great, for which I am afraid: but I hope in thy mercies, of which there is no end. Look therefore upon me with the eyes of thy mercy, O Lord Jesus Christ, eternal King, God and Man, crucified for man. Hearken unto me whose trust is in thee: have mercy upon me who am full of misery and sin, thou Fountain of mercy that will never cease to flow. Hail, Victim of Salvation, offered for me and for all mankind upon the Altar of the Cross! Hail, noble and precious Blood, flowing from the wounds of my crucified Lord Jesus Christ, and washing away the sins of the whole world! Remember O Lord, thy creature, whom thou hast redeemed with thine own Blood. It repents me that I have sinned, and I desire to amend what I have done. Take away therefore from me, O most merciful Father, all my sins and iniquities; that being purified both in soul and body, I may be made meet worthily to taste the Holy of Holies; and grant that this holy foretaste of thy Body and Blood, which I, unworthy, purpose to take, may be for the remission of my sins; the perfect cleansing of my faults; the driving away of shameful thoughts, and the renewal of good desires; the healthful performance of works well pleasing unto thee; and the most sure protection of soul and body against the wiles of my enemies. Amen.

A DEVOTIONAL PRAYER OF ST. AUGUSTINE

AGAINST thee only have I sinned, O Lord, for no man is without sin: and therefore against thee only have I sinned, because thou alone art without sin. O Lord, who hast so long spared the guilty, shew forth thy mercy upon the miserable offender. Behold the unhappy, O Unfathomable Piety. Regard the cruel ones, O Mercy of All. As one about to despair, I come unto the Almighty. I run, wounded, unto the Physician. Keep, O Lord, the compassion of thy gentleness, who hast so long stayed the sword of vengeance. Blot out the great number of my crimes by the greatness of thy mercy.

Unto thee have I cried, O Lord: and early shall my prayer come before thee. Lord, why abhorrest thou my soul: and hidest thou thy face from me? I am in misery, and like unto him that is at the point to die: even from my youth up thy terrors have I suffered with a troubled mind. Thy wrathful displeasure goeth over me: and the fear of thee hath undone me. They came round about me daily like water: and compassed me together on every side. My lovers and friends hast thou put away from me: and hid mine acquaintance out of my sight.

But thou, O Redeemer of all, ineffable Saviour God, who didst enter hell for us, and wast made free among the dead: hear our morning prayer, and have mercy, O Lord, unto thy family, and deliver us from the most grievous bondage of the lurking enemy. Who livest and reignest with the Father, in the unity of the Holy Ghost, God, throughout all ages, world without end. Amen.

ANOTHER DEVOTIONAL PRAYER BEFORE COMMUNION

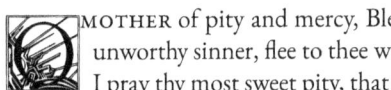MOTHER of pity and mercy, Blessed Virgin Mary, I, a miserable and unworthy sinner, flee to thee with my whole heart and affection, and I pray thy most sweet pity, that as thou didst stand by thy most sweet Son hanging upon the Cross, so thou wouldest vouchsafe mercifully to stand by me a miserable offender and all who here and in all the holy Church offer the Most Holy Sacrifice of the Mass this day, that, aided by thy merits and prayers, we may be enabled to offer a worthy and acceptable Victim in the sight of the most high and undivided Trinity. Amen.

DECLARATION OF INTENTION BEFORE MASS

INTEND to [assist at this celebration of the Mass and at the consecration of][j] the Body and Blood of our Lord Jesus Christ, according to the rite of Holy Church, to the praise of Almighty God, and of the whole Church triumphant; for my own benefit; for the benefit of the whole Church militant and expectant; for all who have commended themselves to my prayers in general and in particular, . . . and for the good estate of the Holy Catholic Church.

[j] *celebrate Mass and to consecrate*

HE Almighty and merciful Lord grant unto us joy with peace, amendment of life, time for true repentance, the grace and comfort of the Holy Ghost, and perseverance in good works. Amen.

Eucharistic Devotions

Thanksgiving for Holy Communion

Ant. Let us sing † the song of the three children, which the Saints sang in the furnace of fire, blessing the Lord (Alleluia).

BENEDICITE

ALL ye Works of the Lord, bless ye the Lord: * praise him, and magnify him for ever.

O ye Angels of the Lord, bless ye the Lord: * O ye heavens, bless ye the Lord.

O ye waters that be above the firmament, bless ye the Lord: * O all ye powers of the Lord, bless ye the Lord.

O ye sun and moon, bless ye the Lord: * O ye stars of heaven, bless ye the Lord.

O ye showers and dew, bless ye the Lord: * O ye winds of God, bless ye the Lord.

O ye fire and heat, bless ye the Lord: * O ye winter and summer, bless ye the Lord.

O ye dews and frosts, bless ye the Lord: * O ye frost and cold, bless ye the Lord.

O ye ice and snow, bless ye the Lord: * O ye nights and days, bless ye the Lord.

O ye light and darkness, bless ye the Lord: * O ye lightnings and clouds, bless ye the Lord.

LET the earth bless the Lord: yea, let it praise him, and magnify him for ever.

O ye mountains and hills, bless ye the Lord: * O all ye green things upon the earth, bless ye the Lord.

O ye wells, bless ye the Lord: * O ye Seas and Floods, bless ye the Lord.

O ye whales, and all that move in the waters, bless ye the Lord: * O all ye fowls of the air, bless ye the Lord.

O all ye beasts and cattle, bless ye the Lord: * O ye children of men, bless ye the Lord.

LET Israel bless the Lord: * praise him, and magnify him for ever.

O ye priests of the Lord, bless ye the Lord: * O ye servants of the Lord, bless ye the Lord.

O ye spirits and souls of the righteous, bless ye the Lord: * O ye holy and humble men of heart, bless ye the Lord.

O Ananias, Azarias, and Misael, bless ye the Lord: * praise him, and magnify him for ever.

ET us bless the Father and the Son with the Holy Ghost: * let us praise him and magnify him for ever.

Blessed art thou, O Lord, in the firmament of heaven: * and to be praised and glorified and exalted above all for ever.

¶ Here neither Glory be nor Amen is said.

PSALM 150

PRAISE God in his holiness : * praise him in the firmament of his power.

2 Praise him in his noble acts : * praise him according to his excellent greatness.

3 Praise him in the sound of the trumpet : * praise him upon the lute and harp.

4 Praise him in the cymbals and dances : * praise him upon the strings and pipe.

5 Praise him upon the well-tuned cymbals : * praise him upon the loud cymbals.

6 Let every thing that hath breath * praise the Lord.

℣. Glory be to the Father, and to the Son, and to the Holy Ghost.

℟. As it was in the beginning, is now, and ever shall be, world without end. Amen.

Ant. Let us sing the song of the three children, which the Saints sang in the furnace of fire, blessing the Lord (Alleluia).

℣. Lord, have mercy upon us.
℟. Christ, have mercy upon us.
℣. Lord, have mercy upon us.

¶ The Lord's Prayer is here said, in secret, kneeling, ending with,

℣. And lead us not into temptation.
℟. But deliver us from evil.
℣. All thy works praise thee, O Lord.
℟. And thy Saints give thanks unto thee.
℣. Let thy Saints be joyful in glory,
℟. Let them rejoice in their beds.
℣. Not unto us, O Lord, not unto us,
℟. But unto thy name give the praise.
℣. O Lord, hear my prayer.
℟. And let my cry come unto thee.
℣. The Lord be with you.
℟. And with thy spirit.

Let us pray.

GOD, who to the three children didst assuage the flames of fire: mercifully grant; that the flames of sin may not kindle upon thy servants.

REVENT us, O Lord, in all our doings with thy most gracious favour, and further us with thy continual help: that all our prayer and work may be begun, continued, and ended in thee.

RANT to us, we beseech thee, O Lord, that we may quench the flames of our sins: as thou didst enable blessed Lawrence to overcome the fires of his torments. Through Christ, our Lord. *Amen.*

Antecommunion

Collect for Purity

¶ The Minister, remaining at his place, saith the Collect for Purity, as followeth, in an audible voice.

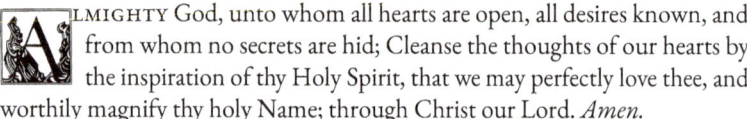

LMIGHTY God, unto whom all hearts are open, all desires known, and from whom no secrets are hid; Cleanse the thoughts of our hearts by the inspiration of thy Holy Spirit, that we may perfectly love thee, and worthily magnify thy holy Name; through Christ our Lord. *Amen.*

¶ Then shall the Minister, turning to the People, rehearse distinctly—in an audible voice—The Ten Commandments; and the People, still kneeling, shall, after every Commandment, ask God mercy for their transgressions for the time past, and grace to keep the law for the time to come.

¶ And NOTE, that in rehearsing the Ten Commandments, the Minister may omit that part of the Commandment which is inset.

¶ The Decalogue may be omitted. But NOTE, That when ever it is omitted, the Minister shall say the Summary of the Law, beginning, Hear what our Lord Jesus Christ saith.

Ten Commandments

God spake these words, and said:

I am the LORD thy God; Thou shalt have none other gods but me.
Lord, have mercy upon us, and incline our hearts to keep this law.
Thou shalt not make to thyself any graven image, nor the likeness of any thing that is in heaven above, or in the earth beneath, or in the water under the earth; thou shalt not bow down to them, nor worship them:
> for I the Lord thy God am a jealous God, and visit the sins of the fathers upon the children, unto the third and fourth generation of them that hate me; and show mercy unto thousands in them that love me and keep my commandments.
Lord, have mercy upon us, and incline our hearts to keep this law.
Thou shalt not take the Name of the Lord thy God in vain;
> for the Lord will not hold him guiltless, that taketh his Name in vain.
Lord, have mercy upon us, and incline our hearts to keep this law.
Remember that thou keep holy the Sabbath-day.
> Six days shalt thou labour, and do all that thou hast to do; but the seventh day is the Sabbath of the Lord thy God. In it thou shalt do no manner of work; thou, and thy son, and thy daughter, thy man-servant, and thy maid-servant, thy cattle,

and the stranger that is within thy gates. For in six days the Lord made heaven and earth, the sea, and all that in them is, and rested the seventh day: wherefore the Lord blessed the seventh day, and hallowed it.

Lord, have mercy upon us, and incline our hearts to keep this law.
Honour thy father and thy mother;
> that thy days may be long in the land which the Lord thy God giveth thee.

Lord, have mercy upon us, and incline our hearts to keep this law.
Thou shalt do no murder.

Lord, have mercy upon us, and incline our hearts to keep this law.
Thou shalt not commit adultery.

Lord, have mercy upon us, and incline our hearts to keep this law.
Thou shalt not steal.

Lord, have mercy upon us, and incline our hearts to keep this law.
Thou shalt not bear false witness against thy neighbour.

Lord, have mercy upon us, and incline our hearts to keep this law.
Thou shalt not covet.
> thy neighbour's house, thou shalt not covet thy neighbour's wife, nor his servant, nor his maid, nor his ox, nor his ass, nor any thing that is his.

Lord, have mercy upon us, and write all these thy laws in our hearts, we beseech thee.

❡ Then may the Minister say the Summary of the Law, as followeth, in an audible voice.

SUMMARY OF THE LAW

HEAR WHAT OUR LORD JESUS CHRIST SAITH.

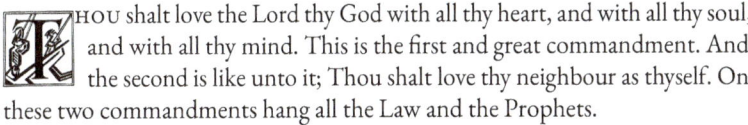HOU shalt love the Lord thy God with all thy heart, and with all thy soul, and with all thy mind. This is the first and great commandment. And the second is like unto it; Thou shalt love thy neighbour as thyself. On these two commandments hang all the Law and the Prophets.

❡ Then shall the Minister, signing himself with the sign of the Cross, begin the Introit: which finished, with joined hands, he saith alternately with the other Ministers the Kyrie,

KYRIE

℣. Lord, have mercy upon us.
℞. Lord, have mercy upon us.
℣. Lord, have mercy upon us.
℞. Christ, have mercy upon us.

℣. Kyrie, eléison.
℞. Kyrie, eléison.
℣. Kyrie, eléison.
℞. Christe, eléison.

℣. Christ, have mercy upon us. ℣. Christe, eléison.
℟. Christ, have mercy upon us. ℟. Christe, eléison.
℣. Lord, have mercy upon us. ℣. Kyrie, eléison.
℟. Lord, have mercy upon us. ℟. Kyrie, eléison.
℣. Lord, have mercy upon us. ℣. Kyrie, eléison.

GLORIA IN EXCELSIS

¶ Then the Minister shall extend and join his hands and—bowing his head slightly—say, if it is to be said,

LORY be to God on high, and on earth peace, good will towards men. We praise thee, *a Bow head.* we bless thee, we worship thee,[a] we *b Bow head.* glorify thee, we give thanks[b] to thee for thy great glory, O Lord God, heavenly King, God the Father Almighty.

O Lord, the only-begotten Son, Jesus Christ; O Lord God, Lamb of God, Son of the Father, that takest away the sins of the world, have mercy upon us. Thou that takest away the sins of the *c Bow head.* world, receive our prayer.[c] Thou that sittest at the right hand of God the Father, have mercy upon us.

For thou only art holy; thou only art the Lord; thou only, O Christ, with the Holy Ghost, ✠ art most high in the glory of God the Father. Amen.

LÓRIA in excélsis Deo. Et in terra pax homínibus bonæ voluntátis. Laudámus te. Benedícimus te. Adorámus te.[a] Glorificámus te. Grátias ágimus tibi[b] propter magnam glóriam tuam. Dómine Deus, Rex cæléstis, Deus Pater omnípotens.

Dómine Fili unigénite, Jesu Christe. Dómine Deus, Agnus Dei, Fílius Patris. Qui tollis peccáta mundi, miserére nobis. Qui tollis peccáta mundi, súscipe deprecatiónem nostram.[c] Qui sedes ad déxteram Patris, miserére nobis.

Quóniam tu solus Sanctus. Tu solus Dóminus. Tu solus Altíssimus, Jesu Christe. Cum Sancto Spíritu ✠ in glória Dei Patris. Amen.

¶ Then shall the Minister turn to the People and say,

℣. O Lord, hear our prayer. ℣. Dómine, exáudi oratiónem nostram.
℟. And let our cry come unto thee.
℣. Let us pray. ℟. Et clamor noster ad te véniat.
℣. Orémus.

144

Eucharistic Devotions *Antecommunion*

COLLECT

❡ Then shall the Minister pray the Collect(s) of the Day.

EPISTLE

❡ The Epistle for the Day shall then be read by the Minister, first saying, The Epistle is written in the – Chapter of –, beginning at the – Verse.

❡ The Epistle ended, he shall say, Here endeth the Epistle, the People responding, Thanks be to God.

❡ The Gradual and Alleluia (or Tract) and (if provided) Sequence is here chanted by the Choir.

GOSPEL

❡ Then, all the People standing, the Minister shall say with joined hands,

℣. O Lord, hear our prayer.
℟. And let our cry come unto thee.
℣. The Beginning (or, Continuation) ✝ of the Holy Gospel according to N.
℟. Glory be to thee, O Lord.

℣. Dómine, exáudi oratiónem nostram.
℟. Et clamor noster ad te véniat.
℣. Inítium (vel, Sequéntia) ✝ sancti Evangélii secúndum N.
℟. Glória tibi, Dómine.

❡ Then shall the Minister sign himself on the forehead, the mouth, and the breast: then readeth the Gospel with joined hands.

❡ At the end of the Gospel, the Ministers respond,

℟. Praise be to thee, O Christ.

℟. Laus tibi, Christe.

❡ Then the Minister shall say, if it is to be said, I believe in one God, proceeding with joined hands.

NICENE CREED

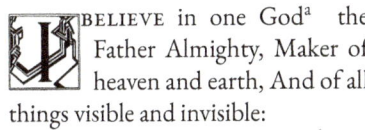BELIEVE in one God[a] the Father Almighty, Maker of heaven and earth, And of all things visible and invisible: And in one Lord Jesus Christ,[b] the only-begotten Son of God; Begotten of his Father before all worlds, God

REDO in unum Deum,[a] Patrem omnipoténtem, factórem cæli et terræ, visibílium ómnium et invisibílium.

Et in unum Dóminum Jesum Christum,[b] Fílium Dei unigénitum. Et ex Patre natum ante ómnia sæcu-

[a] *Bow head to Cross.*

[b] *Bow head to Cross.*

of God, Light of Light, Very God of very God; Begotten, not made; Being of one substance with the Father; By whom all things were made: Who for us men and for our salvation came down from heaven, (Everyone genuflects.) And was incarnate by the Holy Ghost of the Virgin Mary, And was made man: (Everyone rises.) And was crucified also for us under Pontius Pilate; He suffered and was buried: And the third day he rose again according to the Scriptures: And ascended into heaven, And sitteth on the right hand of the Father: And he shall come again, with glory, to judge both the quick and the dead; Whose kingdom shall have no end.

And I believe in the Holy Ghost, The Lord, and Giver of Life, Who proceedeth from the Father; Who with the Father and the Son together is worshiped[c] and glorified; Who spake by the Prophets: And I believe one, holy, catholic, and apostolic Church: I acknowledge one Baptism for the remission of sins: And I look for the Resurrection of the dead: ✠ And the Life of the world to come. Amen.

[c] Bow head to Cross.

la. Deum de Deo, lumen de lúmine, Deum verum de Deo vero. Génitum, non factum, consubstantiálem Patri: per quem ómnia facta sunt. Qui propter nos hómines et propter nostram salútem descéndit de cælis. (Everyone genuflects.) Et incarnátus est de Spíritu Sancto ex María Vírgine: Et homo factus est. (Everyone rises.) Crucifíxus étiam pro nobis: sub Póntio Piláto passus, et sepúltus est. Et resurréxit tértia die, secúndum Scriptúras. Et ascéndit in cælum: sedet ad déxteram Patris. Et íterum ventúrus est cum glória judicáre vivos et mórtuos: cujus regni non erit finis.

Et in Spíritum Sanctum, Dóminum et vivificántem: qui ex Patre procédit. Qui cum Patre et Fílio simul adorátur[c] et conglorificátur: qui locútus est per Prophétas. Et unam sanctam cathólicam et apostólicam Ecclésiam. Confíteor unum baptísma in remissiónem peccatórum. Et exspécto resurrectiónem mortuórum. ✠ Et vitam ventúri sǽculi. Amen.

¶ Then shall be declared unto the People what Holy-days, or Fasting-days, are in the week following to be observed; and (if occasion be) shall Notice be given of the Communion, and of the Banns of Matrimony, and other matters to be published.

¶ Here, or immediately after the Creed, may be said the Bidding Prayer, or other authorised Prayers and intercessions.

¶ Then followeth the Sermon.

¶ After the Sermon, Antecommunion is concluded with the Additional Collects (p. 79).

Propers of the
Church Year

First Sunday of Advent

First Class Semidouble

ALMIGHTY God, give us grace that we may cast away the works of darkness, and put upon us the armour of light, now in the time of this mortal life, in which thy Son Jesus Christ came to visit us in great humility; that in the last day, when he shall come again in his glorious majesty to judge both the quick and the dead, we may rise to the life immortal, through him who liveth and reigneth with thee and the Holy Ghost, now and ever. *Amen.*

¶ This Collect is to be repeated every day, with the other Collects in Advent, until Christmas Day.

Second Sunday of Advent

Second Class Semidouble

BLESSED Lord, who hast caused all holy Scriptures to be written for our learning; Grant that we may in such wise hear them, read, mark, learn, and inwardly digest them, that by patience and comfort of thy holy Word, we may embrace, and ever hold fast, the blessed hope of everlasting life, which thou hast given us in our Saviour Jesus Christ. Who liveth.

Third Sunday of Advent

Second Class Semidouble

O LORD Jesus Christ, who at thy first coming didst send thy messenger to prepare thy way before thee; Grant that the ministers and stewards of thy mysteries may likewise so prepare and make ready thy way, by turning the hearts of the disobedient to the wisdom of the just, that at thy second coming to judge the world we may be found an acceptable people in thy sight, who livest and reignest with the Father and the Holy Spirit ever one God, world without end. *Amen.*

Ember Wednesday in Advent

Greater Feria

GRANT, we beseech thee, almighty God: that the coming solemnity of our redemption may bestow on us thy succour in this present life, and win for us the rewards of everlasting blessedness. Through.

148

EMBER FRIDAY IN ADVENT

Greater Feria

TIR up, we beseech thee, O Lord, thy power, and come among us: that they who put their confidence in thy goodness may speedily be delivered from all adversity. Who livest.

EMBER SATURDAY IN ADVENT

Greater Feria

GOD, who seest us that we are afflicted by reason of our iniquity: mercifully grant; that we may be comforted by thy visitation. Who livest.

FOURTH SUNDAY OF ADVENT

Second Class Semidouble

LORD, raise up, we pray thee, thy power, and come among us, and with great might succour us; that whereas, through our sins and wickedness, we are sore let and hindered in running the race that is set before us, thy bountiful grace and mercy may speedily help and deliver us; through the satisfaction of thy Son our Lord, to whom, with thee and the Holy Ghost, be honour and glory, world without end. *Amen.*

VIGIL OF THE NATIVITY OF OUR LORD

First Class Vigil

Opening Sentence. To-morrow shall the wickedness of the earth be done away. And the Saviour of the world shall be King over us.

GOD, who makest us glad with the yearly expectation of our redemption: vouchsafe; that as we joyfully receive thine Only-begotten Son for our Redeemer, so we may with sure confidence behold him when he shall come to be our judge, even Jesus Christ thy Son our Lord. Who liveth.

NATIVITY OF OUR LORD

First Class Double, Third Class Octave

LMIGHTY God, who hast given us thy only begotten Son to take our nature upon him, and as at this time to be born of a Holy Virgin; Grant that we being regenerate, and made thy children by adoption and grace, may daily be renewed by thy holy Spirit; through the same our Lord Jesus Christ, who liveth and reigneth with thee and the same Spirit ever, one God, world without end. *Amen.*

 RANT, we beseech thee, almighty God: that we who devoutly keep the festival of thy blessed Martyr Anastasia; may know her to be our advocate with thee. Through.

ST. STEPHEN

26 December
Second Class Double, Simple Octave

Opening Sentence. The righteous shall flourish like a palm-tree: and shall spread abroad like a cedar in Libanus.

 RANT, O Lord, that, in all our sufferings here upon earth for the testimony of thy truth, we may stedfastly look up to heaven, and by faith behold the glory that shall be revealed; and, being filled with the Holy Ghost, may learn to love and bless our persecutors by the example of thy first Martyr Saint Stephen, who prayed for his murderers to thee, O blessed Jesus, who standest at the right hand of God to succour all those who suffer for thee, our only Mediator and Advocate. *Amen.*

ST. JOHN

27 December
Second Class Double, Simple Octave

Opening Sentence. Greatly to be had in honour is blessed John. For he leaned on the Lord's bosom at Supper.

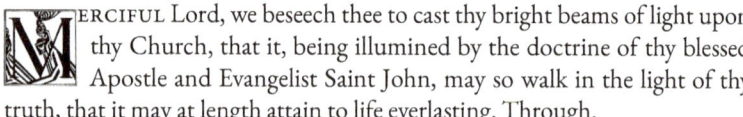 ERCIFUL Lord, we beseech thee to cast thy bright beams of light upon thy Church, that it, being illumined by the doctrine of thy blessed Apostle and Evangelist Saint John, may so walk in the light of thy truth, that it may at length attain to life everlasting. Through.

HOLY INNOCENTS

28 December
Second Class Double, Simple Octave

Opening Sentence. The righteous live for evermore. Their reward also is with the Lord.

ALMIGHTY God, who out of the mouths of babes and sucklings hast ordained strength, and madest infants to glorify thee by their deaths: Mortify and kill all vices in us, and so strengthen us by thy grace, that by the innocency of our lives, and constancy of our faith even unto death, we may glorify thy holy Name. Through.

SUNDAY WITHIN THE NATIVITY OCTAVE

Semidouble

ALMIGHTY God, who hast given us thy only-begotten Son to take our nature upon him, and as at this time to be born of a pure virgin: Grant that we being regenerate, and made thy children by adoption and grace, may daily be renewed by thy Holy Spirit; through the same our Lord Jesus Christ, who liveth and reigneth with thee and the same Spirit ever, one God, world without end. *Amen.*

GRANT, we beseech thee, almighty God: that we, who through our ancient bondage are held beneath the yoke of sin; may by the new Birth of thy only-begotten Son in the flesh obtain deliverance. Through the same.

CIRCUMCISION OF OUR LORD

1 January
Second Class Double

Opening Sentence. The Word was made flesh and dwelt among us. Alleluia.

ALMIGHTY God, who madest thy blessed Son to be circumcised, and obedient to the law for man; Grant us the true circumcision of the Spirit; that, our hearts, and all our members, being mortified from all worldly and carnal lusts, we may in all things obey thy blessed will; through the same thy Son Jesus Christ our Lord. Who liveth.

❡ The same Collect shall serve for every day after unto the Epiphany.

Most Holy Name of Jesus

2 January
Second Class Double

Opening Sentence. Our help is in the Name of the Lord who hath made heaven and earth.

GOD, who didst appoint thine only-begotten Son to be the Saviour of mankind, and didst command that he should be called JESUS: mercifully grant; that as we venerate his holy name on earth, so we may rejoice to behold him in heaven. Through the same.

❡ Commemoration of the Octave Day of St. Stephen, as followeth,

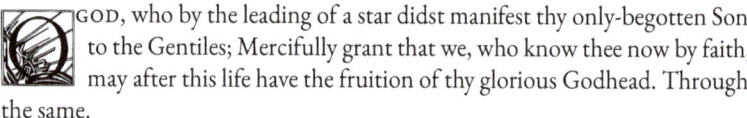LMIGHTY and everlasting God, who, in the blood of the blessed Levite Stephen, didst consecrate the first-fruits of the Martyrs: grant, we beseech thee; that he may intercede for us, who prayed even for his persecutors to our Lord Jesus Christ, thy Son. Who liveth and reigneth with thee.

Second Sunday after Nativity

The Sunday between Circumcision & Epiphany, if there be one.
Semidouble

LMIGHTY God, who hast poured upon us the new light of thine incarnate Word; Grant that the same light enkindled in our hearts may shine forth in our lives. Through.

Epiphany of Our Lord

First Class Double, Second Class Octave

GOD, who by the leading of a star didst manifest thy only-begotten Son to the Gentiles; Mercifully grant that we, who know thee now by faith, may after this life have the fruition of thy glorious Godhead. Through the same.

❡ This Collect to be said daily throughout the Octave.

Sunday within the Octave of the Epiphany

Semidouble

O LORD, we beseech thee mercifully to receive the prayers of thy people who call upon thee: and grant that they may both perceive and know what things they ought to do, and also may have grace and power faithfully to fulfil the same. Through.

❡ *Commemoration is made of the Epiphany (p. 152).*

Baptism of Our Lord

(Octave Day of the Epiphany)

Greater Double

O GOD, whose only-begotten Son hath been made manifest in substance of our flesh: grant, we beseech thee; that, as we have known him after the fashion of our outward likeness, so through him we may be made worthy inwardly to be renewed. Who liveth.

Second Sunday after Epiphany

Semidouble

A LMIGHTY and everlasting God, who dost govern all things in heaven and earth; Mercifully hear the supplications of thy people, and grant us thy peace all the days of our life. Through.

Third Sunday after Epiphany

Semidouble

A LMIGHTY and everlasting God, mercifully look upon our infirmities, and in all our dangers and necessities stretch forth thy right hand to help and defend us. Through.

Fourth Sunday after Epiphany

Semidouble

O GOD, who knowest us to be set in the midst of so many and great dangers, that by reason of the frailty of our nature we cannot always stand upright; Grant to us such strength and protection, as may support us in all dangers, and carry us through all temptations. Through.

Proper of Season

FIFTH SUNDAY AFTER EPIPHANY

Semidouble

LORD, we beseech thee to keep thy Church and household continually in thy true religion; that they who do lean only upon the hope of thy heavenly grace may evermore be defended by thy mighty power. Through.

SIXTH SUNDAY AFTER EPIPHANY

Semidouble

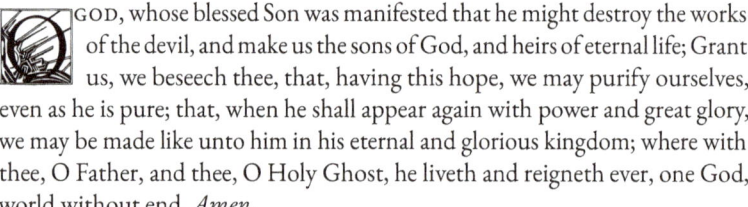GOD, whose blessed Son was manifested that he might destroy the works of the devil, and make us the sons of God, and heirs of eternal life; Grant us, we beseech thee, that, having this hope, we may purify ourselves, even as he is pure; that, when he shall appear again with power and great glory, we may be made like unto him in his eternal and glorious kingdom; where with thee, O Father, and thee, O Holy Ghost, he liveth and reigneth ever, one God, world without end. *Amen.*

¶ If there be more than six Sundays of Epiphany before Septuagesima, then the upcoming unused Sundays after Trinity are used.

SEPTUAGESIMA SUNDAY

Second Class Semidouble

LORD, we beseech thee favourably to hear the prayers of thy people; that we, who are justly punished for our offences, may be mercifully delivered by thy goodness, for the glory of thy Name; through Jesus Christ our Saviour, who liveth and reigneth with thee and the Holy Ghost ever, one God, world without end. *Amen.*

SEXAGESIMA SUNDAY

Second Class Semidouble

GOD, who seest that we put not our trust in any thing that we do: mercifully grant; that by the protection of the Doctor of the Gentiles we may be defended against all adversity. Through.

QUINQUAGESIMA SUNDAY

Second Class Semidouble

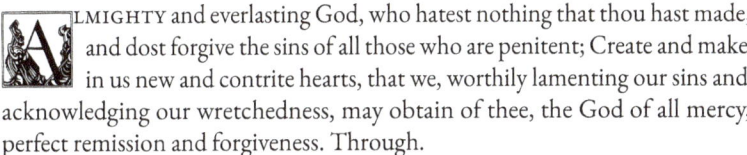LORD, who hast taught us that all our doings without charity are nothing worth; Send thy Holy Ghost, and pour into our hearts that most excellent gift of charity, the very bond of peace and of all virtues, without which whosoever liveth is counted dead before thee. Grant this for thine only Son Jesus Christ's sake. Who liveth.

ASH WEDNESDAY

First Class Feria

❡ On Ash Wednesday, during the Order of Morning Prayer, the Great Litany (p. 86) should said in its appropriate place after the Third Collect followed by A Penitential Office (p. 91).

LMIGHTY and everlasting God, who hatest nothing that thou hast made, and dost forgive the sins of all those who are penitent; Create and make in us new and contrite hearts, that we, worthily lamenting our sins and acknowledging our wretchedness, may obtain of thee, the God of all mercy, perfect remission and forgiveness. Through.

❡ This Collect is to be said every day in Lent, after the Collect appointed for the day, until Palm Sunday.

❡ The Propers of Ash Wednesday shall serve for every day after, unto the next Sunday, except upon a Feast Day.

FIRST SUNDAY OF LENT

First Class Semidouble

LORD, who for our sake didst fast forty days and forty nights; Give us grace to use such abstinence, that, our flesh being subdued to the Spirit, we may ever obey thy godly motions in righteousness, and true holiness, to thy honour and glory, who livest and reignest with the Father and the Holy Ghost, one God, world without end. *Amen.*

EMBER WEDNESDAY IN LENT

Second Class Feria

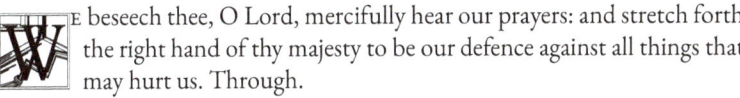E beseech thee, O Lord, mercifully hear our prayers: and stretch forth the right hand of thy majesty to be our defence against all things that may hurt us. Through.

Proper of Season

EMBER FRIDAY IN LENT

Second Class Feria

E favourable, O Lord, to thy people: and mercifully comfort with thy gracious help those whom thou dost make to do thee godly service. Through.

EMBER SATURDAY IN LENT

Second Class Feria

E beseech thee, O Lord, graciously look upon thy people: and mercifully turn away from them the scourges of thy wrath. Through.

SECOND SUNDAY OF LENT

First Class Semidouble

LMIGHTY God, who seest that we have no power of ourselves to help ourselves; Keep us both outwardly in our bodies, and inwardly in our souls; that we may be defended from all adversities which may happen to the body, and from all evil thoughts which may assault and hurt the soul. Through.

THIRD SUNDAY OF LENT

First Class Semidouble

E beseech thee, Almighty God, look upon the hearty desires of thy humble servants, and stretch forth the right hand of thy Majesty, to be our defence against all our enemies. Through.

FOURTH SUNDAY OF LENT

First Class Semidouble

RANT, we beseech thee, Almighty God, that we, who for our evil deeds do worthily deserve to be punished, by the comfort of thy grace may mercifully be relieved; through our Lord and Saviour Jesus Christ. Who liveth.

PASSION SUNDAY

First Class Semidouble

E beseech thee, Almighty God, mercifully to look upon thy people; that by thy great goodness they may be governed and preserved evermore, both in body and soul. Through.

PALM SUNDAY

First Class Semidouble

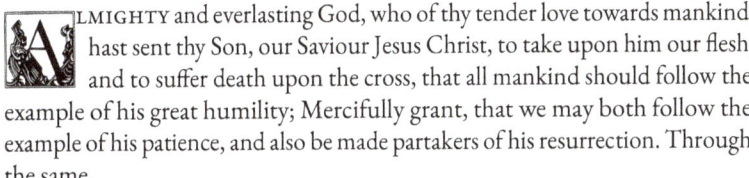LMIGHTY and everlasting God, who of thy tender love towards mankind, hast sent thy Son, our Saviour Jesus Christ, to take upon him our flesh, and to suffer death upon the cross, that all mankind should follow the example of his great humility; Mercifully grant, that we may both follow the example of his patience, and also be made partakers of his resurrection. Through the same.

¶ This Collect is to be said every day, after the Collect appointed for the day, until Good Friday.

HOLY MONDAY

LMIGHTY God, whose most dear Son went not up to joy but first he suffered pain, and entered not into glory before he was crucified; Mercifully grant that we, walking in the way of the cross, may find it none other than the way of life and peace. Through the same.

HOLY TUESDAY

LORD God, whose blessed Son, our Saviour, gave his back to the smiters and hid not his face from shame; Grant us grace to take joyfully the sufferings of the present time, in full assurance of the glory that shall be revealed. Through the same.

SPY WEDNESDAY

SSIST us mercifully with thy help, O Lord God of our salvation; that we may enter with joy upon the meditation of those mighty acts, whereby thou hast given unto us life and immortality. Through.

Proper of Season

MAUNDY THURSDAY

LMIGHTY Father, whose dear Son, on the night before he suffered, did institute the Sacrament of his Body and Blood; Mercifully grant that we may thankfully receive the same in remembrance of him, who in these holy mysteries giveth us a pledge of life eternal; through the same thy Son Jesus Christ our Lord, who now liveth and reigneth with thee and the Holy Spirit ever, one God, world without end. *Amen.*

GOOD FRIDAY

LMIGHTY God, we beseech thee graciously to behold this thy family, for which our Lord Jesus Christ was contented to be betrayed and given up into the hands of wicked men, and to suffer death upon the cross; who now liveth and reigneth with thee and the Holy Ghost ever, one God, world without end. *Amen.*

LMIGHTY and everlasting God, by whose Spirit the whole body of the Church is governed and sanctified; Receive our supplications and prayers, which we offer before thee for all estates of men in thy holy Church, that every member of the same, in his vocation and ministry, may truly and godly serve thee. Through.

MERCIFUL God, who hast made all men, and hatest nothing that thou hast made, nor desirest the death of a sinner, but rather that he should be converted and live; Have mercy upon all Jews, Turks, infidels, and heretics; and take from them all ignorance, hardness of heart, and contempt of thy Word; and so fetch them home, blessed Lord, to thy flock, that they may be saved among the remnant of the true Israelites, and be made one fold under one shepherd, Jesus Christ our Lord, who liveth and reigneth with thee and the Holy Spirit, one God, world without end. *Amen.*

EASTER EVEN

RANT, O Lord, that as we are baptized into the death of thy blessed Son, our Saviour Jesus Christ, so by continual mortifying our corrupt affections we may be buried with him; and that through the grave, and gate of death, we may pass to our joyful resurrection; for his merits, who died, and was buried, and rose again for us, the same thy Son Jesus Christ our Lord. Who with thee.

EASTER DAY

First Class Double, First Class Octave

Pascha Nostrum

¶ At Morning Prayer, instead of the **Venite**, the following shall be said, and may be said throughout the Octave.

CHRIST our Passover is sacrificed for us : therefore let us keep the feast, Not with old leaven, neither with the leaven of malice and wickedness : but with the unleavened bread of sincerity and truth. (1 Cor. 5:7)

CHRIST being raised from the dead dieth no more : death hath no more dominion over him.

For in that he died, he died unto sin once : but in that he liveth, he liveth unto God.

Likewise reckon ye also yourselves to be dead indeed unto sin : but alive unto God through Jesus Christ our Lord. (Rom. 6:9)

CHRIST is risen from the dead : and become the firstfruits of them that slept.

For since by man came death : by man came also the resurrection of the dead.

For as in Adam all die : even so in Christ shall all be made alive. (1 Cor. 15:20)

℣. Glory be to the Father, and to the Son : and to the Holy Ghost;

℟. As it was in the beginning, is now, and ever shall be: world without end. Amen.

Collect

ALMIGHTY God, who through thine only-begotten Son Jesus Christ hast overcome death, and opened unto us the gate of everlasting life; We humbly beseech thee that, as by thy special grace preventing us thou dost put into our minds good desires, so by thy continual help we may bring the same to good effect; through the same Jesus Christ our Lord, who liveth and reigneth with thee and the Holy Ghost ever, one God, world without end. *Amen.*

¶ This Collect is to be said daily throughout the Easter Octave.

Proper of Season

EASTER MONDAY

First Class Double

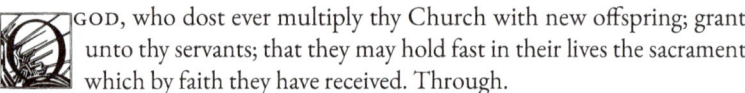

GOD, who by the paschal solemnity hast bestowed healing upon the world: prosper, we beseech thee, thy people with thy heavenly gift; that they may be worthy to attain unto perfect freedom, and may likewise be profited unto everlasting life. Through.

❡ Commemoration of Easter Day (p. 159).

EASTER TUESDAY

First Class Double

GOD, who dost ever multiply thy Church with new offspring; grant unto thy servants; that they may hold fast in their lives the sacrament which by faith they have received. Through.

❡ Commemoration of Easter Day (p. 159).

EASTER WEDNESDAY

Semidouble

GOD, who dost gladden us with the yearly solemnity of the Resurrection of the Lord: mercifully grant; that through this temporal feast which we observe, we may be found worthy to attain unto everlasting joys. Through the same.

❡ Commemoration of Easter Day (p. 159).

EASTER THURSDAY

Semidouble

GOD, who hast united the diversity of nations in the confession of thy name: grant that they who are born again in the font of Baptism may agree in unity of faith and in godliness of conversation. Through.

❡ Commemoration of Easter Day (p. 159).

EASTER FRIDAY

Semidouble

LMIGHTY and everlasting God, who hast bestowed the paschal sacrament for a pledge of man's reconciliation: grant unto our hearts; that what we celebrate in outward profession we may effectually fulfil. Through.

❡ Commemoration of Easter Day (p. 159).

EASTER SATURDAY

Semidouble

RANT, we beseech thee, almighty God: that we who have devoutly kept this paschal festival may thereby be found worthy to attain to everlasting joys. Through.

❡ Commemoration of Easter Day (p. 159).

LOW SUNDAY

First Class Double, Octave Day of Easter

LMIGHTY Father, who hast given thine only Son to die for our sins, and to rise again for our justification; Grant us so to put away the leaven of malice and wickedness, that we may always serve thee in pureness of living and truth; through the merits of the same thy Son Jesus Christ our Lord. Who with.

SECOND SUNDAY AFTER EASTER

Semidouble

LMIGHTY GOD, who hast given thine only Son to be unto us both a sacrifice for sin, and also an ensample of godly life; Give us grace that we may always most thankfully receive that his inestimable benefit, and also daily endeavour ourselves to follow the blessed steps of his most holy life. Through the same.

Proper of Season

PATRONAGE OF ST. JOSEPH

Wednesday after the Second Sunday after Easter
First Class Double, Simple Octave

Opening Sentence. He made him lord also of his house : and ruler of all his substance.

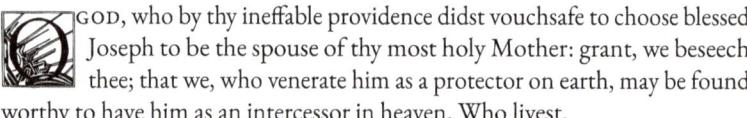GOD, who by thy ineffable providence didst vouchsafe to choose blessed Joseph to be the spouse of thy most holy Mother: grant, we beseech thee; that we, who venerate him as a protector on earth, may be found worthy to have him as an intercessor in heaven. Who livest.

THIRD SUNDAY AFTER EASTER

Semidouble

ALMIGHTY God, who showest to them that are in error the light of thy truth, to the intent that they may return into the way of righteousness; Grant unto all those who are admitted into the fellowship of Christ's Religion, that they may avoid those things that are contrary to their profession, and follow all such things as are agreeable to the same. Through.

FOURTH SUNDAY AFTER EASTER

Semidouble

ALMIGHTY God, who alone canst order the unruly wills and affections of sinful men; Grant unto thy people, that they may love the thing which thou commandest, and desire that which thou dost promise; that so, among the sundry and manifold changes of the world, our hearts may surely there be fixed, where true joys are to be found. Through.

ROGATION SUNDAY

Semidouble

LORD, from whom all good things do come; Grant to us thy humble servants, that by thy holy inspiration we may think those things that are good, and by thy merciful guiding may perform the same. Through.

ROGATION DAYS

❡ Rogation Monday is a 2nd Feria. Rogation Tuesday is a Feria.

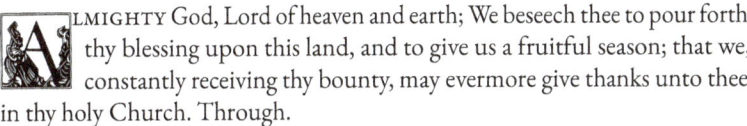LMIGHTY God, Lord of heaven and earth; We beseech thee to pour forth thy blessing upon this land, and to give us a fruitful season; that we, constantly receiving thy bounty, may evermore give thanks unto thee in thy holy Church. Through.

VIGIL OF ASCENSION

Vigil

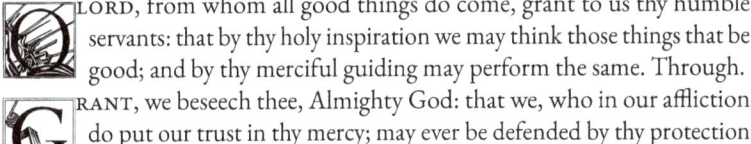LORD, from whom all good things do come, grant to us thy humble servants: that by thy holy inspiration we may think those things that be good; and by thy merciful guiding may perform the same. Through.

RANT, we beseech thee, Almighty God: that we, who in our affliction do put our trust in thy mercy; may ever be defended by thy protection against all adversities. (Through.)

ASCENSION THURSDAY

First Class Double, Third Class Octave

RANT, we beseech thee, Almighty God, that like as we do believe thy only-begotten Son our Lord Jesus Christ to have ascended into the heavens; so we may also in heart and mind thither ascend, and with him continually dwell, who liveth and reigneth with thee and the Holy Ghost, one God, world without end. *Amen.*

SUNDAY WITHIN THE ASCENSION OCTAVE

Semidouble

GOD, the King of glory, who hast exalted thine only Son Jesus Christ with great triumph unto thy kingdom in heaven; We beseech thee, leave us not comfortless; but send to us thine Holy Ghost to comfort us, and exalt us unto the same place whither our Saviour Christ is gone before, who liveth and reigneth with thee and the Holy Ghost, one God, world without end. *Amen.*

❡ Commemoration of Ascension Thursday, as followeth,

RANT, we beseech thee, almighty God: that like as we do believe thy only-begotten Son our Lord Jesus Christ to have ascended into the heavens; so we may also in heart and mind thither ascend and with him continually dwell. Who liveth and reigneth with thee.

Proper of Season

WHITSUNDAY

First Class Double, First Class Octave

GOD, who as at this time didst teach the hearts of thy faithful people, by sending to them the light of thy Holy Spirit; Grant us by the same Spirit to have a right judgment in all things, and evermore to rejoice in his holy comfort. Through.

WHIT-MONDAY

First Class Double

SEND, we beseech thee, Almighty God, thy Holy Spirit into our hearts, that he may direct and rule us according to thy will, comfort us in all our afflictions, defend us from all error, and lead us into all truth; through Jesus Christ our Lord, who with thee and the same Holy Spirit liveth and reigneth, one God, world without end. *Amen.*

WHIT-TUESDAY

First Class Double

RANT, we beseech thee, merciful God, that thy Church, being gathered together in unity by thy Holy Spirit, may manifest thy power among all peoples, to the glory of thy Name; through Jesus Christ our Lord, who liveth and reigneth with thee and the same Spirit, one God, world without end. *Amen.*

EMBER WEDNESDAY IN WHITSUNTIDE

Semidouble

E beseech thee, O Lord, that the Paraclete, who proceedeth from thee, may enlighten our minds: and lead us, as thy Son hath promised, into all truth; Who liveth.

WHIT-THURSDAY

Semidouble

OD, who as at this time didst teach the hearts of thy faithful people, by sending to them the light of thy Holy Spirit; grant us by the same Spirit to have a right judgment in all things, and evermore to rejoice in his holy comfort. Through.

164

EMBER FRIDAY IN WHITSUNTIDE

Semidouble

RANT, we beseech thee, O merciful God, to thy Church: that, being gathered together in the Holy Ghost, she may be disturbed by no assaults of the enemy. Through.

EMBER SATURDAY IN WHITSUNTIDE

Semidouble

E beseech thee, O Lord, graciously pour the Holy Ghost into our hearts: by whose wisdom we were created, and by whose providence we are governed. Through.

TRINITY SUNDAY

First Class Double

LMIGHTY and everlasting God, who hast given unto us thy servants grace by the confession of a true faith to acknowledge the glory of the eternal Trinity, and in the power of the Divine Majesty to worship the Unity: We beseech thee; that thou wouldest keep us stedfast in this faith, and evermore defend us from all adversities. Who livest and reignest, one God, world without end. *Amen.*

THE MOST HOLY BODY OF CHRIST

Thursday after Trinity Sunday
First Class Double, Second Class Octave

Opening Sentence. Thou gavest them Bread from heaven. Containing in itself all sweetness.

GOD, who under a wonderful sacrament hast left unto us a memorial of thy Passion: grant us, we beseech thee, so to venerate the sacred mysteries of thy Body and Blood; that we may ever perceive within ourselves the fruit of thy redemption. Who livest and reignest with God the Father.

Proper of Season

SUNDAY IN THE OCTAVE OF CORPUS CHRISTI

(First Sunday after Trinity)

Semidouble

GOD, the strength of all those who put their trust in thee, mercifully accept our prayers: and because through the weakness of our mortal nature we can do no good thing without thee, grant us the help of thy grace; that in keeping thy commandments we may please thee, both in will and deed. Through.

¶ Commemoration of the Most Holy Body of Christ, as followeth.

GOD, who under a wonderful sacrament hast left unto us a memorial of thy Passion: grant us, we beseech thee, so to venerate the sacred mysteries of thy Body and Blood; that we may ever perceive within ourselves the fruit of thy redemption. Who livest and reignest with God the Father.

COMPASSION OF OUR LORD JESUS CHRIST

Friday after Trinity I
Second Class Double, Simple Octave

Opening Sentence. The Lord is full of compassion and mercy: long-suffering, and of great goodness.

GOD, who in the Heart of thy Son, wounded by our sins, dost vouchsafe mercifully to bestow upon us the infinite treasures of love: grant, we beseech thee; that we, giving him the homage of our devotion and piety, may likewise perform the duty of worthy satisfaction. Through the same.

SECOND SUNDAY AFTER TRINITY

Semidouble

LORD, who never failest to help and govern those whom thou dost bring up in thy stedfast fear and love; Keep us, we beseech thee, under the protection of thy good providence, and make us to have a perpetual fear and love of thy holy Name. Through.

THIRD SUNDAY AFTER TRINITY

Semidouble

LORD, we beseech thee mercifully to hear us; and grant that we, to whom thou hast given an hearty desire to pray, may, by thy mighty aid, be defended and comforted in all dangers and adversities. Through.

FOURTH SUNDAY AFTER TRINITY

Semidouble

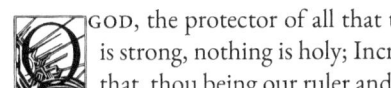GOD, the protector of all that trust in thee, without whom nothing is strong, nothing is holy; Increase and multiply upon us thy mercy; that, thou being our ruler and guide, we may so pass through things temporal, that we finally lose not the things eternal. Grant this, O heavenly Father, for the sake of Jesus Christ our Lord. Who liveth.

FIFTH SUNDAY AFTER TRINITY

Semidouble

RANT, O Lord, we beseech thee, that the course of this world may be so peaceably ordered by thy governance, that thy Church may joyfully serve thee in all godly quietness. Through.

SIXTH SUNDAY AFTER TRINITY

Semidouble

GOD, who hast prepared for them that love thee such good things as pass man's understanding: pour into our hearts such love toward thee: that we, loving thee above all things, may obtain thy promises, which exceed all that we can desire. Through.

SEVENTH SUNDAY AFTER TRINITY

Semidouble

ORD of all power and might, who art the author and giver of all good things; Graft in our hearts the love of thy Name, increase in us true religion, nourish us with all goodness, and of thy great mercy keep us in the same. Through.

Proper of Season

EIGHTH SUNDAY AFTER TRINITY

Semidouble

GOD, whose never-failing providence ordereth all things both in heaven and earth; We humbly beseech thee to put away from us all hurtful things, and to give us those things which are profitable for us. Through.

NINTH SUNDAY AFTER TRINITY

Semidouble

RANT to us, Lord, we beseech thee, the spirit to think and do always such things as be rightful: that we, who cannot exist without thee; may by thee be enabled to live according to thy will. Through.

TENTH SUNDAY AFTER TRINITY

Semidouble

ET thy merciful ears, O Lord, be open to the prayers of thy humble servants; and that they may obtain their petitions make them to ask such things as shall please thee. Through.

ELEVENTH SUNDAY AFTER TRINITY

Semidouble

GOD, who declarest thy almighty power chiefly in showing mercy and pity; Mercifully grant unto us such a measure of thy grace, that we, running the way of thy commandments, may obtain thy gracious promises, and be made partakers of thy heavenly treasure. Through.

TWELFTH SUNDAY AFTER TRINITY

Semidouble

LMIGHTY and everlasting God, who art always more ready to hear than we to pray, and art wont to give more than either we desire or deserve; Pour down upon us the abundance of thy mercy; forgiving us those things whereof our conscience is afraid, and giving us those good things which we are not worthy to ask, but through the merits and mediation of Jesus Christ, thy Son, our Lord. Who liveth.

THIRTEENTH SUNDAY AFTER TRINITY

Semidouble

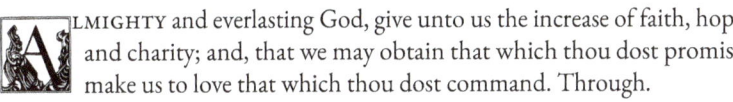

LMIGHTY and merciful God, of whose only gift it cometh that thy faithful people do unto thee true and laudable service; Grant, we beseech thee, that we may so faithfully serve thee in this life, that we fail not finally to attain thy heavenly promises. Through.

FOURTEENTH SUNDAY AFTER TRINITY

Semidouble

LMIGHTY and everlasting God, give unto us the increase of faith, hope, and charity; and, that we may obtain that which thou dost promise, make us to love that which thou dost command. Through.

FIFTEENTH SUNDAY AFTER TRINITY

Semidouble

EEP, we beseech thee, O Lord, thy Church with thy perpetual mercy; and, because the frailty of man without thee cannot but fall, keep us ever by thy help from all things hurtful, and lead us to all things profitable to our salvation. Through.

SIXTEENTH SUNDAY AFTER TRINITY

Semidouble

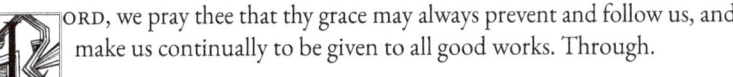

LORD, we beseech thee, let thy continual pity cleanse and defend thy Church; and, because it cannot continue in safety without thy succour, preserve it evermore by thy help and goodness. Through.

SEVENTEENTH SUNDAY AFTER TRINITY

Semidouble

ORD, we pray thee that thy grace may always prevent and follow us, and make us continually to be given to all good works. Through.

Proper of Season

EIGHTEENTH SUNDAY AFTER TRINITY

Semidouble

ORD, we beseech thee, grant thy people grace to withstand the temptations of the world, the flesh, and the devil; and with pure hearts and minds to follow thee, the only God. Through.

NINETEENTH SUNDAY AFTER TRINITY

Semidouble

GOD, forasmuch as without thee we are not able to please thee; Mercifully grant that thy Holy Spirit may in all things direct and rule our hearts. Through.

TWENTIETH SUNDAY AFTER TRINITY

Semidouble

ALMIGHTY and most merciful God, of thy bountiful goodness keep us, we beseech thee, from all things that may hurt us; that we, being ready both in body and soul, may cheerfully accomplish those things which thou commandest. Through.

TWENTY-FIRST SUNDAY AFTER TRINITY

Semidouble

RANT, we beseech thee, merciful Lord, to thy faithful people pardon and peace, that they may be cleansed from all their sins, and serve thee with a quiet mind. Through.

TWENTY-SECOND SUNDAY AFTER TRINITY

Semidouble

ORD, we beseech thee to keep thy household the Church in continual godliness; that through thy protection it may be free from all adversities, and devoutly given to serve thee in good works, to the glory of thy Name. Through.

Twenty-Third Sunday after Trinity

Semidouble

GOD, our refuge and strength, who art the author of all godliness; Be ready, we beseech thee, to hear the devout prayers of thy Church; and grant that those things which we ask faithfully we may obtain effectually. Through.

Twenty-Fourth Sunday after Trinity

Semidouble

❡ If this Sunday be hindered by the Sunday Next before Advent, it is anticipated on Saturday with all the privileges proper to a Sunday occurring.

LORD, we beseech thee, absolve thy people from their offences; that through thy bountiful goodness we may all be delivered from the bands of those sins, which by our frailty we have committed. Through.

Sunday Next before Advent

Semidouble

TIR up, we beseech thee, O Lord, the wills of thy faithful people; that they, plenteously bringing forth the fruit of good works, may by thee be plenteously rewarded. Through.

St. Andrew

Second Class Double
30 November

Opening Sentence. The Lord loved Andrew in the odour of sweetness.

E humbly entreat thy majesty, O Lord: that as blessed Andrew the Apostle was to thy Church a preacher and governor; so he may be a perpetual intercessor for us in thy sight. Through.

❡ In Advent, Commemoration is made of the Feria.

Conception of the Blessed Virgin Mary

Second Class Double with a Common Octave
8 December

GOD, mercifully hear the supplication of thy servants; that we who are assembled together on the Conception of the Virgin Mother of God, may at her intercession be delivered by thee from the dangers which beset us. Through.

❡ In Advent, Commemoration is made of the Feria.

St. Thomas

Second Class Double
21 December

RANT us, we beseech thee, O Lord, to glory in the solemnity of thy blessed Apostle Thomas: that we may ever be succoured by his protection; and follow his faith with worthy devotion. Through.

❡ Commemoration of the Feria.

CONVERSION OF ST. PAUL

Greater Double
25 January

Opening Sentence. Thou hast given an heritage unto those that fear thy Name, O Lord.

GOD, who, through the preaching of the blessed Apostle Saint Paul, hast caused the light of the Gospel to shine throughout the world; Grant, we beseech thee, that we, having his wonderful conversion in remembrance, may show forth our thankfulness unto thee for the same, by following the holy doctrine which he taught. Through.

GOD, who didst bestow upon thy blessed Apostle Peter the keys of the kingdom of heaven, and didst appoint unto him the high priesthood of binding and loosing: vouchsafe; that by the help of his intercession we may be delivered from the bonds of our iniquities. Who livest.

PURIFICATION OF THE BLESSED VIRGIN MARY

Second Class Double
2 February

Opening Sentence. It was revealed unto Simeon by the Holy Ghost, that he should not see death, until he had seen the Lord's Christ.

LMIGHTY and everliving God, we humbly beseech thy Majesty, that, as thy only-begotten Son was this day presented in the temple in substance of our flesh, so we may be presented unto thee with pure and clean hearts. By the same thy Son Jesus Christ our Lord. Who liveth.

ST. SCHOLASTICA

Second Class Double
10 February

GOD, who didst reveal in a vision the soul of blessed Scholastica thy Virgin entering heaven in the likeness of a dove, that thou mightest shew the way of the undefiled: grant us by the aid of her merits and prayers so innocently to live, that we may worthily attain unto joys eternal. Through.

173

CHAIR OF ST. PETER AT ANTIOCH

Second Class Double
22 February

Opening Sentence. That they would exalt him also in the congregation of the people : and praise him in the seat of the elders!

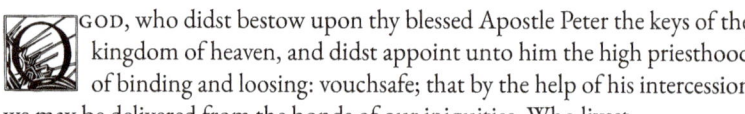GOD, who didst bestow upon thy blessed Apostle Peter the keys of the kingdom of heaven, and didst appoint unto him the high priesthood of binding and loosing: vouchsafe; that by the help of his intercession we may be delivered from the bonds of our iniquities. Who livest.

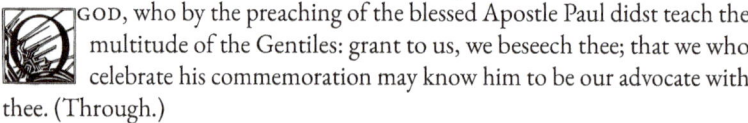GOD, who by the preaching of the blessed Apostle Paul didst teach the multitude of the Gentiles: grant to us, we beseech thee; that we who celebrate his commemoration may know him to be our advocate with thee. (Through.)

❡ In Lent, Commemoration is made of the Feria.

❡ If this Feast fall on a Saturday—not in a Leap Year—the following Commemoration is made of the Vigil of St. Matthias.

RANT, we beseech thee, almighty God: that the venerable solemnity of blessed Matthias thine Apostle, which we here prevent, may increase our devotion and set forward our salvation. Through.

ST. MATTHIAS

Second Class Double
24 February (25 February in a Leap Year)

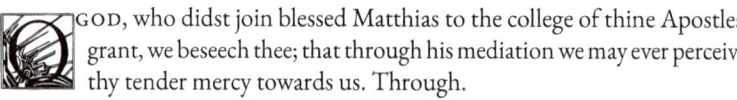GOD, who didst join blessed Matthias to the college of thine Apostles: grant, we beseech thee; that through his mediation we may ever perceive thy tender mercy towards us. Through.

❡ In Lent, Commemoration is made of the Feria.

Pope St. Gregory

Second Class Double
12 March

GOD, who on the soul of thy servant Gregory, hast bestowed the rewards of everlasting bliss: mercifully grant; that we, who are oppressed by the burden of our sins, may by his prayers before thee be relieved. Through.

❧ In Lent, Commemoration is made of the Feria.

St. Joseph, Spouse of the Blessed Virgin Mary

First Class Double
19 March

E beseech thee, O Lord, that we may be aided through the merits of the Spouse of thy most holy Mother: that those things, which by our own power we cannot obtain, may through his intercession be granted unto us. Who livest.

❧ In Lent, Commemoration is made of the Feria.

St. Benedict

Second Class Double
21 March

LMIGHTY and everlasting God, who on this day didst release thy most blessed Confessor Benedict from the bondage of the flesh and take him up to heaven, grant, we beseech thee, to us thy servants who celebrate this feast pardon of all our sins, that we who with joyful hearts take pleasure in his renown may for his sake, and at his intercession, have fellowship with him. Through.

❧ In Lent, Commemoration is made of the Feria.

ANNUNCIATION OF THE BLESSED VIRGIN MARY

First Class Double
25 March

Opening Sentence. Send, O Lord, the Lamb, the Ruler of the land. From the rock of the wilderness unto the mountain of the daughter of Sion.

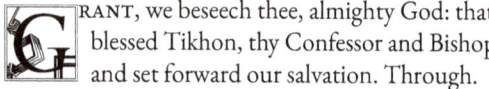GOD, who wast pleased that thy Word should take flesh of the womb of the Blessed Virgin Mary at the message of an Angel: grant to thy humble servants; that we who believe her to be truly the Mother of God may be aided by her intercession in thy sight. Through the same.

❡ In Lent, Commemoration is made of the Feria.

❡ NOTE, If any Feast fall during Holy Week or the Easter Octave, it is transferred to the next available day.

ST. TIKHON OF MOSCOW

First Class Double with a Common Octave
7 April

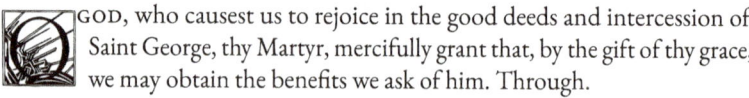RANT, we beseech thee, almighty God: that the venerable solemnity of blessed Tikhon, thy Confessor and Bishop may increase our devotion and set forward our salvation. Through.

❡ In Lent, Commemoration is made of the Feria.

ST. GEORGE

First Class Double with a Common Octave
23 April

GOD, who causest us to rejoice in the good deeds and intercession of Saint George, thy Martyr, mercifully grant that, by the gift of thy grace, we may obtain the benefits we ask of him. Through.

❡ In Lent, Commemoration is made of the Feria.

St. Mark

Second Class Double
25 April

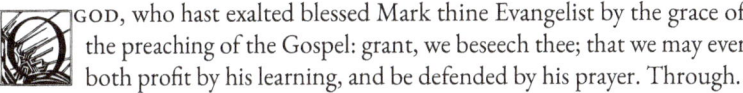 GOD, who hast exalted blessed Mark thine Evangelist by the grace of the preaching of the Gospel: grant, we beseech thee; that we may ever both profit by his learning, and be defended by his prayer. Through.

¶ In Lent, Commemoration is made of the Feria.

Sts. Philip & James

Second Class Double
1 May

Opening Sentence. He was known of them in breaking of bread. Alleluia.

ALMIGHTY God, whom truly to know is everlasting life; Grant us perfectly to know thy Son Jesus Christ to be the way, the truth, and the life; that, following the steps of thy holy Apostles, Saint Philip and Saint James, we may stedfastly walk in the way that leadeth to eternal life through the same thy Son Jesus Christ our Lord. Who liveth.

Invention of the Holy Cross

Second Class Double
3 May

Opening Sentence. Tell it out among the nations that the Lord reigneth from the tree.

GOD, who in the wondrous Finding of the Cross of salvation didst renew the miracles of thy Passion: vouchsafe; that by the ransom of the tree of life we may attain thy succour unto life eternal. Who livest.

¶ On 3 May, Commemoration of Sts. Alexander, Eventius, Theodulus, & Juvenalis, as followeth,

RANT, we beseech thee, almighty God: that we, who devoutly celebrate the birthday of thy Saints Alexander, Eventius, Theodulus, and Juvenal; may, by their intercession, be delivered from all evils that beset us. Through.

ST. JOHN BEFORE THE LATIN GATE

Greater Double
6 May

GOD, who seest that we are beset by evils on every side: grant, we beseech thee; that the glorious intercession of blessed John, thine Apostle and Evangelist, may protect us. Through.

ST. BARNABAS

Greater Double
11 June

E beseech thee, O Lord, let the prayers of thy Apostle, Saint Barnabas, commend thy Church to thee, and let him continue to intercede for her whom by his doctrine and death he doth glorify. Through.

ST. JOHN BAPTIST

First Class Double with a Common Octave
24 June

Opening Sentence. There was a man sent from God whose name was John.

LMIGHTY God, by whose providence thy servant John Baptist was wonderfully born, and sent to prepare the way of thy Son our Saviour by preaching repentance; Make us so to follow his doctrine and holy life, that we may truly repent according to his preaching; and after his example constantly speak the truth, boldly rebuke vice, and patiently suffer for the truth's sake. Through the same.

Proper of Saints

STS. PETER & PAUL

(St. Peter)

First Class Double with a Common Octave

29 June

Opening Sentence. Thou art Peter and upon this rock I will build my Church.

GOD, who hast hallowed this day by the martyrdom of thine Apostles Peter and Paul: grant unto thy Church in all things to follow the commandment of those; through whom she received the beginning of religion. Through.

ALMIGHTY God, who by thy Son Jesus Christ didst give to thy Apostle Saint Peter many excellent gifts, and commandedst him earnestly to feed thy flock; Make, we beseech thee, all Bishops and Pastors diligently to preach thy holy Word, and the people obediently to follow the same, that they may receive the crown of everlasting glory. Through the same.

COMMEMORATION OF ST. PAUL THE APOSTLE

Greater Double

30 June

GOD, who by the preaching of the blessed Apostle Paul didst teach the multitude of the Gentiles: grant to us, we beseech thee; that we who celebrate his birthday (commemoration) may know him to be our advocate with thee. Through.

❧ Commemoration of St. Peter is made before all other Commemorations.

GOD, who didst bestow upon thy blessed Apostle Peter the keys of the kingdom of heaven, and didst appoint unto him the high priesthood of binding and loosing: vouchsafe; that by the help of his intercession we may be delivered from the bonds of our iniquities. (Who livest.)

❧ Commemoration is also made of the Octave of St. John (p. 178).

The Most Precious Blood of Our Lord Jesus Christ

Second Class Double
1 July

Opening Sentence. We therefore pray thee, help thy servants, whom thou hast redeemed with thy precious blood.

ALMIGHTY and everlasting God, who didst appoint thine only-begotten Son to be the Redeemer of the world, and hast vouchsafed to be reconciled to us by his Blood: grant us, we beseech thee, so to venerate with solemn worship the price of our salvation, that by its power we may be defended from the evils of this present life on earth; and may rejoice in the everlasting fruit thereof in heaven. Through.

❡ Commemoration is made of the Octave Day of St. John Baptist (p. 178).

Visitation of the Blessed Virgin Mary

Second Class Double
2 July

WE beseech thee, O Lord, to grant unto us thy servants the gift of heavenly grace: that as the child-bearing of the blessed Virgin was unto us the beginning of salvation; so the devout observance of her Visitation may bestow on us an increase of peace. Through.

❡ On 2 July, Commemoration of St. John of San Francisco, as followeth,

WE beseech thee, O Lord, graciously to hear the prayers which we offer unto thee on the solemnity of blessed John, thy Confessor and Bishop: that, like as he was found worthy to do thee faithful service, so by his merits and intercession we may be absolved from all our sins. Through.

❡ On 2 July, Commemoration of Sts. Processus and Martinian, as followeth,

O GOD, who dost encompass and protect us by the glorious confession of thy holy Martyrs Processus and Martinian: grant us both to profit by their example, and to rejoice in their intercession. Through.

ST. MARY MAGDALENE, PENITENT

Greater Double
22 July

Opening Sentence. Mary hath chosen that good part, which shall not be taken away from her.

RANT us, most merciful Father, like as St. Mary Magdalene, by loving thy Only Begotten Son above all things, obtained forgiveness of her sins, so she may procure for us in thy compassionate presence everlasting blessedness. Through.

ST. JAMES

Second Class Double
25 July

E thou, O Lord, the sanctifier and guardian of thy people, that under the protection of thy Apostle, James, they may please thee in their conversation, and serve thee in all quietness. Through.

¶ On 25 July, Commemoration of St. Christopher, as followeth,

RANT, we beseech thee, almighty God: that we, who devoutly celebrate the birthday of blessed Christopher, thy Martyr, may by his intercession be stablished in the love of thy name. Through.

ST. ANNE

Second Class Double
26 July

GOD, who on blessed Anne didst vouchsafe to bestow grace, that she might be made worthy to become the mother of her who bore thine only-begotten Son: mercifully grant; that we, who celebrate her festival (commemoration) may be aided by her intercession with thee. Through the same.

St. Peter in Chains

Greater Double
1 August

Opening Sentence. I will call upon the Lord, which is worthy to be praised. So shall I be saved from mine enemies.

GOD, who didst deliver blessed Peter the Apostle from his chains, and didst cause him to depart unhurt: loose, we beseech thee, the chains of our sins; and graciously keep from us all evils. Through.

¶ Commemoration of St. Paul, as followeth,

GOD, who by the preaching of the blessed Apostle Paul didst teach the multitude of the Gentiles: grant to us, we beseech thee; that we who celebrate his commemoration may know him to be our advocate with thee. (Through.)

¶ Commemoration of the Holy Maccabees, as followeth,

LORD, let the crown of the brethren, thy Martyrs, cause us to rejoice: that we may thereby be strengthened and increased in our faith; and comforted by their manifold intercession. Through.

Transfiguration of Our Lord Jesus Christ

Second Class Double
6 August

Opening Sentence. Let us worship the Father, the Son, and the Holy Ghost, reigning in his Majesty.

GOD, who on this day didst reveal from heaven thine only-begotten Son, transfigured in a wonderful manner, to the fathers of both testaments, grant unto us, we beseech thee, that by actions acceptable unto thee we may attain unto the perpetual contemplation of his glory in whom thou hast testified that thou, the Father, wast well pleased. Through the same.

GOD, who on the mount didst reveal to chosen witnesses thine only-begotten Son wonderfully transfigured, in raiment white and glistering; Mercifully grant that we, being delivered from the disquietude of this world, may be permitted to behold the King in his beauty, who with thee, O Father, and thee, O Holy Ghost, liveth and reigneth, one God, world without end. *Amen.*

❡ On 6 August, Commemoration of Sts. Sixtus II, Felicissimus, & Agapitus, as followeth,

GOD, who vouchsafest unto us to celebrate the birthday of thy holy Martyrs Sixtus, Felicissimus, and Agapitus: grant that we may rejoice in the everlasting felicity of their fellowship. Through.

Most Holy Name of Jesus Christ

Second Class Double
7 August

❡ The propers are the same as on the Christmastide Feast Day of the same name (p. 152).

St. Lawrence

Second Class Double with Simple Octave
10 August

Opening Sentence. He hath dispersed abroad, and given to the poor : and his righteousness remaineth for ever.

RANT to us, we beseech thee, almighty God: that we may quench the flames of our sins; as thou didst enable blessed Lawrence to overcome the fires of his torments. Through.

Assumption of the Blessed Virgin Mary

First Class Double with Common Octave
15 August

E beseech thee, O Lord, let us be continually aided by the sacred feast of this day, whereon the holy Mother of God underwent death in this world, and yet could not be holden by the chains of death: who did bring forth thy Son our Lord. Who liveth.

St. Joachim, Father of the Blessed Virgin Mary

Second Class Double
16 August

GOD, who from amongst all thy Saints didst choose blessed Joachim to be the father of the Mother of thy Son: grant, we beseech thee; that we who venerate his festival may also continually perceive his advocacy. Through the same.

ST. BARTHOLOMEW

Second Class Double
24 August

ALMIGHTY and everlasting God, who didst give to thine Apostle Bartholomew grace truly to believe and to preach thy Word; Grant, we beseech thee, unto thy Church to love that Word which he believed, and both to preach and receive the same. Through.

DECOLLATION OF ST. JOHN BAPTIST

Greater Double
29 August

WE beseech thee, O Lord: that the venerable festival of thy Forerunner and Martyr, Saint John Baptist, may effectually bestow upon us thy succour unto our salvation. Who livest.

¶ Commemoration of St. Sabina, as followeth,

GOD, who among the manifold works of thy power hast bestowed even upon the weakness of women the victory of martyrdom: mercifully grant; that we, who celebrate the birthday of blessed Sabina, thy Virgin and Martyr, may by her example be drawn nearer unto thee. Through.

NATIVITY OF THE BLESSED VIRGIN MARY

Second Class Double with a Simple Octave
8 September

Opening Sentence. The Lord shall come down like the rain into a fleece of wool. Even as the drops that water the earth.

WE beseech thee, O Lord, to grant unto us thy servants the gift of heavenly grace: that as the childbearing of the blessed Virgin was unto us the beginning of salvation; so the devout observance of her Nativity may bestow an increase of peace. Through.

EXALTATION OF THE HOLY CROSS

Greater Double
14 September

 GOD, who on this day dost gladden us with the yearly solemnity of the exaltation of the holy Cross: grant, we beseech thee; that as we have known the mystery of thy Son on earth, so we may attain unto the rewards of his redemption in heaven. Through the same

EMBER WEDNESDAY IN AUTUMN

Second Class Feria
Wednesday after the Exaltation of the Holy Cross (14 September)
On this day and the following Friday and Saturday, no Feast is kept unless it be a First or Second Class Double.

 E beseech thee, O Lord, that our frailty may be upheld by the healing of thy loving kindness: that what by its own nature is ready to decay, may by thy mercy be renewed. Through.

EMBER FRIDAY IN AUTUMN

Second Class Feria
Friday after Ember Wednesday

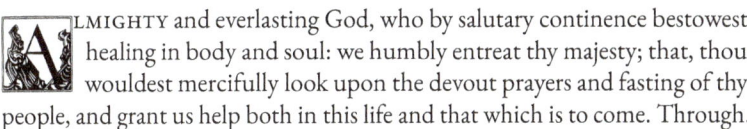 RANT, we beseech thee, almighty God: that we, who year by year devoutly keep this holy observance, may be acceptable unto thee both in body and in soul. Through.

EMBER SATURDAY IN AUTUMN

Second Class Feria
Saturday after Ember Friday

LMIGHTY and everlasting God, who by salutary continence bestowest healing in body and soul: we humbly entreat thy majesty; that, thou wouldest mercifully look upon the devout prayers and fasting of thy people, and grant us help both in this life and that which is to come. Through.

Seven Sorrows of the Blessed Virgin Mary

Second Class Double
15 September

GOD, in whose passion according to the prophecy of Simeon, a sword of sorrow did pierce the most sweet soul of the glorious Virgin Mother Mary: mercifully grant; that we, who devoutly call to mind her sorrows, may obtain the blessed effects of thy passion. Who livest.

¶ On 15 September, Commemoration of St. Nicomedes, as followeth,

SSIST, O Lord, thy people: that as they do profit by the glorious merits of blessed Nicomedes thy Martyr, so his advocacy may at all times succour them to the obtaining of thy mercy. Through.

St. Matthew

Second Class Double
21 September

Opening Sentence. Thou hast given an heritage unto those that fear thy Name, O Lord.

AY we be assisted, O Lord, by the prayers of blessed Matthew, the Apostle and Evangelist: that those things, which of ourselves we cannot obtain, may be vouchsafed unto us by his intercession. Through.

St. Michael

First Class Double
29 September

Opening Sentence. The smoke of the incense ascended up before God out of the Angel's hand.

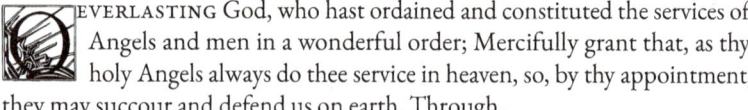EVERLASTING God, who hast ordained and constituted the services of Angels and men in a wonderful order; Mercifully grant that, as thy holy Angels always do thee service in heaven, so, by thy appointment, they may succour and defend us on earth. Through.

HOLY GUARDIAN ANGELS

Greater Double

2 October

Opening Sentence. O praise the Lord, ye Angels of his. Ye that excel in strength, and hearken unto the voice of his words.

GOD, who of thy ineffable providence dost vouchsafe to send thy holy Angels to be our guardians: grant unto us thy humble servants; that we may ever both be defended by their protection, and rejoice in their everlasting fellowship. Through.

HOLY ROSARY OF THE BLESSED VIRGIN MARY

Greater Double

7 October

GOD, whose only-begotten Son by his life, death, and resurrection hath purchased for us the rewards of everlasting salvation: grant, we beseech thee; that we, who meditate upon these mysteries in the most sacred Rosary of the blessed Virgin Mary, may both imitate those things which they set forth, and attain unto those things which they promise. Through.

❡ Commemoration of St. Mark of Rome, as followeth,

RACIOUSLY hear our prayers, O Lord: and at the intercession of blessed Mark, thy Confessor and Bishop, mercifully grant us pardon and peace. Through.

❡ Commemoration of Sts. Sergius, Bacchus, Marcellus, & Apuleius, as followeth,

AY the blessed merits of thy holy Martyrs Sergius, Bacchus, Marcellus, and Apuleius uphold us, O Lord: and ever make us fervent in thy love. Through.

MOTHERHOOD OF THE BLESSED VIRGIN MARY

Second Class Double

11 October

GOD, who wast pleased that thy Word should take flesh of the womb of the Blessed Virgin Mary at the message of an Angel: grant to thy humble servants; that we, who believe her to be truly the Mother of God, may be aided by her intercession in thy sight. Through the same.

OUR LADY OF WALSINGHAM

Double
15 October

Opening Sentence. How dreadful is this place! this is none other but the house of God, and this is the gate of heaven.

GOD, who in the blessed Virgin Mary didst make a fit dwelling-place for thy Son: grant, we beseech thee, that we who honour her shrine at Walsingham may also become temples of thy Holy Ghost. Through the same.

ST. LUKE

Second Class Double
18 October

E beseech thee, O Lord: that thy holy Evangelist Luke may intercede for us: who for the honour of thy name continually bare in his own body the mortification of the Cross. Through.

ST. RAPHAEL

Greater Double
24 October

Opening Sentence. And there appeared an angel unto him from heaven strengthening him.

GOD, who didst give blessed Raphael the Archangel unto thy servant Tobias for a companion on his way: grant to us thy servants; that we may ever be guarded by his protection and strengthened by his help. Through.

STS. SIMON AND JUDE

Second Class Double
28 October

LMIGHTY God, who hast built thy Church upon the foundation of the Apostles and Prophets, Jesus Christ himself being the head cornerstone; Grant us so to be joined together in unity of spirit by their doctrine, that we may be made an holy temple acceptable unto thee. Through.

Our Lord Jesus Christ the King

First Class Double
Last Sunday in October

Opening Sentence. All power is given unto me in heaven and in earth.

ALMIGHTY and everlasting God, who in thy beloved Son, the King of all, hast been pleased to make all things new: mercifully grant; that all the families of the Gentiles, dispersed by the wounds of sin, may be made subject to his most gracious governance. Who liveth.

❡ Commemoration is made of the Sunday occurring.

All Hallows

Second Class Double
1 November

Opening Sentence. The righteous live for evermore, but their reward is with the Lord.

ALMIGHTY and everlasting God, who in one solemnity hast vouchsafed unto us to venerate the merits of all thy Saints: we beseech thee; that, at the intercession of so great a multitude, thou wouldest bestow upon us, who entreat thee, the abundance of thy mercy. Through.

All Souls

Double
2 November

❡ The Office of the Dead is said, with the relevant rubrics for All Souls' Day.

189

Through the Year

EVENSONG

Office Hymn

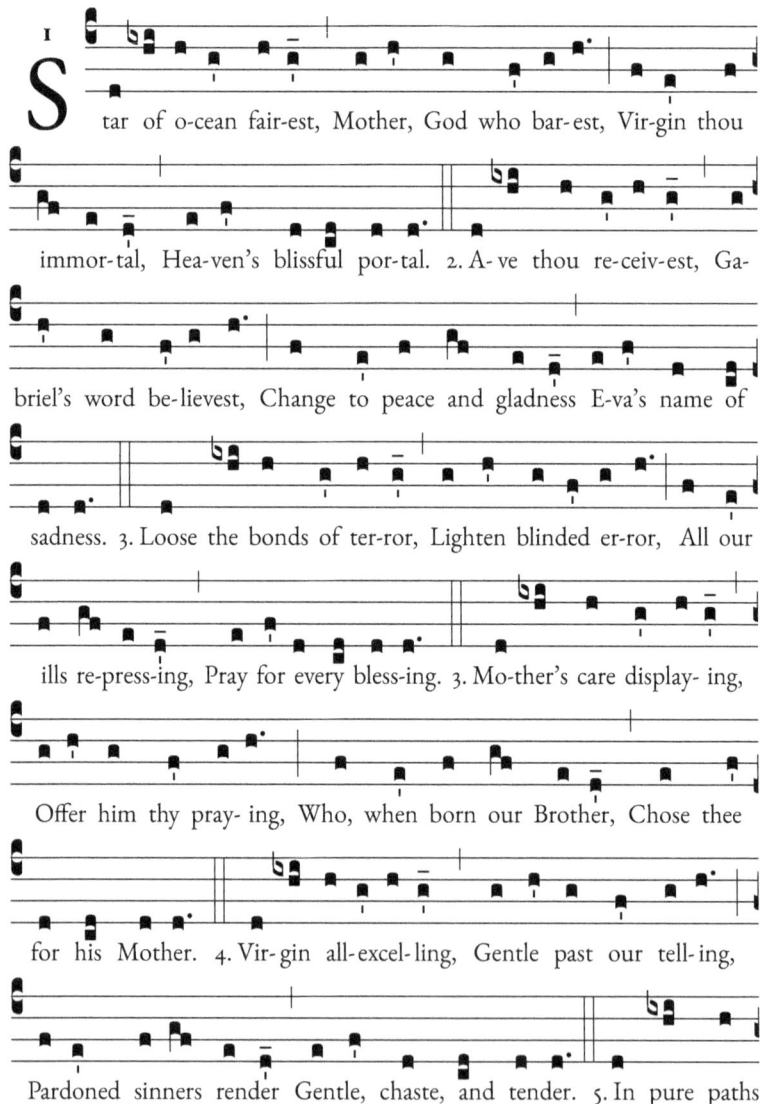

S tar of o-cean fair-est, Mother, God who bar-est, Vir-gin thou

immor-tal, Hea-ven's blissful por-tal. 2. A- ve thou re-ceiv-est, Ga-

briel's word be-lievest, Change to peace and gladness E-va's name of

sadness. 3. Loose the bonds of ter-ror, Lighten blinded er-ror, All our

ills re-press-ing, Pray for every bless-ing. 3. Mo-ther's care display- ing,

Offer him thy pray- ing, Who, when born our Brother, Chose thee

for his Mother. 4. Vir- gin all-excel- ling, Gentle past our tell- ing,

Pardoned sinners render Gentle, chaste, and tender. 5. In pure paths

Office of St. Mary on Saturday Year

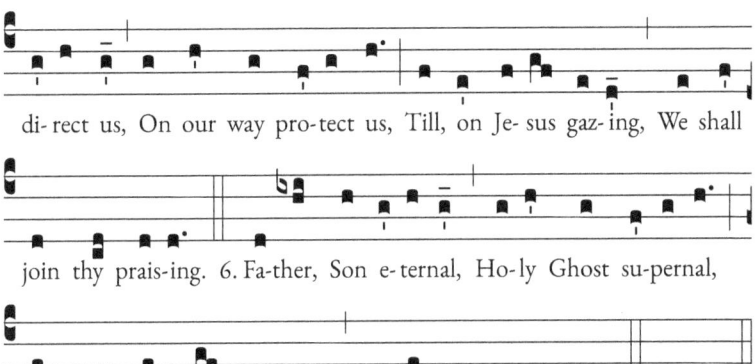

di- rect us, On our way pro-tect us, Till, on Je- sus gaz- ing, We shall

join thy prais-ing. 6. Fa-ther, Son e- ternal, Ho- ly Ghost su-pernal,

With one praise we bless thee, Three in One confess thee.   A- men.

℣. Full of grace are thy lips.

℟. Because God hath blessed thee for ever.

Mag. Ant. O blessed Mother † and spotless Virgin, thou glorious Queen of the world, intercede for us to the Lord.

Collect

RANT, we beseech thee, O Lord God, that we thy servants may enjoy perpetual health of mind and of body: and, at the glorious intercession of blessed Mary ever Virgin, be delivered from present sadness, and rejoice in everlasting gladness. Through.

EFEND us, we beseech thee, O Lord, from all perils of mind and body: and at the intercession of blessed Joseph, of thy blessed Apostles Peter and Paul, of blessed *N.* and of all Saints, graciously bestow upon us both peace and safety: that all adversity and error being done away, thy Church may serve thee in untroubled freedom. Through.

MATTINS

Invitatory Hymn

IV

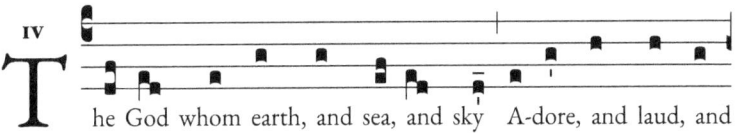

T he God whom earth, and sea, and sky A-dore, and laud, and

magni- fy, Who o'er their three-fold fabric reigns, The Vir-gin's

spot-less womb contains. 2. The God whose will by moon, and sun,

And all things in due course is done, Is borne up-on a Maid-en's

breast, By full-est heav'nly grace pos-sessed. 3. How blest that Moth-

er, in whose shrine The great Artif- i- cer Di- vine, Whose hand

contains the earth and sky, Vouch-safed, as in his ark, to lie.

4. Blest, in the mes-sage Gabriel brought; Blest, by the work the

Spir- it wrought; From whom the great De- sire of earth Took hu-

man flesh and hu-man birth. 5. All hon-our, laud, and glo- ry be,

O Je-su Vir-gin-born, to thee, Whom with the Fa-ther we a-dore,

And Ho-ly Ghost for ev- ermore. A- men.

Office Hymn

II

O glor- ious La-dy, throned in rest, Amidst the star-ry

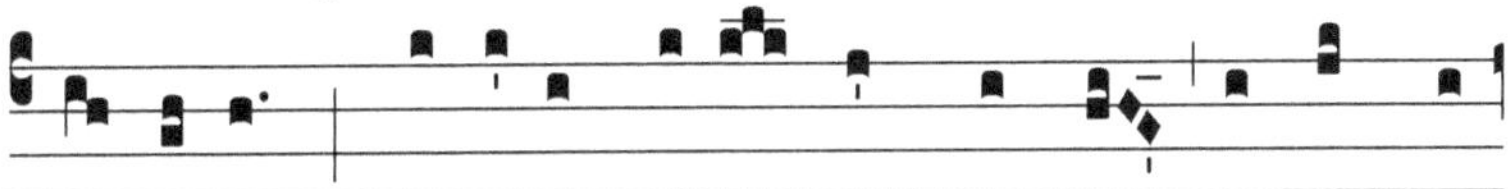

host a-bove, Who gav-est nurture from thy breast To God, with

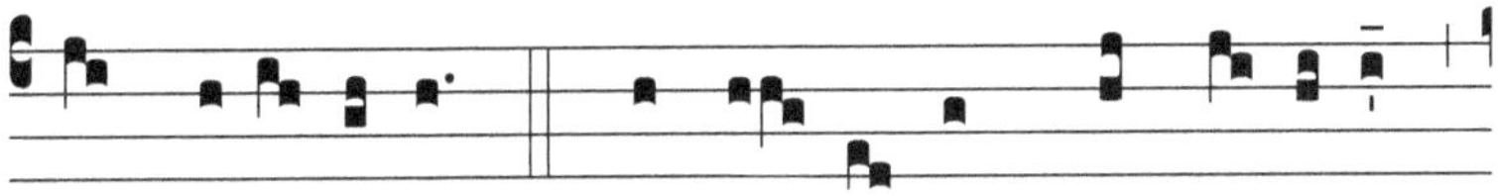

pure ma- ter-nal love. 2. What we had lost through sin-ful Eve

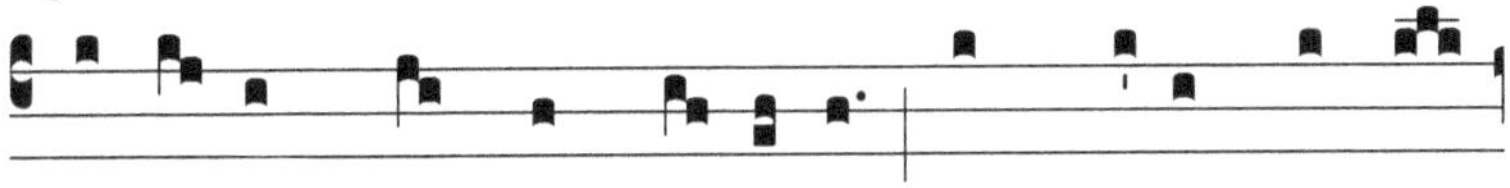

The Blos-som sprung from thee re-stores, And, granting bliss to

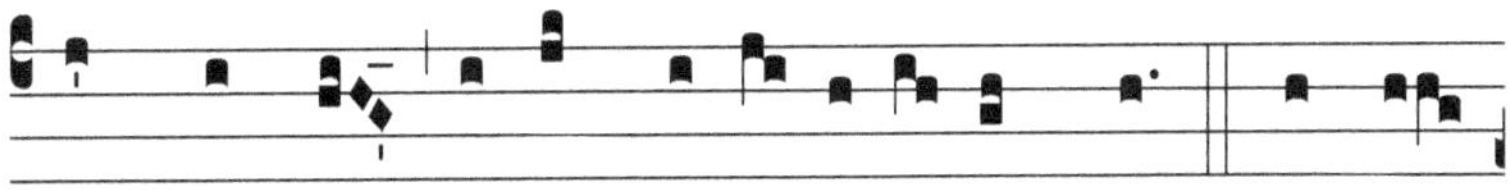

souls that grieve, Unbars the ev- er- last- ing doors. 3. O Gate,

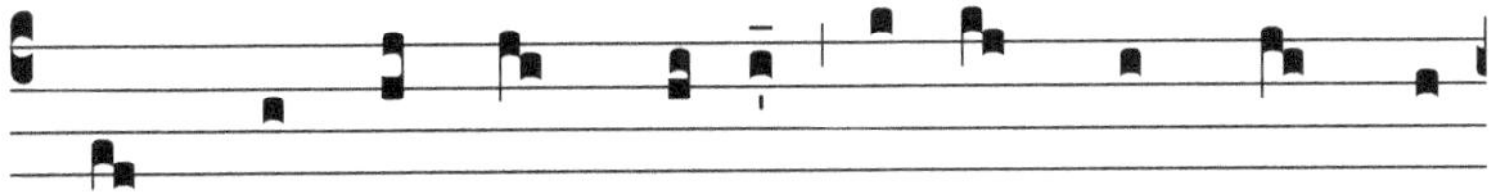

through which hath passed the King, O Hall, whence Light shone

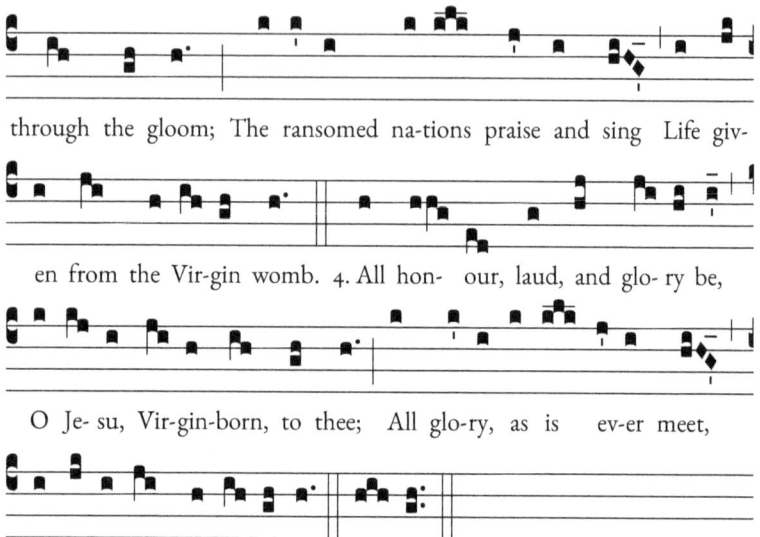

through the gloom; The ransomed na-tions praise and sing Life giv-

en from the Vir-gin womb. 4. All hon- our, laud, and glo- ry be,

O Je- su, Vir-gin-born, to thee; All glo-ry, as is   ev-er meet,

To Father and to Par- a-clete. A- men.

℣. Blessed art thou amongst women.

℞. And blessed is the fruit of thy womb.

Ben. Ant. O ever blessed Mother of God, † Mary ever Virgin, temple of the Godhead, hallowed shrine of the Holy Spirit, thou only, above all others, wast acceptable to our Lord Jesus Christ: pray for the people, entreat for the clergy, intercede for all womankind vowed unto God.

Collect

GRANT, we beseech thee, O Lord God, that we thy servants may enjoy perpetual health of mind and of body: and, at the glorious intercession of blessed Mary ever Virgin, be delivered from present sadness, and rejoice in everlasting gladness. Through.

DEFEND us, we beseech thee, O Lord, from all perils of mind and body: and at the intercession of blessed Joseph, of thy blessed Apostles Peter and Paul, of blessed *N.* and of all Saints, graciously bestow upon us both peace and safety: that all adversity and error being done away, thy Church may serve thee in untroubled freedom. Through.

Office of St. Mary on Saturday *Christmas*

After Christmas

❡ From Saturday after the Epiphany Octave through Saturday before Purification.
❡ NOTE, The Hymns are as above.

EVENSONG

℣. Full of grace are thy lips.

℞. Because God hath blessed thee for ever.

Mag. Ant. Great † is the mystery of the inheritance: the womb of her that knew not man is become the temple of the Godhead: by taking flesh of her, he was no way defiled: all the nations shall gather, saying: Glory be to thee, O Lord.

Collect

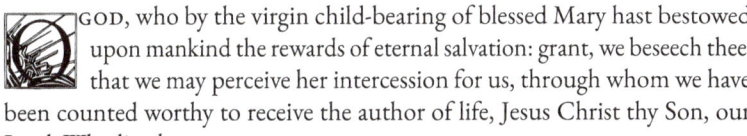GOD, who by the virgin child-bearing of blessed Mary hast bestowed upon mankind the rewards of eternal salvation: grant, we beseech thee; that we may perceive her intercession for us, through whom we have been counted worthy to receive the author of life, Jesus Christ thy Son, our Lord. Who liveth.

EFEND us, we beseech thee, O Lord, from all perils of mind and body: and at the intercession of blessed Joseph, of thy blessed Apostles Peter and Paul, of blessed *N.* and of all Saints, graciously bestow upon us both peace and safety: that all adversity and error being done away, thy Church may serve thee in untroubled freedom. Through.

MATTINS

℣. Blessed art thou amongst women.

℞. And blessed is the fruit of thy womb.

Ben. Ant. A great and wondrous mystery † is made known to us this day; a new thing is wrought in both natures: God is made man; that which was, remained, and that which was not, he assumed; suffering no confusion, nor yet division.

Collect

GOD, who by the virgin child-bearing of blessed Mary hast bestowed upon mankind the rewards of eternal salvation: grant, we beseech thee; that we may perceive her intercession for us, through whom we have been counted worthy to receive the author of life, Jesus Christ thy Son, our Lord. Who liveth.

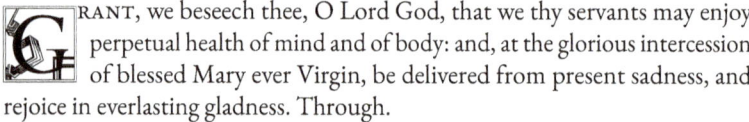EFEND us, we beseech thee, O Lord, from all perils of mind and body: and at the intercession of blessed Joseph, of thy blessed Apostles Peter and Paul, of blessed *N.* and of all Saints, graciously bestow upon us both peace and safety: that all adversity and error being done away, thy Church may serve thee in untroubled freedom. Through.

Eastertide

EVENSONG

℣. Full of grace art thy lips, alleluia.

℟. Because God hath blessed thee for ever, alleluia.

Mag. Ant. O Queen of heaven, † be joyful, alleluia; Because he whom so meetly thou barest, alleluia, Hath arisen, as he promised, alleluia: Pray for us to the Father, alleluia.

Collect

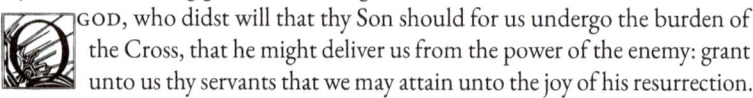RANT, we beseech thee, O Lord God, that we thy servants may enjoy perpetual health of mind and of body: and, at the glorious intercession of blessed Mary ever Virgin, be delivered from present sadness, and rejoice in everlasting gladness. Through.

GOD, who didst will that thy Son should for us undergo the burden of the Cross, that he might deliver us from the power of the enemy: grant unto us thy servants that we may attain unto the joy of his resurrection. Through the same.

MATTINS

❡ Mattins is as in Evensong.

Forms of Prayer to be used in Families

Forms of Prayer to be used in Families

Morning Prayer

UR Father, who art in heaven, Hallowed be thy Name. Thy kingdom come. Thy will be done, On earth as it is in heaven. Give us this day our daily bread. And forgive us our trespasses, As we forgive those who trespass against us. And lead us not into temptation, But deliver us from evil. For thine is the kingdom, and the power, and the glory, for ever and ever. Amen.

AIL Mary, full of grace; The Lord is with thee; Blessed art thou amongst women, And blessed is the fruit of thy womb, Jesus. Holy Mary, Mother of God, Pray for us sinners, now and at the hour of our death. Amen.

¶ Here may follow the Collect for the day.

ACKNOWLEDGMENT OF GOD'S MERCY AND PRESERVATION, ESPECIALLY THROUGH THE NIGHT PAST.

LMIGHTY and everlasting God, in whom we live and move and have our being; We, thy needy creatures, render thee our humble praises, for thy preservation of us from the beginning of our lives to this day, and especially for having delivered us from the dangers of the past night. For these thy mercies, we bless and magnify thy glorious Name; humbly beseeching thee to accept this our morning sacrifice of praise and thanksgiving; for his sake who lay down in the grave, and rose again for us, thy Son our Saviour Jesus Christ. *Amen.*

DEDICATION OF SOUL AND BODY TO GOD'S SERVICE, WITH A RESOLUTION TO BE GROWING DAILY IN GOODNESS.

ND since it is of thy mercy, O gracious Father, that another day is added to our lives; We here dedicate both our souls and our bodies to thee and thy service, in a sober, righteous, and godly life: in which resolution, do thou, O merciful God, confirm and strengthen us; that, as we grow in age, we may grow in grace, and in the knowledge of our Lord and Saviour Jesus Christ. *Amen.*

Forms of Prayer to be used in Families

Prayer for Grace to enable us to perform that Resolution.

UT, O God, who knowest the weakness and corruption of our nature, and the manifold temptations which we daily meet with; We humbly beseech thee to have compassion on our infirmities, and to give us the constant assistance of thy Holy Spirit; that we may be effectually restrained from sin, and incited to our duty. Imprint upon our hearts such a dread of thy judgments, and such a grateful sense of thy goodness to us, as may make us both afraid and ashamed to offend thee. And, above all, keep in our minds a lively remembrance of that great day, in which we must give a strict account of our thoughts, words, and actions to him whom thou hast appointed the Judge of quick and dead, thy Son Jesus Christ our Lord. *Amen.*

For Grace to guide and keep us the following Day, and for God's Blessing on the business of the Same.

N particular, we implore thy grace and protection for the ensuing day. Keep us temperate in all things, and diligent in our several callings. Grant us patience under our afflictions. Give us grace to be just and upright in all our dealings; quiet and peaceable; full of compassion; and ready to do good to all men, according to our abilities and opportunities. Direct us in all our ways. Defend us from all dangers and adversities; and be graciously pleased to take us, and all who are dear to us, under thy fatherly care and protection. These things, and whatever else thou shalt see to be necessary and convenient to us, we humbly beg, through the merits and mediation of thy Son Jesus Christ, our Lord and Saviour. *Amen.*

HE grace of our Lord Jesus Christ, ✠ and the love of God, and the fellowship of the Holy Ghost, be with us all evermore. *Amen.*

Forms of Prayer to be used in Families

Evening Prayer

❡ The Family being together, a little before bedtime, let the Master or Mistress, or any other who may be appointed, say as followeth, all kneeling, and repeating with him the Lord's Prayer & Angelic Salutation.

OUR Father, who art in heaven, Hallowed be thy Name. Thy kingdom come. Thy will be done, On earth as it is in heaven. Give us this day our daily bread. And forgive us our trespasses, As we forgive those who trespass against us. And lead us not into temptation, But deliver us from evil. For thine is the kingdom, and the power, and the glory, for ever and ever. Amen.

HAIL Mary, full of grace; The Lord is with thee; Blessed art thou amongst women, And blessed is the fruit of thy womb, Jesus. Holy Mary, Mother of God, Pray for us sinners, now and at the hour of our death. Amen.

❡ Here may follow the Collect for the day.

CONFESSION OF SINS, WITH A PRAYER FOR CONTRITION AND PARDON.

MOST merciful God, who art of purer eyes than to behold iniquity, and hast promised forgiveness to all those who confess and forsake their sins; We come before thee in an humble sense of our own unworthiness, *a Here let him* acknowledging our manifold transgressions of thy righteous laws.[a] But, O *who reads make* gracious Father, who desirest not the death of a sinner, look upon us, we beseech *a short pause,* thee, in mercy, and forgive us all our transgressions. Make us deeply sensible of *that every one* the great evil of them; and work in us an hearty contrition; that we may obtain *may secretly* forgiveness at thy hands, who art ever ready to receive humble and penitent *confess the sins* *and failings* sinners; for the sake of thy Son Jesus Christ, our only Saviour and Redeemer. *of that day.* *Amen.*

PRAYER FOR GRACE TO REFORM AND GROW BETTER.

AND lest, through our own frailty, or the temptations which encompass us, we be drawn again into sin, vouchsafe us, we beseech thee, the direction and assistance of thy Holy Spirit. Reform whatever is amiss in the temper and disposition of our souls; that no unclean thoughts, unlawful designs, or inordinate desires, may rest there. Purge our hearts from envy, hatred, and malice; that we may never suffer the sun to go down upon our wrath; but may always go to our rest in peace, charity, and good-will, with a conscience void of offence towards thee, and towards men; that so we may be preserved pure and blameless, unto the coming of our Lord and Saviour Jesus Christ. *Amen.*

THE INTERCESSION.

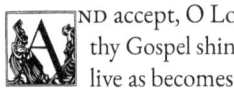ND accept, O Lord, our intercessions for all mankind. Let the light of thy Gospel shine upon all nations; and may as many as have received it, live as becomes it. Be gracious unto thy Church; and grant that every member of the same, in his vocation and ministry, may serve thee faithfully. Bless all in authority over us; and so rule their hearts and strengthen their hands, that they may punish wickedness and vice, and maintain thy true religion and virtue. Send down thy blessings, temporal and spiritual, upon all our relations, friends, and neighbours. Reward all who have done us good, and pardon all those who have done or wish us evil, and give them repentance and better minds. Be merciful to all who are in any trouble; and do thou, the God of pity, administer to them according to their several necessities; for his sake who went about doing good, thy Son our Saviour Jesus Christ. *Amen.*

THE THANKSGIVING.

TO our prayers, O Lord, we join our unfeigned thanks for all thy mercies; for our being, our reason, and all other endowments and faculties of soul and body; for our health, friends, food, and raiment, and all the other comforts and conveniences of life. Above all, we adore thy mercy in sending thy only Son into the world, to redeem us from sin and eternal death, and in giving us the knowledge and sense of our duty towards thee. We bless thee for thy patience with us, notwithstanding our many and great provocations; for all the directions, assistances, and comforts of thy Holy Spirit; for thy continual care and watchful providence over us through the whole course of our lives; and particularly for the mercies and benefits of the past day; beseeching thee to continue these thy blessings to us, and to give us grace to show our thankfulness in a sincere obedience to his laws, through whose merits and inter-cession we received them all, thy Son our Saviour Jesus Christ. *Amen.*

PRAYER FOR GOD'S PROTECTION THROUGH THE NIGHT FOLLOWING.

IN particular, we beseech thee to continue thy gracious protection to us this night. Defend us from all dangers and mischiefs, and from the fear of them; that we may enjoy such refreshing sleep as may fit us for the duties of the coming day. And grant us grace always to live in such a state that we may never be afraid to die; so that, living and dying, we may be thine,

Forms of Prayer to be used in Families

through the merits and satisfaction of thy Son Christ Jesus, in whose Name we offer up these our imperfect prayers. *Amen.*

HE grace of our Lord Jesus Christ, ✠ and the love of God, and the fellowship of the Holy Ghost, be with us all evermore. *Amen.*

❡ On Sundays, and on other days when it may be convenient, it will be proper to begin with a Chapter, or part of a Chapter, from the New Testament.

A Shorter Form of Morning Prayer

❡ After the reading of a brief portion of Holy Scripture, let the Head of the Household, or some other member of the family, say as followeth, all kneeling, and repeating with him the Lord's Prayer & Angelic Salutation.

UR Father, who art in heaven, Hallowed be thy Name. Thy kingdom come. Thy will be done, On earth as it is in heaven. Give us this day our daily bread. And forgive us our trespasses, As we forgive those who trespass against us. And lead us not into temptation, But deliver us from evil. For thine is the kingdom, and the power, and the glory, for ever and ever. Amen.

AIL Mary, full of grace; The Lord is with thee; Blessed art thou amongst women, And blessed is the fruit of thy womb, Jesus. Holy Mary, Mother of God, Pray for us sinners, now and at the hour of our death. Amen.

LORD, our heavenly Father, Almighty and everlasting God, who hast safely brought us to the beginning of this day; Defend us in the same with thy mighty power; and grant that this day we fall into no sin, neither run into any kind of danger; but that all our doings, being ordered by thy governance, may be righteous in thy sight; through Jesus Christ our Lord. *Amen.*

❡ Here may be added any special Prayers.

HE grace of our Lord Jesus Christ, ✠ and the love of God, and the fellowship of the Holy Ghost, be with us all evermore. *Amen.*

Forms of Prayer to be used in Families

A Shorter Form of Evening Prayer

¶ After the reading of a brief portion of Holy Scripture, let the Head of the Household, or some other member of the family, say as followeth, all kneeling and repeating with him the Lord's Prayer & Angelic Salutation.

OUR Father, who art in heaven, Hallowed be thy Name. Thy kingdom come. Thy will be done, On earth as it is in heaven. Give us this day our daily bread. And forgive us our trespasses, As we forgive those who trespass against us. And lead us not into temptation, But deliver us from evil. For thine is the kingdom, and the power, and the glory, for ever and ever. Amen.

HAIL Mary, full of grace; The Lord is with thee; Blessed art thou amongst women, And blessed is the fruit of thy womb, Jesus. Holy Mary, Mother of God, Pray for us sinners, now and at the hour of our death. Amen.

LIGHTEN our darkness, we beseech thee, O Lord; and by thy great mercy defend us from all perils and dangers of this night; for the love of thy only Son, our Saviour, Jesus Christ. *Amen.*

¶ Here may be added any special Prayers.

THE Lord bless us and keep us. The Lord make his face to shine upon us, and be gracious unto us. The Lord ✠ lift up his countenance upon us, and give us peace, this night and evermore. *Amen.*

Forms of Prayer to be used in Families

Additional Prayers

For the Spirit of Prayer.

LMIGHTY God, who pourest out on all who desire it, the spirit of grace and of supplication; Deliver us, when we draw nigh to thee, from coldness of heart and wanderings of mind, that with stedfast thoughts and kindled affections, we may worship thee in spirit and in truth; through Jesus Christ our Lord. *Amen.*

In the Morning.

GOD, the King eternal, who dividest the day from the darkness, and turnest the shadow of death into the morning; Drive far off from us all wrong desires, incline our hearts to keep thy law, and guide our feet into the way of peace; that having done thy will with cheerfulness while it was day, we may, when the night cometh, rejoice to give thee thanks; through Jesus Christ our Lord. *Amen.*

LMIGHTY God, who alone gavest us the breath of life, and alone canst keep alive in us the holy desires thou dost impart; We beseech thee, for thy compassion's sake, to sanctify all our thoughts and endeavours; that we may neither begin an action without a pure intention nor continue it without thy blessing. And grant that, having the eyes of the mind opened to behold things invisible and unseen, we may in heart be inspired by thy wisdom, and in work be upheld by thy strength, and in the end be accepted of thee as thy faithful servants; through Jesus Christ our Saviour. *Amen.*

At Night.

LORD, support us all the day long, until the shadows lengthen and the evening comes, and the busy world is hushed, and the fever of life is over, and our work is done. Then in thy mercy grant us a safe lodging, and a holy rest, and peace at the last. *Amen.*

GOD, who art the life of mortal men, the light of the faithful, the strength of those who labour, and the repose of the dead; We thank thee for the timely blessings of the day, and humbly supplicate thy merciful protection all this night. Bring us, we beseech thee, in safety to the morning hours; through him who died for us and rose again, thy Son, our Saviour Jesus Christ. *Amen.*

Forms of Prayer to be used in Families

Sunday Morning.

GOD, who makest us glad with the weekly remembrance of the glorious resurrection of thy Son our Lord; Vouchsafe us this day such blessing through our worship of thee, that the days to come may be spent in thy service; through the same Jesus Christ our Lord. *Amen.*

For Quiet Confidence.

GOD of peace, who hast taught us that in returning and rest we shall be saved, in quietness and in confidence shall be our strength; By the might of thy Spirit lift us, we pray thee, to thy presence, where we may be still and know that thou art God; through Jesus Christ our Lord. *Amen.*

For Guidance.

GOD, by whom the meek are guided in judgment, and light riseth up in darkness for the godly; Grant us, in all our doubts and uncertainties, the grace to ask what thou wouldest have us to do, that the Spirit of Wisdom may save us from all false choices, and that in thy light we may see light, and in thy straight path may not stumble; through Jesus Christ our Lord. *Amen.*

For Trustfulness.

MOST loving Father, who willest us to give thanks for all things, to dread nothing but the loss of thee, and to cast all our care on thee, who carest for us; Preserve us from faithless fears and worldly anxieties, and grant that no clouds of this mortal life may hide from us the light of that love which is immortal, and which thou hast manifested unto us in thy Son, Jesus Christ our Lord. *Amen.*

HEAVENLY Father, thou understandest all thy children; through thy gift of faith we bring our perplexities to the light of thy wisdom, and receive the blessed encouragement of thy sympathy, and a clearer knowledge of thy will. Glory be to thee for all thy gracious gifts. *Amen.*

For Joy in God's Creation.

HEAVENLY Father, who hast filled the world with beauty; Open, we beseech thee, our eyes to behold thy gracious hand in all thy works; that rejoicing in thy whole creation, we may learn to serve thee with gladness; for the sake of him by whom all things were made, thy Son, Jesus Christ our Lord. *Amen.*

For the Children.

LMIGHTY God, heavenly Father, who hast blessed us with the joy and care of children; Give us light and strength so to train them, that they may love whatsoever things are true and pure and lovely and of good report, following the example of their Saviour Jesus Christ. *Amen.*

For the Absent.

GOD, whose fatherly care reacheth to the uttermost parts of the earth; We humbly beseech thee graciously to behold and bless those whom we love, now absent from us. Defend them from all dangers of soul and body; and grant that both they and we, drawing nearer to thee, may be bound together by thy love in the communion of thy Holy Spirit, and in the fellowship of thy saints; through Jesus Christ our Lord. *Amen.*

For Those We Love.

LMIGHTY God, we entrust all who are dear to us to thy never-failing care and love, for this life and the life to come; knowing that thou art doing for them better things than we can desire or pray for; through Jesus Christ our Lord. *Amen.*

For the Recovery of a Sick Person.

MERCIFUL God, giver of life and health; Bless, we pray thee, thy *servant*, *N.*, and those who administer to *him* of thy healing gifts; that *he* may be restored to health of body and of mind; through Jesus Christ our Lord. *Amen.*

For One about to undergo an Operation.

LMIGHTY God our heavenly Father, we beseech thee graciously to comfort thy servant in his suffering, and to bless the means made use of for his cure. Fill his heart with confidence, that though he be sometime afraid, he yet may put his trust in thee; through Jesus Christ our Lord. *Amen.*

Forms of Prayer to be used in Families

FOR A BIRTHDAY.

ATCH over thy child, O Lord, as his days increase; bless and guide him wherever he may be, keeping him unspotted from the world. Strengthen him when he stands; comfort him when discouraged or sorrowful; raise him up if he fall; and in his heart may thy peace which passeth understanding abide all the days of his life; through Jesus Christ our Lord. *Amen.*

FOR AN ANNIVERSARY OF ONE DEPARTED.

LMIGHTY God, we remember this day before thee thy faithful servant *N.,* and we pray thee that, having opened to him the gates of larger life, thou wilt receive him more and more into thy joyful service; that he may win, with thee and thy servants everywhere, the eternal victory; through Jesus Christ our Lord. *Amen.*

FOR THOSE IN MENTAL DARKNESS.

HEAVENLY Father, we beseech thee to have mercy upon all thy children who are living in mental darkness. Restore them to strength of mind and cheerfulness of spirit, and give them health and peace; through Jesus Christ our Lord. *Amen.*

FOR A BLESSING ON THE FAMILIES OF THE LAND.

LMIGHTY God, our heavenly Father, who settest the solitary in families; We commend to thy continual care the homes in which thy people dwell. Put far from them, we beseech thee, every root of bitterness, the desire of vain-glory, and the pride of life. Fill them with faith, virtue, knowledge, temperance, patience, godliness. Knit together in constant affection those who, in holy wedlock, have been made one flesh; turn the heart of the fathers to the children, and the heart of the children to the fathers; and so enkindle fervent charity among us all, that we be evermore kindly affectioned with brotherly love; through Jesus Christ our Lord. *Amen.*

FOR ALL POOR, HOMELESS, AND NEGLECTED FOLK.

GOD, Almighty and merciful, who healest those that are broken in heart, and turnest the sadness of the sorrowful to joy; Let thy fatherly goodness be upon all that thou hast made. Remember in pity such as are this day destitute, homeless, or forgotten of their fellow-men. Bless the

Forms of Prayer to be used in Families

congregation of thy poor. Uplift those who are cast down. Mightily befriend innocent sufferers, and sanctify to them the endurance of their wrongs. Cheer with hope all discouraged and unhappy people, and by thy heavenly grace preserve from falling those whose penury tempteth them to sin; though they be troubled on every side, suffer them not to be distressed; though they be perplexed, save them from despair. Grant this, O Lord, for the love of him, who for our sakes became poor, thy Son, our Saviour Jesus Christ. *Amen.*

FOR FAITHFULNESS IN THE USE OF THIS WORLD'S GOODS.

ALMIGHTY God, whose loving hand hath given us all that we possess; Grant us grace that we may honour thee with our substance, and remembering the account which we must one day give, may be faithful stewards of thy bounty; through Jesus Christ our Lord. *Amen.*

A GENERAL INTERCESSION.

O GOD, at whose word man goeth forth to his work and to his labour until the evening; Be merciful to all whose duties are difficult or burdensome, and comfort them concerning their toil. Shield from bodily accident and harm the workmen at their work. Protect the efforts of sober and honest industry, and suffer not the hire of the labourers to be kept back by fraud. Incline the heart of employers and of those whom they employ to mutual forbearance, fairness, and good-will. Give the spirit of governance and of a sound mind to all in places of authority. Bless all those who labour in works of mercy or in schools of good learning. Care for all aged persons, and all little children, the sick and the afflicted, and those who travel by land or by sea. Remember all who by reason of weakness are overtasked, or because of poverty are forgotten. Let the sorrowful sighing of the prisoners come before thee; and according to the greatness of thy power, preserve thou those that are appointed to die. Give ear unto our prayer, O merciful and gracious Father, for the love of thy dear Son, our Saviour Jesus Christ. *Amen.*

GRACE BEFORE MEAT.

BLESS, O Father, thy gifts to our use and us to thy service; for Christ's sake. *Amen.*

GIVE us grateful hearts, our Father, for all thy mercies, and make us mindful of the needs of others; through Jesus Christ our Lord. *Amen.*

EXPOSITIO
PATRVM
GRÆCORVM
IN
PSALMOS,

PSALTER OF DAVID

Day 1. Morning Prayer

Psalm 1. *Beatus vir, qui non abiit, &c.*

LESSED is the man that hath not walked in the counsel of the ungodly, nor stood in the way of sinners : and hath not sat in the seat of the scornful.

2 But his delight is in the law of the Lord : and in his law will he exercise himself day and night.

3 And he shall be like a tree planted by the water-side : that will bring forth his fruit in due season.

4 His leaf also shall not wither : and look, whatsoever he doeth, it shall prosper.

5 As for the ungodly, it is not so with them : but they are like the chaff, which the wind scattereth away from the face of the earth.

6 Therefore the ungodly shall not be able to stand in the judgement : neither the sinners in the congregation of the righteous.

7 But the Lord knoweth the way of the righteous : and the way of the ungodly shall perish.

Psalm 2. *Quare fremuerunt gentes?*

HY do the heathen so furiously rage together : and why do the people imagine a vain thing?

2 The kings of the earth stand up, and the rulers take counsel together : against the Lord, and against his Anointed.

3 Let us break their bonds asunder : and cast away their cords from us.

4 He that dwelleth in heaven shall laugh them to scorn : the Lord shall have them in derision.

5 Then shall he speak unto them in his wrath : and vex them in his sore displeasure.

6 Yet have I set my King : upon my holy hill of Sion.

7 I will preach the law, whereof the Lord hath said unto me : Thou art my Son, this day have I begotten thee.

8 Desire of me, and I shall give thee the heathen for thine inheritance : and the utmost parts of the earth for thy possession.

9 Thou shalt bruise them with a rod of iron : and break them in pieces like a potter's vessel.

10 Be wise now therefore, O ye kings : be learned, ye that are judges of the earth.

11 Serve the Lord in fear : and rejoice unto him with reverence.

12 Kiss the Son, lest he be angry, and so ye perish from the right way : if his wrath be kindled, (yea, but a little,) blessed are all they that put their trust in him.

PSALM 3. *DOMINE, QUID MULTIPLICATI,*

ORD, how are they increased that trouble me : many are they that rise against me.

2 Many one there be that say of my soul : There is no help for him in his God.

3 But thou, O Lord, art my defender : thou art my worship, and the lifter up of my head.

4 I did call upon the Lord with my voice : and he heard me out of his holy hill.

5 I laid me down and slept, and rose up again : for the Lord sustained me.

6 I will not be afraid for ten thousands of the people : that have set themselves against me round about.

7 Up, Lord, and help me, O my God : for thou smitest all mine enemies upon the cheekbone; thou hast broken the teeth of the ungodly.

8 Salvation belongeth unto the Lord : and thy blessing is upon thy people.

PSALM 4. *CUM INVOCAREM*

EAR me when I call, O God of my righteousness : thou hast set me at liberty when I was in trouble; have mercy upon me, and hearken unto my prayer.

2 O ye sons of men, how long will ye blaspheme mine honour : and have such pleasure in vanity, and seek after leasing?

3 Know this also, that the Lord hath chosen to himself the man that is godly : when I call upon the Lord, he will hear me.

4 Stand in awe, and sin not : commune with your own heart, and in your chamber, and be still.

5 Offer the sacrifice of righteousness : and put your trust in the Lord.

6 There be many that say : Who will shew us any good?

7 Lord, lift thou up : the light of thy countenance upon us.

8 Thou hast put gladness in my heart : since the time that their corn and wine and oil increased.

9 I will lay me down in peace, and take my rest : for it is thou, Lord, only, that makest me dwell in safety.

PSALM 5. *VERBA MEA AURIBUS.*

PONDER my words, O Lord : consider my meditation

2 O hearken thou unto the voice of my calling, my King, and my God : for unto thee will I make my prayer.

3 My voice shalt thou hear betimes, O Lord : early in the morning will I direct my prayer unto thee, and will look up.

4 For thou art the God that hast no pleasure in wickedness : neither shall any evil dwell with thee.

5 Such as be foolish shall not stand in thy sight : for thou hatest all them that work vanity.

6 Thou shalt destroy them that speak leasing : the Lord will abhor both the blood-thirsty and deceitful man.

7 But as for me, I will come into thine house, even upon the multitude of thy mercy : and in thy fear will I worship toward thy holy temple.

8 Lead me, O Lord, in thy righteousness, because of mine enemies : make thy way plain before my face.

9 For there is no faithfulness in his mouth : their inward parts are very wickedness.

10 Their throat is an open sepulchre : they flatter with their tongue.

11 Destroy thou them, O God; let them perish through their own imaginations : cast them out in the multitude of their ungodliness; for they have rebelled against thee.

12 And let all them that put their trust in thee rejoice : they shall ever be giving of thanks, because thou defendest them; they that love thy Name shall be joyful in thee;

13 For thou, Lord, wilt give thy blessing unto the righteous : and with thy favourable kindness wilt thou defend him as with a shield.

Day 1. Evening Prayer

PSALM 6. *DOMINE, NE IN FURORE*

LORD, rebuke me not in thine indignation : neither chasten me in thy displeasure.

2 Have mercy upon me, O Lord, for I am weak : O Lord, heal me, for my bones are vexed.

3 My soul also is sore troubled : but, Lord, how long wilt thou punish me?

4 Turn thee, O Lord, and deliver my soul : O save me for thy mercy's sake.

5 For in death no man remembereth thee : and who will give thee thanks in the pit?

6 I am weary of my groaning; every night wash I my bed : and water my couch with my tears.

7 My beauty is gone for very trouble : and worn away because of all mine enemies.

8 Away from me, all ye that work vanity : for the Lord hath heard the voice of my weeping.

9 The Lord hath heard my petition : the Lord will receive my prayer.

10 All mine enemies shall be confounded, and sore vexed : they shall be turned back, and put to shame suddenly.

Psalm 7. *Domine, Deus meus*

LORD my God, in thee have I put my trust : save me from all them that persecute me, and deliver me;

2 Lest he devour my soul, like a lion, and tear it in pieces : while there is none to help.

3 O Lord my God, if I have done any such thing : or if there be any wickedness in my hands;

4 If I have rewarded evil unto him that dealt friendly with me : yea, I have delivered him that without any cause is mine enemy,

5 Then let mine enemy persecute my soul, and take me : yea, let him tread my life down upon the earth, and lay mine honour in the dust.

6 Stand up, O Lord, in thy wrath, and lift up thyself, because of the indignation of mine enemies : arise up for me in the judgement that thou hast commanded.

7 And so shall the congregation of the people come about thee : for their sakes therefore lift up thyself again.

8 The Lord shall judge the people; give sentence with me, O Lord : according to my righteousness, and according to the innocency that is in me.

9 O let the wickedness of the ungodly come to an end : but guide thou the just.

10 For the righteous God : trieth the very hearts and reins.

11 My help cometh of God : who preserveth them that are true of heart.

12 God is a righteous Judge, strong and patient : and God is provoked every day.

13 If a man will not turn, he will whet his sword : he hath bent his bow, and made it ready.

14 He hath prepared for him the instruments of death : he ordaineth his arrows against the persecutors.

15 Behold, he travaileth with mischief : he hath conceived sorrow, and brought forth ungodliness.

16 He hath graven and digged up a pit : and is fallen on himself into the destruction that he made for other.

17 For his travail shall come upon his own head : and his wickedness shall fall on his own pate.

18 I will give thanks unto the Lord, according to his righteousness : and I will praise the Name of the Lord most High.

PSALM 8. *DOMINE, DOMINUS NOSTER*

LORD our Governor, how excellent is thy Name in all the world : thou that hast set thy glory above the heavens!

2 Out of the mouth of very babes and sucklings hast thou ordained strength, because of thine enemies : that thou mightest still the enemy and the avenger.

3 For I will consider thy heavens, even the works of thy fingers : the moon and the stars, which thou hast ordained.

4 What is man, that thou art mindful of him : and the son of man, that thou visitest him?

5 Thou madest him lower than the angels : to crown him with glory and worship.

6 Thou makest him to have dominion of the works of thy hands : and thou hast put all things in subjection under his feet;

7 All sheep and oxen : yea, and the beasts of the field;

8 The fowls of the air, and the fishes of the sea : and whatsoever walketh through the paths of the seas.

9 O Lord our Governor : how excellent is thy Name in all the world!

Day 2. Morning Prayer

PSALM 9. *CONFITEBOR TIBI*

WILL give thanks unto thee, O Lord, with my whole heart : I will speak of all thy marvellous works.

2 I will be glad and rejoice in thee : yea, my songs will I make of thy Name, O thou most Highest.

3 While mine enemies are driven back : they shall fall and perish at thy presence.

4 For thou hast maintained my right and my cause : thou art set in the throne that judgest right.

5 Thou hast rebuked the heathen, and destroyed the ungodly : thou hast put out their name for ever and ever.

6 O thou enemy, destructions are come to a perpetual end : even as the cities which thou hast destroyed, their memorial is perished with them.

7 But the Lord shall endure for ever : he hath also prepared his seat for judgement.

8 For he shall judge the world in righteousness : and minister true judgement unto the people.

9 The Lord also will be a defence for the oppressed : even a refuge in due time of trouble.

10 And they that know thy Name will put their trust in thee : for thou, Lord, hast never failed them that seek thee.

11 O praise the Lord which dwelleth in Sion : shew the people of his doings.

12 For when he maketh inquisition for blood, he remembereth them : and forgetteth not the complaint of the poor.

13 Have mercy upon me, O Lord; consider the trouble which I suffer of them that hate me : thou that liftest me up from the gates of death.

14 That I may shew all thy praises within the ports of the daughter of Sion : I will rejoice in thy salvation.

15 The heathen are sunk down in the pit that they made : in the same net which they hid privily, is their foot taken.

16 The Lord is known to execute judgement : the ungodly is trapped in the work of his own hands.

17 The wicked shall be turned into hell : and all the people that forget God.

18 For the poor shall not alway be forgotten : the patient abiding of the meek shall not perish for ever.

19 Up, Lord, and let not man have the upper hand : let the heathen be judged in thy sight.

20 Put them in fear, O Lord : that the heathen may know themselves to be but men.

PSALM 10. *UT QUID, DOMINE?*

WHY standest thou so far off, O Lord : and hidest thy face in the needful time of trouble?

2 The ungodly for his own lust doth persecute the poor : let them be taken in the crafty wiliness that they have imagined.

3 For the ungodly hath made boast of his own heart's desire : and speaketh good of the covetous, whom God abhorreth.

4 The ungodly is so proud, that he careth not for God : neither is God in all his thoughts.

5 His ways are alway grievous : thy judgements are far above out of his sight, and therefore defieth he all his enemies.

6 For he hath said in his heart, Tush, I shall never be cast down : there shall no harm happen unto me.

7 His mouth is full of cursing, deceit, and fraud : under his tongue is ungodliness and vanity.

8 He sitteth lurking in the thievish corners of the streets : and privily in his lurking dens doth he murder the innocent; his eyes are set against the poor.

9 For he lieth waiting secretly, even as a lion lurketh he in his den : that he may ravish the poor.

10 He doth ravish the poor : when he getteth him into his net.

11 He falleth down, and humbleth himself : that the congregation of the poor may fall into the hands of his captains.

12 He hath said in his heart, Tush, God hath forgotten : he hideth away his face, and he will never see it.

13 Arise, O Lord God, and lift up thine hand : forget not the poor.

14 Wherefore should the wicked blaspheme God : while he doth say in his heart, Tush, thou God carest not for it.

15 Surely thou hast seen it : for thou beholdest ungodliness and wrong.

16 That thou mayest take the matter into thy hand : the poor committeth himself unto thee; for thou art the helper of the friendless.

17 Break thou the power of the ungodly and malicious : take away his ungodliness, and thou shalt find none.

18 The Lord is King for ever and ever : and the heathen are perished out of the land.

19 Lord, thou hast heard the desire of the poor : thou preparest their heart, and thine ear hearkeneth thereto;

20 To help the fatherless and poor unto their right : that the man of the earth be no more exalted against them.

PSALM 11. *IN DOMINO CONFIDO*

IN the Lord put I my trust : how say ye then to my soul, that she should flee as a bird unto the hill?

2 For lo, the ungodly bend their bow, and make ready their arrows within the quiver : that they may privily shoot at them which are true of heart.

3 For the foundations will be cast down : and what hath the righteous done?

4 The Lord is in his holy temple : the Lord's seat is in heaven.

5 His eyes consider the poor : and his eye-lids try the children of men.

6 The Lord alloweth the righteous : but the ungodly, and him that delighteth in wickedness, doth his soul abhor.

7 Upon the ungodly he shall rain snares, fire and brimstone, storm and tempest : this shall be their portion to drink.

8 For the righteous Lord loveth righteousness : his countenance will behold the thing that is just.

Day 2. Evening Prayer

PSALM 12. *SALVUM ME FAC*

HELP me, Lord, for there is not one godly man left : for the faithful are minished from among the children of men,

2 They talk of vanity every one with his neighbour : they do but flatter with their lips, and dissemble in their double heart.

3 The Lord shall root out all deceitful lips : and the tongue that speaketh proud things;

4 Which have said, With our tongue will we prevail : we are they that ought to speak, who is lord over us?

5 Now for the comfortless trouble's sake of the needy : and because of the deep sighing of the poor,

6 I will up, saith the Lord : and will help every one from him that swelleth against him, and will set him at rest.

7 The words of the Lord are pure words : even as the silver, which from the earth is tried, and purified seven times in the fire.

8 Thou shalt keep them, O Lord : thou shalt preserve him from this generation for ever.

9 The ungodly walk on every side : when they are exalted, the children of men are put to rebuke.

PSALM 13. *USQUE QUO, DOMINE?*

OW long wilt thou forget me, O Lord, for ever : how long wilt thou hide thy face from me?

2 How long shall I seek counsel in my soul, and be so vexed in my heart : how long shall mine enemies triumph over me?

3 Consider, and hear me, O Lord my God : lighten mine eyes, that I sleep not in death.

4 Lest mine enemy say, I have prevailed against him : for if I be cast down, they that trouble me will rejoice at it.

5 But my trust is in thy mercy : and my heart is joyful in thy salvation.

6 I will sing of the Lord, because he hath dealt so lovingly with me : yea, I will praise the Name of the Lord most Highest.

PSALM 14. *DIXIT INSIPIENS*

HE fool hath said in his heart : There is no God.

2 They are corrupt, and become abominable in their doings : there is none that doeth good, no not one.

3 The Lord looked down from heaven upon the children of men : to see if there were any that would understand, and seek after God.

4 But they are all gone out of the way, they are altogether become abominable : there is none that doeth good, no not one.

5 Their throat is an open sepulchre, with their tongues have they deceived : the poison of asps is under their lips.

6 Their mouth is full of cursing and bitterness : their feet are swift to shed blood.

7 Destruction and unhappiness is in their ways, and the way of peace have they not known : there is no fear of God before their eyes.

8 Have they no knowledge, that they are all such workers of mischief : eating up my people as it were bread, and call not upon the Lord?

9 There were they brought in great fear, even where no fear was : for God is in the generation of the righteous.

10 As for you, ye have made a mock at the counsel of the poor : because he putteth his trust in the Lord.

11 Who shall give salvation unto Israel out of Sion? When the Lord turneth the captivity of his people : then shall Jacob rejoice, and Israel shall be glad.

Day 3. Morning Prayer

PSALM 15. *DOMINE, QUIS HABITABIT?*

ORD, who shall dwell in thy tabernacle : or who shall rest upon thy holy hill?

2 Even he that leadeth an uncorrupt life : and doeth the thing which is right, and speaketh the truth from his heart.

3 He that hath used no deceit in his tongue, nor done evil to his neighbour : and hath not slandered his neighbour.

4 He that setteth not by himself, but is lowly in his own eyes : and maketh much of them that fear the Lord.

5 He that sweareth unto his neighbour, and disappointeth him not : though it were to his own hindrance.

6 He that hath not given his money upon usury : nor taken reward against the innocent.

7 Whoso doeth these things : shall never fall.

PSALM 16. *CONSERVA ME, DOMINE*

RESERVE me, O God : for in thee have I put my trust.

2 O my soul, thou hast said unto the Lord : Thou art my God, my goods are nothing unto thee.

3 All my delight is upon the saints, that are in the earth : and upon such as excel in virtue.

4 But they that run after another god : shall have great trouble.

5 Their drink-offerings of blood will I not offer : neither make mention of their names within my lips.

6 The Lord himself is the portion of mine inheritance, and of my cup : thou shalt maintain my lot.

7 The lot is fallen unto me in a fair ground : yea, I have a goodly heritage.

8 I will thank the Lord for giving me warning : my reins also chasten me in the night-season.

9 I have set God always before me : for he is on my right hand, therefore I shall not fall.

10 Wherefore my heart was glad, and my glory rejoiced : my flesh also shall rest in hope.

11 For why? thou shalt not leave my soul in hell : neither shalt thou suffer thy Holy One to see corruption.

12 Thou shalt shew me the path of life; in thy presence is the fulness of joy : and at thy right hand there is pleasure for evermore.

PSALM 17. *EXAUDI, DOMINE*

HEAR the right, O Lord, consider my complaint : and hearken unto my prayer, that goeth not out of feigned lips.

2 Let my sentence come forth from thy presence : and let thine eyes look upon the thing that is equal.

3 Thou hast proved and visited mine heart in the night-season; thou hast tried me, and shalt find no wickedness in me : for I am utterly purposed that my mouth shall not offend.

4 Because of men's works, that are done against the words of thy lips : I have kept me from the ways of the destroyer.

5 O hold thou up my goings in thy paths : that my footsteps slip not.

6 I have called upon thee, O God, for thou shalt hear me : incline thine ear to me, and hearken unto my words.

7 Shew thy marvellous loving-kindness, thou that art the Saviour of them which put their trust in thee : from such as resist thy right hand.

8 Keep me as the apple of an eye : hide me under the shadow of thy wings.

9 From the ungodly that trouble me : mine enemies compass me round about to take away my soul.

10 They are inclosed in their own fat : and their mouth speaketh proud things.

11 They lie waiting in our way on every side : turning their eyes down to the ground.

12 Like as a lion that is greedy of his prey : and as it were a lion's whelp, lurking in secret places.

13 Up, Lord, disappoint him, and cast him down : deliver my soul from the ungodly, which is a sword of thine;

14 From the men of thy hand, O Lord, from the men, I say, and from the evil world : which have their portion in this life, whose bellies thou fillest with thy hid treasure.

15 They have children at their desire : and leave the rest of their substance for their babes.

16 But as for me, I will behold thy presence in righteousness : and when I awake up after thy likeness, I shall be satisfied with it.

Day 3. Evening Prayer

Psalm 18. *Diligam te, Domine*

WILL love thee, O Lord, my strength; the Lord is my stony rock, and my defence : my saviour, my God, and my might, in whom I will trust, my buckler, the horn also of my salvation, and my refuge.

2 I will call upon the Lord, which is worthy to be praised : so shall I be safe from mine enemies.

3 The sorrows of death compassed me : and the overflowings of ungodliness made me afraid.

4 The pains of hell came about me : the snares of death overtook me.

5 In my trouble I will call upon the Lord : and complain unto my God.

6 So shall he hear my voice out of his holy temple : and my complaint shall come before him, it shall enter even into his ears.

7 The earth trembled and quaked : the very foundations also of the hills shook, and were removed, because he was wroth.

8 There went a smoke out in his presence : and a consuming fire out of his mouth, so that coals were kindled at it.

9 He bowed the heavens also, and came down : and it was dark under his feet.

10 He rode upon the cherubins, and did fly : he came flying upon the wings of the wind.

11 He made darkness his secret place : his pavilion round about him, with dark water and thick clouds to cover him.

12 At the brightness of his presence his clouds removed : hail-stones, and coals of fire.

13 The Lord also thundered out of heaven, and the Highest gave his thunder : hail-stones, and coals of fire.

14 He sent out his arrows, and scattered them : he cast forth lightnings, and destroyed them.

15 The springs of water were seen, and the foundations of the round world were discovered, at thy chiding, O Lord : at the blasting of the breath of thy displeasure.

16 He shall send down from on high to fetch me : and shall take me out of many waters.

17 He shall deliver me from my strongest enemy, and from them which hate me : for they are too mighty for me.

18 They prevented me in the day of my trouble : but the Lord was my up-holder.

19 He brought me forth also into a place of liberty : he brought me forth, even because he had a favour unto me.

20 The Lord shall reward me after my righteous dealing : according to the cleanness of my hands shall he recompense me.

21 Because I have kept the ways of the Lord : and have not forsaken my God, as the wicked doth.

22 For I have an eye unto all his laws : and will not cast out his commandments from me.

23 I was also uncorrupt before him : and eschewed mine own wickedness.

24 Therefore shall the Lord reward me after my righteous dealing : and according unto the cleanness of my hands in his eye-sight.

25 With the holy thou shalt be holy : and with a perfect man thou shalt be perfect.

26 With the clean thou shalt be clean : and with the froward thou shalt learn frowardness.

27 For thou shalt save the people that are in adversity : and shalt bring down the high looks of the proud.

28 Thou also shalt light my candle : the Lord my God shall make my darkness to be light.

29 For in thee I shall discomfit an host of men : and with the help of my God I shall leap over the wall.

30 The way of God is an undefiled way : the word of the Lord also is tried in the fire; he is the defender of all them that put their trust in him.

31 For who is God, but the Lord : or who hath any strength, except our God?

32 It is God, that girdeth me with strength of war : and maketh my way perfect.

33 He maketh my feet like harts' feet : and setteth me up on high.

34 He teacheth mine hands to fight : and mine arms shall break even a bow of steel.

35 Thou hast given me the defence of thy salvation : thy right hand also shall hold me up, and thy loving correction shall make me great.

36 Thou shalt make room enough under me for to go : that my footsteps shall not slide.

37 I will follow upon mine enemies, and overtake them : neither will I turn again till I have destroyed them.

38 I will smite them, that they shall not be able to stand : but fall under my feet.

39 Thou hast girded me with strength unto the battle : thou shalt throw down mine enemies under me.

40 Thou hast made mine enemies also to turn their backs upon me : and I shall destroy them that hate me.

41 They shall cry, but there shall be none to help them : yea, even unto the Lord shall they cry, but he shall not hear them.

42 I will beat them as small as the dust before the wind : I will cast them out as the clay in the streets.

43 Thou shalt deliver me from the strivings of the people : and thou shalt make me the head of the heathen.

44 A people whom I have not known : shall serve me.

45 As soon as they hear of me, they shall obey me : but the strange children shall dissemble with me.

46 The strange children shall fail : and be afraid out of their prisons.

47 The Lord liveth, and blessed be my strong helper : and praised be the Lord of my salvation;

48 Even the God that seeth that I be avenged : and subdueth the people unto me.

49 It is he that delivereth me from my cruel enemies, and setteth me up above mine adversaries : thou shalt rid me from the wicked man.

50 For this cause will I give thanks unto thee, O Lord, among the Gentiles : and sing praises unto thy Name.

51 Great prosperity giveth he unto his King : and sheweth loving-kindness unto David his Anointed, and unto his seed for evermore.

Day 4. Morning Prayer

Psalm 19. *Caeli enarrant*

THE heavens declare the glory of God : and the firmament sheweth his handywork.

2 One day telleth another : and one night certifieth another.

3 There is neither speech nor language : but their voices are heard among them.

4 Their sound is gone out into all lands : and their words into the ends of the world.

5 In them hath he set a tabernacle for the sun : which cometh forth as a bridegroom out of his chamber, and rejoiceth as a giant to run his course.

6 It goeth forth from the uttermost part of the heaven, and runneth about unto the end of it again : and there is nothing hid from the heat thereof.

7 The law of the Lord is an undefiled law, converting the soul : the testimony of the Lord is sure, and giveth wisdom unto the simple.

8 The statutes of the Lord are right, and rejoice the heart : the commandment of the Lord is pure, and giveth light unto the eyes.

9 The fear of the Lord is clean, and endureth for ever : the judgements of the Lord are true, and righteous altogether.

10 More to be desired are they than gold, yea, than much fine gold : sweeter also than honey, and the honey-comb.

11 Moreover, by them is thy servant taught : and in keeping of them there is great reward.

12 Who can tell how oft he offendeth : O cleanse thou me from my secret faults.

13 Keep thy servant also from presumptuous sins, lest they get the dominion over me : so shall I be undefiled, and innocent from the great offence.

14 Let the words of my mouth, and the meditation of my heart : be alway acceptable in thy sight,

15 O Lord : my strength, and my redeemer.

PSALM 20. *EXAUDIAT TE DOMINUS*

HE Lord hear thee in the day of trouble : the Name of the God of Jacob defend thee;

2 Send thee help from the sanctuary : and strengthen thee out of Sion;

3 Remember all thy offerings : and accept thy burnt-sacrifice;

4 Grant thee thy heart's desire : and fulfil all thy mind.

5 We will rejoice in thy salvation, and triumph in the Name of the Lord our God : the Lord perform all thy petitions.

6 Now know I that the Lord helpeth his Anointed, and will hear him from his holy heaven : even with the wholesome strength of his right hand.

7 Some put their trust in chariots, and some in horses : but we will remember the Name of the Lord our God.

8 They are brought down, and fallen : but we are risen, and stand upright.

9 Save, Lord, and hear us, O King of heaven : when we call upon thee.

PSALM 21. *DOMINE, IN VIRTUTE TUA*

HE King shall rejoice in thy strength, O Lord : exceeding glad shall he be of thy salvation.

2 Thou hast given him his heart's desire : and hast not denied him the request of his lips.

3 For thou shalt prevent him with the blessings of goodness : and shalt set a crown of pure gold upon his head.

4 He asked life of thee, and thou gavest him a long life : even for ever and ever.

5 His honour is great in thy salvation : glory and great worship shalt thou lay upon him.

6 For thou shalt give him everlasting felicity : and make him glad with the joy of thy countenance.

7 And why? because the King putteth his trust in the Lord : and in the mercy of the most Highest he shall not miscarry.

8 All thine enemies shall feel thine hand : thy right hand shall find out them that hate thee.

9 Thou shalt make them like a fiery oven in time of thy wrath : the Lord shall destroy them in his displeasure, and the fire shall consume them.

10 Their fruit shalt thou root out of the earth : and their seed from among the children of men.

11 For they intended mischief against thee : and imagined such a device as they are not able to perform.

12 Therefore shalt thou put them to flight : and the strings of thy bow shalt thou make ready against the face of them.

13 Be thou exalted, Lord, in thine own strength : so we will sing, and praise thy power.

Day 4. Evening Prayer

PSALM 22. *DEUS, DEUS MEUS*

MY God, my God, look upon me; why hast thou forsaken me : and art so far from my health, and from the words of my complaint?

2 O my God, I cry in the day-time, but thou hearest not : and in the night-season also I take no rest.

3 And thou continuest holy : O thou worship of Israel.

4 Our fathers hoped in thee : they trusted in thee, and thou didst deliver them.

5 They called upon thee, and were holpen : they put their trust in thee, and were not confounded.

6 But as for me, I am a worm, and no man : a very scorn of men, and the outcast of the people.

7 All they that see me laugh me to scorn : they shoot out their lips, and shake their heads, saying,

8 He trusted in God, that he would deliver him : let him deliver him, if he will have him.

9 But thou art he that took me out of my mother's womb : thou wast my hope, when I hanged yet upon my mother's breasts.

10 I have been left unto thee ever since I was born : thou art my God, even from my mother's womb.

11 O go not from me, for trouble is hard at hand : and there is none to help me.

12 Many oxen are come about me : fat bulls of Basan close me in on every side.

13 They gape upon me with their mouths : as it were a ramping and a roaring lion.

14 I am poured out like water, and all my bones are out of joint : my heart also in the midst of my body is even like melting wax.

15 My strength is dried up like a potsherd, and my tongue cleaveth to my gums : and thou shalt bring me into the dust of death.

16 For many dogs are come about me : and the council of the wicked layeth siege against me.

17 They pierced my hands and my feet; I may tell all my bones : they stand staring and looking upon me.

18 They part my garments among them : and casts lots upon my vesture.

19 But be not thou far from me, O Lord : thou art my succour, haste thee to help me.

20 Deliver my soul from the sword : my darling from the power of the dog.

21 Save me from the lion's mouth : thou hast heard me also from among the horns of the unicorns.

22 I will declare thy Name unto my brethren : in the midst of the congregation will I praise thee.

23 O praise the Lord, ye that fear him : magnify him, all ye of the seed of Jacob, and fear him, all ye seed of Israel.

24 For he hath not despised, nor abhorred, the low estate of the poor : he hath not hid his face from him, but when he called unto him he heard him.

25 My praise is of thee in the great congregation : my vows will I perform in the sight of them that fear him.

26 The poor shall eat and be satisfied : they that seek after the Lord shall praise him; your heart shall live for ever.

27 All the ends of the world shall remember themselves, and be turned unto the Lord : and all the kindreds of the nations shall worship before him.

28 For the kingdom is the Lord's : and he is the Governor among the people.

29 All such as be fat upon earth : have eaten and worshipped.

30 All they that go down into the dust shall kneel before him : and no man hath quickened his own soul.

31 My seed shall serve him : they shall be counted unto the Lord for a generation.

32 They shall come, and the heavens shall declare his righteousness : unto a people that shall be born, whom the Lord hath made.

PSALM 23. *DOMINUS REGIT ME.*

THE Lord is my shepherd : therefore can I lack nothing.

2 He shall feed me in a green pasture : and lead me forth beside the waters of comfort.

3 He shall convert my soul : and bring me forth in the paths of righteousness, for his Name's sake.

4 Yea, though I walk through the valley of the shadow of death, I will fear no evil : for thou art with me; thy rod and thy staff comfort me.

5 Thou shalt prepare a table before me against them that trouble me : thou hast anointed my head with oil, and my cup shall be full.

6 But thy loving-kindness and mercy shall follow me all the days of my life : and I will dwell in the house of the Lord for ever.

Day 5. Morning Prayer

PSALM 24. *DOMINI EST TERRA*

THE earth is the Lord's, and all that therein is : the compass of the world, and they that dwell therein.

2 For he hath founded it upon the seas : and prepared it upon the floods.

3 Who shall ascend into the hill of the Lord : or who shall rise up in his holy place?

4 Even he that hath clean hands, and a pure heart : and that hath not lift up his mind unto vanity, nor sworn to deceive his neighbour.

5 He shall receive the blessing from the Lord : and righteousness from the God of his salvation.

6 This is the generation of them that seek him : even of them that seek thy face, O Jacob.

7 Lift up your heads, O ye gates, and be ye lift up, ye everlasting doors : and the King of glory shall come in.

8 Who is the King of glory : it is the Lord strong and mighty, even the Lord mighty in battle.

9 Lift up your heads, O ye gates, and be ye lift up, ye everlasting doors : and the King of glory shall come in.

10 Who is the King of glory : even the Lord of hosts, he is the King of glory.

Psalm 25. *Ad te, Domine, levavi*

NTO thee, O Lord, will I lift up my soul; my God, I have put my trust in thee : O let me not be confounded, neither let mine enemies triumph over me.

2 For all they that hope in thee shall not be ashamed : but such as transgress without a cause shall be put to confusion.

3 Shew me thy ways, O Lord : and teach me thy paths.

4 Lead me forth in thy truth, and learn me : for thou art the God of my salvation; in thee hath been my hope all the day long.

5 Call to remembrance, O Lord, thy tender mercies : and thy loving-kindnesses, which have been ever of old.

6 O remember not the sins and offences of my youth : but according to thy mercy think thou upon me, O Lord, for thy goodness.

7 Gracious and righteous is the Lord : therefore will he teach sinners in the way.

8 Them that are meek shall he guide in judgement : and such as are gentle, them shall he learn his way.

9 All the paths of the Lord are mercy and truth : unto such as keep his covenant and his testimonies.

10 For thy Name's sake, O Lord : be merciful unto my sin, for it is great.

11 What man is he that feareth the Lord : him shall he teach in the way that he shall choose.

12 His soul shall dwell at ease : and his seed shall inherit the land.

13 The secret of the Lord is among them that fear him : and he will shew them his covenant.

14 Mine eyes are ever looking unto the Lord : for he shall pluck my feet out of the net.

15 Turn thee unto me, and have mercy upon me : for I am desolate and in misery.

16 The sorrows of my heart are enlarged : O bring thou me out of my troubles.

17 Look upon my adversity and misery : and forgive me all my sin.

18 Consider mine enemies, how many they are : and they bear a tyrannous hate against me.

19 O keep my soul, and deliver me : let me not be confounded, for I have put my trust in thee.

20 Let perfectness and righteous dealing wait upon me : for my hope hath been in thee.

21 Deliver Israel, O God : out of all his troubles.

Psalm 26. *Judica me, Domine*

ᴮE thou my judge, O Lord, for I have walked innocently : my trust hath been also in the Lord, therefore shall I not fall.

2 Examine me, O Lord, and prove me : try out my reins and my heart.

3 For thy loving-kindness is ever before mine eyes : and I will walk in thy truth.

4 I have not dwelt with vain persons : neither will I have fellowship with the deceitful.

5 I have hated the congregation of the wicked : and will not sit among the ungodly.

6 I will wash my hands in innocency, O Lord : and so will I go to thine altar.

7 That I may shew the voice of thanksgiving : and tell of all thy wondrous works.

8 Lord, I have loved the habitation of thy house : and the place where thine honour dwelleth.

9 O shut not up my soul with the sinners : nor my life with the blood-thirsty.

10 In whose hands is wickedness : and their right hand is full of gifts.

11 But as for me, I will walk innocently : O deliver me, and be merciful unto me.

12 My foot standeth right : I will praise the Lord in the congregations.

Day 5. Evening Prayer

Psalm 27. *Dominus illuminatio*

ᵀHE Lord is my light and my salvation; whom then shall I fear : the Lord is the strength of my life; of whom then shall I be afraid?

2 When the wicked, even mine enemies and my foes, came upon me to eat up my flesh : they stumbled and fell.

3 Though an host of men were laid against me, yet shall not my heart be afraid : and though there rose up war against me, yet will I put my trust in him.

4 One thing have I desired of the Lord, which I will require : even that I may dwell in the house of the Lord all the days of my life, to behold the fair beauty of the Lord, and to visit his temple.

5 For in the time of trouble he shall hide me in his tabernacle : yea, in the secret place of his dwelling shall he hide me, and set me up upon a rock of stone.

6 And now shall he lift up mine head : above mine enemies round about me.

7 Therefore will I offer in his dwelling an oblation with great gladness : I will sing, and speak praises unto the Lord.

8 Hearken unto my voice, O Lord, when I cry unto thee : have mercy upon me, and hear me.

9 My heart hath talked of thee, Seek ye my face : Thy face, Lord, will I seek.

10 O hide not thou thy face from me : nor cast thy servant away in displeasure.

11 Thou hast been my succour : leave me not, neither forsake me, O God of my salvation.

12 When my father and my mother forsake me : the Lord taketh me up.

13 Teach me thy way, O Lord : and lead me in the right way, because of mine enemies.

14 Deliver me not over into the will of mine adversaries : for there are false witnesses risen up against me, and such as speak wrong.

15 I should utterly have fainted : but that I believe verily to see the goodness of the Lord in the land of the living.

16 O tarry thou the Lord's leisure : be strong, and he shall comfort thine heart; and put thou thy trust in the Lord.

Psalm 28. *Ad te, Domine*

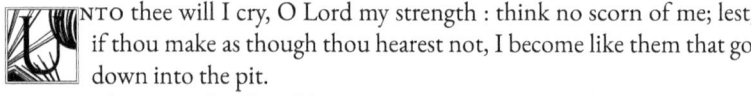 NTO thee will I cry, O Lord my strength : think no scorn of me; lest, if thou make as though thou hearest not, I become like them that go down into the pit.

2 Hear the voice of my humble petitions, when I cry unto thee : when I hold up my hands towards the mercy-seat of thy holy temple.

3 O pluck me not away, neither destroy me, with the ungodly and wicked doers : which speak friendly to their neighbours, but imagine mischief in their hearts.

4 Reward them according to their deeds : and according to the wickedness of their own inventions.

5 Recompense them after the work of their hands : pay them that they have deserved.

6 For they regard not in their mind the works of the Lord, nor the operation of his hands : therefore shall he break them down, and not build them up.

7 Praised be the Lord : for he hath heard the voice of my humble petitions.

8 The Lord is my strength and my shield; my heart hath trusted in him, and I am helped : therefore my heart danceth for joy, and in my song will I praise him.

9 The Lord is my strength : and he is the wholesome defence of his Anointed.

10 O save thy people, and give thy blessing unto thine inheritance : feed them, and set them up for ever.

PSALM 29. *AFFERTE DOMINO*

RING unto the Lord, O ye mighty, bring young rams unto the Lord : ascribe unto the Lord worship and strength.

2 Give the Lord the honour due unto his Name : worship the Lord with holy worship.

3 It is the Lord that commandeth the waters : it is the glorious God that maketh the thunder.

4 It is the Lord that ruleth the sea; the voice of the Lord is mighty in operation : the voice of the Lord is a glorious voice.

5 The voice of the Lord breaketh the cedar-trees : yea, the Lord breaketh the cedars of Libanus.

6 He maketh them also to skip like a calf : Libanus also, and Sirion, like a young unicorn.

7 The voice of the Lord divideth the flames of fire; the voice of the Lord shaketh the wilderness : yea, the Lord shaketh the wilderness of Cades.

8 The voice of the Lord maketh the hinds to bring forth young, and discovereth the thick bushes : in his temple doth every man speak of his honour.

9 The Lord sitteth above the water-flood : and the Lord remaineth a King for ever.

10 The Lord shall give strength unto his people : the Lord shall give his people the blessing of peace.

Day 6. Morning Prayer

PSALM 30. *EXALTABO TE, DOMINE*

WILL magnify thee, O Lord, for thou hast set me up : and not made my foes to triumph over me.

2 O Lord my God, I cried unto thee : and thou hast healed me.

3 Thou, Lord, hast brought my soul out of hell : thou hast kept my life from them that go down to the pit.

4 Sing praises unto the Lord, O ye saints of his : and give thanks unto him for a remembrance of his holiness.

5 For his wrath endureth but the twinkling of an eye, and in his pleasure is life : heaviness may endure for a night, but joy cometh in the morning.

6 And in my prosperity I said, I shall never be removed : thou, Lord, of thy goodness hast made my hill so strong.

7 Thou didst turn thy face from me : and I was troubled.

8 Then cried I unto thee, O Lord : and gat me to my Lord right humbly.

9 What profit is there in my blood : when I go down to the pit?

10 Shall the dust give thanks unto thee : or shall it declare thy truth?

11 Hear, O Lord, and have mercy upon me : Lord, be thou my helper.

12 Thou hast turned my heaviness into joy : thou hast put off my sackcloth, and girded me with gladness.

13 Therefore shall every good man sing of thy praise without ceasing : O my God, I will give thanks unto thee for ever.

Psalm 31. *In te, Domine, speravi*

IN thee, O Lord, have I put my trust : let me never be put to confusion, deliver me in thy righteousness.

2 Bow down thine ear to me : make haste to deliver me.

3 And be thou my strong rock, and house of defence : that thou mayest save me.

4 For thou art my strong rock, and my castle : be thou also my guide, and lead me for thy Name's sake.

5 Draw me out of the net that they have laid privily for me : for thou art my strength.

6 Into thy hands I commend my spirit : for thou hast redeemed me, O Lord, thou God of truth.

7 I have hated them that hold of superstitious vanities : and my trust hath been in the Lord.

8 I will be glad and rejoice in thy mercy : for thou hast considered my trouble, and hast known my soul in adversities.

9 Thou hast not shut me up into the hand of the enemy : but hast set my feet in a large room.

10 Have mercy upon me, O Lord, for I am in trouble : and mine eye is consumed for very heaviness; yea, my soul and my body.

11 For my life is waxen old with heaviness : and my years with mourning.

12 My strength faileth me, because of mine iniquity : and my bones are consumed.

13 I became a reproof among all mine enemies, but especially among my neighbours : and they of mine acquaintance were afraid of me; and they that did see me without conveyed themselves from me.

14 I am clean forgotten, as a dead man out of mind : I am become like a broken vessel.

15 For I have heard the blasphemy of the multitude : and fear is on every side, while they conspire together against me, and take their counsel to take away my life.

16 But my hope hath been in thee, O Lord : I have said, Thou art my God.

17 My time is in thy hand; deliver me from the hand of mine enemies : and from them that persecute me.

18 Shew thy servant the light of thy countenance : and save me for thy mercy's sake.

19 Let me not be confounded, O Lord, for I have called upon thee : let the ungodly be put to confusion, and be put to silence in the grave.

20 Let the lying lips be put to silence : which cruelly, disdainfully, and despitefully, speak against the righteous.

21 O how plentiful is thy goodness, which thou hast laid up for them that fear thee : and that thou hast prepared for them that put their trust in thee, even before the sons of men!

22 Thou shalt hide them privily by thine own presence from the provoking of all men : thou shalt keep them secretly in thy tabernacle from the strife of tongues.

23 Thanks be to the Lord : for he hath shewed me marvellous great kindness in a strong city.

24 And when I made haste, I said : I am cast out of the sight of thine eyes.

25 Nevertheless, thou heardest the voice of my prayer : when I cried unto thee.

26 O love the Lord, all ye his saints : for the Lord preserveth them that are faithful, and plenteously rewardeth the proud doer.

27 Be strong, and he shall establish your heart : all ye that put your trust in the Lord.

Day 6. Evening Prayer

PSALM 32. *BEATI, QUORUM*

LESSED is he whose unrighteousness is forgiven : and whose sin is covered.

2 Blessed is the man unto whom the Lord imputeth no sin : and in whose spirit there is no guile.

3 For while I held my tongue : my bones consumed away through my daily complaining.

4 For thy hand is heavy upon me day and night : and my moisture is like the drought in summer.

5 I will acknowledge my sin unto thee : and mine unrighteousness have I not hid.

6 I said, I will confess my sins unto the Lord : and so thou forgavest the wickedness of my sin.

7 For this shall every one that is godly make his prayer unto thee, in a time when thou mayest be found : but in the great water-floods they shall not come nigh him.

8 Thou art a place to hide me in, thou shalt preserve me from trouble : thou shalt compass me about with songs of deliverance.

9 I will inform thee, and teach thee in the way wherein thou shalt go : and I will guide thee with mine eye.

10 Be ye not like to horse and mule, which have no understanding : whose mouths must be held with bit and bridle, lest they fall upon thee.

11 Great plagues remain for the ungodly : but whoso putteth his trust in the Lord, mercy embraceth him on every side.

12 Be glad, O ye righteous, and rejoice in the Lord : and be joyful, all ye that are true of heart.

PSALM 33. *EXULTATE, JUSTI*

REJOICE in the Lord, O ye righteous : for it becometh well the just to be thankful.

2 Praise the Lord with harp : sing praises unto him with the lute, and instrument of ten strings.

3 Sing unto the Lord a new song : sing praises lustily unto him with a good courage.

4 For the word of the Lord is true : and all his works are faithful.

5 He loveth righteousness and judgement : the earth is full of the goodness of the Lord.

6 By the word of the Lord were the heavens made : and all the hosts of them by the breath of his mouth.

7 He gathereth the waters of the sea together, as it were upon an heap : and layeth up the deep, as in a treasure-house.

8 Let all the earth fear the Lord : stand in awe of him, all ye that dwell in the world.

9 For he spake, and it was done : he commanded, and it stood fast.

10 The Lord bringeth the counsel of the heathen to nought : and maketh the devices of the people to be of none effect, and casteth out the counsels of princes.

11 The counsel of the Lord shall endure for ever : and the thoughts of his heart from generation to generation.

12 Blessed are the people, whose God is the Lord JEHOVAH : and blessed are the folk, that he hath chosen to him to be his inheritance.

13 The Lord looked down from heaven, and beheld all the children of men : from the habitation of his dwelling he considereth all them that dwell on the earth.

14 He fashioneth all the hearts of them : and understandeth all their works.

15 There is no king that can be saved by the multitude of an host : neither is any mighty man delivered by much strength.

16 A horse is counted but a vain thing to save a man : neither shall he deliver any man by his great strength.

17 Behold, the eye of the Lord is upon them that fear him : and upon them that put their trust in his mercy;

18 To deliver their soul from death : and to feed them in the time of dearth.

19 Our soul hath patiently tarried for the Lord : for he is our help and our shield.

20 For our heart shall rejoice in him : because we have hoped in his holy Name.

21 Let thy merciful kindness, O Lord, be upon us : like as we do put our trust in thee.

PSALM 34. *BENEDICAM DOMINO*

I WILL alway give thanks unto the Lord : his praise shall ever be in my mouth.

2 My soul shall make her boast in the Lord : the humble shall hear thereof, and be glad.

3 O praise the Lord with me : and let us magnify his Name together.

4 I sought the Lord, and he heard me : yea, he delivered me out of all my fear.

5 They had an eye unto him, and were lightened : and their faces were not ashamed.

6 Lo, the poor crieth, and the Lord heareth him : yea, and saveth him out of all his troubles.

7 The angel of the Lord tarrieth round about them that fear him : and delivereth them.

8 O taste, and see, how gracious the Lord is : blessed is the man that trusteth in him.

9 O fear the Lord, ye that are his saints : for they that fear him lack nothing.

10 The lions do lack, and suffer hunger : but they who seek the Lord shall want no manner of thing that is good.

11 Come, ye children, and hearken unto me : I will teach you the fear of the Lord.

12 What man is he that lusteth to live : and would fain see good days?

13 Keep thy tongue from evil : and thy lips, that they speak no guile.

14 Eschew evil, and do good : seek peace, and ensue it.

15 The eyes of the Lord are over the righteous : and his ears are open unto their prayers.

16 The countenance of the Lord is against them that do evil : to root out the remembrance of them from the earth.

17 The righteous cry, and the Lord heareth them : and delivereth them out of all their troubles.

18 The Lord is nigh unto them that are of a contrite heart : and will save such as be of an humble spirit.

19 Great are the troubles of the righteous : but the Lord delivereth him out of all.

20 He keepeth all his bones : so that not one of them is broken.

21 But misfortune shall slay the ungodly : and they that hate the righteous shall be desolate.

22 The Lord delivereth the souls of his servants : and all they that put their trust in him shall not be destitute.

Day 7. Morning Prayer

PSALM 35. *JUDICA, DOMINE*

PLEAD thou my cause, O Lord, with them that strive with me : and fight thou against them that fight against me.

2 Lay hand upon the shield and buckler : and stand up to help me.

3 Bring forth the spear, and stop the way against them that persecute me : say unto my soul, I am thy salvation.

4 Let them be confounded and put to shame, that seek after my soul : let them be turned back and brought to confusion, that imagine mischief for me.

5 Let them be as the dust before the wind : and the angel of the Lord scattering them.

6 Let their way be dark and slippery : and let the angel of the Lord persecute them.

7 For they have privily laid their net to destroy me without a cause : yea, even without a cause have they made a pit for my soul.

8 Let a sudden destruction come upon him unawares, and his net, that he hath laid privily, catch himself : that he may fall into his own mischief.

9 And, my soul, be joyful in the Lord : it shall rejoice in his salvation.

10 All my bones shall say, Lord, who is like unto thee, who deliverest the poor from him that is too strong for him : yea, the poor, and him that is in misery, from him that spoileth him?

11 False witnesses did rise up : they laid to my charge things that I knew not.

12 They rewarded me evil for good : to the great discomfort of my soul.

13 Nevertheless, when they were sick, I put on sackcloth, and humbled my soul with fasting : and my prayer shall turn into mine own bosom.

14 I behaved myself as though it had been my friend or my brother : I went heavily, as one that mourneth for his mother.

15 But in mine adversity they rejoiced, and gathered themselves together : yea, the very abjects came together against me unawares, making mouths at me, and ceased not.

16 With the flatterers were busy mockers : who gnashed upon me with their teeth.

17 Lord, how long wilt thou look upon this : O deliver my soul from the calamities which they bring on me, and my darling from the lions.

18 So will I give thee thanks in the great congregation : I will praise thee among much people.

19 O let not them that are mine enemies triumph over me ungodly : neither let them wink with their eyes that hate me without a cause.

20 And why? their communing is not for peace : but they imagine deceitful words against them that are quiet in the land.

21 They gaped upon me with their mouths, and said : Fie on thee, fie on thee, we saw it with our eyes.

22 This thou hast seen, O Lord : hold not thy tongue then, go not far from me, O Lord.

23 Awake, and stand up to judge my quarrel : avenge thou my cause, my God, and my Lord.

24 Judge me, O Lord my God, according to thy righteousness : and let them not triumph over me.

25 Let them not say in their hearts, There, there, so would we have it : neither let them say, We have devoured him.

26 Let them be put to confusion and shame together, that rejoice at my trouble : let them be clothed with rebuke and dishonour, that boast themselves against me.

27 Let them be glad and rejoice, that favour my righteous dealing : yea, let them say alway, Blessed be the Lord, who hath pleasure in the prosperity of his servant.

28 And as for my tongue, it shall be talking of thy righteousness : and of thy praise all the day long.

PSALM 36. *DIXIT INJUSTUS*

MY heart sheweth me the wickedness of the ungodly : that there is no fear of God before his eyes.

2 For he flattereth himself in his own sight : until his abominable sin be found out.

3 The words of his mouth are unrighteous, and full of deceit : he hath left off to behave himself wisely, and to do good.

4 He imagineth mischief upon his bed, and hath set himself in no good way : neither doth he abhor any thing that is evil.

5 Thy mercy, O Lord, reacheth unto the heavens : and thy faithfulness unto the clouds.

6 Thy righteousness standeth like the strong mountains : thy judgements are like the great deep.

7 Thou, Lord, shalt save both man and beast; How excellent is thy mercy, O God : and the children of men shall put their trust under the shadow of thy wings.

8 They shall be satisfied with the plenteousness of thy house : and thou shalt give them drink of thy pleasures, as out of the river.

9 For with thee is the well of life : and in thy light shall we see light.

10 O continue forth thy loving-kindness unto them that know thee : and thy righteousness unto them that are true of heart.

11 O let not the foot of pride come against me : and let not the hand of the ungodly cast me down.

12 There are they fallen, all that work wickedness : they are cast down, and shall not be able to stand.

Day 7. Evening Prayer

PSALM 37. *NOLI AEMULARI*

FRET not thyself because of the ungodly : neither be thou envious against the evil-doers.

2 For they shall soon be cut down like the grass : and be withered even as the green herb.

3 Put thou thy trust in the Lord, and be doing good : dwell in the land, and verily thou shalt be fed.

4 Delight thou in the Lord : and he shall give thee thy heart's desire.

5 Commit thy way unto the Lord, and put thy trust in him : and he shall bring it to pass.

6 He shall make thy righteousness as clear as the light : and thy just dealing as the noon-day.

7 Hold thee still in the Lord, and abide patiently upon him : but grieve not thyself at him whose way doth prosper, against the man that doeth after evil counsels.

8 Leave off from wrath, and let go displeasure : fret not thyself, else shalt thou be moved to do evil.

9 Wicked doers shall be rooted out : and they that patiently abide the Lord, those shall inherit the land.

10 Yet a little while, and the ungodly shall be clean gone : thou shalt look after his place, and he shall be away.

11 But the meek-spirited shall possess the earth : and shall be refreshed in the multitude of peace.

12 The ungodly seeketh counsel against the just : and gnasheth upon him with his teeth.

13 The Lord shall laugh him to scorn : for he hath seen that his day is coming.

14 The ungodly have drawn out the sword, and have bent their bow : to cast down the poor and needy, and to slay such as are of a right conversation.

15 Their sword shall go through their own heart : and their bow shall be broken.

16 A small thing that the righteous hath : is better than great riches of the ungodly.

17 For the arms of the ungodly shall be broken : and the Lord upholdeth the righteous.

18 The Lord knoweth the days of the godly : and their inheritance shall endure for ever.

19 They shall not be confounded in the perilous time : and in the days of dearth they shall have enough.

20 As for the ungodly, they shall perish; and the enemies of the Lord shall consume as the fat of lambs : yea, even as the smoke shall they consume away.

21 The ungodly borroweth, and payeth not again : but the righteous is merciful and liberal.

22 Such as are blessed of God shall possess the land : and they that are cursed of him shall be rooted out.

23 The Lord ordereth a good man's going : and maketh his way acceptable to himself.

24 Though he fall, he shall not be cast away : for the Lord upholdeth him with his hand.

25 I have been young, and now am old : and yet saw I never the righteous forsaken, nor his seed begging their bread.

26 The righteous is ever merciful, and lendeth : and his seed is blessed.

27 Flee from evil, and do the thing that is good : and dwell for evermore.

28 For the Lord loveth the thing that is right : he forsaketh not his that be godly, but they are preserved for ever.

29 The unrighteous shall be punished : as for the seed of the ungodly, it shall be rooted out.

30 The righteous shall inherit the land : and dwell therein for ever.

31 The mouth of the righteous is exercised in wisdom : and his tongue will be talking of judgement.

32 The law of his God is in his heart : and his goings shall not slide.

33 The ungodly seeth the righteous : and seeketh occasion to slay him.

34 The Lord will not leave him in his hand : nor condemn him when he is judged.

35 Hope thou in the Lord, and keep his way, and he shall promote thee, that thou shalt possess the land : when the ungodly shall perish, thou shalt see it.

36 I myself have seen the ungodly in great power : and flourishing like a green bay-tree.

37 I went by, and lo, he was gone : I sought him, but his place could no where be found.

38 Keep innocency, and take heed unto the thing that is right : for that shall bring a man peace at the last.

39 As for the transgressors, they shall perish together : and the end of the ungodly is, they shall be rooted out at the last.

40 But the salvation of the righteous cometh of the Lord : who is also their strength in the time of trouble.

41 And the Lord shall stand by them, and save them : he shall deliver them from the ungodly, and shall save them, because they put their trust in him.

Day 8. Morning Prayer

Psalm 38. *Domine, ne in furore*

UT me not to rebuke, O Lord, in thine anger : neither chasten me in thy heavy displeasure.

2 For thine arrows stick fast in me : and thy hand presseth me sore.

3 There is no health in my flesh, because of thy displeasure : neither is there any rest in my bones, by reason of my sin.

4 For my wickednesses are gone over my head : and are like a sore burden, too heavy for me to bear.

5 My wounds stink, and are corrupt : through my foolishness.

6 I am brought into so great trouble and misery : that I go mourning all the day long.

7 For my loins are filled with a sore disease : and there is no whole part in my body.

8 I am feeble, and sore smitten : I have roared for the very disquietness of my heart.

9 Lord, thou knowest all my desire : and my groaning is not hid from thee.

10 My heart panteth, my strength hath failed me : and the sight of mine eyes is gone from me.

11 My lovers and my neighbours did stand looking upon my trouble : and my kinsmen stood afar off.

12 They also that sought after my life laid snares for me : and they that went about to do me evil talked of wickedness, and imagined deceit all the day long.

13 As for me, I was like a deaf man, and heard not : and as one that is dumb, who doth not open his mouth.

14 I became even as a man that heareth not : and in whose mouth are no reproofs.

15 For in thee, O Lord, have I put my trust : thou shalt answer for me, O Lord my God.

16 I have required that they, even mine enemies, should not triumph over me : for when my foot slipped, they rejoiced greatly against me.

17 And I, truly, am set in the plague : and my heaviness is ever in my sight.

18 For I will confess my wickedness : and be sorry for my sin.

19 But mine enemies live, and are mighty : and they that hate me wrongfully are many in number.

20 They also that reward evil for good are against me : because I follow the thing that good is.

21 Forsake me not, O Lord my God : be not thou far from me.

22 Haste thee to help me : O Lord God of my salvation.

PSALM 39. *DIXI, CUSTODIAM*

SAID, I will take heed to my ways : that I offend not in my tongue.

2 I will keep my mouth as it were with a bridle : while the ungodly is in my sight.

3 I held my tongue, and spake nothing : I kept silence, yea, even from good words; but it was pain and grief to me.

4 My heart was hot within me, and while I was thus musing the fire kindled : and at the last I spake with my tongue;

5 Lord, let me know mine end, and the number of my days : that I may be certified how long I have to live.

6 Behold, thou hast made my days as it were a span long : and mine age is even as nothing in respect of thee; and verily every man living is altogether vanity.

7 For man walketh in a vain shadow, and disquieteth himself in vain : he heapeth up riches, and cannot tell who shall gather them.

8 And now, Lord, what is my hope : truly my hope is even in thee.

9 Deliver me from all mine offences : and make me not a rebuke unto the foolish.

10 I became dumb, and opened not my mouth : for it was thy doing.

11 Take thy plague away from me : I am even consumed by the means of thy heavy hand.

12 When thou with rebukes dost chasten man for sin, thou makest his beauty to consume away, like as it were a moth fretting a garment : every man therefore is but vanity.

13 Hear my prayer, O Lord, and with thine ears consider my calling : hold not thy peace at my tears.

14 For I am a stranger with thee : and a sojourner, as all my fathers were.

15 O spare me a little, that I may recover my strength : before I go hence, and be no more seen.

Psalm 40. *Expectans expectavi*

WAITED patiently for the Lord : and he inclined unto me, and heard my calling.

2 He brought me also out of the horrible pit, out of the mire and clay : and set my feet upon the rock, and ordered my goings.

3 And he hath put a new song in my mouth : even a thanksgiving unto our God.

4 Many shall see it, and fear : and shall put their trust in the Lord.

5 Blessed is the man that hath set his hope in the Lord : and turned not unto the proud, and to such as go about with lies.

6 O Lord my God, great are the wondrous works which thou hast done, like as be also thy thoughts which are to us-ward : and yet there is no man that ordereth them unto thee:

7 If I should declare them, and speak of them : they should be more than I am able to express.

8 Sacrifice and meat-offering thou wouldest not : but mine ears hast thou opened.

9 Burnt-offerings, and sacrifice for sin, hast thou not required : then said I, Lo, I come,

10 In the volume of the book it is written of me, that I should fulfil thy will, O my God : I am content to do it; yea, thy law is within my heart.

11 I have declared thy righteousness in the great congregation : lo, I will not refrain my lips, O Lord, and that thou knowest.

12 I have not hid thy righteousness within my heart : my talk hath been of thy truth and of thy salvation.

13 I have not kept back thy loving mercy and truth : from the great congregation.

14 Withdraw not thou thy mercy from me, O Lord : let thy loving-kindness and thy truth alway preserve me.

15 For innumerable troubles are come about me; my sins have taken such hold upon me that I am not able to look up : yea, they are more in number than the hairs of my head, and my heart hath failed me.

16 O Lord, let it be thy pleasure to deliver me : make haste, O Lord, to help me.

17 Let them be ashamed and confounded together, that seek after my soul to destroy it : let them be driven backward and put to rebuke, that wish me evil.

18 Let them be desolate, and rewarded with shame : that say unto me, Fie upon thee, fie upon thee.

19 Let all those that seek thee be joyful and glad in thee : and let such as love thy salvation say alway, The Lord be praised.

20 As for me, I am poor and needy : but the Lord careth for me.

21 Thou art my helper and redeemer : make no long tarrying, O my God.

Day 8. Evening Prayer

PSALM 41. *BEATUS QUI INTELLIGIT*

BLESSED is he that considereth the poor and needy : the Lord shall deliver him in the time of trouble.

2 The Lord preserve him, and keep him alive, that he may be blessed upon earth : and deliver not thou him into the will of his enemies.

3 The Lord comfort him, when he lieth sick upon his bed : make thou all his bed in his sickness.

4 I said, Lord, be merciful unto me : heal my soul, for I have sinned against thee.

5 Mine enemies speak evil of me : When shall he die, and his name perish?

6 And if he come to see me, he speaketh vanity : and his heart conceiveth falsehood within himself, and when he cometh forth he telleth it.

7 All mine enemies whisper together against me : even against me do they imagine this evil.

8 Let the sentence of guiltiness proceed against him : and now that he lieth, let him rise up no more.

9 Yea, even mine own familiar friend, whom I trusted : who did also eat of my bread, hath laid great wait for me.

10 But be thou merciful unto me, O Lord : raise thou me up again, and I shall reward them.

11 By this I know thou favourest me : that mine enemy doth not triumph against me.

12 And when I am in my health, thou upholdest me : and shalt set me before thy face for ever.

13 Blessed be the Lord God of Israel : world without end. Amen.

PSALM 42. *QUEMADMODUM*

LIKE as the hart desireth the water-brooks : so longeth my soul after thee, O God.

2 My soul is athirst for God, yea, even for the living God : when shall I come to appear before the presence of God?

3 My tears have been my meat day and night : while they daily say unto me, Where is now thy God?

4 Now when I think thereupon, I pour out my heart by myself : for I went with the multitude, and brought them forth into the house of God;

5 In the voice of praise and thanksgiving : among such as keep holy-day.

6 Why art thou so full of heaviness, O my soul : and why art thou so disquieted within me?

7 Put thy trust in God : for I will yet give him thanks for the help of his countenance.

8 My God, my soul is vexed within me : therefore will I remember thee concerning the land of Jordan, and the little hill of Hermon.

9 One deep calleth another, because of the noise of the water-pipes : all thy waves and storms are gone over me.

10 The Lord hath granted his loving-kindness in the day-time : and in the night-season did I sing of him, and made my prayer unto the God of my life.

11 I will say unto the God of my strength, Why hast thou forgotten me : why go I thus heavily, while the enemy oppresseth me?

12 My bones are smitten asunder as with a sword : while mine enemies that trouble me cast me in the teeth;

13 Namely, while they say daily unto me : Where is now thy God?

14 Why art thou so vexed, O my soul : and why art thou so disquieted within me?

15 O put thy trust in God : for I will yet thank him, which is the help of my countenance, and my God.

PSALM 43. *JUDICA ME, DEUS*

IVE sentence with me, O God, and defend my cause against the ungodly people : O deliver me from the deceitful and wicked man.

2 For thou art the God of my strength, why hast thou put me from thee : and why go I so heavily, while the enemy oppresseth me?

3 O send out thy light and thy truth, that they may lead me : and bring me unto thy holy hill, and to thy dwelling.

4 And that I may go unto the altar of God, even unto the God of my joy and gladness : and upon the harp will I give thanks unto thee, O God, my God.

5 Why art thou so heavy, O my soul : and why art thou so disquieted within me?

6 O put thy trust in God : for I will yet give him thanks, which is the help of my countenance, and my God.

Day 9. Morning Prayer

PSALM 44. *DEUS, AURIBUS*

W E have heard with our ears, O God, our fathers have told us : what thou hast done in their time of old;

2 How thou hast driven out the heathen with thy hand, and planted them in : how thou hast destroyed the nations and cast them out.

3 For they gat not the land in possession through their own sword : neither was it their own arm that helped them;

4 But thy right hand, and thine arm, and the light of thy countenance : because thou hadst a favour unto them.

5 Thou art my King, O God : send help unto Jacob.

6 Through thee will we overthrow our enemies : and in thy Name will we tread them under, that rise up against us.

7 For I will not trust in my bow : it is not my sword that shall help me;

8 But it is thou that savest us from our enemies : and puttest them to confusion that hate us.

9 We make our boast of God all day long : and will praise thy Name for ever.

10 But now thou art far off, and puttest us to confusion : and goest not forth with our armies.

11 Thou makest us to turn our backs upon our enemies : so that they which hate us spoil our goods.

12 Thou lettest us be eaten up like sheep : and hast scattered us among the heathen.

13 Thou sellest thy people for nought : and takest no money for them.

14 Thou makest us to be rebuked of our neighbours : to be laughed to scorn, and had in derision of them that are round about us.

15 Thou makest us to be a by-word among the heathen : and that the people shake their heads at us.

16 My confusion is daily before me : and the shame of my face hath covered me;

17 For the voice of the slanderer and blasphemer : for the enemy and avenger.

18 And though all this be come upon us, yet do we not forget thee : nor behave ourselves frowardly in thy covenant.

19 Our heart is not turned back : neither our steps gone out of thy way;

20 No, not when thou hast smitten us into the place of dragons : and covered us with the shadow of death.

21 If we have forgotten the Name of our God, and holden up our hands to any strange god : shall not God search it out? for he knoweth the very secrets of

the heart.

22 For thy sake also are we killed all the day long : and are counted as sheep appointed to be slain.

23 Up, Lord, why sleepest thou : awake, and be not absent from us for ever.

24 Wherefore hidest thou thy face : and forgettest our misery and trouble?

25 For our soul is brought low, even unto the dust : our belly cleaveth unto the ground.

26 Arise, and help us : and deliver us for thy mercy's sake.

PSALM 45. *ERUCTAVIT COR MEUM*

Y heart is inditing of a good matter : I speak of the things which I have made unto the King.

2 My tongue is the pen : of a ready writer.

3 Thou art fairer than the children of men : full of grace are thy lips, because God hath blessed thee for ever.

4 Gird thee with thy sword upon thy thigh, O thou most Mighty : according to thy worship and renown.

5 Good luck have thou with thine honour : ride on, because of the word of truth, of meekness, and righteousness; and thy right hand shall teach thee terrible things.

6 Thy arrows are very sharp, and the people shall be subdued unto thee : even in the midst among the King's enemies.

7 Thy seat, O God, endureth for ever : the sceptre of thy kingdom is a right sceptre.

8 Thou hast loved righteousness, and hated iniquity : wherefore God, even thy God, hath anointed thee with the oil of gladness above thy fellows.

9 All thy garments smell of myrrh, aloes, and cassia : out of the ivory palaces, whereby they have made thee glad.

10 Kings' daughters were among thy honourable women : upon thy right hand did stand the queen in a vesture of gold, wrought about with divers colours.

11 Hearken, O daughter, and consider, incline thine ear : forget also thine own people, and thy father's house.

12 So shall the King have pleasure in thy beauty : for he is thy Lord God, and worship thou him.

13 And the daughter of Tyre shall be there with a gift : like as the rich also among the people shall make their supplication before thee.

14 The King's daughter is all glorious within : her clothing is of wrought gold.

15 She shall be brought unto the King in raiment of needle-work : the virgins that be her fellows shall bear her company, and shall be brought unto thee.

16 With joy and gladness shall they be brought : and shall enter into the King's palace.

17 Instead of thy fathers thou shalt have children : whom thou mayest make princes in all lands.

18 I will remember thy Name from one generation to another : therefore shall the people give thanks unto thee, world without end.

PSALM 46. *DEUS NOSTER REFUGIUM*

OD is our hope and strength : a very present help in trouble.

2 Therefore will we not fear, though the earth be moved : and though the hills be carried into the midst of the sea;

3 Though the waters thereof rage and swell : and though the mountains shake at the tempest of the same.

4 The rivers of the flood thereof shall make glad the city of God : the holy place of the tabernacle of the most Highest.

5 God is in the midst of her, therefore shall she not be removed : God shall help her, and that right early.

6 The heathen make much ado, and the kingdoms are moved : but God hath shewed his voice, and the earth shall melt away.

7 The Lord of hosts is with us : the God of Jacob is our refuge.

8 O come hither, and behold the works of the Lord : what destruction he hath brought upon the earth.

9 He maketh wars to cease in all the world : he breaketh the bow, and knappeth the spear in sunder, and burneth the chariots in the fire.

10 Be still then, and know that I am God : I will be exalted among the heathen, and I will be exalted in the earth.

11 The Lord of hosts is with us : the God of Jacob is our refuge.

Day 9. Evening Prayer

PSALM 47. *OMNES GENTES, PLAUDITE*

CLAP your hands together, all ye people : O sing unto God with the voice of melody.

2 For the Lord is high, and to be feared : he is the great King upon all the earth.

3 He shall subdue the people under us : and the nations under our feet.

4 He shall choose out an heritage for us : even the worship of Jacob, whom he loved.

5 God is gone up with a merry noise : and the Lord with the sound of the trump.

6 O sing praises, sing praises unto our God : O sing praises, sing praises unto our King.

7 For God is the King of all the earth : sing ye praises with understanding.

8 God reigneth over the heathen : God sitteth upon his holy seat.

9 The princes of the people are joined unto the people of the God of Abraham : for God, which is very high exalted, doth defend the earth, as it were with a shield.

PSALM 48. *MAGNUS DOMINUS*

GREAT is the Lord, and highly to be praised : in the city of our God, even upon his holy hill.

2 The hill of Sion is a fair place, and the joy of the whole earth : upon the north-side lieth the city of the great King; God is well known in her palaces as a sure refuge.

3 For lo, the kings of the earth : are gathered, and gone by together.

4 They marvelled to see such things : they were astonished, and suddenly cast down.

5 Fear came there upon them, and sorrow : as upon a woman in her travail.

6 Thou shalt break the ships of the sea : through the east-wind.

7 Like as we have heard, so have we seen in the city of the Lord of hosts, in the city of our God : God upholdeth the same for ever.

8 We wait for thy loving-kindness, O God : in the midst of thy temple.

9 O God, according to thy Name, so is thy praise unto the world's end : thy right hand is full of righteousness.

10 Let the mount Sion rejoice, and the daughters of Judah be glad : because of thy judgements.

11 Walk about Sion, and go round about her : and tell the towers thereof.

12 Mark well her bulwarks, set up her houses : that ye may tell them that come after.

13 For this God is our God for ever and ever : he shall be our guide unto death.

PSALM 49. *AUDITE HAEC, OMNES*

HEAR ye this, all ye people : ponder it with your ears, all ye that dwell in the world;

2 High and low, rich and poor : one with another.

3 My mouth shall speak of wisdom : and my heart shall muse of understanding.

4 I will incline mine ear to the parable : and shew my dark speech upon the harp.

5 Wherefore should I fear in the days of wickedness : and when the wickedness of my heels compasseth me round about?

6 There be some that put their trust in their goods : and boast themselves in the multitude of their riches.

7 But no man may deliver his brother : nor make agreement unto God for him;

8 For it cost more to redeem their souls : so that he must let that alone for ever;

9 Yea, though he live long : and see not the grave.

10 For he seeth that wise men also die, and perish together : as well as the ignorant and foolish, and leave their riches for other.

11 And yet they think that their houses shall continue for ever : and that their dwelling-places shall endure from one generation to another; and call the lands after their own names.

12 Nevertheless, man will not abide in honour : seeing he may be compared unto the beasts that perish; this is the way of them.

13 This is their foolishness : and their posterity praise their saying.

14 They lie in the hell like sheep, death gnaweth upon them, and the righteous shall have domination over them in the morning : their beauty shall consume in the sepulchre out of their dwelling.

15 But God hath delivered my soul from the place of hell : for he shall receive me.

16 Be not thou afraid, though one be made rich : or if the glory of his house be increased;

17 For he shall carry nothing away with him when he dieth : neither shall his pomp follow him.

18 For while he lived, he counted himself an happy man : and so long as thou doest well unto thyself, men will speak good of thee.

19 He shall follow the generation of his fathers : and shall never see light.

20 Man being in honour hath no understanding : but is compared unto the beasts that perish.

Day 10. Morning Prayer

PSALM 50. *DEUS DEORUM*

THE Lord, even the most mighty God, hath spoken : and called the world, from the rising up of the sun unto the going down thereof.

2 Out of Sion hath God appeared : in perfect beauty.

3 Our God shall come, and shall not keep silence : there shall go before him a consuming fire, and a mighty tempest shall be stirred up round about him.

4 He shall call the heaven from above : and the earth, that he may judge his people.

5 Gather my saints together unto me : those that have made a covenant with me with sacrifice.

6 And the heavens shall declare his righteousness : for God is Judge himself.

7 Hear, O my people, and I will speak : I myself will testify against thee, O Israel; for I am God, even thy God.

8 I will not reprove thee because of thy sacrifices, or for thy burnt-offerings : because they were not alway before me.

9 I will take no bullock out of thine house : nor he-goat out of thy folds.

10 For all the beasts of the forest are mine : and so are the cattle upon a thousand hills.

11 I know all the fowls upon the mountains : and the wild beasts of the field are in my sight.

12 If I be hungry, I will not tell thee : for the whole world is mine, and all that is therein.

13 Thinkest thou that I will eat bulls' flesh : and drink the blood of goats?

14 Offer unto God thanksgiving : and pay thy vows unto the most Highest.

15 And call upon me in the time of trouble : so will I hear thee, and thou shalt praise me.

16 But unto the ungodly said God : Why dost thou preach my laws, and takest my covenant in thy mouth;

17 Whereas thou hatest to be reformed : and hast cast my words behind thee?

18 When thou sawest a thief, thou consentedst unto him : and hast been partaker with the adulterers.

19 Thou hast let thy mouth speak wickedness : and with thy tongue thou hast set forth deceit.

20 Thou satest, and spakest against thy brother : yea, and hast slandered thine own mother's son.

21 These things hast thou done, and I held my tongue, and thou thoughtest wickedly, that I am even such a one as thyself : but I will reprove thee, and set

before thee the things that thou hast done.

22 O consider this, ye that forget God : lest I pluck you away, and there be none to deliver you.

23 Whoso offereth me thanks and praise, he honoureth me : and to him that ordereth his conversation right will I shew the salvation of God.

PSALM 51. *MISERERE MEI, DEUS*

AVE mercy upon me, O God, after thy great goodness : according to the multitude of thy mercies do away mine offences.

2 Wash me throughly from my wickedness : and cleanse me from my sin.

3 For I acknowledge my faults : and my sin is ever before me.

4 Against thee only have I sinned, and done this evil in thy sight : that thou mightest be justified in thy saying, and clear when thou art judged.

5 Behold, I was shapen in wickedness : and in sin hath my mother conceived me.

6 But lo, thou requirest truth in the inward parts : and shalt make me to understand wisdom secretly.

7 Thou shalt purge me with hyssop, and I shall be clean : thou shalt wash me, and I shall be whiter than snow.

8 Thou shalt make me hear of joy and gladness : that the bones which thou hast broken may rejoice.

9 Turn thy face from my sins : and put out all my misdeeds.

10 Make me a clean heart, O God : and renew a right spirit within me.

11 Cast me not away from thy presence : and take not thy holy Spirit from me.

12 O give me the comfort of thy help again : and stablish me with thy free Spirit.

13 Then shall I teach thy ways unto the wicked : and sinners shall be converted unto thee.

14 Deliver me from blood-guiltiness, O God, thou that art the God of my health : and my tongue shall sing of thy righteousness.

15 Thou shalt open my lips, O Lord : and my mouth shall shew thy praise.

16 For thou desirest no sacrifice, else would I give it thee : but thou delightest not in burnt-offerings.

17 The sacrifice of God is a troubled spirit : a broken and contrite heart, O God, shalt thou not despise.

18 O be favourable and gracious unto Sion : build thou the walls of Jerusalem.

19 Then shalt thou be pleased with the sacrifice of righteousness, with the burnt-offerings and oblations : then shall they offer young bullocks upon thine altar.

PSALM 52. *QUID GLORIARIS?*

HY boastest thou thyself, thou tyrant : that thou canst do mischief;
2 Whereas the goodness of God : endureth yet daily?
3 Thy tongue imagineth wickedness : and with lies thou cuttest like a sharp rasor.

4 Thou hast loved unrighteousness more than goodness : and to talk of lies more than righteousness.

5 Thou hast loved to speak all words that may do hurt : O thou false tongue.

6 Therefore shall God destroy thee for ever : he shall take thee, and pluck thee out of thy dwelling, and root thee out of the land of the living.

7 The righteous also shall see this, and fear : and shall laugh him to scorn;

8 Lo, this is the man that took not God for his strength : but trusted unto the multitude of his riches, and strengthened himself in his wickedness.

9 As for me, I am like a green olive-tree in the house of God : my trust is in the tender mercy of God for ever and ever.

10 I will always give thanks unto thee for that thou hast done : and I will hope in thy Name, for thy saints like it well.

Day 10. Evening Prayer

PSALM 53. *DIXIT INSIPIENS*

HE foolish body hath said in his heart : There is no God.
2 Corrupt are they, and become abominable in their wickedness : there is none that doeth good.

3 God looked down from heaven upon the children of men : to see if there were any that would understand, and seek after God.

4 But they are all gone out of the way, they are altogether become abominable : there is also none that doeth good, no not one.

5 Are not they without understanding, that work wickedness : eating up my people as if they would eat bread? they have not called upon God.

6 They were afraid where no fear was : for God hath broken the bones of him that besieged thee; thou hast put them to confusion, because God hath despised them.

7 O that the salvation were given unto Israel out of Sion : O that the Lord would deliver his people out of captivity!

8 Then should Jacob rejoice : and Israel should be right glad.

PSALM 54. *DEUS, IN NOMINE*

AVE me, O God, for thy Name's sake : and avenge me in thy strength.

2 Hear my prayer, O God : and hearken unto the words of my mouth.

3 For strangers are risen up against me : and tyrants, which have not God before their eyes, seek after my soul.

4 Behold, God is my helper : the Lord is with them that uphold my soul.

5 He shall reward evil unto mine enemies : destroy thou them in thy truth.

6 An offering of a free heart will I give thee, and praise thy Name, O Lord : because it is so comfortable.

7 For he hath delivered me out of all my trouble : and mine eye hath seen his desire upon mine enemies.

PSALM 55. *EXAUDI, DEUS*

EAR my prayer, O God : and hide not thyself from my petition.

2 Take heed unto me, and hear me : how I mourn in my prayer, and am vexed.

3 The enemy crieth so, and the ungodly cometh on so fast : for they are minded to do me some mischief; so maliciously are they set against me.

4 My heart is disquieted within me : and the fear of death is fallen upon me.

5 Fearfulness and trembling are come upon me : and an horrible dread hath overwhelmed me.

6 And I said, O that I had wings like a dove : for then would I flee away, and be at rest.

7 Lo, then would I get me away far off : and remain in the wilderness.

8 I would make haste to escape : because of the stormy wind and tempest.

9 Destroy their tongues, O Lord, and divide them : for I have spied unright-eousness and strife in the city.

10 Day and night they go about within the walls thereof : mischief also and sorrow are in the midst of it.

11 Wickedness is therein : deceit and guile go not out of their streets.

12 For it is not an open enemy, that hath done me this dishonour : for then I could have borne it.

13 Neither was it mine adversary, that did magnify himself against me : for then peradventure I would have hid myself from him.

14 But it was even thou, my companion : my guide, and mine own familiar friend.

15 We took sweet counsel together : and walked in the house of God as friends.

16 Let death come hastily upon them, and let them go down quick into hell : for wickedness is in their dwellings, and among them.

17 As for me, I will call upon God : and the Lord shall save me.

18 In the evening, and morning, and at noonday will I pray, and that instantly : and he shall hear my voice.

19 It is he that hath delivered my soul in peace from the battle that was against me : for there were many with me.

20 Yea, even God, that endureth for ever, shall hear me, and bring them down : for they will not turn, nor fear God.

21 He laid his hands upon such as be at peace with him : and he brake his covenant.

22 The words of his mouth were softer than butter, having war in his heart : his words were smoother than oil, and yet be they very swords.

23 O cast thy burden upon the Lord, and he shall nourish thee : and shall not suffer the righteous to fall for ever.

24 And as for them : thou, O God, shalt bring them into the pit of destruction.

25 The blood-thirsty and deceitful men shall not live out half their days : nevertheless, my trust shall be in thee, O Lord.

Day 11. Morning Prayer

PSALM 56. *MISERERE MEI, DEUS*

BE merciful unto me, O God, for man goeth about to devour me : he is daily fighting, and troubling me.

2 Mine enemies are daily in hand to swallow me up : for they be many that fight against me, O thou most Highest.

3 Nevertheless, though I am sometime afraid : yet put I my trust in thee.

4 I will praise God, because of his word : I have put my trust in God, and will not fear what flesh can do unto me.

5 They daily mistake my words : all that they imagine is to do me evil.

6 They hold all together, and keep themselves close : and mark my steps, when they lay wait for my soul.

7 Shall they escape for their wickedness : thou, O God, in thy displeasure shalt cast them down.

8 Thou tellest my flittings; put my tears into thy bottle : are not these things noted in thy book?

9 Whensoever I call upon thee, then shall mine enemies be put to flight : this I know; for God is on my side.

10 In God's word I will rejoice : in the Lord's word will I comfort me.

11 Yea, in God have I put my trust : I will not be afraid what man can do unto me.

12 Unto thee, O God, will I pay my vows : unto thee will I give thanks.

13 For thou hast delivered my soul from death, and my feet from falling : that I may walk before God in the light of the living.

PSALM 57. *MISERERE MEI, DEUS*

E merciful unto me, O God, be merciful unto me, for my soul trusteth in thee : and under the shadow of thy wings shall be my refuge, until this tyranny be over-past.

2 I will call unto the most high God : even unto the God that shall perform the cause which I have in hand.

3 He shall send from heaven : and save me from the reproof of him that would eat me up.

4 God shall send forth his mercy and truth : my soul is among lions.

5 And I lie even among the children of men, that are set on fire : whose teeth are spears and arrows, and their tongue a sharp sword.

6 Set up thyself, O God, above the heavens : and thy glory above all the earth.

7 They have laid a net for my feet, and pressed down my soul : they have digged a pit before me, and are fallen into the midst of it themselves.

8 My heart is fixed, O God, my heart is fixed : I will sing, and give praise.

9 Awake up, my glory; awake, lute and harp : I myself will awake right early.

10 I will give thanks unto thee, O Lord, among the people : and I will sing unto thee among the nations.

11 For the greatness of thy mercy reacheth unto the heavens : and thy truth unto the clouds.

12 Set up thyself, O God, above the heavens : and thy glory above all the earth.

PSALM 58. *SI VERE UTIQUE*

RE your minds set upon righteousness, O ye congregation : and do ye judge the thing that is right, O ye sons of men?

2 Yea, ye imagine mischief in your heart upon the earth : and your hands deal with wickedness.

3 The ungodly are froward, even from their mother's womb : as soon as they are born, they go astray, and speak lies.

4 They are as venomous as the poison of a serpent : even like the deaf adder that stoppeth her ears;

5 Which refuseth to hear the voice of the charmer : charm he never so wisely.

6 Break their teeth, O God, in their mouths; smite the jaw-bones of the lions, O Lord : let them fall away like water that runneth apace; and when they shoot their arrows let them be rooted out.

7 Let them consume away like a snail, and be like the untimely fruit of a woman : and let them not see the sun.

8 Or ever your pots be made hot with thorns : so let indignation vex him, even as a thing that is raw.

9 The righteous shall rejoice when he seeth the vengeance : he shall wash his footsteps in the blood of the ungodly.

10 So that a man shall say, Verily there is a reward for the righteous : doubtless there is a God that judgeth the earth.

Day 11. Evening Prayer

PSALM 59. *ERIPE ME DE INIMICIS*

DELIVER me from mine enemies, O God : defend me from them that rise up against me.

2 O deliver me from the wicked doers : and save me from the blood-thirsty men.

3 For lo, they lie waiting for my soul : the mighty men are gathered against me, without any offence or fault of me, O Lord.

4 They run and prepare themselves without my fault : arise thou therefore to help me, and behold.

5 Stand up, O Lord God of hosts, thou God of Israel, to visit all the heathen : and be not merciful unto them that offend of malicious wickedness.

6 They go to and fro in the evening : they grin like a dog, and run about through the city.

7 Behold, they speak with their mouth, and swords are in their lips : for who doth hear?

8 But thou, O Lord, shalt have them in derision : and thou shalt laugh all the heathen to scorn.

9 My strength will I ascribe unto thee : for thou art the God of my refuge.

10 God sheweth me his goodness plenteously : and God shall let me see my desire upon mine enemies.

11 Slay them not, lest my people forget it : but scatter them abroad among the people, and put them down, O Lord, our defence.

12 For the sin of their mouth, and for the words of their lips, they shall be taken in their pride : and why? their preaching is of cursing and lies.

13 Consume them in thy wrath, consume them, that they may perish : and know that it is God that ruleth in Jacob, and unto the ends of the world.

14 And in the evening they will return : grin like a dog, and will go about the city.

15 They will run here and there for meat : and grudge if they be not satisfied.

16 As for me, I will sing of thy power, and will praise thy mercy betimes in the morning : for thou hast been my defence and refuge in the day of my trouble.

17 Unto thee, O my strength, will I sing : for thou, O God, art my refuge, and my merciful God.

PSALM 60. *DEUS, REPULISTI NOS*

GOD, thou hast cast us out, and scattered us abroad : thou hast also been displeased; O turn thee unto us again.

2 Thou hast moved the land, and divided it : heal the sores thereof, for it shaketh.

3 Thou hast shewed thy people heavy things : thou hast given us a drink of deadly wine.

4 Thou hast given a token for such as fear thee : that they may triumph because of the truth.

5 Therefore were thy beloved delivered : help me with thy right hand, and hear me.

6 God hath spoken in his holiness, I will rejoice, and divide Sichem : and mete out the valley of Succoth.

7 Gilead is mine, and Manasses is mine : Ephraim also is the strength of my head; Judah is my law-giver;

8 Moab is my wash-pot; over Edom will I cast out my shoe : Philistia, be thou glad of me.

9 Who will lead me into the strong city : who will bring me into Edom?

10 Hast not thou cast us out, O God : wilt not thou, O God, go out with our hosts?

11 O be thou our help in trouble : for vain is the help of man.

12 Through God will we do great acts : for it is he that shall tread down our enemies.

Psalm 61. *Exaudi, Deus*

EAR my crying, O God : give ear unto my prayer.

2 From the ends of the earth will I call upon thee : when my heart is in heaviness.

3 O set me up upon the rock that is higher than I : for thou hast been my hope, and a strong tower for me against the enemy.

4 I will dwell in thy tabernacle for ever : and my trust shall be under the covering of thy wings.

5 For thou, O Lord, hast heard my desires : and hast given an heritage unto those that fear thy Name.

6 Thou shalt grant the King a long life : that his years may endure throughout all generations.

7 He shall dwell before God for ever : O prepare thy loving mercy and faithfulness, that they may preserve him.

8 So will I always sing praise unto thy Name : that I may daily perform my vows.

Day 12. Morning Prayer

Psalm 62. *Nonne Deo?*

Y soul truly waiteth still upon God : for of him cometh my salvation.

2 He verily is my strength and my salvation : he is my defence, so that I shall not greatly fall.

3 How long will ye imagine mischief against every man : ye shall be slain all the sort of you; yea, as a tottering wall shall ye be, and like a broken hedge.

4 Their device is only how to put him out whom God will exalt : their delight is in lies; they give good words with their mouth, but curse with their heart.

5 Nevertheless, my soul, wait thou still upon God : for my hope is in him.

6 He truly is my strength and my salvation : he is my defence, so that I shall not fall.

7 In God is my health, and my glory : the rock of my might, and in God is my trust.

8 O put your trust in him alway, ye people : pour out your hearts before him, for God is our hope.

9 As for the children of men, they are but vanity : the children of men are deceitful upon the weights, they are altogether lighter than vanity itself.

10 O trust not in wrong and robbery, give not yourselves unto vanity : if riches increase, set not your heart upon them.

11 God spake once, and twice I have also heard the same : that power belongeth unto God;

12 And that thou, Lord, art merciful : for thou rewardest every man according to his work.

PSALM 63. *DEUS, DEUS MEUS*

GOD, thou art my God : early will I seek thee.

2 My soul thirsteth for thee, my flesh also longeth after thee : in a barren and dry land where no water is.

3 Thus have I looked for thee in holiness : that I might behold thy power and glory.

4 For thy loving-kindness is better than the life itself : my lips shall praise thee.

5 As long as I live will I magnify thee on this manner : and lift up my hands in thy Name.

6 My soul shall be satisfied, even as it were with marrow and fatness : when my mouth praiseth thee with joyful lips.

7 Have I not remembered thee in my bed : and thought upon thee when I was waking?

8 Because thou hast been my helper : therefore under the shadow of thy wings will I rejoice.

9 My soul hangeth upon thee : thy right hand hath upholden me.

10 These also that seek the hurt of my soul : they shall go under the earth.

11 Let them fall upon the edge of the sword : that they may be a portion for foxes.

12 But the King shall rejoice in God; all they also that swear by him shall be commended : for the mouth of them that speak lies shall be stopped.

PSALM 64. *EXAUDI, DEUS*

HEAR my voice, O God, in my prayer : preserve my life from fear of the enemy.

2 Hide me from the gathering together of the froward : and from the insurrection of wicked doers;

3 Who have whet their tongue like a sword : and shoot out their arrows, even bitter words;

4 That they may privily shoot at him that is perfect : suddenly do they hit him, and fear not.

5 They encourage themselves in mischief : and commune among themselves how they may lay snares, and say that no man shall see them.

6 They imagine wickedness, and practise it : that they keep secret among themselves, every man in the deep of his heart.

7 But God shall suddenly shoot at them with a swift arrow : that they shall be wounded.

8 Yea, their own tongues shall make them fall : insomuch that whoso seeth them shall laugh them to scorn.

9 And all men that see it shall say, This hath God done : for they shall perceive that it is his work.

10 The righteous shall rejoice in the Lord, and put his trust in him : and all they that are true of heart shall be glad.

Day 12. Evening Prayer

Psalm 65. *Te decet hymnus*

THOU, O God, art praised in Sion : and unto thee shall the vow be performed in Jerusalem.

2 Thou that hearest the prayer : unto thee shall all flesh come.

3 My misdeeds prevail against me : O be thou merciful unto our sins.

4 Blessed is the man whom thou choosest, and receivest unto thee : he shall dwell in thy court, and shall be satisfied with the pleasures of thy house, even of thy holy temple.

5 Thou shalt shew us wonderful things in thy righteousness, O God of our salvation : thou that art the hope of all the ends of the earth, and of them that remain in the broad sea.

6 Who in his strength setteth fast the mountains : and is girded about with power.

7 Who stilleth the raging of the sea : and the noise of his waves, and the madness of the people.

8 They also that dwell in the uttermost parts of the earth shall be afraid at thy tokens : thou that makest the outgoings of the morning and evening to praise thee.

9 Thou visitest the earth, and blessest it : thou makest it very plenteous.

10 The river of God is full of water : thou preparest their corn, for so thou providest for the earth.

11 Thou waterest her furrows, thou sendest rain into the little valleys thereof : thou makest it soft with the drops of rain, and blessest the increase of it.

12 Thou crownest the year with thy goodness : and thy clouds drop fatness.

13 They shall drop upon the dwellings of the wilderness : and the little hills shall rejoice on every side.

14 The folds shall be full of sheep : the valleys also shall stand so thick with corn, that they shall laugh and sing.

PSALM 66. *JUBILATE DEO*

BE joyful in God, all ye lands : sing praises unto the honour of his Name, make his praise to be glorious.

2 Say unto God, O how wonderful art thou in thy works : through the greatness of thy power shall thine enemies be found liars unto thee.

3 For all the world shall worship thee : sing of thee, and praise thy Name.

4 O come hither, and behold the works of God : how wonderful he is in his doing toward the children of men.

5 He turned the sea into dry land : so that they went through the water on foot; there did we rejoice thereof.

6 He ruleth with his power for ever; his eyes behold the people : and such as will not believe shall not be able to exalt themselves.

7 O praise our God, ye people : and make the voice of his praise to be heard;

8 Who holdeth our soul in life : and suffereth not our feet to slip.

9 For thou, O God, hast proved us : thou also hast tried us, like as silver is tried.

10 Thou broughtest us into the snare : and laidest trouble upon our loins.

11 Thou sufferedst men to ride over our heads : we went through fire and water, and thou broughtest us out into a wealthy place.

12 I will go into thine house with burnt-offerings : and will pay thee my vows, which I promised with my lips, and spake with my mouth, when I was in trouble.

13 I will offer unto thee fat burnt-sacrifices, with the incense of rams : I will offer bullocks and goats.

14 O come hither, and hearken, all ye that fear God : and I will tell you what he hath done for my soul.

15 I called unto him with my mouth : and gave him praises with my tongue.

16 If I incline unto wickedness with mine heart : the Lord will not hear me.

17 But God hath heard me : and considered the voice of my prayer.

18 Praised be God, who hath not cast out my prayer : nor turned his mercy from me.

Psalm 67. *Deus misereatur*

God be merciful unto us, and bless us : and shew us the light of his countenance, and be merciful unto us;

2 That thy way may be known upon earth : thy saving health among all nations.

3 Let the people praise thee, O God : yea, let all the people praise thee.

4 O let the nations rejoice and be glad : for thou shalt judge the folk righteously, and govern the nations upon earth.

5 Let the people praise thee, O God : let all the people praise thee.

6 Then shall the earth bring forth her increase : and God, even our own God, shall give us his blessing.

7 God shall bless us : and all the ends of the world shall fear him.

Day 13. Morning Prayer

Psalm 68. *Exurgat Deus*

Let God arise, and let his enemies be scattered : let them also that hate him flee before him.

2 Like as the smoke vanisheth, so shalt thou drive them away : and like as wax melteth at the fire, so let the ungodly perish at the presence of God.

3 But let the righteous be glad and rejoice before God : let them also be merry and joyful.

4 O sing unto God, and sing praises unto his Name : magnify him that rideth upon the heavens, as it were upon an horse; praise him in his Name Jah, and rejoice before him.

5 He is a father of the fatherless, and defendeth the cause of the widows : even God in his holy habitation.

6 He is the God that maketh men to be of one mind in an house, and bringeth the prisoners out of captivity : but letteth the runagates continue in scarceness.

7 O God, when thou wentest forth before the people : when thou wentest through the wilderness;

8 The earth shook, and the heavens dropped at the presence of God : even as Sinai also was moved at the presence of God, who is the God of Israel.

9 Thou, O God, sentest a gracious rain upon thine inheritance : and refreshedst it when it was weary.

10 Thy congregation shall dwell therein : for thou, O God, hast of thy goodness prepared for the poor.

11 The Lord gave the word : great was the company of the preachers.

12 Kings with their armies did flee, and were discomfited : and they of the household divided the spoil.

13 Though ye have lien among the pots, yet shall ye be as the wings of a dove : that is covered with silver wings, and her feathers like gold.

14 When the Almighty scattered kings for their sake : then were they as white as snow in Salmon.

15 As the hill of Basan, so is God's hill : even an high hill, as the hill of Basan.

16 Why hop ye so, ye high hills? this is God's hill, in the which it pleaseth him to dwell : yea, the Lord will abide in it for ever.

17 The chariots of God are twenty thousand, even thousands of angels : and the Lord is among them, as in the holy place of Sinai.

18 Thou art gone up on high, thou hast led captivity captive, and received gifts for men : yea, even for thine enemies, that the Lord God might dwell among them.

19 Praised be the Lord daily : even the God who helpeth us, and poureth his benefits upon us.

20 He is our God, even the God of whom cometh salvation : God is the Lord, by whom we escape death.

21 God shall wound the head of his enemies : and the hairy scalp of such a one as goeth on still in his wickedness.

22 The Lord hath said, I will bring my people again, as I did from Basan : mine own will I bring again, as I did sometime from the deep of the sea.

23 That thy foot may be dipped in the blood of thine enemies : and that the tongue of thy dogs may be red through the same.

24 It is well seen, O God, how thou goest : how thou, my God and King, goest in the sanctuary.

25 The singers go before, the minstrels follow after : in the midst are the damsels playing with the timbrels.

26 Give thanks, O Israel, unto God the Lord in the congregations : from the ground of the heart.

27 There is little Benjamin their ruler, and the princes of Judah their counsel : the princes of Zabulon, and the princes of Nephthali.

28 Thy God hath sent forth strength for thee : stablish the thing, O God, that thou hast wrought in us,

29 For thy temple's sake at Jerusalem : so shall kings bring presents unto thee.

30 When the company of the spear-men, and multitude of the mighty are scattered abroad among the beasts of the people, so that they humbly bring pieces of silver : and when he hath scattered the people that delight in war;

31 Then shall the princes come out of Egypt : the Morians' land shall soon stretch our her hands unto God.

32 Sing unto God, O ye kingdoms of the earth : O sing praises unto the Lord;

33 Who sitteth in the heavens over all from the beginning : lo, he doth send out his voice, yea, and that a mighty voice.

34 Ascribe ye the power to God over Israel : his worship and strength is in the clouds.

35 O God, wonderful art thou in thy holy places : even the God of Israel, he will give strength and power unto his people; blessed be God.

Day 13. Evening Prayer

Psalm 69. *Salvum me fac*

HAVE me, O God : for the waters are come in, even unto my soul.

2 I stick fast in the deep mire, where no ground is : I am come into deep waters, so that the floods run over me.

3 I am weary of crying; my throat is dry : my sight faileth me for waiting so long upon my God.

4 They that hate me without a cause are more than the hairs of my head : they that are mine enemies, and would destroy me guiltless, are mighty.

5 I paid them the things that I never took : God, thou knowest my simpleness, and my faults are not hid from thee.

6 Let not them that trust in thee, O Lord God of hosts, be ashamed for my cause : let not those that seek thee be confounded through me, O Lord God of Israel.

7 And why? for thy sake have I suffered reproof : shame hath covered my face.

8 I am become a stranger unto my brethren : even an alien unto my mother's children.

9 For the zeal of thine house hath even eaten me : and the rebukes of them that rebuked thee are fallen upon me.

10 I wept, and chastened myself with fasting : and that was turned to my reproof.

11 I put on sackcloth also : and they jested upon me.

12 They that sit in the gate speak against me : and the drunkards make songs upon me.

13 But, Lord, I make my prayer unto thee : in an acceptable time.

14 Hear me, O God, in the multitude of thy mercy : even in the truth of thy salvation.

15 Take me out of the mire, that I sink not : O let me be delivered from them that hate me, and out of the deep waters.

16 Let not the water-flood drown me, neither let the deep swallow me up : and let not the pit shut her mouth upon me.

17 Hear me, O Lord, for thy loving-kindness is comfortable : turn thee unto me according to the multitude of thy mercies.

18 And hide not thy face from thy servant, for I am in trouble : O haste thee, and hear me.

19 Draw nigh unto my soul, and save it : O deliver me, because of mine enemies.

20 Thou hast known my reproof, my shame, and my dishonour : mine adversaries are all in thy sight.

21 Thy rebuke hath broken my heart; I am full of heaviness : I looked for some to have pity on me, but there was no man, neither found I any to comfort me.

22 They gave me gall to eat : and when I was thirsty they gave me vinegar to drink.

23 Let their table be made a snare to take themselves withal : and let the things that should have been for their wealth be unto them an occasion of falling.

24 Let their eyes be blinded, that they see not : and ever bow thou down their backs.

25 Pour out thine indignation upon them : and let thy wrathful displeasure take hold of them.

26 Let their habitation be void : and no man to dwell in their tents.

27 For they persecute him whom thou hast smitten : and they talk how they may vex them whom thou hast wounded.

28 Let them fall from one wickedness to another : and not come into thy righteousness.

29 Let them be wiped out of the book of the living : and not be written among the righteous.

30 As for me, when I am poor and in heaviness : thy help, O God, shall lift me up.

31 I will praise the Name of God with a song : and magnify it with thanksgiving.

32 This also shall please the Lord : better than a bullock that hath horns and hoofs.

33 The humble shall consider this, and be glad : seek ye after God, and your soul shall live.

34 For the Lord heareth the poor : and despiseth not his prisoners.

35 Let heaven and earth praise him : the sea, and all that moveth therein.

36 For God will save Sion, and build the cities of Judah : that men may dwell there, and have it in possession.

37 The posterity also of his servants shall inherit it : and they that love his Name shall dwell therein.

PSALM 70. *DEUS, IN ADJUTORIUM*

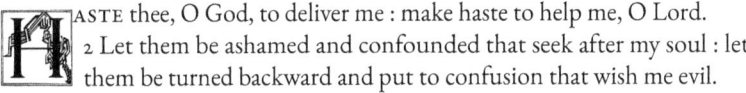

ASTE thee, O God, to deliver me : make haste to help me, O Lord. 2 Let them be ashamed and confounded that seek after my soul : let them be turned backward and put to confusion that wish me evil.

3 Let them for their reward be soon brought to shame : that cry over me, There, there.

4 But let all those that seek thee be joyful and glad in thee : and let all such as delight in thy salvation say alway, The Lord be praised.

5 As for me, I am poor and in misery : haste thee unto me, O God.

6 Thou art my helper and my redeemer : O Lord, make no long tarrying.

Day 14. Morning Prayer

PSALM 71. *IN TE, DOMINE, SPERAVI*

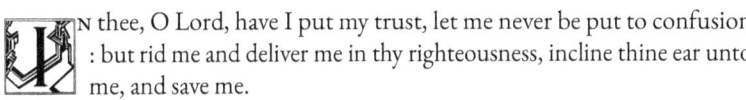

N thee, O Lord, have I put my trust, let me never be put to confusion : but rid me and deliver me in thy righteousness, incline thine ear unto me, and save me.

2 Be thou my strong hold, whereunto I may alway resort : thou hast promised to help me, for thou art my house of defence and my castle.

3 Deliver me, O my God, out of the hand of the ungodly : out of the hand of the unrighteous and cruel man.

4 For thou, O Lord God, art the thing that I long for : thou art my hope, even from my youth.

5 Through thee have I been holden up ever since I was born : thou art he that took me out of my mother's womb; my praise shall be always of thee.

6 I am become as it were a monster unto many : but my sure trust is in thee.

7 O let my mouth be filled with thy praise : that I may sing of thy glory and honour all the day long.

8 Cast me not away in the time of age : forsake me not when my strength faileth me.

9 For mine enemies speak against me, and they that lay wait for my soul take their counsel together, saying : God hath forsaken him; persecute him, and take him, for there is none to deliver him.

10 Go not far from me, O God : my God, haste thee to help me.

11 Let them be confounded and perish that are against my soul : let them be covered with shame and dishonour that seek to do me evil.

12 As for me, I will patiently abide alway : and will praise thee more and more.

13 My mouth shall daily speak of thy righteousness and salvation : for I know no end thereof.

14 I will go forth in the strength of the Lord God : and will make mention of thy righteousness only.

15 Thou, O God, hast taught me from my youth up until now : therefore will I tell of thy wondrous works.

16 Forsake me not, O God, in mine old age, when I am gray-headed : until I have shewed thy strength unto this generation, and thy power to all them that are yet for to come.

17 Thy righteousness, O God, is very high : and great things are they that thou hast done; O God, who is like unto thee?

18 O what great troubles and adversities hast thou shewed me, and yet didst thou turn and refresh me : yea, and broughtest me from the deep of the earth again.

19 Thou hast brought me to great honour : and comforted me on every side.

20 Therefore will I praise thee and thy faithfulness, O God, playing upon an instrument of musick : unto thee will I sing upon the harp, O thou Holy One of Israel.

21 My lips will be fain when I sing unto thee : and so will my soul whom thou hast delivered.

22 My tongue also shall talk of thy righteousness all the day long : for they are confounded and brought unto shame that seek to do me evil.

PSALM 72. *DEUS, JUDICIUM*

GIVE the King thy judgements, O God : and thy righteousness unto the King's son.

2 Then shall he judge thy people according unto right : and defend the poor.

3 The mountains also shall bring peace : and the little hills righteousness unto the people.

4 He shall keep the simple folk by their right : defend the children of the poor, and punish the wrong-doer.

5 They shall fear thee, as long as the sun and moon endureth : from one generation to another.

6 He shall come down like the rain into a fleece of wool : even as the drops that water the earth.

7 In his time shall the righteous flourish : yea, and abundance of peace, so long as the moon endureth.

8 His dominion shall be also from the one sea to the other : and from the flood unto the world's end.

9 They that dwell in the wilderness shall kneel before him : his enemies shall lick the dust.

10 The kings of Tharsis and of the isles shall give presents : the kings of Arabia and Saba shall bring gifts.

11 All kings shall fall down before him : all nations shall do him service.

12 For he shall deliver the poor when he crieth : the needy also, and him that hath no helper.

13 He shall be favourable to the simple and needy : and shall preserve the souls of the poor.

14 He shall deliver their souls from falsehood and wrong : and dear shall their blood be in his sight.

15 He shall live, and unto him shall be given of the gold of Arabia : prayer shall be made ever unto him, and daily shall he be praised.

16 There shall be an heap of corn in the earth, high upon the hills : his fruit shall shake like Libanus, and shall be green in the city like grass upon the earth.

17 His Name shall endure for ever; his Name shall remain under the sun among the posterities : which shall be blessed through him; and all the heathen shall praise him.

18 Blessed be the Lord God, even the God of Israel : which only doeth wondrous things;

19 And blessed be the Name of his majesty for ever : and all the earth shall be filled with his majesty. Amen, Amen.

Day 14. Evening Prayer

Psalm 73. *Quam bonus Israel!*

RULY God is loving unto Israel : even unto such as are of a clean heart.

2 Nevertheless, my feet were almost gone : my treadings had well-nigh slipt.

3 And why? I was grieved at the wicked : I do also see the ungodly in such prosperity.

4 For they are in no peril of death : but are lusty and strong.

5 They come in no misfortune like other folk : neither are they plagued like other men.

6 And this is the cause that they are so holden with pride : and overwhelmed with cruelty.

7 Their eyes swell with fatness : and they do even what they lust.

8 They corrupt other, and speak of wicked blasphemy : their talking is against the most High.

9 For they stretch forth their mouth unto the heaven : and their tongue goeth through the world.

10 Therefore fall the people unto them : and thereout suck they no small advantage.

11 Tush, say they, how should God perceive it : is there knowledge in the most High?

12 Lo, these are the ungodly, these prosper in the world, and these have riches in possession : and I said, Then have I cleansed my heart in vain, and washed mine hands in innocency.

13 All the day long have I been punished : and chastened every morning.

14 Yea, and I had almost said even as they : but lo, then I should have condemned the generation of thy children.

15 Then thought I to understand this : but it was too hard for me,

16 Until I went into the sanctuary of God : then understood I the end of these men;

17 Namely, how thou dost set them in slippery places : and castest them down, and destroyest them.

18 O how suddenly do they consume : perish, and come to a fearful end!

19 Yea, even like as a dream when one awaketh : so shalt thou make their image to vanish out of the city.

20 Thus my heart was grieved : and it went even through my reins.

21 So foolish was I, and ignorant : even as it were a beast before thee.

22 Nevertheless, I am alway by thee : for thou hast holden me by my right hand.

23 Thou shalt guide me with thy counsel : and after that receive me with glory.

24 Whom have I in heaven but thee : and there is none upon earth that I desire in comparison of thee.

25 My flesh and my heart faileth : but God is the strength of my heart, and my portion for ever.

26 For lo, they that forsake thee shall perish : thou hast destroyed all them that commit fornication against thee.

27 But it is good for me to hold me fast by God, to put my trust in the Lord God : and to speak of all thy works in the gates of the daughter of Sion.

PSALM 74. *UT QUID, DEUS?*

GOD, wherefore art thou absent from us so long : why is thy wrath so hot against the sheep of thy pasture?

2 O think upon thy congregation : whom thou hast purchased and redeemed of old.

3 Think upon the tribe of thine inheritance : and mount Sion, wherein thou hast dwelt.

4 Lift up thy feet, that thou mayest utterly destroy every enemy : which hath done evil in thy sanctuary.

5 Thine adversaries roar in the midst of thy congregations : and set up their banners for tokens.

6 He that hewed timber afore out of the thick trees : was known to bring it to an excellent work.

7 But now they break down all the carved work thereof : with axes and hammers.

8 They have set fire upon thy holy places : and have defiled the dwelling-place of thy Name, even unto the ground.

9 Yea, they said in their hearts, Let us make havock of them altogether : thus have they burnt up all the houses of God in the land.

10 We see not our tokens, there is not one prophet more : no, not one is there among us, that understandeth any more.

11 O God, how long shall the adversary do this dishonour : how long shall the enemy blaspheme thy Name, for ever?

12 Why withdrawest thou thy hand : why pluckest thou not thy right hand out of thy bosom to consume the enemy?

13 For God is my King of old : the help that is done upon earth he doeth it himself.

14 Thou didst divide the sea through thy power : thou brakest the heads of the dragons in the waters.

15 Thou smotest the heads of Leviathan in pieces : and gavest him to be meat for the people in the wilderness.

16 Thou broughtest out fountains and waters out of the hard rocks : thou driedst up mighty waters.

17 The day is thine, and the night is thine : thou hast prepared the light and the sun.

18 Thou hast set all the borders of the earth : thou hast made summer and winter.

19 Remember this, O Lord, how the enemy hath rebuked : and how the foolish people hath blasphemed thy Name.

20 O deliver not the soul of thy turtle-dove unto the multitude of the enemies : and forget not the congregation of the poor for ever.

21 Look upon the covenant : for all the earth is full of darkness and cruel habitations.

22 O let not the simple go away ashamed : but let the poor and needy give praise unto thy Name.

23 Arise, O God, maintain thine own cause : remember how the foolish man blasphemeth thee daily.

24 Forget not the voice of thine enemies : the presumption of them that hate thee increaseth ever more and more.

Day 15. Morning Prayer

Psalm 75. *Confitebimur tibi*

NTO thee, O God, do we give thanks : yea, unto thee do we give thanks.

2 Thy Name also is so nigh : and that do thy wondrous works declare.

3 When I receive the congregation : I shall judge according unto right.

4 The earth is weak, and all the inhabiters thereof : I bear up the pillars of it.

5 I said unto the fools, Deal not so madly : and to the ungodly, Set not up your horn.

6 Set not up your horn on high : and speak not with a stiff neck.

7 For promotion cometh neither from the east, nor from the west : nor yet from the south.

8 And why? God is the Judge : he putteth down one, and setteth up another.

9 For in the hand of the Lord there is a cup, and the wine is red : it is full mixed, and he poureth out of the same.

10 As for the dregs thereof : all the ungodly of the earth shall drink them, and suck them out.

11 But I will talk of the God of Jacob : and praise him for ever.

12 All the horns of the ungodly also will I break : and the horns of the righteous shall be exalted.

Psalm 76. *Notus in Judaea*

N Jewry is God known : his Name is great in Israel.

2 At Salem is his tabernacle : and his dwelling in Sion.

3 There brake he the arrows of the bow : the shield, the sword, and the battle.

4 Thou art of more honour and might : than the hills of the robbers.

5 The proud are robbed, they have slept their sleep : and all the men whose hands were mighty have found nothing.

6 At thy rebuke, O God of Jacob : both the chariot and horse are fallen.

7 Thou, even thou art to be feared : and who may stand in thy sight when thou art angry?

8 Thou didst cause thy judgement to be heard from heaven : the earth trembled, and was still;

9 When God arose to judgement : and to help all the meek upon earth.

10 The fierceness of man shall turn to thy praise : and the fierceness of them shalt thou refrain.

11 Promise unto the Lord your God, and keep it, all ye that are round about him : bring presents unto him that ought to be feared.

12 He shall refrain the spirit of princes : and is wonderful among the kings of the earth.

Psalm 77. *Voce mea ad Dominum*

WILL cry unto God with my voice : even unto God will I cry with my voice, and he shall hearken unto me.

2 In the time of my trouble I sought the Lord : my sore ran and ceased not in the night-season; my soul refused comfort.

3 When I am in heaviness, I will think upon God : when my heart is vexed, I will complain.

4 Thou holdest mine eyes waking : I am so feeble, that I cannot speak.

5 I have considered the days of old : and the years that are past.

6 I call to remembrance my song : and in the night I commune with mine own heart, and search out my spirits.

7 Will the Lord absent himself for ever : and will he be no more intreated?

8 Is his mercy clean gone for ever : and is his promise come utterly to an end for evermore?

9 Hath God forgotten to be gracious : and will he shut up his loving-kindness in displeasure?

10 And I said, It is mine own infirmity : but I will remember the years of the right hand of the most Highest.

11 I will remember the works of the Lord : and call to mind thy wonders of old time.

12 I will think also of all thy works : and my talking shall be of thy doings.

13 Thy way, O God, is holy : who is so great a God as our God?

14 Thou art the God that doeth wonders : and hast declared thy power among the people.

15 Thou hast mightily delivered thy people : even the sons of Jacob and Joseph.

16 The waters saw thee, O God, the waters saw thee, and were afraid : the depths also were troubled.

17 The clouds poured out water, the air thundered : and thine arrows went abroad.

18 The voice of thy thunder was heard round about : the lightnings shone upon the ground; the earth was moved, and shook withal.

19 Thy way is in the sea, and thy paths in the great waters : and thy footsteps are not known.

20 Thou leddest thy people like sheep : by the hand of Moses and Aaron.

Day 15. Evening Prayer

PSALM 78. *ATTENDITE, POPULE*

HEAR my law, O my people : incline your ears unto the words of my mouth.

2 I will open my mouth in a parable : I will declare hard sentences of old;

3 Which we have heard and known : and such as our fathers have told us;

4 That we should not hide them from the children of the generations to come : but to shew the honour of the Lord, his mighty and wonderful works that he hath done.

5 He made a covenant with Jacob, and gave Israel a law : which he commanded our forefathers to teach their children;

6 That their posterity might know it : and the children which were yet unborn;

7 To the intent that when they came up : they might shew their children the same;

8 That they might put their trust in God : and not to forget the works of God, but to keep his commandments;

9 And not to be as their forefathers, a faithless and stubborn generation : a generation that set not their heart aright, and whose spirit cleaveth not stedfastly unto God;

10 Like as the children of Ephraim : who being harnessed, and carrying bows, turned themselves back in the day of battle.

11 They kept not the covenant of God : and would not walk in his law;

12 But forgat what he had done : and the wonderful works that he had shewed for them.

13 Marvellous things did he in the sight of our forefathers, in the land of Egypt : even in the field of Zoan.

14 He divided the sea, and let them go through : he made the waters to stand on an heap.

15 In the day-time also he led them with a cloud : and all the night through with a light of fire.

16 He clave the hard rocks in the wilderness : and gave them drink thereof, as it had been out of the great depth.

17 He brought waters out of the stony rock : so that it gushed out like the rivers.

18 Yet for all this they sinned more against him : and provoked the most Highest in the wilderness.

19 They tempted God in their hearts : and required meat for their lust.

20 They spake against God also, saying : Shall God prepare a table in the wilderness?

21 He smote the stony rock indeed, that the waters gushed out, and the streams flowed withal : but can he give bread also, or provide flesh for his people?

22 When the Lord heard this, he was wroth : so the fire was kindled in Jacob, and there came up heavy displeasure against Israel;

23 Because they believed not in God : and put not their trust in his help.

24 So he commanded the clouds above : and opened the doors of heaven.

25 He rained down manna also upon them for to eat : and gave them food from heaven.

26 So man did eat angels' food : for he sent them meat enough.

27 He caused the east-wind to blow under heaven : and through his power he brought in the south-west-wind.

28 He rained flesh upon them as thick as dust : and feathered fowls like as the sand of the sea.

29 He let it fall among their tents : even round about their habitation.

30 So they did eat and were well filled, for he gave them their own desire : they were not disappointed of their lust.

31 But while the meat was yet in their mouths, the heavy wrath of God came upon them, and slew the wealthiest of them : yea, and smote down the chosen men that were in Israel.

32 But for all this they sinned yet more : and believed not his wondrous works.

33 Therefore their days did he consume in vanity : and their years in trouble.

34 When he slew them, they sought him : and turned them early, and inquired after God.

35 And they remembered that God was their strength : and that the high God was their redeemer.

36 Nevertheless, they did but flatter him with their mouth : and dissembled with him in their tongue.

37 For their heart was not whole with him : neither continued they stedfast in his covenant.

38 But he was so merciful, that he forgave their misdeeds : and destroyed them not.

39 Yea, many a time turned he his wrath away : and would not suffer his whole displeasure to arise.

40 For he considered that they were but flesh : and that they were even a wind that passeth away, and cometh not again.

41 Many a time did they provoke him in the wilderness : and grieved him in the desert.

42 They turned back, and tempted God : and moved the Holy One in Israel.

43 They thought not of his hand : and of the day when he delivered them from the hand of the enemy;

44 How he had wrought his miracles in Egypt : and his wonders in the field of Zoan.

45 He turned their waters into blood : so that they might not drink of the rivers.

46 He sent lice among them, and devoured them up : and frogs to destroy them.

47 He gave their fruit unto the caterpillar : and their labour unto the grasshopper.

48 He destroyed their vines with hail-stones : and their mulberry-trees with the frost.

49 He smote their cattle also with hail-stones : and their flocks with hot thunderbolts.

50 He cast upon them the furiousness of his wrath, anger, displeasure, and trouble : and sent evil angels among them.

51 He made a way to his indignation, and spared not their soul from death : but gave their life over to the pestilence;

52 And smote all the first-born in Egypt : the most principal and mightiest in the dwellings of Ham.

53 But as for his own people, he led them forth like sheep : and carried them in the wilderness like a flock.

54 He brought them out safely, that they should not fear : and overwhelmed their enemies with the sea.

55 And brought them within the borders of his sanctuary : even to his mountain which he purchased with his right hand.

56 He cast out the heathen also before them : caused their land to be divided among them for an heritage, and made the tribes of Israel to dwell in their tents.

57 So they tempted and displeased the most high God : and kept not his testimonies;

58 But turned their backs, and fell away like their forefathers : starting aside like a broken bow.

59 For they grieved him with their hill-altars : and provoked him to displeasure with their images.

60 When God heard this, he was wroth : and took sore displeasure at Israel.

61 So that he forsook the tabernacle in Silo : even the tent that he had pitched among men.

62 He delivered their power into captivity : and their beauty into the enemy's hand.

63 He gave his people over also unto the sword : and was wroth with his inheritance.

64 The fire consumed their young men : and their maidens were not given to marriage.

65 Their priests were slain with the sword : and there were no widows to make lamentation.

66 So the Lord awaked as one out of sleep : and like a giant refreshed with wine.

67 He smote his enemies in the hinder parts : and put them to a perpetual shame.

68 He refused the tabernacle of Joseph : and chose not the tribe of Ephraim;

69 But chose the tribe of Judah : even the hill of Sion which he loved.

70 And there he built his temple on high : and laid the foundation of it like the ground which he hath made continually.

71 He chose David also his servant : and took him away from the sheep-folds.

72 As he was following the ewes great with young ones he took him : that he might feed Jacob his people, and Israel his inheritance.

73 So he fed them with a faithful and true heart : and ruled them prudently with all his power.

Day 16. Morning Prayer

PSALM 79. *DEUS, VENERUNT*

GOD, the heathen are come into thine inheritance : thy holy temple have they defiled, and made Jerusalem an heap of stones.

2 The dead bodies of thy servants have they given to be meat unto the fowls of the air : and the flesh of thy saints unto the beasts of the land.

3 Their blood have they shed like water on every side of Jerusalem : and there was no man to bury them.

4 We are become an open shame to our enemies : a very scorn and derision unto them that are round about us.

5 Lord, how long wilt thou be angry : shall thy jealousy burn like fire for ever?

6 Pour out thine indignation upon the heathen that have not known thee : and upon the kingdoms that have not called upon thy Name.

7 For they have devoured Jacob : and laid waste his dwelling-place.

8 O remember not our old sins, but have mercy upon us, and that soon : for we are come to great misery.

9 Help us, O God of our salvation, for the glory of thy Name : O deliver us, and be merciful unto our sins, for thy Name's sake.

10 Wherefore do the heathen say : Where is now their God?

11 O let the vengeance of thy servants' blood that is shed : be openly shewed upon the heathen in our sight.

12 O let the sorrowful sighing of the prisoners come before thee : according to the greatness of thy power, preserve thou those that are appointed to die.

13 And for the blasphemy wherewith our neighbours have blasphemed thee : reward thou them, O Lord, seven-fold into their bosom.

14 So we, that are thy people, and sheep of thy pasture, shall give thee thanks for ever : and will alway be shewing forth thy praise from generation to generation.

PSALM 80. *QUI REGIS ISRAEL*

HEAR, O thou Shepherd of Israel, thou that leadest Joseph like a sheep : shew thyself also, thou that sittest upon the cherubims.

2 Before Ephraim, Benjamin, and Manasses : stir up thy strength, and come, and help us.

3 Turn us again, O God : shew the light of thy countenance, and we shall be whole.

4 O Lord God of hosts : how long wilt thou be angry with thy people that prayeth?

5 Thou feedest them with the bread of tears : and givest them plenteousness of tears to drink.

6 Thou hast made us a very strife unto our neighbours : and our enemies laugh us to scorn.

7 Turn us again, thou God of hosts : shew the light of thy countenance, and we shall be whole.

8 Thou hast brought a vine out of Egypt : thou hast cast out the heathen, and planted it.

9 Thou madest room for it : and when it had taken root it filled the land.

10 The hills were covered with the shadow of it : and the boughs thereof were like the goodly cedar-trees.

11 She stretched out her branches unto the sea : and her boughs unto the river.

12 Why hast thou then broken down her hedge : that all they that go by pluck off her grapes?

13 The wild boar out of the wood doth root it up : and the wild beasts of the field devour it.

14 Turn thee again, thou God of hosts, look down from heaven : behold, and visit this vine;

15 And the place of the vineyard that thy right hand hath planted : and the branch that thou madest so strong for thyself.

16 It is burnt with fire, and cut down : and they shall perish at the rebuke of thy countenance.

17 Let thy hand be upon the man of thy right hand : and upon the son of man, whom thou madest so strong for thine own self.

18 And so will not we go back from thee : O let us live, and we shall call upon thy Name.

19 Turn us again, O Lord God of hosts : shew the light of thy countenance, and we shall be whole.

Psalm 81. *Exultate Deo*

SING we merrily unto God our strength : make a cheerful noise unto the God of Jacob.

2 Take the psalm, bring hither the tabret : the merry harp with the lute.

3 Blow up the trumpet in the new-moon : even in the time appointed, and upon our solemn feast-day.

4 For this was made a statute for Israel : and a law of the God of Jacob.

5 This he ordained in Joseph for a testimony : when he came out of the land of Egypt, and had heard a strange language.

6 I eased his shoulder from the burden : and his hands were delivered from making the pots.

7 Thou calledst upon me in troubles, and I delivered thee : and heard thee what time as the storm fell upon thee.

8 I proved thee also : at the waters of strife.

9 Hear, O my people, and I will assure thee, O Israel : if thou wilt hearken unto me,

10 There shall no strange god be in thee : neither shalt thou worship any other god.

11 I am the Lord thy God, who brought thee out of the land of Egypt : open thy mouth wide, and I shall fill it.

12 But my people would not hear my voice : and Israel would not obey me.

13 So I gave them up unto their own hearts' lusts : and let them follow their own imaginations.

14 O that my people would have hearkened unto me : for if Israel had walked in my ways,

15 I should soon have put down their enemies : and turned my hand against their adversaries.

16 The haters of the Lord should have been found liars : but their time should have endured for ever.

17 He should have fed them also with the finest wheat-flour : and with honey out of the stony rock should I have satisfied thee.

Day 16. Evening Prayer

Psalm 82. *Deus stetit*

OD standeth in the congregation of princes : he is a Judge among gods. 2 How long will ye give wrong judgement : and accept the persons of the ungodly?

3 Defend the poor and fatherless : see that such as are in need and necessity have right.

4 Deliver the outcast and poor : save them from the hand of the ungodly.

5 They will not be learned nor understand, but walk on still in darkness : all the foundations of the earth are out of course.

6 I have said, Ye are gods : and ye are all the children of the most Highest.

7 But ye shall die like men : and fall like one of the princes.

8 Arise, O God, and judge thou the earth : for thou shalt take all heathen to thine inheritance.

PSALM 83. *DEUS, QUIS SIMILIS?*

HOLD not thy tongue, O God, keep not still silence : refrain not thyself, O God.

2 For lo, thine enemies make a murmuring : and they that hate thee have lift up their head.

3 They have imagined craftily against thy people : and taken counsel against thy secret ones.

4 They have said, Come, and let us root them out, that they be no more a people : and that the name of Israel may be no more in remembrance.

5 For they have cast their heads together with one consent : and are confederate against thee;

6 The tabernacles of the Edomites, and the Ismaelites : the Moabites and Hagarenes;

7 Gebal, and Ammon, and Amalek : the Philistines, with them that dwell at Tyre.

8 Assur also is joined with them : and have holpen the children of Lot.

9 But do thou to them as unto the Madianites : unto Sisera, and unto Jabin at the brook of Kison;

10 Who perished at Endor : and became as the dung of the earth.

11 Make them and their princes like Oreb and Zeb : yea, make all their princes like as Zeba and Salmana;

12 Who say, Let us take to ourselves : the houses of God in possession.

13 O my God, make them like unto a wheel : and as the stubble before the wind;

14 Like as the fire that burneth up the wood : and as the flame that consumeth the mountains.

15 Persecute them even so with thy tempest : and make them afraid with thy storm.

16 Make their faces ashamed, O Lord : that they may seek thy Name.

17 Let them be confounded and vexed ever more and more : let them be put to shame, and perish.

18 And they shall know that thou, whose Name is JEHOVAH : art only the most Highest over all the earth.

PSALM 84. *QUAM DILECTA!*

HOW amiable are thy dwellings : thou Lord of hosts!

2 My soul hath a desire and longing to enter into the courts of the Lord : my heart and my flesh rejoice in the living God.

3 Yea, the sparrow hath found her an house, and the swallow a nest where she may lay her young : even thy altars, O Lord of hosts, my King and my God.

4 Blessed are they that dwell in thy house : they will be alway praising thee.

5 Blessed is the man whose strength is in thee : in whose heart are thy ways.

6 Who going through the vale of misery use it for a well : and the pools are filled with water.

7 They will go from strength to strength : and unto the God of gods appeareth every one of them in Sion.

8 O Lord God of hosts, hear my prayer : hearken, O God of Jacob.

9 Behold, O God our defender : and look upon the face of thine Anointed.

10 For one day in thy courts : is better than a thousand.

11 I had rather be a door-keeper in the house of my God : than to dwell in the tents of ungodliness.

12 For the Lord God is a light and defence : the Lord will give grace and worship, and no good thing shall he withhold from them that live a godly life.

13 O Lord God of hosts : blessed is the man that putteth his trust in thee.

PSALM 85. *BENEDIXISTI, DOMINE*

ORD, thou art become gracious unto thy land : thou hast turned away the captivity of Jacob.

2 Thou hast forgiven the offence of thy people : and covered all their sins.

3 Thou hast taken away all thy displeasure : and turned thyself from thy wrathful indignation.

4 Turn us then, O God our Saviour : and let thine anger cease from us.

5 Wilt thou be displeased at us for ever : and wilt thou stretch out thy wrath from one generation to another?

6 Wilt thou not turn again, and quicken us : that thy people may rejoice in thee?

7 Shew us thy mercy, O Lord : and grant us thy salvation.

8 I will hearken what the Lord God will say concerning me : for he shall speak peace unto his people, and to his saints, that they turn not again.

9 For his salvation is nigh them that fear him : that glory may dwell in our land.

10 Mercy and truth are met together : righteousness and peace have kissed each other.

11 Truth shall flourish out of the earth : and righteousness hath looked down from heaven.

12 Yea, the Lord shall shew loving-kindness : and our land shall give her increase.

13 Righteousness shall go before him : and he shall direct his going in the way.

Day 17. Morning Prayer

PSALM 86. *INCLINA, DOMINE*

ow down thine ear, O Lord, and hear me : for I am poor, and in misery. 2 Preserve thou my soul, for I am holy : my God, save thy servant that putteth his trust in thee.

3 Be merciful unto me, O Lord : for I will call daily upon thee.

4 Comfort the soul of thy servant : for unto thee, O Lord, do I lift up my soul.

5 For thou, Lord, art good and gracious : and of great mercy unto all them that call upon thee.

6 Give ear, Lord, unto my prayer : and ponder the voice of my humble desires.

7 In the time of my trouble I will call upon thee : for thou hearest me.

8 Among the gods there is none like unto thee, O Lord : there is not one that can do as thou doest.

9 All nations whom thou hadst made shall come and worship thee, O Lord : and shall glorify thy Name.

10 For thou art great, and doest wondrous things : thou art God alone.

11 Teach me thy way, O Lord, and I will walk in thy truth : O knit my heart unto thee, that I may fear thy Name.

12 I will thank thee, O Lord my God, with all my heart : and will praise thy Name for evermore.

13 For great is thy mercy toward me : and thou hast delivered my soul from the nethermost hell.

14 O God, the proud are risen against me : and the congregations of naughty men have sought after my soul, and have not set thee before their eyes.

15 But thou, O Lord God, art full of compassion and mercy : long-suffering, plenteous in goodness and truth.

16 O turn thee then unto me, and have mercy upon me : give thy strength unto thy servant, and help the son of thine handmaid.

17 Shew some token upon me for good, that they who hate me may see it and be ashamed : because thou, Lord, hast holpen me and comforted me.

PSALM 87. *FUNDAMENTA EJUS*

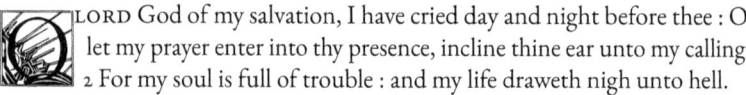

HER foundations are upon the holy hills : the Lord loveth the gates of Sion more than all the dwellings of Jacob.

2 Very excellent things are spoken of thee : thou city of God.

3 I will think upon Rahab and Babylon : with them that know me.

4 Behold ye the Philistines also : and they of Tyre, with the Morians; lo, there was he born.

5 And of Sion it shall be reported that he was born in her : and the most High shall stablish her.

6 The Lord shall rehearse it when he writeth up the people : that he was born there.

7 The singers also and trumpeters shall he rehearse : All my fresh springs shall be in thee.

PSALM 88. *DOMINE DEUS*

LORD God of my salvation, I have cried day and night before thee : O let my prayer enter into thy presence, incline thine ear unto my calling.

2 For my soul is full of trouble : and my life draweth nigh unto hell.

3 I am counted as one of them that go down into the pit : and I have been even as a man that hath no strength.

4 Free among the dead, like unto them that are wounded, and lie in the grave : who are out of remembrance, and are cut away from thy hand.

5 Thou hast laid me in the lowest pit : in a place of darkness, and in the deep.

6 Thine indignation lieth hard upon me : and thou hast vexed me with all thy storms.

7 Thou hast put away mine acquaintance far from me : and made me to be abhorred of them.

8 I am so fast in prison : that I cannot get forth.

9 My sight faileth for very trouble : Lord, I have called daily upon thee, I have stretched forth my hands unto thee.

10 Dost thou shew wonders among the dead : or shall the dead rise up again, and praise thee?

11 Shall thy loving-kindness be shewed in the grave : or thy faithfulness in destruction?

12 Shall thy wondrous works be known in the dark : and thy righteousness in the land where all things are forgotten?

13 Unto thee have I cried, O Lord : and early shall my prayer come before thee.

14 Lord, why abhorrest thou my soul : and hidest thou thy face from me?

15 I am in misery, and like unto him that is at the point to die : even from my youth up thy terrors have I suffered with a troubled mind.

16 Thy wrathful displeasure goeth over me : and the fear of thee hath undone me.

17 They came round about me daily like water : and compassed me together on every side.

18 My lovers and friends hast thou put away from me : and hid mine acquaintance out of my sight.

Day 17. Evening Prayer

Psalm 89. *Misericordias Domini*

MY song shall be alway of the loving-kindness of the Lord : with my mouth will I ever be shewing thy truth from one generation to another.

2 For I have said, Mercy shall be set up for ever : thy truth shalt thou stablish in the heavens.

3 I have made a covenant with my chosen : I have sworn unto David my servant;

4 Thy seed will I stablish for ever : and set up thy throne from one generation to another.

5 O Lord, the very heavens shall praise thy wondrous works : and thy truth in the congregation of the saints.

6 For who is he among the clouds : that shall be compared unto the Lord?

7 And what is he among the gods : that shall be like unto the Lord?

8 God is very greatly to be feared in the council of the saints : and to be had in reverence of all them that are round about him.

9 O Lord God of hosts, who is like unto thee : thy truth, most mighty Lord, is on every side.

10 Thou rulest the raging of the sea : thou stillest the waves thereof when they arise.

11 Thou hast subdued Egypt, and destroyed it : thou hast scattered thine enemies abroad with thy mighty arm.

12 The heavens are thine, the earth also is thine : thou hast laid the foundation of the round world, and all that therein is.

13 Thou hast made the north and the south : Tabor and Hermon shall rejoice in thy Name.

14 Thou hast a mighty arm : strong is thy hand, and high is thy right hand.

15 Righteousness and equity are the habitation of thy seat : mercy and truth shall go before thy face.

16 Blessed is the people, O Lord, that can rejoice in thee : they shall walk in the light of thy countenance.

17 Their delight shall be daily in thy Name : and in thy righteousness shall they make their boast.

18 For thou art the glory of their strength : and in thy loving-kindness thou shalt lift up our horns.

19 For the Lord is our defence : the Holy One of Israel is our King.

20 Thou spakest sometime in visions unto thy saints, and saidst : I have laid help upon one that is mighty; I have exalted one chosen out of the people.

21 I have found David my servant : with my holy oil have I anointed him.

22 My hand shall hold him fast : and my arm shall strengthen him.

23 The enemy shall not be able to do him violence : the son of wickedness shall not hurt him.

24 I will smite down his foes before his face : and plague them that hate him.

25 My truth also and my mercy shall be with him : and in my Name shall his horn be exalted.

26 I will set his dominion also in the sea : and his right hand in the floods.

27 He shall call me, Thou art my Father : my God, and my strong salvation.

28 And I will make him my first-born : higher than the kings of the earth.

29 My mercy will I keep for him for evermore : and my covenant shall stand fast with him.

30 His seed also will I make to endure for ever : and his throne as the days of heaven.

31 But if his children forsake my law : and walk not in my judgements;

32 If they break my statutes, and keep not my commandments : I will visit their offences with the rod, and their sin with scourges.

33 Nevertheless, my loving-kindness will I not utterly take from him : nor suffer my truth to fail.

34 My covenant I will not break, nor alter the thing that is gone out of my lips : I have sworn once by my holiness, that I will not fail David.

35 His seed shall endure for ever : and his seat is like as the sun before me.

36 He shall stand fast for evermore as the moon : and as the faithful witness in heaven.

37 But thou hast abhorred and forsaken thine Anointed : and art displeased at him.

38 Thou hast broken the covenant of thy servant : and cast his crown to the ground.

39 Thou hast overthrown all his hedges : and broken down his strong holds.

40 All they that go by spoil him : and he is become a reproach to his neighbours.

41 Thou hast set up the right hand of his enemies : and made all his adversaries to rejoice.

42 Thou hast taken away the edge of his sword : and givest him not victory in the battle.

43 Thou hast put out his glory : and cast his throne down to the ground.

44 The days of his youth hast thou shortened : and covered him with dishonour.

45 Lord, how long wilt thou hide thyself, for ever : and shall thy wrath burn like fire?

46 O remember how short my time is : wherefore hast thou made all men for nought?

47 What man is he that liveth, and shall not see death : and shall he deliver his soul from the hand of hell?

48 Lord, where are thy old loving-kindnesses : which thou swarest unto David in thy truth?

49 Remember, Lord, the rebuke that thy servants have : and how I do bear in my bosom the rebukes of many people.

50 Wherewith thine enemies have blasphemed thee, and slandered the footsteps of thine Anointed : Praised be the Lord for evermore. Amen, and Amen.

Day 18. Morning Prayer

Psalm 90. *Domine, refugium*

ORD, thou hast been our refuge : from one generation to another.

2 Before the mountains were brought forth, or ever the earth and the world were made : thou art God from everlasting, and world without end.

3 Thou turnest man to destruction : again thou sayest, Come again, ye children of men.

4 For a thousand years in thy sight are but as yesterday : seeing that is past as a watch in the night.

5 As soon as thou scatterest them they are even as a sleep : and fade away suddenly like the grass.

6 In the morning it is green, and groweth up : but in the evening it is cut down, dried up, and withered.

7 For we consume away in thy displeasure : and are afraid at thy wrathful indignation.

8 Thou hast set our misdeeds before thee : and our secret sins in the light of thy countenance.

9 For when thou art angry all our days are gone : we bring our years to an end, as it were a tale that is told.

10 The days of our age are threescore years and ten; and though men be so strong that they come to fourscore years : yet is their strength then but labour and sorrow; so soon passeth it away, and we are gone.

11 But who regardeth the power of thy wrath : for even thereafter as a man feareth, so is thy displeasure.

12 So teach us to number our days : that we may apply our hearts unto wisdom.

13 Turn thee again, O Lord, at the last : and be gracious unto thy servants.

14 O satisfy us with thy mercy, and that soon : so shall we rejoice and be glad all the days of our life.

15 Comfort us again now after the time that thou hast plagued us : and for the years wherein we have suffered adversity.

16 Shew thy servants thy work : and their children thy glory.

17 And the glorious majesty of the Lord our God be upon us : prosper thou the work of our hands upon us, O prosper thou our handywork.

PSALM 91. *QUI HABITAT*

WHOSO dwelleth under the defence of the most High : shall abide under the shadow of the Almighty.

2 I will say unto the Lord, Thou art my hope, and my strong hold : my God, in him will I trust.

3 For he shall deliver thee from the snare of the hunter : and from the noisome pestilence.

4 He shall defend thee under his wings, and thou shalt be safe under his feathers : his faithfulness and truth shall be thy shield and buckler.

5 Thou shalt not be afraid for any terror by night : nor for the arrow that flieth by day;

6 For the pestilence that walketh in darkness : nor for the sickness that destroyeth in the noon-day.

7 A thousand shall fall beside thee, and ten thousand at thy right hand : but it shall not come nigh thee.

8 Yea, with thine eyes shalt thou behold : and see the reward of the ungodly.

9 For thou, Lord, art my hope : thou hast set thine house of defence very high.

10 There shall no evil happen unto thee : neither shall any plague come nigh thy dwelling.

11 For he shall give his angels charge over thee : to keep thee in all thy ways.

12 They shall bear thee in their hands : that thou hurt not thy foot against a stone.

13 Thou shalt go upon the lion and adder : the young lion and the dragon shalt thou tread under thy feet.

14 Because he hath set his love upon me, therefore will I deliver him : I will set him up, because he hath known my Name.

15 He shall call upon me, and I will hear him : yea, I am with him in trouble; I will deliver him, and bring him to honour.

16 With long life will I satisfy him : and shew him my salvation.

Psalm 92. *Bonum est confiteri*

IT is a good thing to give thanks unto the Lord : and to sing praises unto thy Name, O most Highest;

2 To tell of thy loving-kindness early in the morning : and of thy truth in the night-season;

3 Upon an instrument of ten strings, and upon the lute : upon a loud instrument, and upon the harp.

4 For thou, Lord, hast made me glad through thy works : and I will rejoice in giving praise for the operations of thy hands.

5 O Lord, how glorious are thy works : thy thoughts are very deep.

6 An unwise man doth not well consider this : and a fool doth not understand it.

7 When the ungodly are green as the grass, and when all the workers of wickedness do flourish : then shall they be destroyed for ever; but thou, Lord, art the most Highest for evermore.

8 For lo, thine enemies, O Lord, lo, thine enemies shall perish : and all the workers of wickedness shall be destroyed.

9 But mine horn shall be exalted like the horn of an unicorn : for I am anointed with fresh oil.

10 Mine eye also shall see his lust of mine enemies : and mine ear shall hear his desire of the wicked that arise up against me.

11 The righteous shall flourish like a palm-tree : and shall spread abroad like a cedar in Libanus.

12 Such as are planted in the house of the Lord : shall flourish in the courts of the house of our God.

13 They also shall bring forth more fruit in their age : and shall be fat and well-liking.

14 That they may shew how true the Lord my strength is : and that there is no unrighteousness in him.

Day 18. Evening Prayer

PSALM 93. *DOMINUS REGNAVIT*

THE Lord is King, and hath put on glorious apparel : the Lord hath put on his apparel, and girded himself with strength.

2 He hath made the round world so sure : that it cannot be moved.

3 Ever since the world began hath thy seat been prepared : thou art from everlasting.

4 The floods are risen, O Lord, the floods have lift up their voice : the floods lift up their waves.

5 The waves of the sea are mighty, and rage horribly : but yet the Lord, who dwelleth on high, is mightier.

6 Thy testimonies, O Lord, are very sure : holiness becometh thine house for ever.

PSALM 94. *DEUS ULTIONUM*

LORD God, to whom vengeance belongeth : thou God, to whom vengeance belongeth, shew thyself.

2 Arise, thou Judge of the world : and reward the proud after their deserving.

3 Lord, how long shall the ungodly : how long shall the ungodly triumph?

4 How long shall all wicked doers speak so disdainfully : and make such proud boasting?

5 They smite down thy people, O Lord : and trouble thine heritage.

6 They murder the widow and the stranger : and put the fatherless to death.

7 And yet they say, Tush, the Lord shall not see : neither shall the God of Jacob regard it.

8 Take heed, ye unwise among the people : O ye fools, when will ye understand?

9 He that planted the ear, shall he not hear : or he that made the eye, shall he not see?

10 Or he that nurtureth the heathen : it is he that teacheth man knowledge, shall not he punish?

11 The Lord knoweth the thoughts of man : that they are but vain.

12 Blessed is the man whom thou chastenest, O Lord : and teachest him in thy law;

13 That thou mayest give him patience in time of adversity : until the pit be digged up for the ungodly.

14 For the Lord will not fail his people : neither will he forsake his inheritance;

15 Until righteousness turn again unto judgement : all such as are true in heart shall follow it.

16 Who will rise up with me against the wicked : or who will take my part against the evil-doers?

17 If the Lord had not helped me : it had not failed but my soul had been put to silence.

18 But when I said, My foot hath slipt : thy mercy, O Lord, held me up.

19 In the multitude of the sorrows that I had in my heart : thy comforts have refreshed my soul.

20 Wilt thou have any thing to do with the stool of wickedness : which imagineth mischief as a law?

21 They gather them together against the soul of the righteous : and condemn the innocent blood.

22 But the Lord is my refuge : and my God is the strength of my confidence.

23 He shall recompense them their wickedness, and destroy them in their own malice : yea, the Lord our God shall destroy them.

Day 19. Morning Prayer

PSALM 95. *VENITE, EXULTEMUS*

COME, let us sing unto the Lord : let us heartily rejoice in the strength of our salvation.

2 Let us come before his presence with thanksgiving : and shew ourselves glad in him with psalms.

3 For the Lord is a great God : and a great King above all gods.

4 In his hand are all the corners of the earth : and the strength of the hills is his also.

5 The sea is his, and he made it : and his hands prepared the dry land.

6 O come, let us worship and fall down : and kneel before the Lord our Maker.

7 For he is the Lord our God : and we are the people of his pasture, and the sheep of his hand.

8 To-day if ye will hear his voice, harden not your hearts : as in the provocation, and as in the day of temptation in the wilderness.

9 When your fathers tempted me : proved me, and saw my works.

10 Forty years long was I grieved with this generation, and said : It is a people that do err in their hearts, for they have not known my ways;

11 Unto whom I sware in my wrath : that they should not enter into my rest.

PSALM 96. *CANTATE DOMINO*

SING unto the Lord a new song : sing unto the Lord, all the whole earth.

2 Sing unto the Lord, and praise his Name : be telling of his salvation from day to day.

3 Declare his honour unto the heathen : and his wonders unto all people.

4 For the Lord is great, and cannot worthily be praised : he is more to be feared than all gods.

5 As for all the gods of the heathen, they are but idols : but it is the Lord that made the heavens.

6 Glory and worship are before him : power and honour are in his sanctuary.

7 Ascribe unto the Lord, O ye kindreds of the people : ascribe unto the Lord worship and power.

8 Ascribe unto the Lord the honour due unto his Name : bring presents, and come into his courts.

9 O worship the Lord in the beauty of holiness : let the whole earth stand in awe of him.

10 Tell it out among the heathen that the Lord is King : and that it is he who hath made the round world so fast that it cannot be moved; and how that he shall judge the people righteously.

11 Let the heavens rejoice, and let the earth be glad : let the sea make a noise, and all that therein is.

12 Let the field be joyful, and all that is in it : then shall all the trees of the wood rejoice before the Lord.

13 For he cometh, for he cometh to judge the earth : and with righteousness to judge the world, and the people with his truth.

Psalm 97. *Dominus regnavit*

THE Lord is King, the earth may be glad thereof : yea, the multitude of the isles may be glad thereof.

2 Clouds and darkness are round about him : righteousness and judgement are the habitation of his seat.

3 There shall go a fire before him : and burn up his enemies on every side.

4 His lightnings gave shine unto the world : the earth saw it, and was afraid.

5 The hills melted like wax at the presence of the Lord : at the presence of the Lord of the whole earth.

6 The heavens have declared his righteousness : and all the people have seen his glory.

7 Confounded be all they that worship carved images, and that delight in vain gods : worship him, all ye gods.

8 Sion heard of it, and rejoiced : and the daughters of Judah were glad, because of thy judgements, O Lord.

9 For thou, Lord, art higher than all that are in the earth : thou art exalted far above all gods.

10 O ye that love the Lord, see that ye hate the thing which is evil : the Lord preserveth the souls of his saints; he shall deliver them from the hand of the ungodly.

11 There is sprung up a light for the righteous : and joyful gladness for such as are true-hearted.

12 Rejoice in the Lord, ye righteous : and give thanks for a remembrance of his holiness.

Day 19. Evening Prayer

Psalm 98. *Cantate Domino*

SING unto the Lord a new song : for he hath done marvellous things.

2 With his own right hand, and with his holy arm : hath he gotten himself the victory.

3 The Lord declared his salvation : his righteousness hath he openly shewed in the sight of the heathen.

4 He hath remembered his mercy and truth toward the house of Israel : and all the ends of the world have seen the salvation of our God.

5 Shew yourselves joyful unto the Lord, all ye lands : sing, rejoice, and give thanks.

6 Praise the Lord upon the harp : sing to the harp with a psalm of thanksgiving.

7 With trumpets also and shawms : O shew yourselves joyful before the Lord the King.

8 Let the sea make a noise, and all that therein is : the round world, and they that dwell therein.

9 Let the floods clap their hands, and let the hills be joyful together before the Lord : for he is come to judge the earth.

10 With righteousness shall he judge the world : and the people with equity.

PSALM 99. *DOMINUS REGNAVIT*

THE Lord is King, be the people never so unpatient : he sitteth between the cherubims, be the earth never so unquiet.

2 The Lord is great in Sion : and high above all people.

3 They shall give thanks unto thy Name : which is great, wonderful, and holy.

4 The King's power loveth judgement; thou hast prepared equity : thou hast executed judgement and righteousness in Jacob.

5 O magnify the Lord our God : and fall down before his footstool, for he is holy.

6 Moses and Aaron among his priests, and Samuel among such as call upon his Name : these called upon the Lord, and he heard them.

7 He spake unto them out of the cloudy pillar : for they kept his testimonies, and the law that he gave them.

8 Thou heardest them, O Lord our God : thou forgavest them, O God, and punishedst their own inventions.

9 O magnify the Lord our God, and worship him upon his holy hill : for the Lord our God is holy.

PSALM 100. *JUBILATE DEO*

BE joyful in the Lord, all ye lands : serve the Lord with gladness, and come before his presence with a song.

2 Be ye sure that the Lord he is God : it is he that hath made us, and not we ourselves; we are his people, and the sheep of his pasture.

3 O go your way into his gates with thanksgiving, and into his courts with praise : be thankful unto him, and speak good of his Name.

4 For the Lord is gracious, his mercy is everlasting : and his truth endureth from generation to generation.

PSALM 101. *MISERICORDIAM ET JUDICIUM*

Y song shall be of mercy and judgement : unto thee, O Lord, will I sing.

2 O let me have understanding : in the way of godliness.

3 When wilt thou come unto me : I will walk in my house with a perfect heart.

4 I will take no wicked thing in hand; I hate the sins of unfaithfulness : there shall no such cleave unto me.

5 A froward heart shall depart from me : I will not know a wicked person.

6 Whoso privily slandereth his neighbour : him will I destroy.

7 Whoso hath also a proud look and high stomach : I will not suffer him.

8 Mine eyes look upon such as are faithful in the land : that they may dwell with me.

9 Whoso leadeth a godly life : he shall be my servant.

10 There shall no deceitful person dwell in my house : he that telleth lies shall not tarry in my sight.

11 I shall soon destroy all the ungodly that are in the land : that I may root out all wicked doers from the city of the Lord.

Day 20. Morning Prayer

PSALM 102. *DOMINE, EXAUDI*

EAR my prayer, O Lord : and let my crying come unto thee.

2 Hide not thy face from me in the time of my trouble : incline thine ear unto me when I call; O hear me, and that right soon.

3 For my days are consumed away like smoke : and my bones are burnt up as it were a firebrand.

4 My heart is smitten down, and withered liked grass : so that I forget to eat my bread.

5 For the voice of my groaning : my bones will scarce cleave to my flesh.

6 I am become like a pelican in the wilderness : and like an owl that is in the desert.

7 I have watched, and am even as it were a sparrow : that sitteth alone upon the house-top.

8 Mine enemies revile me all the day long : and they that are mad upon me are sworn together against me.

9 For I have eaten ashes as it were bread : and mingled my drink with weeping;

10 And that because of thine indignation and wrath : for thou hast taken me up, and cast me down.

11 My days are gone like a shadow : and I am withered like grass.

12 But thou, O Lord, shalt endure for ever : and thy remembrance throughout all generations.

13 Thou shalt arise, and have mercy upon Sion : for it is time that thou have mercy upon her, yea, the time is come.

14 And why? thy servants think upon her stones : and it pitieth them to see her in the dust.

15 The heathen shall fear thy Name, O Lord : and all the kings of the earth thy majesty;

16 When the Lord shall build up Sion : and when his glory shall appear;

17 When he turneth him unto the prayer of the poor destitute : and despiseth not their desire.

18 This shall be written for those that come after : and the people which shall be born shall praise the Lord.

19 For he hath looked down from his sanctuary : out of the heaven did the Lord behold the earth;

20 That he might hear the mournings of such as are in captivity : and deliver the children appointed unto death;

21 That they may declare the Name of the Lord in Sion : and his worship at Jerusalem;

22 When the people are gathered together : and the kingdoms also, to serve the Lord.

23 He brought down my strength in my journey : and shortened my days.

24 But I said, O my God, take me not away in the midst of mine age : as for thy years, they endure throughout all generations.

25 Thou, Lord, in the beginning hast laid the foundation of the earth : and the heavens are the work of thy hands.

26 They shall perish, but thou shalt endure : they all shall wax old as doth a garment;

27 And as a vesture shalt thou change them, and they shall be changed : but thou art the same, and thy years shall not fail.

28 The children of thy servants shall continue : and their seed shall stand fast in thy sight.

PSALM 103. *BENEDIC, ANIMA MEA*

RAISE the Lord, O my soul : and all that is within me praise his holy Name.

2 Praise the Lord, O my soul : and forget not all his benefits;

3 Who forgiveth all thy sin : and healeth all thine infirmities;

4 Who saveth thy life from destruction : and crowneth thee with mercy and loving-kindness;

5 Who satisfieth thy mouth with good things : making thee young and lusty as an eagle.

6 The Lord executeth righteousness and judgement : for all them that are oppressed with wrong.

7 He shewed his ways unto Moses : his works unto the children of Israel.

8 The Lord is full of compassion and mercy : long-suffering, and of great goodness.

9 He will not alway be chiding : neither keepeth he his anger for ever.

10 He hath not dealt with us after our sins : nor rewarded us according to our wickednesses.

11 For look how high the heaven is in comparison of the earth : so great is his mercy also toward them that fear him.

12 Look how wide also the east is from the west : so far hath he set our sins from us.

13 Yea, like as a father pitieth his own children : even so is the Lord merciful unto them that fear him.

14 For he knoweth whereof we are made : he remembereth that we are but dust.

15 The days of man are but as grass : for he flourisheth as a flower of the field.

16 For as soon as the wind goeth over it, it is gone : and the place thereof shall know it no more.

17 But the merciful goodness of the Lord endureth for ever and ever upon them that fear him : and his righteousness upon children's children;

18 Even upon such as keep his covenant : and think upon his commandments to do them.

19 The Lord hath prepared his seat in heaven : and his kingdom ruleth over all.

20 O praise the Lord, ye angels of his, ye that excel in strength : ye that fulfil his commandment, and hearken unto the voice of his words.

21 O praise the Lord, all ye his hosts : ye servants of his that do his pleasure.

22 O speak good of the Lord, all ye works of his, in all places of his dominion : praise thou the Lord, O my soul.

Day 20. Evening Prayer

PSALM 104. *BENEDIC, ANIMA MEA*

RAISE the Lord, O my soul : O Lord my God, thou art become exceeding glorious; thou art clothed with majesty and honour.

2 Thou deckest thyself with light as it were with a garment : and spreadest out the heavens like a curtain.

3 Who layeth the beams of his chambers in the waters : and maketh the clouds his chariot, and walketh upon the wings of the wind.

4 He maketh his angels spirits : and his ministers a flaming fire.

5 He laid the foundations of the earth : that it never should move at any time.

6 Thou coveredst it with the deep like as with a garment : the waters stand in the hills.

7 At thy rebuke they flee : at the voice of thy thunder they are afraid.

8 They go up as high as the hills, and down to the valleys beneath : even unto the place which thou hast appointed for them.

9 Thou hast set them their bounds which they shall not pass : neither turn again to cover the earth.

10 He sendeth the springs into the rivers : which run among the hills.

11 All beasts of the field drink thereof : and the wild asses quench their thirst.

12 Beside them shall the fowls of the air have their habitation : and sing among the branches.

13 He watereth the hills from above : the earth is filled with the fruit of thy works.

14 He bringeth forth grass for the cattle : and green herb for the service of men;

15 That he may bring food out of the earth, and wine that maketh glad the heart of man : and oil to make him a cheerful countenance, and bread to strengthen man's heart.

16 The trees of the Lord also are full of sap : even the cedars of Libanus which he hath planted;

17 Wherein the birds make their nests : and the fir-trees are a dwelling for the stork.

18 The high hills are a refuge for the wild goats : and so are the stony rocks for the conies.

19 He appointed the moon for certain seasons : and the sun knoweth his going down.

20 Thou makest darkness that it may be night : wherein all the beasts of the forest do move.

21 The lions roaring after their prey : do seek their meat from God.

22 The sun ariseth, and they get them away together : and lay them down in their dens.

23 Man goeth forth to his work, and to his labour : until the evening.

24 O Lord, how manifold are thy works : in wisdom hast thou made them all; the earth is full of thy riches.

25 So is the great and wide sea also : wherein are things creeping innumerable, both small and great beasts.

26 There go the ships, and there is that Leviathan : whom thou hast made to take his pastime therein.

27 These wait all upon thee : that thou mayest give them meat in due season.

28 When thou givest it them they gather it : and when thou openest thy hand they are filled with good.

29 When thou hidest thy face they are troubled : when thou takest away their breath they die, and are turned again to their dust.

30 When thou lettest thy breath go forth they shall be made : and thou shalt renew the face of the earth.

31 The glorious majesty of the Lord shall endure for ever : the Lord shall rejoice in his works.

32 The earth shall tremble at the look of him : if he do but touch the hills, they shall smoke.

33 I will sing unto the Lord as long as I live : I will praise my God while I have my being.

34 And so shall my words please him : my joy shall be in the Lord.

35 As for sinners, they shall be consumed out of the earth, and the ungodly shall come to an end : praise thou the Lord, O my soul, praise the Lord.

Day 21. Morning Prayer

PSALM 105. CONFITEMINI DOMINO

GIVE thanks unto the Lord, and call upon his Name : tell the people what things he hath done.

2 O let your songs be of him, and praise him : and let your talking be of all his wondrous works.

3 Rejoice in his holy Name : let the heart of them rejoice that seek the Lord.

4 Seek the Lord and his strength : seek his face evermore.

5 Remember the marvellous works that he hath done : his wonders, and the judgements of his mouth.

6 O ye seed of Abraham his servant : ye children of Jacob his chosen.

7 He is the Lord our God : his judgements are in all the world.

8 He hath been alway mindful of his covenant and promise : that he made to a thousand generations;

9 Even the covenant that he made with Abraham : and the oath that he sware unto Isaac;

10 And appointed the same unto Jacob for a law : and to Israel for an everlasting testament;

11 Saying, Unto thee will I give the land of Canaan : the lot of your inheritance;

12 When there were yet but a few of them : and they strangers in the land;

13 What time as they went from one nation to another : from one kingdom to another people;

14 He suffered no man to do them wrong : but reproved even kings for their sakes;

15 Touch not mine Anointed : and do my prophets no harm.

16 Moreover, he called for a dearth upon the land : and destroyed all the provision of bread.

17 But he had sent a man before them : even Joseph, who was sold to be a bond-servant;

18 Whose feet they hurt in the stocks : the iron entered into his soul;

19 Until the time came that his cause was known : the word of the Lord tried him.

20 The king sent, and delivered him : the prince of the people let him go free.

21 He made him lord also of his house : and ruler of all his substance;

22 That he might inform his princes after his will : and teach his senators wisdom.

23 Israel also came into Egypt : and Jacob was a stranger in the land of Ham.

24 And he increased his people exceedingly : and made them stronger than their enemies;

25 Whose heart turned, so that they hated his people : and dealt untruly with his servants.

26 Then sent he Moses his servant : and Aaron whom he had chosen.

27 And these shewed his tokens among them : and wonders in the land of Ham.

28 He sent darkness, and it was dark : and they were not obedient unto his word.

29 He turned their waters into blood : and slew their fish.

30 Their land brought forth frogs : yea, even in their kings' chambers.

31 He spake the word, and there came all manner of flies : and lice in all their quarters.

32 He gave them hail-stones for rain : and flames of fire in their land.

33 He smote their vines also and fig-trees : and destroyed the trees that were in their coasts.

34 He spake the word, and the grasshoppers came, and caterpillars innumerable : and did eat up all the grass in their land, and devoured the fruit of their ground.

35 He smote all the first-born in their land : even the chief of all their strength.

36 He brought them forth also with silver and gold : there was not one feeble person among their tribes.

37 Egypt was glad at their departing : for they were afraid of them.

38 He spread out a cloud to be a covering : and fire to give light in the night-season.

39 At their desire he brought quails : and he filled them with the bread of heaven.

40 He opened the rock of stone, and the waters flowed out : so that rivers ran in the dry places.

41 For why? he remembered his holy promise : and Abraham his servant.

42 And he brought forth his people with joy : and his chosen with gladness;

43 And gave them the lands of the heathen : and they took the labours of the people in possession;

44 That they might keep his statutes : and observe his laws.

Day 21. Evening Prayer

PSALM 106. *CONFITEMINI DOMINO*

GIVE thanks unto the Lord, for he is gracious : and his mercy endureth for ever.

2 Who can express the noble acts of the Lord : or shew forth all his praise?

3 Blessed are they that alway keep judgement : and do righteousness.

4 Remember me, O Lord, according to the favour that thou bearest unto thy people : O visit me with thy salvation;

5 That I may see the felicity of thy chosen : and rejoice in the gladness of thy people, and give thanks with thine inheritance.

6 We have sinned with our fathers : we have done amiss, and dealt wickedly.

7 Our fathers regarded not thy wonders in Egypt, neither kept they thy great goodness in remembrance : but were disobedient at the sea, even at the Red sea.

8 Nevertheless, he helped them for his Name's sake : that he might make his power to be known.

9 He rebuked the Red sea also, and it was dried up : so he led them through the deep, as through a wilderness.

10 And he saved them from the adversaries' hand : and delivered them from the hand of the enemy.

11 As for those that troubled them, the waters overwhelmed them : there was not one of them left.

12 Then believed they his words : and sang praise unto him.

13 But within a while they forgat his works : and would not abide his counsel.

14 But lust came upon them in the wilderness : and they tempted God in the desert.

15 And he gave them their desire : and sent leanness withal into their soul.

16 They angered Moses also in the tents : and Aaron the saint of the Lord.

17 So the earth opened, and swallowed up Dathan : and covered the congregation of Abiram.

18 And the fire was kindled in their company : the flame burnt up the ungodly.

19 They made a calf in Horeb : and worshipped the molten image.

20 Thus they turned their glory : into the similitude of a calf that eateth hay.

21 And they forgat God their Saviour : who had done so great things in Egypt;

22 Wondrous works in the land of Ham : and fearful things by the Red sea.

23 So he said, he would have destroyed them, had not Moses his chosen stood before him in the gap : to turn away his wrathful indignation, lest he should destroy them.

24 Yea, they thought scorn of that pleasant land : and gave no credence unto his word;

25 But murmured in their tents : and hearkened not unto the voice of the Lord.

26 Then lift he up his hand against them : to overthrow them in the wilderness;

27 To cast out their seed among the nations : and to scatter them in the lands.

28 They joined themselves unto Baal-peor : and ate the offerings of the dead.

29 Thus they provoked him to anger with their own inventions : and the plague was great among them.

30 Then stood up Phinees and prayed : and so the plague ceased.

31 And that was counted unto him for righteousness : among all posterities for evermore.

32 They angered him also at the waters of strife : so that he punished Moses for their sakes;

33 Because they provoked his spirit : so that he spake unadvisedly with his lips.

34 Neither destroyed they the heathen : as the Lord commanded them;

35 But were mingled among the heathen : and learned their works.

36 Insomuch that they worshipped their idols, which turned to their own decay : yea, they offered their sons and their daughters unto devils;

37 And shed innocent blood, even the blood of their sons and of their daughters : whom they had offered unto the idols of Canaan; and the land was defiled with blood.

38 Thus were they stained with their own works : and went a whoring with their own inventions.

39 Therefore was the wrath of the Lord kindled against his people : insomuch that he abhorred his own inheritance.

40 And he gave them over into the hands of the heathen : and they that hated them were lords over them.

41 Their enemies oppressed them : and had them in subjection.

42 Many a time did he deliver them : but they rebelled against him with their own inventions, and were brought down in their wickedness.

43 Nevertheless, when he saw their adversity : he heard their complaint.

44 He thought upon his covenant, and pitied them according unto the multitude of his mercies : yea, he made all those that led them away captive to pity them.

45 Deliver us, O Lord our God, and gather us from among the heathen : that we may give thanks unto thy holy Name, and make our boast of thy praise.

46 Blessed be the Lord God of Israel from everlasting and world without end : and let all the people say, Amen.

Day 22. Morning Prayer

Psalm 107. *Confitemini Domino*

GIVE thanks unto the Lord, for he is gracious : and his mercy endureth for ever.

2 Let them give thanks whom the Lord hath redeemed : and delivered from the hand of the enemy;

3 And gathered them out of the lands, from the east and from the west : from the north and from the south.

4 They went astray in the wilderness out of the way : and found no city to dwell in;

5 Hungry and thirsty : their soul fainted in them.

6 So they cried unto the Lord in their trouble : and he delivered them from their distress.

7 He led them forth by the right way : that they might go to the city where they dwelt.

8 O that men would therefore praise the Lord for his goodness : and declare the wonders that he doeth for the children of men!

9 For he satisfieth the empty soul : and filleth the hungry soul with goodness.

10 Such as sit in darkness, and in the shadow of death : being fast bound in misery and iron;

11 Because they rebelled against the words of the Lord : and lightly regarded the counsel of the most Highest;

12 He also brought down their heart through heaviness : they fell down, and there was none to help them.

13 So when they cried unto the Lord in their trouble : he delivered them out of their distress.

14 For he brought them out of darkness, and out of the shadow of death : and brake their bonds in sunder.

15 O that men would therefore praise the Lord for his goodness : and declare the wonders that he doeth for the children of men!

16 For he hath broken the gates of brass : and smitten the bars of iron in sunder.

17 Foolish men are plagued for their offence : and because of their wickedness.

18 Their soul abhorred all manner of meat : and they were even hard at death's door.

19 So when they cried unto the Lord in their trouble : he delivered them out of their distress.

20 He sent his word, and healed them : and they were saved from their destruction.

21 O that men would therefore praise the Lord for his goodness : and declare the wonders that he doeth for the children of men!

22 That they would offer unto him the sacrifice of thanksgiving : and tell out his works with gladness!

23 They that go down to the sea in ships : and occupy their business in great waters;

24 These men see the works of the Lord : and his wonders in the deep.

25 For at his word the stormy wind ariseth : which lifteth up the waves thereof.

26 They are carried up to the heaven, and down again to the deep : their soul melteth away because of the trouble.

27 They reel to and fro, and stagger like a drunken man : and are at their wits' end.

28 So when they cry unto the Lord in their trouble : he delivereth them out of their distress.

29 For he maketh the storm to cease : so that the waves thereof are still.

30 Then are they glad, because they are at rest : and so he bringeth them unto the haven where they would be.

31 O that men would therefore praise the Lord for his goodness : and declare the wonders that he doeth for the children of men!

32 That they would exalt him also in the congregation of the people : and praise him in the seat of the elders!

33 Who turneth the floods into a wilderness : and drieth up the water-springs.

34 A fruitful land maketh he barren : for the wickedness of them that dwell therein.

35 Again, he maketh the wilderness a standing water : and water-springs of a dry ground.

36 And there he setteth the hungry : that they may build them a city to dwell in;

37 That they may sow their land, and plant vineyards : to yield them fruits of increase.

38 He blesseth them so that they multiply exceedingly : and suffereth not their cattle to decrease.

39 And again, when they are minished and brought low : through oppression, through any plague or trouble;

40 Though he suffer them to be evil intreated through tyrants : and let them wander out of the way in the wilderness;

41 Yet helpeth he the poor out of misery : and maketh him households like a flock of sheep.

42 The righteous will consider this, and rejoice : and the mouth of all wickedness shall be stopped.

43 Whoso is wise will ponder these things : and they shall understand the loving-kindness of the Lord.

Day 22. Evening Prayer

Psalm 108. *Paratum cor meum*

O GOD, my heart is ready, my heart is ready : I will sing and give praise with the best member that I have.

2 Awake, thou lute, and harp : I myself will awake right early.

3 I will give thanks unto thee, O Lord, among the people : I will sing praises unto thee among the nations.

4 For thy mercy is greater than the heavens : and thy truth reacheth unto the clouds.

5 Set up thyself, O God, above the heavens : and thy glory above all the earth.

6 That thy beloved may be delivered : let thy right hand save them, and hear thou me.

7 God hath spoken in his holiness : I will rejoice therefore, and divide Sichem, and mete out the valley of Succoth.

8 Gilead is mine, and Manasses is mine : Ephraim also is the strength of my head.

9 Judah is my law-giver, Moab is my wash-pot : over Edom will I cast out my shoe, upon Philistia will I triumph.

10 Who will lead me into the strong city : and who will bring me into Edom?

11 Hast not thou forsaken us, O God : and wilt not thou, O God, go forth with our hosts?

12 O help us against the enemy : for vain is the help of man.

13 Through God we shall do great acts : and it is he that shall tread down our enemies.

Psalm 109. *Deus, laudem*

HOLD not thy tongue, O God of my praise : for the mouth of the ungodly, yea, the mouth of the deceitful is opened upon me.

2 And they have spoken against me with false tongues : they compassed me about also with words of hatred, and fought against me without a cause.

3 For the love that I had unto them, lo, they take now my contrary part : but I give myself unto prayer.

4 Thus have they rewarded me evil for good : and hatred for my good will.

5 Set thou an ungodly man to be ruler over him : and let Satan stand at his right hand.

6 When sentence is given upon him, let him be condemned : and let his prayer be turned into sin.

7 Let his days be few : and let another take his office.

8 Let his children be fatherless : and his wife a widow.

9 Let his children be vagabonds, and beg their bread : let them seek it also out of desolate places.

10 Let the extortioner consume all that he hath : and let the stranger spoil his labour.

11 Let there be no man to pity him : nor to have compassion upon his fatherless children.

12 Let his posterity be destroyed : and in the next generation let his name be clean put out.

13 Let the wickedness of his fathers be had in remembrance in the sight of the Lord : and let not the sin of his mother be done away.

14 Let them alway be before the Lord : that he may root out the memorial of them from off the earth.

15 And that, because his mind was not to do good : but persecuted the poor helpless man, that he might slay him that was vexed at the heart.

16 His delight was in cursing, and it shall happen unto him : he loved not blessing, therefore shall it be far from him.

17 He clothed himself with cursing, like as with a raiment : and it shall come into his bowels like water, and like oil into his bones.

18 Let it be unto him as the cloke that he hath upon him : and as the girdle that he is alway girded withal.

19 Let it thus happen from the Lord unto mine enemies : and to those that speak evil against my soul.

20 But deal thou with me, O Lord God, according unto thy Name : for sweet is thy mercy.

21 O deliver me, for I am helpless and poor : and my heart is wounded within me.

22 I go hence like the shadow that departeth : and am driven away as the grasshopper.

23 My knees are weak through fasting : my flesh is dried up for want of fatness.

24 I became also a reproach unto them : they that looked upon me shaked their heads.

25 Help me, O Lord my God : O save me according to thy mercy.

26 And they shall know, how that this is thy hand : and that thou, Lord, hast done it.

27 Though they curse, yet bless thou : and let them be confounded that rise up against me; but let thy servant rejoice.

28 Let mine adversaries be clothed with shame : and let them cover themselves with their own confusion, as with a cloke.

29 As for me, I will give great thanks unto the Lord with my mouth : and praise him among the multitude.

30 For he shall stand at the right hand of the poor : to save his soul from the unrighteous judges.

Day 23. Morning Prayer

PSALM 110. *DIXIT DOMINUS*

THE Lord said unto my Lord : Sit thou on my right hand, until I make thine enemies thy footstool.

2 The Lord shall send the rod of thy power out of Sion : be thou ruler, even in the midst among thine enemies.

3 In the day of thy power shall the people offer thee free-will offerings with an holy worship : the dew of thy birth is of the womb of the morning.

4 The Lord sware, and will not repent : Thou art a priest for ever after the order of Melchisedech.

5 The Lord upon thy right hand : shall wound even kings in the day of his wrath.

6 He shall judge among the heathen; he shall fill the places with the dead bodies : and smite in sunder the heads over divers countries.

7 He shall drink of the brook in the way : therefore shall he lift up his head.

PSALM 111. *CONFITEBOR TIBI*

I WILL give thanks unto the Lord with my whole heart : secretly among the faithful, and in the congregation.

2 The works of the Lord are great : sought out of all them that have pleasure therein.

3 His work is worthy to be praised and had in honour : and his righteousness endureth for ever.

4 The merciful and gracious Lord hath so done his marvellous works : that they ought to be had in remembrance.

5 He hath given meat unto them that fear him : he shall ever be mindful of his covenant.

6 He hath shewed his people the power of his works : that he may give them the heritage of the heathen.

7 The works of his hands are verity and judgement : all his commandments are true.

8 They stand fast for ever and ever : and are done in truth and equity.

9 He sent redemption unto his people : he hath commanded his covenant for ever; holy and reverend is his Name.

10 The fear of the Lord is the beginning of wisdom : a good understanding have all they that do thereafter; the praise of it endureth for ever.

PSALM 112. *BEATUS VIR*

BLESSED is the man that feareth the Lord : he hath great delight in his commandments.

2 His seed shall be mighty upon earth : the generation of the faithful shall be blessed.

3 Riches and plenteousness shall be in his house : and his righteousness endureth for ever.

4 Unto the godly there ariseth up light in the darkness : he is merciful, loving, and righteous.

5 A good man is merciful, and lendeth : and will guide his words with discretion.

6 For he shall never be moved : and the righteous shall be had in everlasting remembrance.

7 He will not be afraid of any evil tidings : for his heart standeth fast, and believeth in the Lord.

8 His heart is established, and will not shrink : until he see his desire upon his enemies.

9 He hath dispersed abroad, and given to the poor : and his righteousness remaineth for ever; his horn shall be exalted with honour.

10 The ungodly shall see it, and it shall grieve him : he shall gnash with his teeth, and consume away; the desire of the ungodly shall perish.

PSALM 113. *LAUDATE, PUERI*

PRAISE the Lord, ye servants : O praise the Name of the Lord.

2 Blessed be the Name of the Lord : from this time forth for evermore.

3 The Lord's Name is praised : from the rising up of the sun unto the going down of the same.

4 The Lord is high above all heathen : and his glory above the heavens.

5 Who is like unto the Lord our God, that hath his dwelling so high : and yet humbleth himself to behold the things that are in heaven and earth?

6 He taketh up the simple out of the dust : and lifteth the poor out of the mire;

7 That he may set him with the princes : even with the princes of his people.

8 He maketh the barren woman to keep house : and to be a joyful mother of children.

Day 23. Evening Prayer

Psalm 114. *In exitu Israel*

WHEN Israel came out of Egypt : and the house of Jacob from among the strange people,

2 Judah was his sanctuary : and Israel his dominion.

3 The sea saw that, and fled : Jordan was driven back.

4 The mountains skipped like rams : and the little hills like young sheep.

5 What aileth thee, O thou sea, that thou fleddest : and thou Jordan, that thou wast driven back?

6 Ye mountains, that ye skipped like rams : and ye little hills, like young sheep?

7 Tremble, thou earth, at the presence of the Lord : at the presence of the God of Jacob;

8 Who turned the hard rock into a standing water : and the flint-stone into a springing well.

Psalm 115. *Non nobis, Domine*

NOT unto us, O Lord, not unto us, but unto thy Name give the praise : for thy loving mercy and for thy truth's sake.

2 Wherefore shall the heathen say : Where is now their God?

3 As for our God, he is in heaven : he hath done whatsoever pleased him.

4 Their idols are silver and gold : even the work of men's hands.

5 They have mouths, and speak not : eyes have they, and see not.

6 They have ears, and hear not : noses have they, and smell not.

7 They have hands, and handle not; feet have they, and walk not : neither speak they through their throat.

8 They that make them are like unto them : and so are all such as put their trust in them.

9 But thou, house of Israel, trust thou in the Lord : he is their succour and defence.

10 Ye house of Aaron, put your trust in the Lord : he is their helper and defender.

11 Ye that fear the Lord, put your trust in the Lord : he is their helper and defender.

12 The Lord hath been mindful of us, and he shall bless us : even he shall bless the house of Israel, he shall bless the house of Aaron.

13 He shall bless them that fear the Lord : both small and great.

14 The Lord shall increase you more and more : you and your children.

15 Ye are the blessed of the Lord : who made heaven and earth.

16 All the whole heavens are the Lord's : the earth hath he given to the children of men.

17 The dead praise not thee, O Lord : neither all they that go down into silence.

18 But we will praise the Lord : from this time forth for evermore. Praise the Lord.

Day 24. Morning Prayer

Psalm 116. *Dilexi, quoniam*

AM well pleased : that the Lord hath heard the voice of my prayer;

2 That he hath inclined his ear unto me : therefore will I call upon him as long as I live.

3 The snares of death compassed me round about : and the pains of hell gat hold upon me.

4 I shall find trouble and heaviness, and I will call upon the Name of the Lord : O Lord, I beseech thee, deliver my soul.

5 Gracious is the Lord, and righteous : yea, our God is merciful.

6 The Lord preserveth the simple : I was in misery, and he helped me.

7 Turn again then unto thy rest, O my soul : for the Lord hath rewarded thee.

8 And why? thou hast delivered my soul from death : mine eyes from tears, and my feet from falling.

9 I will walk before the Lord : in the land of the living.

10 I believed, and therefore will I speak; but I was sore troubled : I said in my haste, All men are liars.

11 What reward shall I give unto the Lord : for all the benefits that he hath done unto me?

12 I will receive the cup of salvation : and call upon the Name of the Lord.

13 I will pay my vows now in the presence of all his people : right dear in the sight of the Lord is the death of his saints.

14 Behold, O Lord, how that I am thy servant : I am thy servant, and the son of thine handmaid; thou hast broken my bonds in sunder.

15 I will offer to thee the sacrifice of thanksgiving : and will call upon the Name of the Lord.

16 I will pay my vows unto the Lord, in the sight of all his people : in the courts of the Lord's house, even in the midst of thee, O Jerusalem. Praise the Lord.

PSALM 117. *LAUDATE DOMINUM*

PRAISE the Lord, all ye heathen : praise him, all ye nations.

2 For his merciful kindness is ever more and more towards us : and the truth of the Lord endureth for ever. Praise the Lord.

PSALM 118. *CONFITEMINI DOMINO*

GIVE thanks unto the Lord, for he is gracious : because his mercy endureth for ever.

2 Let Israel now confess that he is gracious : and that his mercy endureth for ever.

3 Let the house of Aaron now confess : that his mercy endureth for ever.

4 Yea, let them now that fear the Lord confess : that his mercy endureth for ever.

5 I called upon the Lord in trouble : and the Lord heard me at large.

6 The Lord is on my side : I will not fear what man doeth unto me.

7 The Lord taketh my part with them that help me : therefore shall I see my desire upon mine enemies.

8 It is better to trust in the Lord : than to put any confidence in man.

9 It is better to trust in the Lord : than to put any confidence in princes.

10 All nations compassed me round about : but in the Name of the Lord will I destroy them.

11 They kept me in on every side, they kept me in, I say, on every side : but in the Name of the Lord will I destroy them.

12 They came about me like bees, and are extinct even as the fire among the thorns : for in the Name of the Lord I will destroy them.

13 Thou hast thrust sore at me, that I might fall : but the Lord was my help.

14 The Lord is my strength, and my song : and is become my salvation.

15 The voice of joy and health is in the dwellings of the righteous : the right hand of the Lord bringeth mighty things to pass.

16 The right hand of the Lord hath the pre-eminence : the right hand of the Lord bringeth mighty things to pass.

17 I shall not die, but live : and declare the works of the Lord.

18 The Lord hath chastened and corrected me : but he hath not given me over unto death.

19 Open me the gates of righteousness : that I may go into them, and give thanks unto the Lord.

20 This is the gate of the Lord : the righteous shall enter into it.

21 I will thank thee, for thou hast heard me : and art become my salvation.

22 The same stone which the builders refused : is become the head-stone in the corner.

23 This is the Lord's doing : and it is marvellous in our eyes.

24 This is the day which the Lord hath made : we will rejoice and be glad in it.

25 Help me now, O Lord : O Lord, send us now prosperity.

26 Blessed be he that cometh in the Name of the Lord : we have wished you good luck, ye that are of the house of the Lord.

27 God is the Lord who hath shewed us light : bind the sacrifice with cords, yea, even unto the horns of the altar.

28 Thou art my God, and I will thank thee : thou art my God, and I will praise thee.

29 O give thanks unto the Lord, for he is gracious : and his mercy endureth for ever.

Day 24. Evening Prayer

PSALM 119. *BEATI IMMACULATI*

BLESSED are those that are undefiled in the way : and walk in the law of the Lord.

2 Blessed are they that keep his testimonies : and seek him with their whole heart.

3 For they who do no wickedness : walk in his ways.

4 Thou hast charged : that we shall diligently keep thy commandments.

5 O that my ways were made so direct : that I might keep thy statutes!

6 So shall I not be confounded : while I have respect unto all thy commandments.

7 I will thank thee with an unfeigned heart : when I shall have learned the judgements of thy righteousness.

8 I will keep thy ceremonies : O forsake me not utterly.

IN QUO CORRIGET?

WHEREWITHAL shall a young man cleanse his way : Even by ruling himself after thy word.

10 With my whole heart have I sought thee : O let me not go wrong out of thy commandments.

11 Thy words have I hid within my heart : that I should not sin against thee.

12 Blessed art thou, O Lord : O teach me thy statutes.

13 With my lips have I been telling : of all the judgements of thy mouth.

14 I have had as great delight in the way of thy testimonies : as in all manner of riches.

15 I will talk of thy commandments : and have respect unto thy ways.

16 My delight shall be in thy statutes : and I will not forget thy word.

RETRIBUE SERVO TUO

DO well unto thy servant : that I may live, and keep thy word.

18 Open thou mine eyes : that I may see the wondrous things of thy law.

19 I am a stranger upon earth : O hide not thy commandments from me.

20 My soul breaketh out for the very fervent desire : that it hath alway unto thy judgements.

21 Thou hast rebuked the proud : and cursed are they that do err from thy commandments.

22 O turn from me shame and rebuke : for I have kept thy testimonies.

23 Princes also did sit and speak against me : but thy servant is occupied in thy statutes.

24 For thy testimonies are my delight : and my counsellors.

ADHÆSIT PAVIMENTO

MY soul cleaveth to the dust : O quicken thou me, according to thy word.

26 I have acknowledged my ways, and thou heardest me : O teach me thy statutes.

27 Make me to understand the way of thy commandments : and so shall I talk of thy wondrous works.

28 My soul melteth away for very heaviness : comfort thou me according unto thy word.

29 Take from me the way of lying : and cause thou me to make much of thy law.

30 I have chosen the way of truth : and thy judgements have I laid before me.

31 I have stuck unto thy testimonies : O Lord, confound me not.

32 I will run the way of thy commandments : when thou hast set my heart at liberty.

Day 25. Morning Prayer

Legem pone

EACH me, O Lord, the way of thy statutes : and I shall keep it unto the end.

34 Give me understanding, and I shall keep thy law : yea, I shall keep it with my whole heart.

35 Make me to go in the path of thy commandments : for therein is my desire.

36 Incline my heart unto thy testimonies : and not to covetousness.

37 O turn away mine eyes, lest they behold vanity : and quicken thou me in thy way.

38 O stablish thy word in thy servant : that I may fear thee.

39 Take away the rebuke that I am afraid of : for thy judgements are good.

40 Behold, my delight is in thy commandments : O quicken me in thy righteousness.

Et veniat super me

ET thy loving mercy come also unto me, O Lord : even thy salvation, according unto thy word.

42 So shall I make answer unto my blasphemers : for my trust is in thy word.

43 O take not the word of thy truth utterly out of my mouth : for my hope is in thy judgements.

44 So shall I alway keep thy law : yea, for ever and ever.

45 And I will walk at liberty : for I seek thy commandments.

46 I will speak of thy testimonies also, even before kings : and will not be ashamed.

47 And my delight shall be in thy commandments : which I have loved.

48 My hands also will I lift up unto thy commandments, which I have loved : and my study shall be in thy statutes.

MEMOR ESTO SERVI TUI

THINK upon thy servant, as concerning thy word : wherein thou hast caused me to put my trust.

50 The same is my comfort in my trouble : for thy word hath quickened me.

51 The proud have had me exceedingly in derision : yet have I not shrinked from thy law.

52 For I remembered thine everlasting judgements, O Lord : and received comfort.

53 I am horribly afraid : for the ungodly that forsake thy law.

54 Thy statutes have been my songs : in the house of my pilgrimage.

55 I have thought upon thy Name, O Lord, in the night-season : and have kept thy law.

56 This I had : because I kept thy commandments.

PORTIO MEA, DOMINE

THOU art my portion, O Lord : I have promised to keep thy law.

58 I made my humble petition in thy presence with my whole heart : O be merciful unto me, according to thy word.

59 I called mine own ways to remembrance : and turned my feet unto thy testimonies.

60 I made haste, and prolonged not the time : to keep thy commandments.

61 The congregations of the ungodly have robbed me : but I have not forgotten thy law.

62 At midnight I will rise to give thanks unto thee : because of thy righteous judgements.

63 I am a companion of all them that fear thee : and keep thy commandments.

64 The earth, O Lord, is full of thy mercy : O teach me thy statutes.

BONITATEM FECISTI

LORD, thou hast dealt graciously with thy servant : according unto thy word.

66 O learn me true understanding and knowledge : for I have believed thy commandments.

67 Before I was troubled, I went wrong : but now have I kept thy word.

68 Thou art good and gracious : O teach me thy statutes.

69 The proud have imagined a lie against me : but I will keep thy commandments with my whole heart.

70 Their heart is as fat as brawn : but my delight hath been in thy law.

71 It is good for me that I have been in trouble : that I may learn thy statutes.

72 The law of thy mouth is dearer unto me : than thousands of gold and silver.

Day 25. Evening Prayer

Manus tuae fecerunt me

THY hands have made me and fashioned me : O give me understanding, that I may learn thy commandments.

74 They that fear thee will be glad when they see me : because I have put my trust in thy word.

75 I know, O Lord, that thy judgements are right : and that thou of very faithfulness hast caused me to be troubled.

76 O let thy merciful kindness be my comfort : according to thy word unto thy servant.

77 O let thy loving mercies come unto me, that I may live : for thy law is my delight.

78 Let the proud be confounded, for they go wickedly about to destroy me : but I will be occupied in thy commandments.

79 Let such as fear thee, and have known thy testimonies : be turned unto me.

80 O let my heart be sound in thy statutes : that I be not ashamed.

Defecit anima mea

MY soul hath longed for thy salvation : and I have a good hope because of thy word.

82 Mine eyes long sore for thy word : saying, O when wilt thou comfort me?

83 For I am become like a bottle in the smoke : yet do I not forget thy statutes.

84 How many are the days of thy servant : when wilt thou be avenged of them that persecute me?

85 The proud have digged pits for me : which are not after thy law.

86 All thy commandments are true : they persecute me falsely; O be thou my help.

87 They had almost made an end of me upon earth : but I forsook not thy commandments.

88 O quicken me after thy loving-kindness : and so shall I keep the testimonies of thy mouth.

In aeternum, Domine

LORD, thy word : endureth for ever in heaven.

90 Thy truth also remaineth from one generation to another : thou hast laid the foundation of the earth, and it abideth.

91 They continue this day according to thine ordinance : for all things serve thee.

92 If my delight had not been in thy law : I should have perished in my trouble.

93 I will never forget thy commandments : for with them thou hast quickened me.

94 I am thine, O save me : for I have sought thy commandments.

95 The ungodly laid wait for me to destroy me : but I will consider thy testimonies.

96 I see that all things come to an end : but thy commandment is exceeding broad.

Quomodo dilexi!

ORD, what love have I unto thy law : all the day long is my study in it.

98 Thou through thy commandments hast made me wiser than mine enemies : for they are ever with me.

99 I have more understanding than my teachers : for thy testimonies are my study.

100 I am wiser than the aged : because I keep thy commandments.

101 I have refrained my feet from every evil way : that I may keep thy word.

102 I have not shrunk from thy judgements : for thou teachest me.

103 O how sweet are thy words unto my throat : yea, sweeter than honey unto my mouth.

104 Through thy commandments I get understanding : therefore I hate all evil ways.

Day 26. Morning Prayer

Lucerna pedibus meis

THY word is a lantern unto my feet : and a light unto my paths.

106 I have sworn, and am stedfastly purposed : to keep thy righteous judgements.

107 I am troubled above measure : quicken me, O Lord, according to thy word.

108 Let the free-will offerings of my mouth please thee, O Lord : and teach me thy judgements.

109 My soul is alway in my hand : yet do I not forget thy law.

110 The ungodly have laid a snare for me : but yet I swerved not from thy commandments.

111 Thy testimonies have I claimed as mine heritage for ever : and why? they are the very joy of my heart.

112 I have applied my heart to fulfil thy statutes alway : even unto the end.

Iniquos odio habui

I HATE them that imagine evil things : but thy law do I love.

114 Thou art my defence and shield : and my trust is in thy word.

115 Away from me, ye wicked : I will keep the commandments of my God.

116 O stablish me according to thy word, that I may live : and let me not be disappointed of my hope.

117 Hold thou me up, and I shall be safe : yea, my delight shall be ever in thy statutes.

118 Thou hast trodden down all them that depart from thy statutes : for they imagine but deceit.

119 Thou puttest away all the ungodly of the earth like dross : therefore I love thy testimonies.

120 My flesh trembleth for fear of thee : and I am afraid of thy judgements.

Feci judicium

I DEAL with the thing that is lawful and right : O give me not over unto mine oppressors.

122 Make thou thy servant to delight in that which is good : that the proud do me no wrong.

123 Mine eyes are wasted away with looking for thy health : and for the word of thy righteousness.

124 O deal with thy servant according unto thy loving mercy : and teach me thy statutes.

125 I am thy servant, O grant me understanding : that I may know thy testimonies.

126 It is time for thee, Lord, to lay to thine hand : for they have destroyed thy law.

127 For I love thy commandments : above gold and precious stone.

128 Therefore hold I straight all thy commandments : and all false ways I utterly abhor.

Mirabilia

HY testimonies are wonderful : therefore doth my soul keep them.

130 When thy word goeth forth : it giveth light and understanding unto the simple.

131 I opened my mouth, and drew in my breath : for my delight was in thy commandments.

132 O look thou upon me, and be merciful unto me : as thou usest to do unto those that love thy Name.

133 Order my steps in thy word : and so shall no wickedness have dominion over me.

134 O deliver me from the wrongful dealings of men : and so shall I keep thy commandments.

135 Shew the light of thy countenance upon thy servant : and teach me thy statutes.

136 Mine eyes gush out with water : because men keep not thy law.

Justus es, Domine

IGHTEOUS art thou, O Lord : and true is thy judgement.

138 The testimonies that thou hast commanded : are exceeding righteous and true.

139 My zeal hath even consumed me : because mine enemies have forgotten thy words.

140 Thy word is tried to the uttermost : and thy servant loveth it.

141 I am small, and of no reputation : yet do I not forget thy commandments.

142 Thy righteousness is an everlasting righteousness : and thy law is the truth.

143 Trouble and heaviness have taken hold upon me : yet is my delight in thy commandments.

144 The righteousness of thy testimonies is everlasting : O grant me understanding, and I shall live.

Day 26. Evening Prayer

Clamavi in toto corde meo

CALL with my whole heart : hear me, O Lord, I will keep thy statutes.

146 Yea, even unto thee do I call : help me, and I shall keep thy testimonies.

147 Early in the morning do I cry unto thee : for in thy word is my trust.

148 Mine eyes prevent the night-watches : that I might be occupied in thy words.

149 Hear my voice, O Lord, according unto thy loving-kindness : quicken me, according as thou art wont.

150 They draw nigh that of malice persecute me : and are far from thy law.

151 Be thou nigh at hand, O Lord : for all thy commandments are true.

152 As concerning thy testimonies, I have known long since : that thou hast grounded them for ever.

Vide humilitatem

CONSIDER mine adversity, and deliver me : for I do not forget thy law.

154 Avenge thou my cause, and deliver me : quicken me, according to thy word.

155 Health is far from the ungodly : for they regard not thy statutes.

156 Great is thy mercy, O Lord : quicken me, as thou art wont.

157 Many there are that trouble me, and persecute me : yet do I not swerve from thy testimonies.

158 It grieveth me when I see the transgressors : because they keep not thy law.

159 Consider, O Lord, how I love thy commandments : O quicken me, according to thy loving-kindness.

160 Thy word is true from everlasting : all the judgements of thy righteousness endure for evermore.

Principes persecuti sunt

RINCES have persecuted me without a cause : but my heart standeth in awe of thy word.

162 I am as glad of thy word : as one that findeth great spoils.

163 As for lies, I hate and abhor them : but thy law do I love.

164 Seven times a day do I praise thee : because of thy righteous judgements.

165 Great is the peace that they have who love thy law : and they are not offended at it.

166 Lord, I have looked for thy saving health : and done after thy commandments.

167 My soul hath kept thy testimonies : and loved them exceedingly.

168 I have kept thy commandments and testimonies : for all my ways are before thee.

Appropinquet deprecatio

ET my complaint come before thee, O Lord : give me understanding, according to thy word.

170 Let my supplication come before thee : deliver me, according to thy word.

171 My lips shall speak of thy praise : when thou hast taught me thy statutes.

172 Yea, my tongue shall sing of thy word : for all thy commandments are righteous.

173 Let thine hand help me : for I have chosen thy commandments.

174 I have longed for thy saving health, O Lord : and in thy law is my delight.

175 O let my soul live, and it shall praise thee : and thy judgements shall help me.

176 I have gone astray like a sheep that is lost : O seek thy servant, for I do not forget thy commandments.

Day 27. Morning Prayer

Psalm 120. *Ad Dominum*

HEN I was in trouble I called upon the Lord : and he heard me.

2 Deliver my soul, O Lord, from lying lips : and from a deceitful tongue.

3 What reward shall be given or done unto thee, thou false tongue : even mighty and sharp arrows, with hot burning coals.

4 Woe is me, that I am constrained to dwell with Mesech : and to have my habitation among the tents of Kedar.

5 My soul hath long dwelt among them : that are enemies unto peace.

6 I labour for peace, but when I speak unto them thereof : they make them ready to battle.

PSALM 121. *LEVAVI OCULUS*

WILL lift up mine eyes unto the hills : from whence cometh my help.

2 My help cometh even from the Lord : who hath made heaven and earth.

3 He will not suffer thy foot to be moved : and he that keepeth thee will not sleep.

4 Behold, he that keepeth Israel : shall neither slumber nor sleep.

5 The Lord himself is thy keeper : the Lord is thy defence upon thy right hand;

6 So that the sun shall not burn thee by day : neither the moon by night.

7 The Lord shall preserve thee from all evil : yea, it is even he that shall keep thy soul.

8 The Lord shall preserve thy going out, and thy coming in : from this time forth for evermore.

PSALM 122. *LAETATUS SUM*

WAS glad when they said unto me : We will go into the house of the Lord.

2 Our feet shall stand in thy gates : O Jerusalem.

3 Jerusalem is built as a city : that is at unity in itself.

4 For thither the tribes go up, even the tribes of the Lord : to testify unto Israel, to give thanks unto the Name of the Lord.

5 For there is the seat of judgement : even the seat of the house of David.

6 O pray for the peace of Jerusalem : they shall prosper that love thee.

7 Peace be within thy walls : and plenteousness within thy palaces.

8 For my brethren and companions' sakes : I will wish thee prosperity.

9 Yea, because of the house of the Lord our God : I will seek to do thee good.

PSALM 123. *AD TE LEVAVI OCULOS MEOS*

NTO thee lift I up mine eyes : O thou that dwellest in the heavens.

2 Behold, even as the eyes of servants look unto the hand of their masters, and as the eyes of a maiden unto the hand of her mistress : even

so our eyes wait upon the Lord our God, until he have mercy upon us.

3 Have mercy upon us, O Lord, have mercy upon us : for we are utterly despised.

4 Our soul is filled with the scornful reproof of the wealthy : and with the despitefulness of the proud.

PSALM 124. *NISI QUIA DOMINUS*

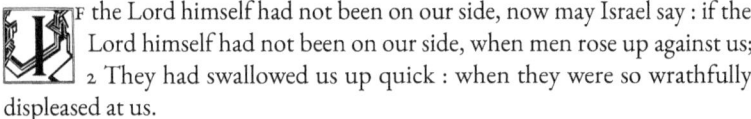F the Lord himself had not been on our side, now may Israel say : if the Lord himself had not been on our side, when men rose up against us; 2 They had swallowed us up quick : when they were so wrathfully displeased at us.

3 Yea, the waters had drowned us : and the stream had gone over our soul.

4 The deep waters of the proud : had gone even over our soul.

5 But praised be the Lord : who hath not given us over for a prey unto their teeth.

6 Our soul is escaped even as a bird out of the snare of the fowler : the snare is broken, and we are delivered.

7 Our help standeth in the Name of the Lord : who hath made heaven and earth.

PSALM 125. *QUI CONFIDUNT*

HEY that put their trust in the Lord shall be even as the mount Sion : which may not be removed, but standeth fast for ever. 2 The hills stand about Jerusalem : even so standeth the Lord round about his people, from this time forth for evermore.

3 For the rod of the ungodly cometh not into the lot of the righteous : lest the righteous put their hand unto wickedness.

4 Do well, O Lord : unto those that are good and true of heart.

5 As for such as turn back unto their own wickedness : the Lord shall lead them forth with the evil-doers; but peace shall be upon Israel.

Day 27. Evening Prayer

PSALM 126. *IN CONVERTENDO*

HEN the Lord turned again the captivity of Sion : then were we like unto them that dream. 2 Then was our mouth filled with laughter : and our tongue with joy.

3 Then said they among the heathen : The Lord hath done great things for them.

4 Yea, the Lord hath done great things for us already : whereof we rejoice.

5 Turn our captivity, O Lord : as the rivers in the south.

6 They that sow in tears : shall reap in joy.

7 He that now goeth on his way weeping, and beareth forth good seed : shall doubtless come again with joy, and bring his sheaves with him.

PSALM 127. *NISI DOMINUS*

EXCEPT the Lord build the house : their labour is but lost that build it.

2 Except the Lord keep the city : the watchman waketh but in vain.

3 It is but lost labour that ye haste to rise up early, and so late take rest, and eat the bread of carefulness : for so he giveth his beloved sleep.

4 Lo, children and the fruit of the womb : are an heritage and gift that cometh of the Lord.

5 Like as the arrows in the hand of the giant : even so are the young children.

6 Happy is the man that hath his quiver full of them : they shall not be ashamed when they speak with their enemies in the gate.

PSALM 128. *BEATI OMNES*

BLESSED are all they that fear the Lord : and walk in his ways.

2 For thou shalt eat the labours of thine hands : O well is thee, and happy shalt thou be.

3 Thy wife shall be as the fruitful vine : upon the walls of thine house.

4 Thy children like the olive-branches : round about thy table.

5 Lo, thus shall the man be blessed : that feareth the Lord.

6 The Lord from out of Sion shall so bless thee : that thou shalt see Jerusalem in prosperity all thy life long.

7 Yea, that thou shalt see thy children's children : and peace upon Israel.

PSALM 129. *SAEPE EXPUGNAVERUNT*

MANY a time have they fought against me from my youth up : may Israel now say.

2 Yea, many a time have they vexed me from my youth up : but they have not prevailed against me.

3 The plowers plowed upon my back : and made long furrows.

4 But the righteous Lord : hath hewn the snares of the ungodly in pieces.

5 Let them be confounded and turned backward : as many as have evil will at Sion.

6 Let them be even as the grass growing upon the house-tops : which withereth afore it be plucked up;

7 Whereof the mower filleth not his hand : neither he that bindeth up the sheaves his bosom.

8 So that they who go by say not so much as, The Lord prosper you : we wish you good luck in the Name of the Lord.

PSALM 130. *DE PROFUNDIS*

OUT of the deep have I called unto thee, O Lord : Lord, hear my voice.

2 O let thine ears consider well : the voice of my complaint.

3 If thou, Lord, wilt be extreme to mark what is done amiss : O Lord, who may abide it?

4 For there is mercy with thee : therefore shalt thou be feared.

5 I look for the Lord; my soul doth wait for him : in his word is my trust.

6 My soul fleeth unto the Lord : before the morning watch, I say, before the morning watch.

7 O Israel, trust in the Lord, for with the Lord there is mercy : and with him is plenteous redemption.

8 And he shall redeem Israel : from all his sins.

PSALM 131. *DOMINE, NON EST*

LORD, I am not high-minded : I have no proud looks.

2 I do not exercise myself in great matters : which are too high for me.

3 But I refrain my soul, and keep it low, like as a child that is weaned from his mother : yea, my soul is even as a weaned child.

4 O Israel, trust in the Lord : from this time forth for evermore.

Day 28. Morning Prayer

PSALM 132. *MEMENTO, DOMINE*

LORD, remember David : and all his trouble;

2 How he sware unto the Lord : and vowed a vow unto the Almighty God of Jacob;

3 I will not come within the tabernacle of mine house : nor climb up into my bed;

4 I will not suffer mine eyes to sleep, nor mine eye-lids to slumber : neither the temples of my head to take any rest;

5 Until I find out a place for the temple of the Lord : an habitation for the mighty God of Jacob.

6 Lo, we heard of the same at Ephrata : and found it in the wood.

7 We will go into his tabernacle : and fall low on our knees before his footstool.

8 Arise, O Lord, into thy resting-place : thou, and the ark of thy strength.

9 Let thy priests be clothed with righteousness : and let thy saints sing with joyfulness.

10 For thy servant David's sake : turn not away the presence of thine Anointed.

11 The Lord hath made a faithful oath unto David : and he shall not shrink from it;

12 Of the fruit of thy body : shall I set upon thy seat.

13 If thy children will keep my covenant, and my testimonies that I shall learn them : their children also shall sit upon thy seat for evermore.

14 For the Lord hath chosen Sion to be an habitation for himself : he hath longed for her.

15 This shall be my rest for ever : here will I dwell, for I have a delight therein.

16 I will bless her victuals with increase : and will satisfy her poor with bread.

17 I will deck her priests with health : and her saints shall rejoice and sing.

18 There shall I make the horn of David to flourish : I have ordained a lantern for mine Anointed.

19 As for his enemies, I shall clothe them with shame : but upon himself shall his crown flourish.

Psalm 133. *Ecce, quam bonum!*

BEHOLD, how good and joyful a thing it is : brethren, to dwell together in unity!

2 It is like the precious ointment upon the head, that ran down unto the beard : even unto Aaron's beard, and went down to the skirts of his clothing.

3 Like as the dew of Hermon : which fell upon the hill of Sion.

4 For there the Lord promised his blessing : and life for evermore.

Psalm 134. *Ecce nunc*

BEHOLD now, praise the Lord : all ye servants of the Lord;

2 Ye that by night stand in the house of the Lord : even in the courts of the house of our God.

3 Lift up your hands in the sanctuary : and praise the Lord.

4 The Lord that made heaven and earth : give thee blessing out of Sion.

PSALM 135. *LAUDATE NOMEN*

PRAISE the Lord, laud ye the Name of the Lord : praise it, O ye servants of the Lord;

2 Ye that stand in the house of the Lord : in the courts of the house of our God.

3 O praise the Lord, for the Lord is gracious : O sing praises unto his Name, for it is lovely.

4 For why? the Lord hath chosen Jacob unto himself : and Israel for his own possession.

5 For I know that the Lord is great : and that our Lord is above all gods.

6 Whatsoever the Lord pleased, that did he in heaven and in earth : and in the sea, and in all deep places.

7 He bringeth forth the clouds from the ends of the world : and sendeth forth lightnings with the rain, bringing the winds out of his treasures.

8 He smote the first-born of Egypt : both of man and beast.

9 He hath sent tokens and wonders into the midst of thee, O thou land of Egypt : upon Pharaoh, and all his servants.

10 He smote divers nations : and slew mighty kings;

11 Sehon king of the Amorites, and Og the king of Basan : and all the kingdoms of Canaan;

12 And gave their land to be an heritage : even an heritage unto Israel his people.

13 Thy Name, O Lord, endureth for ever : so doth thy memorial, O Lord, from one generation to another.

14 For the Lord will avenge his people : and be gracious unto his servants.

15 As for the images of the heathen, they are but silver and gold : the work of men's hands.

16 They have mouths, and speak not : eyes have they, but they see not.

17 They have ears, and yet they hear not : neither is there any breath in their mouths.

18 They that make them are like unto them : and so are all they that put their trust in them.

19 Praise the Lord, ye house of Israel : praise the Lord, ye house of Aaron.

20 Praise the Lord, ye house of Levi : ye that fear the Lord, praise the Lord.

21 Praised be the Lord out of Sion : who dwelleth at Jerusalem.

Day 28. Evening Prayer

PSALM 136. *CONFITEMINI*

GIVE thanks unto the LORD, for he is gracious : and his mercy endureth for ever.

2 O give thanks unto the God of all gods : for his mercy endureth for ever.

3 O thank the Lord of all lords : for his mercy endureth for ever.

4 Who only doeth great wonders : for his mercy endureth for ever.

5 Who by his excellent wisdom made the heavens : for his mercy endureth for ever.

6 Who laid out the earth above the waters : for his mercy endureth for ever.

7 Who hath made great lights : for his mercy endureth for ever;

8 The sun to rule the day : for his mercy endureth for ever;

9 The moon and the stars to govern the night : for his mercy endureth for ever.

10 Who smote Egypt with their first-born : for his mercy endureth for ever;

11 And brought out Israel from among them : for his mercy endureth for ever;

12 With a mighty hand, and stretched out arm : for his mercy endureth for ever.

13 Who divided the Red sea in two parts : for his mercy endureth for ever;

14 And made Israel to go through the midst of it : for his mercy endureth for ever.

15 But as for Pharaoh and his host, he overthrew them in the Red sea : for his mercy endureth for ever.

16 Who led his people through the wilderness : for his mercy endureth for ever.

17 Who smote great kings : for his mercy endureth for ever;

18 Yea, and slew mighty kings : for his mercy endureth for ever;

19 Sehon king of the Amorites : for his mercy endureth for ever;

20 And Og the king of Basan : for his mercy endureth for ever;

21 And gave away their land for an heritage : for his mercy endureth for ever;

22 Even for an heritage unto Israel his servant : for his mercy endureth for ever.

23 Who remembered us when we were in trouble : for his mercy endureth for ever;

24 And hath delivered us from our enemies : for his mercy endureth for ever.

25 Who giveth food to all flesh : for his mercy endureth for ever.

26 O give thanks unto the God of heaven : for his mercy endureth for ever.

27 O give thanks unto the Lord of lords : for his mercy endureth for ever.

PSALM 137. *SUPER FLUMINA*

BY the waters of Babylon we sat down and wept : when we remembered thee, O Sion.

2 As for our harps, we hanged them up : upon the trees that are therein.

3 For they that led us away captive required of us then a song, and melody in our heaviness : Sing us one of the songs of Sion.

4 How shall we sing the Lord's song : in a strange land?

5 If I forget thee, O Jerusalem : let my right hand forget her cunning.

6 If I do not remember thee, let my tongue cleave to the roof of my mouth : yea, if I prefer not Jerusalem in my mirth.

7 Remember the children of Edom, O Lord, in the day of Jerusalem : how they said, Down with it, down with it, even to the ground.

8 O daughter of Babylon, wasted with misery : yea, happy shall he be that rewardeth thee, as thou hast served us.

9 Blessed shall he be that taketh thy children : and throweth them against the stones.

PSALM 138. *CONFITEBOR TIBI*

I WILL give thanks unto thee, O Lord, with my whole heart : even before the gods will I sing praise unto thee.

2 I will worship toward thy holy temple, and praise thy Name, because of thy loving-kindness and truth : for thou hast magnified thy Name and thy word above all things.

3 When I called upon thee, thou heardest me : and enduedst my soul with much strength.

4 All the kings of the earth shall praise thee, O Lord : for they have heard the words of thy mouth.

5 Yea, they shall sing in the ways of the Lord : that great is the glory of the Lord.

6 For though the Lord be high, yet hath he respect unto the lowly : as for the proud, he beholdeth them afar off.

7 Though I walk in the midst of trouble, yet shalt thou refresh me : thou shalt stretch forth thy hand upon the furiousness of mine enemies, and thy right hand shall save me.

8 The Lord shall make good his loving-kindness toward me : yea, thy mercy, O Lord, endureth for ever; despise not then the works of thine own hands.

Day 29. Morning Prayer

Psalm 139. *Domine, probasti*

LORD, thou hast searched me out and known me : thou knowest my down-sitting and mine up-rising, thou understandest my thoughts long before.

2 Thou art about my path, and about my bed : and spiest out all my ways.

3 For lo, there is not a word in my tongue : but thou, O Lord, knowest it altogether.

4 Thou hast fashioned me behind and before : and laid thine hand upon me.

5 Such knowledge is too wonderful and excellent for me : I cannot attain unto it.

6 Whither shall I go then from thy Spirit : or whither shall I go then from thy presence?

7 If I climb up into heaven, thou art there : if I go down to hell, thou art there also.

8 If I take the wings of the morning : and remain in the uttermost parts of the sea;

9 Even there also shall thy hand lead me : and thy right hand shall hold me.

10 If I say, Peradventure the darkness shall cover me : then shall my night be turned to day.

11 Yea, the darkness is no darkness with thee, but the night is as clear as the day : the darkness and light to thee are both alike.

12 For my reins are thine : thou hast covered me in my mother's womb.

13 I will give thanks unto thee, for I am fearfully and wonderfully made : marvellous are thy works, and that my soul knoweth right well.

14 My bones are not hid from thee : though I be made secretly, and fashioned beneath in the earth.

15 Thine eyes did see my substance, yet being unperfect : and in thy book were all my members written;

16 Which day by day were fashioned : when as yet there was none of them.

17 How dear are thy counsels unto me, O God : O how great is the sum of them!

18 If I tell them, they are more in number than the sand : when I wake up I am present with thee.

19 Wilt thou not slay the wicked, O God : depart from me, ye blood-thirsty men.

20 For they speak unrighteously against thee : and thine enemies take thy Name in vain.

21 Do not I hate them, O Lord, that hate thee : and am not I grieved with those that rise up against thee?

22 Yea, I hate them right sore : even as though they were mine enemies.

23 Try me, O God, and seek the ground of my heart : prove me, and examine my thoughts.

24 Look well if there be any way of wickedness in me : and lead me in the way everlasting.

PSALM 140. *ERIPE ME, DOMINE*

ELIVER me, O Lord, from the evil man : and preserve me from the wicked man.

2 Who imagine mischief in their hearts : and stir up strife all the day long.

3 They have sharpened their tongues like a serpent : adders' poison is under their lips.

4 Keep me, O Lord, from the hands of the ungodly : preserve me from the wicked men, who are purposed to overthrow my goings.

5 The proud have laid a snare for me, and spread a net abroad with cords : yea, and set traps in my way.

6 I said unto the Lord, Thou art my God : hear the voice of my prayers, O Lord.

7 O Lord God, thou strength of my health : thou hast covered my head in the day of the battle.

8 Let not the ungodly have his desire, O Lord : let not his mischievous imagination prosper, lest they be too proud.

9 Let the mischief of their own lips fall upon the head of them : that compass me about.

10 Let hot burning coals fall upon them : let them be cast into the fire and into the pit, that they never rise up again.

11 A man full of words shall not prosper upon the earth : evil shall hunt the wicked person to overthrow him.

12 Sure I am that the Lord will avenge the poor : and maintain the cause of the helpless.

13 The righteous also shall give thanks unto thy Name : and the just shall continue in thy sight.

PSALM 141. *DOMINE, CLAMAVI*

ORD, I call upon thee, haste thee unto me : and consider my voice when I cry unto thee.

2 Let my prayer be set forth in thy sight as the incense : and let the lifting up of my hands be an evening sacrifice.

3 Set a watch, O Lord, before my mouth : and keep the door of my lips.

4 O let not mine heart be inclined to any evil thing : let me not be occupied in ungodly works with the men that work wickedness, lest I eat of such things as please them.

5 Let the righteous rather smite me friendly : and reprove me.

6 But let not their precious balms break my head : yea, I will pray yet against their wickedness.

7 Let their judges be overthrown in stony places : that they may hear my words, for they are sweet.

8 Our bones lie scattered before the pit : like as when one breaketh and heweth wood upon the earth.

9 But mine eyes look unto thee, O Lord God : in thee is my trust, O cast not out my soul.

10 Keep me from the snare that they have laid for me : and from the traps of the wicked doers.

11 Let the ungodly fall into their own nets together : and let me ever escape them.

Day 29. Evening Prayer

PSALM 142. *VOCE MEA AD DOMINUM*

CRIED unto the Lord with my voice : yea, even unto the Lord did I make my supplication.

2 I poured out my complaints before him : and shewed him of my trouble.

3 When my spirit was in heaviness thou knewest my path : in the way wherein I walked have they privily laid a snare for me.

4 I looked also upon my right hand : and saw there was no man that would know me.

5 I had no place to flee unto : and no man cared for my soul.

6 I cried unto thee, O Lord, and said : Thou art my hope, and my portion in the land of the living.

7 Consider my complaint : for I am brought very low.

8 O deliver me from my persecutors : for they are too strong for me.

9 Bring my soul out of prison, that I may give thanks unto thy Name : which thing if thou wilt grant me, then shall the righteous resort unto my company.

PSALM 143. *DOMINE, EXAUDI*

HEAR my prayer, O Lord, and consider my desire : hearken unto me for thy truth and righteousness' sake.

2 And enter not into judgement with thy servant : for in thy sight shall no man living be justified.

3 For the enemy hath persecuted my soul; he hath smitten my life down to the ground : he hath laid me in the darkness, as the men that have been long dead.

4 Therefore is my spirit vexed within me : and my heart within me is desolate.

5 Yet do I remember the time past; I muse upon all thy works : yea, I exercise myself in the works of thy hands.

6 I stretch forth my hands unto thee : my soul gaspeth unto thee as a thirsty land.

7 Hear me, O Lord, and that soon, for my spirit waxeth faint : hide not thy face from me, lest I be like unto them that go down into the pit.

8 O let me hear thy loving-kindness betimes in the morning, for in thee is my trust : shew thou me the way that I should walk in, for I lift up my soul unto thee.

9 Deliver me, O Lord, from mine enemies : for I flee unto thee to hide me.

10 Teach me to do the thing that pleaseth thee, for thou art my God : let thy loving Spirit lead me forth into the land of righteousness.

11 Quicken me, O Lord, for thy Name's sake : and for thy righteousness' sake bring my soul out of trouble.

12 And of thy goodness slay mine enemies : and destroy all them that vex my soul; for I am thy servant.

Day 30. Morning Prayer

❡ The Psalms for the 30ᵗʰ Day are repeated on the 31ˢᵗ Day, if there be one.

PSALM 144. *BENEDICTUS DOMINUS*

BLESSED be the Lord my strength : who teacheth my hands to war, and my fingers to fight;

2 My hope and my fortress, my castle and deliverer, my defender in whom I trust : who subdueth my people that is under me.

3 Lord, what is man, that thou hast such respect unto him : or the son of man, that thou so regardest him?

4 Man is like a thing of nought : his time passeth away like a shadow.

5 Bow thy heavens, O Lord, and come down : touch the mountains, and they shall smoke.

6 Cast forth thy lightning, and tear them : shoot out thine arrows, and consume them.

7 Send down thine hand from above : deliver me, and take me out of the great waters, from the hand of strange children;

8 Whose mouth talketh of vanity : and their right hand is a right hand of wickedness.

9 I will sing a new song unto thee, O God : and sing praises unto thee upon a ten-stringed lute.

10 Thou hast given victory unto kings : and hast delivered David thy servant from the peril of the sword.

11 Save me, and deliver me from the hand of strange children : whose mouth talketh of vanity, and their right hand is a right hand of iniquity.

12 That our sons may grow up as the young plants : and that our daughters may be as the polished corners of the temple.

13 That our garners may be full and plenteous with all manner of store : that our sheep may bring forth thousands and ten thousands in our streets.

14 That our oxen may be strong to labour, that there be no decay : no leading into captivity, and no complaining in our streets.

15 Happy are the people that are in such a case : yea, blessed are the people who have the Lord for their God.

Psalm 145. *Exaltabo te, Deus*

I WILL magnify thee, O God, my King : and I will praise thy Name for ever and ever.

2 Every day will I give thanks unto thee : and praise thy Name for ever and ever.

3 Great is the Lord, and marvellous worthy to be praised : there is no end of his greatness.

4 One generation shall praise thy works unto another : and declare thy power.

5 As for me, I will be talking of thy worship : thy glory, thy praise, and wondrous works;

6 So that men shall speak of the might of thy marvellous acts : and I will also tell of thy greatness.

7 The memorial of thine abundant kindness shall be shewed : and men shall sing of thy righteousness.

8 The Lord is gracious and merciful : long-suffering and of great goodness.

9 The Lord is loving unto every man : and his mercy is over all his works.

10 All thy works praise thee, O Lord : and thy saints give thanks unto thee.

11 They shew the glory of thy kingdom : and talk of thy power;

12 That thy power, thy glory, and mightiness of thy kingdom : might be known unto men.

13 Thy kingdom is an everlasting kingdom : and thy dominion endureth throughout all ages.

14 The Lord upholdeth all such as fall : and lifteth up all those that are down.

15 The eyes of all wait upon thee, O Lord : and thou givest them their meat in due season.

16 Thou openest thine hand : and fillest all things living with plenteousness.

17 The Lord is righteous in all his ways : and holy in all his works.

18 The Lord is nigh unto all them that call upon him : yea, all such as call upon him faithfully.

19 He will fulfil the desire of them that fear him : he also will hear their cry, and will help them.

20 The Lord preserveth all them that love him : but scattereth abroad all the ungodly.

21 My mouth shall speak the praise of the Lord : and let all flesh give thanks unto his holy Name for ever and ever.

PSALM 146. *LAUDA, ANIMA MEA*

RAISE the Lord, O my soul; while I live will I praise the Lord : yea, as long as I have any being, I will sing praises unto my God.

2 O put not your trust in princes, nor in any child of man : for there is no help in them.

3 For when the breath of man goeth forth he shall turn again to his earth : and then all his thoughts perish.

4 Blessed is he that hath the God of Jacob for his help : and whose hope is in the Lord his God;

5 Who made heaven and earth, the sea, and all that therein is : who keepeth his promise for ever;

6 Who helpeth them to right that suffer wrong : who feedeth the hungry.

7 The Lord looseth men out of prison : the Lord giveth sight to the blind.

8 The Lord helpeth them that are fallen : the Lord careth for the righteous.

9 The Lord careth for the strangers, he defendeth the fatherless and widow : as for the way of the ungodly, he turneth it upside down.

10 The Lord thy God, O Sion, shall be King for evermore : and throughout all generations.

Day 30. Evening Prayer

PSALM 147. *LAUDATE DOMINUM*

PRAISE the Lord, for it is a good thing to sing praises unto our God : yea, a joyful and pleasant thing it is to be thankful.

2 The Lord doth build up Jerusalem : and gather together the out-casts of Israel.

3 He healeth those that are broken in heart : and giveth medicine to heal their sickness.

4 He telleth the number of the stars : and calleth them all by their names.

5 Great is our Lord, and great is his power : yea, and his wisdom is infinite.

6 The Lord setteth up the meek : and bringeth the ungodly down to the ground.

7 O sing unto the Lord with thanksgiving : sing praises upon the harp unto our God;

8 Who covereth the heaven with clouds, and prepareth rain for the earth : and maketh the grass to grow upon the mountains, and herb for the use of men;

9 Who giveth fodder unto the cattle : and feedeth the young ravens that call upon him.

10 He hath no pleasure in the strength of an horse : neither delighteth he in any man's legs.

11 But the Lord's delight is in them that fear him : and put their trust in his mercy.

12 Praise the Lord, O Jerusalem : praise thy God, O Sion.

13 For he hath made fast the bars of thy gates : and hath blessed thy children within thee.

14 He maketh peace in thy borders : and filleth thee with the flour of wheat.

15 He sendeth forth his commandment upon earth : and his word runneth very swiftly.

16 He giveth snow like wool : and scattereth the hoar-frost like ashes.

17 He casteth forth his ice like morsels : who is able to abide his frost?

18 He sendeth out his word, and melteth them : he bloweth with his wind, and the waters flow.

19 He sheweth his word unto Jacob : his statutes and ordinances unto Israel.

20 He hath not dealt so with any nation : neither have the heathen knowledge of his laws.

Psalm 148. *Laudate Dominum*

PRAISE the Lord of heaven : praise him in the height.

2 Praise him, all ye angels of his : praise him, all his host.

3 Praise him, sun and moon : praise him, all ye stars and light.

4 Praise him, all ye heavens : and ye waters that are above the heavens.

5 Let them praise the Name of the Lord : for he spake the word, and they were made; he commanded, and they were created.

6 He hath made them fast for ever and ever : he hath given them a law which shall not be broken.

7 Praise the Lord upon earth : ye dragons, and all deeps;

8 Fire and hail, snow and vapours : wind and storm, fulfilling his word;

9 Mountains and all hills : fruitful trees and all cedars;

10 Beasts and all cattle : worms and feathered fowls;

11 Kings of the earth and all people : princes and all judges of the world;

12 Young men and maidens, old men and children, praise the Name of the Lord : for his Name only is excellent, and his praise above heaven and earth.

13 He shall exalt the horn of his people; all his saints shall praise him : even the children of Israel, even the people that serveth him.

PSALM 149. *CANTATE DOMINO*

SING unto the Lord a new song : let the congregation of saints praise him.

2 Let Israel rejoice in him that made him : and let the children of Sion be joyful in their King.

3 Let them praise his Name in the dance : let them sing praises unto him with tabret and harp.

4 For the Lord hath pleasure in his people : and helpeth the meek-hearted.

5 Let the saints be joyful with glory : let them rejoice in their beds.

6 Let the praises of God be in their mouth : and a two-edged sword in their hands;

7 To be avenged of the heathen : and to rebuke the people;

8 To bind their kings in chains : and their nobles with links of iron.

9 That they may be avenged of them, as it is written : Such honour have all his saints.

PSALM 150. *LAUDATE DOMINUM*

PRAISE God in his holiness : praise him in the firmament of his power.

2 Praise him in his noble acts : praise him according to his excellent greatness.

3 Praise him in the sound of the trumpet : praise him upon the lute and harp.

4 Praise him in the cymbals and dances : praise him upon the strings and pipe.

5 Praise him upon the well-tuned cymbals : praise him upon the loud cymbals.

6 Let every thing that hath breath : praise the Lord.

Most Holy Trinity, Save Us.
St. Mary Ever-Virgin, Pray for Us.
St. John the Divine, Pray for Us.
St. Alban the Martyr, Pray for Us.
St. Augustine of Canterbury, Pray for Us.
St. Gregory the Great, Pray for Us.
St. Tikhon of Moscow, Pray for Us.
St. John of San Francisco, Pray for Us.
All Ye Holy Angels & Saints, Pray for Us.